THE NORTH AMERICAN WEST IN THE TWENTY-FIRST CENTURY

THE NORTH AMERICAN WEST IN THE TWENTY-FIRST CENTURY

EDITED BY BRENDEN W. RENSINK

University of Nebraska Press
LINCOLN

© 2022 by the Board of Regents of the University of Nebraska

All rights reserved

The University of Nebraska Press is part of a land-grant institution with campuses and programs on the past, present, and future homelands of the Pawnee, Ponca, Otoe-Missouria, Omaha, Dakota, Lakota, Kaw, Cheyenne, and Arapaho Peoples, as well as those of the relocated Ho-Chunk, Sac and Fox, and Iowa Peoples.

Publication of this volume was assisted by a grant from the Charles Redd Center for Western Studies at Brigham Young University.

Library of Congress Cataloging-in-Publication Data
Names: Rensink, Brenden W., editor.
Title: The North American West in the twenty-first century / edited by Brenden W. Rensink.
Description: Lincoln : University of Nebraska Press, [2022] | Includes bibliographical references and index.
Identifiers: LCCN 2022005570
ISBN 9781496230430 (hardback)
ISBN 9781496233028 (paperback)
ISBN 9781496233271 (epub)
ISBN 9781496233288 (pdf)
Subjects: LCSH: West (U.S.)—History—1945 | West (U.S.)—Social conditions. | BISAC: HISTORY / United States / 21st Century | HISTORY / United States / State & Local / West (AK, CA, CO, HI, ID, MT, NV, UT, WY)
Classification: LCC F595.3 .N67 2022 |
DDC 978/.034—dc23/eng/20220727
LC record available at https://lccn.loc.gov/202200557

Set in Arno Pro by Laura Buis.

CONTENTS

List of Illustrations | vii

Foreword, by Patricia Nelson Limerick | ix

Introduction: Updating "Modern West" Histories for the Twenty-First Century | xvii
BRENDEN W. RENSINK

Part 1. Environmental Reckonings

1. Poisoned Wilderness: Superfund and Libby, Montana | 3
JENNIFER DUNN

2. Vulnerable Harvests: Agricultural Risk and Environmental Hazard in the Modern Great Plains West | 29
DAVID D. VAIL

Part 2. Indigenous Lands and Sovereignty

3. Sacred Space and Identity: The Fight for Chi'chil Biłdagoteel (Oak Flat) and the History of the San Carlos Apachean Peoples | 59
MARCUS C. MACKTIMA

4. Chess or Checkers?: Fracking in Greater Chaco | 81
SONI GRANT

Part 3. Urban and Rural Transformations

5. Westworld: Life on the High-Tech Frontier | 109
STUART W. LESLIE AND LAYNE R. KARAFANTIS

6. Our Mission, No Eviction: Resisting Gentrification in San Francisco | 141
LINDSEY PASSENGER WIECK

7. Agritourism as Land-Saving Action in the New West | 169
JEFFREY M. WIDENER

Part 4. Migrant Lives and Labor

8. "A Violation of the Most Elementary Human Rights of Children": The Rise of Migrant Youth Detention and Family Separation in the American West | 199
IVÓN PADILLA-RODRÍGUEZ

9. Toxins in the Field: The CRLA, Farmworker Families, and Environmental Justice in Contemporary California | 219
TAYLOR COZZENS

10. NAFTA's Legacy in the High Country: Mexican Migration to Colorado's Western Slope | 251
ERNESTO SAGÁS

Part 5. Unresolved Politics and Law

11. "I Oppose the ERA, but I Do Approve of Equal Rights for Women": Gender and Politics in the Aftermath of the Equal Rights Amendment Campaign in the U.S. West | 281
CHELSEA BALL

12. LGBTQ Civil Rights in Washington State Since 1977: An Unresolved History | 305
PETER BOAG

13. The American West, Native Americans, and Controversies over the Antiquities Act: Bears Ears National Monument, a Utah Case Study | 331
ANDREW GULLIFORD

Afterword | 363
FRANK BERGON

Contributors | 369

Index | 371

ILLUSTRATIONS

Figures

1. Map of Libby, Montana | 4
2. Map of the Great Plains West | 32
3. Drought map of the Great Plains West, 1950s | 37
4. Secretary of Agriculture Ezra Taft Benson's drought tour map | 40
5. Great Plains Agricultural Council activities and accomplishments | 47
6. Map of Apachean homelands | 62
7. Map of Chi'chil Biłdagoteel (Oak Flat) and surrounding region | 63
8. Oil and gas extraction on the checkerboard | 86
9. Amazon Spheres | 114
10. Google walkout protest, November 2018 | 120
11. SpaceX headquarters | 122
12. The Sanford Consortium | 130
13. Altar in front of the SOMArts Cultural Center | 142
14. Map of San Francisco Mission District | 145
15. Eviction mural at Twenty-Fourth and Bryant, 2013 | 151
16. René and Rio Yañez and the Day of the Dead procession, 2013 | 159
17. Community-built altar in remembrance of Yañez after his death, 2018 | 162
18. Map of the Grand Valley | 171
19. Palisade Peach Festival, August 2012 | 175
20. Colorado Mountain Winefest, 2012 | 179

21. Fruit and Wine Scenic Byway signs, 2012 | 184
22. Photograph of a booking form at the San Diego MCC | 206
23. *La amenaza de los pesticidas!* cartoon | 226
24. Oxnard strawberry fields | 233
25. Map of Colorado's Western Slope | 252
26. Graph of Latinx population of western Colorado, 1990–2017 | 261
27. Graph of Latinx population change in western Colorado, 1990–2000 and 2000–2010 | 265
28. Graph of Latinos as percent of western Colorado population, 1990–2010 | 267
29. ERA vote totals by state | 283
30. Map of Bears Ears National Monument boundaries and reduction | 332

Tables

1. Festivals held in the upper Grand Valley | 176
2. Table of Latinx population of Colorado's Western Slope, 1990–2017 | 260

FOREWORD

PATRICIA NELSON LIMERICK

Speaking from the Audience

A writer of a foreword for a collection of articles sometimes resembles a speaker giving the welcoming remarks for a conference.

Not this time.

Introducing readers to this collection, I am seated in the audience. With the equivalent of a lavalier microphone briefly in my possession, I have been given the right amount of amplification to invite people of many different ages, identities, and perspectives to join me in this audience. I hope many young people will join me here, but I also hope I will recruit a good showing of people who join me in unexpected veneration.

Here is why I could be distinctively positioned to make this invitation.

In the late 1980s, guided more by hope than by certainty, I made my one and only successful run at prophecy, declaring that the field of western American history was about to undergo a renaissance in research and writing.

Did I ever get that right!

This prediction of an impending revitalization of the field was at the core of the movement that, in a moment of inadvertent branding, I christened "the New Western History." The work of the fourteen writers who came together to create this collection stands as its own compelling demonstration that the renaissance not only *happened*, but it shows no signs of slowing down. While I hit the target by forecasting the abundance and vitality of publications about to be unleashed, I did not come anywhere near foreseeing the originality of the questions and the expanding significance of the findings that would drive a cascade of productivity that has mocked any dream I ever had of keeping up and keeping track of this inordinately robust field of scholarship.

In a paradox that also moved fast in mockery, it didn't take very long for the adjective "new" in the phrase, the New Western History, to approach and pass its expiration date. By its very title, *The North American West in the Twenty-First Century*, this collection gets its bearings from a recognition that seems to have escaped me a few decades ago. These authors know they are writing in a moment in time that is not going to last; indeed, since they themselves are writing of the transition from the twentieth-century West to the twenty-first-century West, they are necessarily aware that another set of historians—in which they will not be included—will probably write about the transition from the twenty-first-century West to the twenty-second-century West.

Back in the 1980s, when I was completely devoted to the project of exploring the past in order to make sense of the present, I seem not to have noticed that the term "the present" is one of the slipperiest concepts in human cognition. Even as I was working away to enlist the past to help us deal the present, history's outcomes and consequences kept multiplying, proliferating, and layering upon each other in unpredictable juxtapositions and permutations. Perhaps most vexing of all, even as we speak the word "now," the moment we were planning to capture with that word has slipped out of our grip.

Never surrendering its traditional role as a trickster, time dismisses any request to hold still. And, as a further dimension of chrono-trickster achievement, the passage of several decades generated a wild overabundance of historically significant twists and turns, events and episodes. This gave both opportunity and burden to historians, who, it seemed to me in the late 1980s, already had way too much material demanding our attention.

And yet the authors in this collection, apparently immune to fatigue, convey only an eager curiosity and even an urgent ethical commitment to accept the challenge to get to work on researching, narrating, and analyzing the stories that got going in 2000.

Oblivious as I apparently was to the fact that the twenty-first century was stalking me, as the very audible advocate for the New Western History three or four decades ago, the passage of time has reconfigured me into—in some sense—a predecessor to the writers whose work appears here.

No guidebook lays out the proper conduct for a predecessor, and the role can seem, initially, both mystifying and exhausting. And then the light comes up, yielding the insight that makes a predecessor's life worth living: "If all goes as you hope, a renaissance in historical research may make you outmoded and irrelevant, but it will also make you grateful, and *relieved*."

The Invitation

And now, back to the terms of my invitation.

Here's why readers want to join me as receptive and engaged members of the audience assembling for *The North American West in the Twenty-First Century*.

On every page of this collection, you will be in the company of historians acting as ambassadors and diplomats, negotiating—with equal agility and integrity—the terms of understanding between the people of the past and the people of the present. These negotiations demand that these scholars act as translators and interpreters, delivering messages from our predecessors to those of us who now claim our momentary lease on life.

And now, full disclosure: a good share of the messages that these historians deliver to us are unsettling, uncomfortable, and even alarming. The writers are forthright in casting a clear light on the injustices and afflictions, the mishaps and misfortunes, brought into being in the nineteenth and twentieth centuries, and they are equally forthright in bringing attention to the injustices and afflictions, the mishaps and misfortunes, that have emerged in the now not-so-new twenty-first century.

Here is the spirit in which I hope you will respond to these forthright reckonings: *welcome*—and do not invest more than a moment in blaming—these messengers. Quickly convert any irritation or vexation into appreciation for the respect that these scholars show to their readers by addressing us with honesty.

Throughout this collection the reflections of the authors left my own assumptions refreshed, reconfigured, or rattled. Here is my own "travel diary" of unsettled thoughts to keep in mind as you take your own journey through this book:

- Often characterized as unprecedented, megafires of the twenty-first-century West may resemble or even replicate patterns of wildlands fire in the nineteenth and early twentieth centuries.
- Some of the most environmentally devastated western communities have residents who are unshakable in their loyalty to the locales they consider their homes and are determined to find ways to live with the troubled history of these places.
- In the mid-twentieth century, in gatherings convened by little-known federal agencies, issues of climate, water scarcity, and chemical risk provoked collaborative reckonings that now seem prescient and almost improbably ahead of their times.
- Attention to the process of forced relocation that put Indigenous peoples of mixed identity on one reservation can make sense of the otherwise confounding appearance of dissent and disagreement in tribal decision-making.
- When tribal communities confront risks from extractive industry, the tangles of "land status," jurisdictions, and property regimes—especially in access to subsurface resources—have the power to install a barely comprehensible complexity in efforts to slow down or reject resource development.
- Tracking the proliferation of high-tech companies and institutions in the West at once confirms—and challenges—widespread assumptions about change and continuity in patterns of regional economic development in "old" and "new" industries (while also affirming that the scary folks who brought us *Westworld* knew what they were doing).
- The process of gentrification and the displacement of working-class households from thriving neighborhoods in western cities gain a sharpness and poignancy with case studies of the power of art to foster cultural vitality, even as economic vulnerability of those neighborhoods remains undiminished.

- Even when policy-oriented sorts have created and deferred to clear categorizations of agriculture and recreation as inherently different economies, westerners who have not signed on to that categorization prove to be quite capable of merging those economies into a shared enterprise.
- The cruel treatment of immigrant children on the U.S.-Mexico border began years before 2017, even though there are solid reasons why we came to associate this with the Trump administration.
- The exposure of agricultural workers to pesticides registers as one of the most taken-for-granted elements of injustice in the twenty-first-century West, even as efforts to recognize this as a key element of environmental justice have not ended the problem.
- Even in an area, as in Colorado's Western Slope, where "diversity" seems under-represented, careful research can reveal a robust tradition of immigrant families who have cultivated and acquired a strong sense of connection to and continuity in these locales.
- Tracking the course of feminism in western states—through the early securing of women's suffrage to the ups and downs (with a possible return to the "up" setting) of the Equal Rights Amendment—makes a compelling case for observing changes in the meanings of feminism, as well as noting that one defeat at a national scale did not immobilize other actions at the local level.
- While there may be a few generalizations worth considering about western attitudes toward LGBTQ civil rights, those generalizations need to be put to the test by examining the history of particular states over a range of time in order to reveal the complexities and variations of this history.
- In the twenty-first century some dramatic variations from the predictable—as in the crucial role played by an intertribal alliance in the designation of the Bears Ears National Monument—make it clear that there is, every now and then, genuinely something new under the sun, with the promise of those innovations still to be determined.

Hanging Out with Historians

Every one of these articles rests on a shared premise: we will not get anywhere in figuring out the dynamics of the contemporary West, and we will make even less progress in conjuring up resolutions for conflicts and dilemmas, unless we pay rapt attention to the origins and persistence of arrangements, customs, and habits that our predecessors cobbled together over the last two centuries.

Just as important, each article is its own reminder that tracking continuity and change over time requires hyper-alertness on the part of scholars and their readers. In this collection we learn about some precedents that have lasted from their origins to the present day, about other precedents that had barely been set before they petered out, and still other precedents that people purposefully modified or eliminated, even when those precedents seemed to be very entrenched.

Perhaps most illuminating, these articles converge on an important reminder: those of us who are committed to understanding the American West need to stay on constant alert for situations where we might think that we are encountering something new, but we are actually allowing ourselves to be spooked by the resurgence of a pattern or trend that keeps showing up when it was supposed to be consigned to a distant past. The project of distinguishing change from continuity in history may seem simple enough when you first give it a try, but beneath its veneer of simplicity, that project often delivers more mystery than clarity. Throughout this collection, transformations have a way of revealing themselves to be incomplete, with plenty of elements of the previous pre-transformation situation refusing to be evicted.

And yet, in these articles, readers repeatedly encounter stories of westerners putting heart and soul into wrestling with history in very grounded and immediate ways. Particularly in the many western communities attempting to shift from an economy of extraction to an economy of tourism and recreation, people who never contemplated getting the formal study of history are nonetheless drawn, by an almost gravitational pull, into historical deliberations. Whether a community is trying to romanticize its former reliance on mining to attract and amuse tourists, or federal officials are trying to find ways to refresh and modify a long-established system of laws, regulations, and customs, westerners find themselves immersed in the deep waters of historical interpretations—and are very much in need of the company and counsel of historians.

Writing in mid-2021, even as the word "now" moves out of my grip as soon as I think it, I am very aware that I and my fellow historians are worn down by life in a fractured, divided, and contention-saturated nation. Sorrowfully, public disputes over history itself usually lock in contention rather than arouse a greater determination to direct conflict toward cooperation.

I conclude with a hypothesis I have been putting to the test for most of my career.

No problem facing the American West in the present will come near a solution or resolution without the full engagement of historians.

There is no guarantee that most Americans are going to embrace the benefits that hanging out with historians could provide to them.

With or without that guarantee, historians should still take every opportunity to declare their availability, a declaration that the fourteen authors of *The North American West in the Twenty-First Century* have made with energy and grace.

INTRODUCTION

Updating "Modern West" Histories for the Twenty-First Century

BRENDEN W. RENSINK

On February 4, 2020, Pres. Donald J. Trump used nineteenth-century frontier imagery and mythology in his State of the Union address to frame the United States' bright future. "The American nation was carved out of the vast frontier by the toughest, strongest, fiercest, and most determined men and women ever to walk on the face of the Earth," he opined. "Our ancestors braved the unknown; tamed the wilderness; settled the Wild West."[1] The American West—a region that boasts many of the fastest growing metropolises, most vibrant economies, and most demographically dynamic populations—was reduced to a caricature, a set of tropes cemented in a nineteenth-century past. Historian Patricia Nelson Limerick, who kindly provided the foreword for this volume, voiced a response to President Trump's speech that echoes what many western historians likely thought: "When a powerful national leader turns the people of the past into caricatures and thereby drains their lives of dignity and meaning, the response of a conscientious Western American historian condenses into four words: 'Just cut that out.'"[2] Professional historians have largely moved past shallow mythology. The disconnect between recent scholarship and President Trump's address is bracing. It reveals how the divide between public imaginings and scholarly inquiry persists. This matters. Regardless of how "academic" the questions of where, what, who, and when the "West" was, the answers we provide and stories we tell have real impact on the region, its lands, and the "westerners" who call it home in the twenty-first century.

Just as national historical interpretations matter to the modern West, the modern West matters to the nation. Beyond Frederick Jackson Turner's 1893 interpretation that the western "frontier" is what forged American identity and the generations of subsequent scholars who accepted, adapted, or challenged that interpretive lens, the West continues to present America with challenging processes to wrestle, navigate, and overcome.[3] The West may be America's most economically, demographically, and politically dynamic region, and as such, its twenty-first-century developments may shape national narratives now more than ever. "Does the western past have a future?" asked historians William Cronon, George Miles, and Jay Gitlin in 1992. Yes! "We believe that one cannot understand the modern United States without coming to terms with its western past," they replied.[4] Western individuals and communities grappling with complex present realities know all too well that the history must be reckoned with. How the West navigates the transitions between fraught histories, a precarious present, and uncertain futures is of national consequence.

President Trump's invocation of tired frontier tropes will frustrate scholars from multiple overlapping disciplines and fields who have been making careful study of the West in recent decades. In the late twentieth century "New Western" historians dissected the mythologized western histories that Turner and others had long used to embody American triumph and progress. They interrogated the settler conquest of North America that had been accepted as integral to American history and identity by historians for more than a century, highlighted the pervasive influence that one-sided or inaccurate frontier mythologies had on popular literature, film, and public memory, and uncovered forgotten, misrepresented, or actively overlooked experiences of Indigenous peoples, ethnic groups, and other marginalized peoples that had no place in existing popular western imaginings. Subsequent generations of historians have followed and collectively demanded that invocations of the frontier offer more than settler mythologies heard in the 2020 State of the Union address— not for hostility toward settler society, but because the fuller and more complex history offers so much more valuable knowledge and a variety of perspectives to a nation and region still wrestling with past and present problems. Trump's frontier musings suggest these revisions and updates to western scholarship have either failed to enter national consciousness or are being intentionally ignored.

This reads out of step with how mainstream America seemed ready to engage with the New Western History as it evolved in the 1980s–1990s. The national media paid remarkable attention to new landmark western surveys, monographs, and the broad questions they posed.[5] These histories, after all, were revising popular (and profitable) national creation myths. Though not without critique, the academy also demonstrated interest.[6] Western scholars won national awards and honors, suggesting growing acceptance that their regional work was more than quaint and parochial.[7] In recent years western scholars continue to win national awards, and their work is occasionally still reviewed in popular venues, but the broad excitement that attended the heady early days of the New Western History—when the nation seemed to take collective note—seems to have waned in the twenty-first century. Important new works are praised but often by audiences already converted to the importance of revisionist perspectives. Has the broader mainstream of the nation tuned out? It is difficult to measure. But the 2020 State of the Union address suggests that scholars must continue working to successfully weave new perspectives into national consciousness, discourse, and identity.

The Promise of "Modern West" Studies

As studies of the "Modern West" likely explore the issues with which the general public is most familiar, they offer a promising starting point for helping broad audiences engage in historical thinking and using history to better inform our present. The emergence of "modern" studies as a prominent feature in the New Western History merits exploration—revealing the foundations the New Western History laid for ongoing work today and clarifying persistent challenges that demand persistent attention. The very notion of a "Modern West" worth studying has faced "powerful obstacles." "In a way," mused Michael E. McGerr in 1992, "American historiography has conspired against the modern region."[8] When Patricia Limerick cast her gaze across U.S. history survey textbooks from before 1990, her observation confirmed this:

> Nearly all of the textbooks stopped indexing any usage of the word "West" after 1980 because, to their authors, the frontier was the West,

the West was the frontier, and both had departed as significant subjects of study before the twentieth century started. Most unhappily, this closing of the frontier and the West, in a stroke, declared the work of Western historians irrelevant to any understanding of the West today. To study the frontier was to study an era that had definitively and solidly ended, with no narrative or casual ties connecting the past to the present.[9]

She elaborated further on the "deeply worn ruts" into which textbooks relegated western topics—discrete, segregated, and often unimportant to broader narratives.[10] At the time Limerick's oft tongue-in-cheek riffing built on this growing subfield of modern West history that played well with many New Western historians. An exploration of more recent regional histories invited the revisionist mindset so needed to critically reexamine an endless list of more distant historical topics.

So how did late twentieth-century "New Western" historians define the "Modern West"? Historian Gerald D. Nash opened his field-defining 1973 survey textbook, *The American West in the Twentieth Century: A Short History of An Urban Oasis*, with an even more fundamental question: "Is there a twentieth-century West?"[11] He replied in the affirmative. The modern West was vibrant, and the twentieth century might "very well constitute the most significant era in the entire history of the region." This rings more self-evident in the 2020s than it did in 1973.[12] His previous generation of western and American historians had followed Frederick Jackson Turner's assertion that while the "frontier" process had been integral in shaping American history and identity, it was closed. The West's significance in national affairs was a thing of the past. Bold in his defiance, Nash declared that the region's modern history was its *most* significant and continued to determine national fates: "The American West today is America tomorrow."[13] Reviews were mixed, but many hinted that Nash had laid a powerful foundation for additional work.[14] They were prescient. A flood of "Modern West" scholarship followed. Nash's 1973 text "clearly shaped [that] first generation of books and essays," recalled Richard W. Etulain in 2003.[15] However, we must not forget the radical nature of his twofold thesis. The West steered the nation, and its recent past overshadowed the popularized frontier past in relevance.

The modern West scholarship that followed Nash's 1973 survey grew in tandem with (or firmly as a part of) the "New Western History" movement in the field. And while Nash himself became stridently critical of the field's revisionist tack, many of the modern West scholars inspired by him were immersed and engaged with the same.[16] The New Western History emerged as the twentieth century was coming to a close but not quite finished. Conferences and seminars convened to ask big questions, and participants produced an immense body of radically new scholarship. Many included modern western history, linking recent and more distant stories across centuries. Patricia Nelson Limerick built her influential 1987 *The Legacy of Conquest* on this concept—connecting twentieth-century western issues to antecedent historical events. The region cannot escape the influence of history, she argued, and "contemporary Americans ought to be well informed and well warned" of western history, lest we stumble and fall individually or collectively.[17] The West today cannot ignore the West of centuries past. Inherent in this argument is the assertion that the modern West itself continues to be unique, worthy of study, and important in its own right. The region was not frozen in the past, offering up nothing more than frontier morality tales for a nation grappling with daily crises. New Western historians not only argued that the West mattered and demanded renewed historical inquiry, but that its recent past had as much to teach us as centuries more distant.

Now decades removed from the New Western History's emergence, and with multiple academic generations of resulting scholarship to consider, the state of many intersecting subfields is energizing. To celebrate its fifty-year anniversary, the Western History Association dedicated the full Autumn 2011 issue of the *Western Historical Quarterly* to surveying recent historiographies and assessing the health of multiple subfields.[18] The contributions serve as excellent primers for several subfields, and some began to re-ask questions that had permeated early New Western History discussions. Many spirited discussions in conference panels (or at conference bars) highlight an exciting but complicated state of western history. It is simultaneously fractured between subfields and adjacent disciplines as well as pulled back together in new configurations by the growth of interdisciplinary and comparative work. Whether the field or splintering and intersecting subfields have moved beyond the "New Western History" is perhaps a facile query. Suffice it to say that an immense body of scholarship has been built on foundations the New Western History laid. But what of the "Modern West" subfield? It presents a unique paradox as the "modern" content that New Western History textbooks, monographs, anthologies, and articles present become less and less "modern" with each passing year. It is a subfield uniquely prone to aging toward irrelevance.

By way of example, consider some of the prominent American West survey textbooks published since 1980. Ray Allen Billington's *Westward Expansion: A History of the American Frontier*, first published in 1949, largely ended in 1890 and included only a brief twentieth-century coda entitled "The Frontier Heritage."[19] In 1989 Clyde Milner II published the *Major Problems in the History of the American West* reader (with a substantive revised second edition in 1997 with Anne M. Butler and David Rich Lewis as additional editors), dedicating almost half of the documents and essays to the post-1890 era.[20] Subsequent textbooks, readers, and anthologies followed suit in near-equal twentieth-century coverage, including:

> Richard White, *"It's Your Misfortune and None of My Own": A History of the American West* (1991)
>
> Clyde A. Milner II, Carol A. O'Connor, and Martha A. Sandweiss, *The Oxford History of the American West* (1994)
>
> Clyde A. Milner II, *A New Significance: Re-Envisioning the History of the American West* (1996)
>
> Walter Nugent and Martin Ridge, *American West: The Reader* (1999)
>
> Walter Nugent, *Into the West* (1999)
>
> Robert V. Hine and John Mack Faragher, *The American West: A New Interpretive History* (2000)

Anne M. Butler and Michael J. Lansing, *The American West: A Concise History* (2007)

Gary Clayton Anderson and Kathleen P. Chamberlain, *Power and Promise: The Changing American West* (2008)

Carol L. Higham and William H. Katerberg, *Conquests and Consequences: The American West from Frontier to Region* (2009)[21]

Moving beyond surveys that *include* the twentieth century, there have also been generalist studies and anthologies specific to the twentieth-century West: Robert G. Athearn's 1986 *The Mythic West in Twentieth-Century America*, Gerald D. Nash and Richard W. Etulain's edited 1989 *The Twentieth-Century West: Historical Interpretations*, Michael P. Malone and Richard W. Etulain's 1989 *The American West: A Modern History, 1900 to the Present*, Richard W. Etulain's 1996 *Re-Imagining the Modern American West: A Century of Fiction, History, and Art*, Michael L. Johnson's 1996 *New Westers: The West in Contemporary American Culture*, David M. Wrobel and Michael C. Steiner's edited 1997 *Many Wests: Place, Culture, and Regional Identity*, Gerald D. Nash's 2000 *A Brief History of the American West Since 1945*, and Richard W. Etulain and Ferenc Morton Szasz's edited 2003 *The American West in 2000: Essays in Honor of Gerald D. Nash*.[22] These are valuable, but of the above, only two have been subsequently revised to update modern content in significant fashion: Malone and Etulain's received a new preface and final chapter in 2007, and Hine and Faragher's was revised in 2017 with Jon T. Coleman as an additional editor.[23]

Thankfully, those published or revised after 2000 *do* highlight intriguing trends unique to the twenty-first-century West. For example, Higham and Katerberg underscored increasingly varied subregional identities and the influence metropolitan centers had on their peripheries as undermining broader shared western relationships, histories, or experiences.[24] Moreover, western connections with global trade, culture, and populations pull western identities in disparate directions.[25] Anderson and Chamberlain offered the "challenges of change" as a key consideration for the twenty-first-century West, with increased competition for control of resources and belonging between federal and private entities, rural and urban populations, multicultural populations, and other divides.[26] Flipping perspective to how *outsiders* view the West, Coleman used the pop-culture characters of Napoleon Dynamite, from Jared Hess's 2004 film of the same name, and Sherman Alexie's Arnold Spirit Jr., from his 2007 novel *The Absolute True Diary of a Part-Time Indian*, as examples of "unavoidably and recognizably western" characters and stories, but that mainstream (outsider or non-western) audiences do not view as such. "Mainstream audiences no longer recognize Napoleon's casseroles or Junior's fry-bread as western, but they eat up the idiosyncrasies even if they haven't a clue about the historical forces that hatched them."[27] These examples reveal fascinating potential tensions for the region, split and divided by economics and culture that challenge any semblance of a unified "western" identity. These surveys reveal a region whose pace of change is accelerating the intensity of conflict as the twenty-first century progresses.

There are many other essay collections, readers, and survey texts from subfields relevant to western history with modern content. Countless twentieth-century monographs and articles can be added to these texts to form an impressive body of literature. However, their "modern" content that previously so energized scholarship and public awareness are decades old and no longer seem quite so "modern." If our envisioning of the "Modern West" grew from questions asked in the late twentieth century, perhaps it is time to revisit them, consider how those histories have progressed into the early twenty-first century, and attempt to both update and reenergize our study of the "Modern West." What new trends, narratives, or truths might twenty-first-century "Modern West" histories reveal?

Present Approach and Collection Summary

This collection attempts to answer this with essays that explore late twentieth-century histories (which would have been fully "modern" and presentist during the foundational "New Western History" years) and pivot to explicitly trace them across another turn-of-the-century divide and fully into the twenty-first century. We accept the assertions that "modern" West history has unique relevance and forward the thesis that such relevance is only evident if we continually update our scholarship to include new developments. As the goalposts of what constitutes "modern" march on, so must our work. This continual rededication to exploring the very recent aspects of the West can open powerful opportunities to reengage with the general American public, reintroduce nuanced scholarly perspectives into public dialogue, and re-vanquish the frontier myths some hoped had long since been put to rest.

What follows is not a comprehensive or definitive "state of the field" survey. Considering Gerald D. Nash and Richard W. Etulain's excellent 1989 edited volume, *The Twentieth-Century West*, as a template, many crucial topics, fields, and subfields are absent in the present volume. Nash and Etulain curated an astounding selection from premier scholars and offered wide-coverage topics including urban and rural divides, race and ethnicity, Indigenous peoples, migration, economies, the environment from multiple perspectives, politics, and culture. Our collection is less broad in coverage but more focused in analytical scope. Each scholar herein takes Modern West stories from the late twentieth century and carefully pulls them toward the present—explicitly tracing continuity with or unexpected divergence from trajectories established in the 1980s and 1990s. The resulting works both revisit past "modern" topics and update them for our ever-progressing "modern" timeframes.

Most of these essays began as drafts workshopped at a June 2019 seminar hosted by the Charles Redd Center for Western Studies at Brigham Young University. As the seminar organizer and host, I fretted over the participant list, struggling to include a diversity of topics, geography, author backgrounds, and methodology that would eventually be able to fit into a single volume. Quickly realizing that comprehensive coverage was not possible, I focused on finding groups of participants whose papers could work in tandem—both in the context of our workshop and as essays in a published volume. As we workshopped essays together, we foregrounded an across-the-turn-of-the-century analytical framework. While our contributions leave many topics and subfields unexplored, collectively we forward a cohesive set of research questions as explored through a handful of case studies. Just as the New Western History broadly sought to inform national dialogues of important lessons the region had to offer, we contend that *modern* western histories continue to present insight and guidance to a region in turmoil. Our collective hope is that these forays into the twenty-first-century West will inspire more scholars to pull histories to the present and, by so doing, reinsert scholarly findings into contemporary public awareness.

This volume is divided into five parts: Environmental Reckonings, Indigenous Lands and Sovereignty, Urban and Rural Transformations, Migrant Lives and Labor, and Unresolved Politics and Law. The essays in each often blend topics that could easily find a home in a different "part" or as a member of differently divided sections. This is a product of coincidence as well as significant cross-pollination due to the collaborative group workshopping process at the Redd Center. More significant is the designed overlap in approach and thesis. In our workshop and subsequent revising, all authors considered the following questions, along with many others: What was the trajectory of your topic in the late twentieth century? Did it continue along expected paths in the twenty-first century or diverge in unexpected ways? If something unique to the twenty-first century has transpired, how does your work reconfigure our understanding of the "Modern West"? How did scholars treat similar topics in the late twentieth century, and how do you build upon and/or revise their conclusions? With these and other questions in mind, essays were revised, chopped and refashioned, gutted and rebuilt. The process was certainly painful for some, but the collective benefited from framing our work together.

Part 1, Environmental Reckonings, starts our volume with two essays that consider our relationships with the natural world, how we have successfully and unsuccessfully navigated them, present realities we cannot escape, and future possibilities we must consider. Historian Jennifer Dunn explores similar themes of twenty-first-century populations struggling to reckon with inherited environmental crises. In Libby, Montana, Dunn uncovers a community in transition—reacting to a failing extractive industry, living with attendant toxic pollution (asbestos), and weighing options for paths forward. Public health demands acknowledgement and attention to cleaning local environs, but doing so creates stigma that may undermine efforts to recast the town as a destination for heritage tourism. Historian David D. Vail shifts our gaze to the Great Plains. He contextualizes modern debates over protecting agricultural production in the face of drought and natural disasters with the twentieth-century work of the Great Plains Agricultural Council (GPAC). As a collaboration between agricultural scientists, public policy makers, and private entities, GPAC's frank acknowledgment of agricultural vulnerability and environmental risk, as well as its work to find solutions, offers lessons for twenty-first-century agriculture to consider. The essays in part 1 emphasize that current environmental challenges must be met with open dialogue, potentially painful discussions, and a clearer understanding of recent histories at our feet. The urgent and constantly evolving nature of environmental crises in the 2020s underscores the seriousness with which we should approach these essays and adjacent topics. Missing is the pressing topic of wildfire in the West, a now ever-present reality of what Stephen Pyne terms the "pyrocene."[28]

Part 2, Indigenous Lands and Sovereignty, contains two essays from the southwestern United States that intersect Indigenous sovereignty with modern issues of lands, resources, and culture. Historian Marcus C. Macktima (San Carlos Apache) explores Apache history, the recent fights over mining at Chi'chil Biłdagoteel (Oak Flat, Arizona), and the impact of historic federal Indian policies on Apache communities. After forcefully settling multiple Apachean peoples together as a singular "San Carlos Apache Nation," the U.S. government has more recently manipulated the resulting variance of cultural traditions and relationships with sacred lands like Chi'chil Biłdagoteel to push development and mining. Macktima leverages this history to expose a modern lack of sensitivity to and public awareness and protection of Indigenous cultural heritage, sovereignty, and sacred spaces. Anthropologist Soni Grant explores similar issues of resource extraction on culturally important Indigenous lands on the checkerboard areas of the Navajo Nation in New Mexico. From extensive fieldwork in the region and engagement with local residents and interests, Grant attempts to make sense of a complex patchwork of jurisdictions. Moving beyond simply thinking about Indigenous sovereignty, Grant argues that the murky complexity of competing jurisdictions serves to increase private and public interest in exploiting Indigenous natural resources. Increased focus on jurisdiction, or "land status," will help strengthen understanding and respect of Diné sovereignty and presence on the lands. These two essays reveal fraught and ongoing contests that may feature modern factors of oil pipelines or multinational mining interests but echo historical injustices and long-brewing conflicts between Native and non-Native peoples throughout the West. The story of one modern Native community is not the story of all, but they are in conversation. Dynamics explored in these southwestern United States stories resonate powerfully with ongoing Native rights movements and issues across the continent and hemisphere.

Part 3, Urban and Rural Transformations, features three essays that highlight the accelerating pace of economic, cultural, and demographic changes that are reshaping western cities, the neighborhoods within them, and the ever-connected rural hinterlands that surround and connect them. Historians Stuart W. Leslie and Layne R. Karafantis use the lens of high-tech industry and labor markets to view immense new pressures and rapid changes being wrought upon western communities. Along with the economic promise these industries bring, they argue that high-tech development has also reinforced economic privilege, community segregation, social stratification, and gendered inequality. Historian Lindsey Passenger Wieck explores Latino community struggles against gentrification in San Francisco. Drawn from the types of experiences recently popularized in Netflix's 2020–2021 *Gentefied* series, Wieck tracks successive generations of Latinos who resisted eviction due to rising rents and fought against cultural erasure through art. Farther east, geographer Jeffrey M. Widener presents the agricultural landscape of Colorado's Western Slope and the struggle of small farmers to explore new pathways for economic survival. In Grand Valley, Widener offers the local turn to agritourism as a potential model—preserving local traditions and economies by pivoting them to new markets and consumers. These three essays highlight the risk that rapid economic and demographic changes pose to western communities and populations if not rigorously studied, as well as pointing to avenues for carefully and ethically addressing them.

Part 4, Migrant Lives and Labor, contains three essays tracing experiences of immigrant populations, including the violence imposed upon many by the U.S.-Mexico border regime, the western regions where many live, and how they impact the industries and communities for which they provide labor. Historian Ivón Padilla-Rodríguez contextualizes the Trump administration's "zero-tolerance" as well as the deterrence policies toward immigrants and asylum-seekers in already existent late twentieth-century family separation and child detention programs. Padilla-Rodríguez highlights the racialization of migrant childhoods, the politics of childhood innocence, and the long *durée* of inhumane border practices. Shifting to experiences of immigrants already in the United States, historian Taylor Cozzens uncovers the legal history of migrant laborers and workplace safety. Through a series of lawsuits concerning the injuries that pesticides, herbicides, and other chemicals caused migrant agricultural laborers and surrounding communities, Cozzens traces the injustices imposed on migrant communities and links them to ongoing legal fights concerning pollution from waste disposal. The nation relies on the bodies of migrant laborers for much of its food supply but has proven reticent or resistant to protecting their health and safety. Political scientist Ernesto Sagás tracks the movement of historic and post-North American Free Trade Agreement Hispanic and migrant labor along Colorado's Western Slope. While new high-amenity and resort economies are built and serviced by migrant labor populations, the resulting increase in property values and general affordability is pricing them out of the communities where they work. The crisis of affordability they face resonates with countless communities across the West, dependent on but pushed out by tourism-fueled gentrification. These three essays barely scratch the surface of the myriad issues migrants, minorities, and other marginalized communities face in the West, but they successfully illuminate conclusions with broad potential application.

Part 5, Unresolved Politics and Law, concludes the volume with three essays that wrestle with ongoing and unresolved political debates and struggles. Historian Chelsea Ball pulls the late twentieth-century fight over the Equal Rights Amendment (ERA) fully into the present by showcasing the western states where the ERA failed and where recent revivals have spent considerable political capital to resurrect and ratify the dead constitutional amendment. In Nevada, Utah, Oklahoma, and Arizona, she traces efforts of western women and others to complete what is unfinished. This enriches and diversifies our view of modern western women's lives, while also revealing western examples of unresolved and gendered cultural politics. Historian Peter Boag traces the thirty-year history of legislative battles in Washington State to extend civil rights protections to LGBTQ peoples by adding "sexual orientation" as a protected class. The successful inclusion of this language in 2006 only came after decades of organizing and overcoming resistance. In this history, Boag finds a continuity of increased acceptance of LGBTQ peoples and rights in the state *and* increasingly shrill opposition. As expanding efforts continue to be fought and resisted, it is an unresolved and ongoing issue in Washington and across the American West. Finally, historian Andrew Gulliford explores the fight of the Bears Ears National Monument designation and reduction to highlight the broader tableau of unresolved fights of public land use in the American West. In the twenty-first-century West, Gulliford outlines the challenges of balancing local economies, extractive industries, and tourism with the competing existing claims to the landscape by Indigenous peoples, more recent settlers, and new land users. It is as thoroughly "western" a dilemma as it is vexing. These three essays offer in explicit terms a thesis that is woven throughout all of this volume's essays: contest over the West is ongoing, and any hope for resolutions will require equal parts careful reflection and open dialogue.

Final Musings

In the end, what do the essays in this volume offer us? It seems that the closer we pull western histories to the present, the more our investigations muddy the waters, and the less they offer clarity and resolution. As he weighed our current collision of "Old" and "New" Wests, Frank Burgon recently mused, "This is the West—and America—today, a region in conflict with itself."[29] Perhaps it is fitting, therefore, if reviewing modern western history and ongoing twenty-first-century western issues leaves us feeling no less conflicted than when we began. In 1987 and again in 2000, Patricia Nelson Limerick categorized the West as a place of *continuity, convergence, conquest,* and *complexity*.[30] After another twenty years, the authors in this volume find the West no less tied to its past, no less challenged by the peoples and cultures that meet and mix here, no less troubled by the legacies and ongoing forms of settler, environmental, cultural, and other conquests, and no less confused by the ever-accelerating complexities unfolding in this dynamic region. The scholarship of a previous generation of "modern" West scholars resoundingly declared that trouble had long been and still was on the horizon, and that westerners needed to reckon with their past if they were to thrive in the future. Either blinded by the hubris of modern society or swept along by the simple inertia of time, we may not have stopped to pause, think, confer, and plan as much as we should have. We renew the call through these essays. The twenty-first-century West straddles multiple modern frontiers, not the least of which is the temporal frontier between our unsettled past and uncertain future. To chart positive futures for the countless populations, landscapes, and forces that make up the twenty-first-century West, our recent and more distant histories demand that we *do* pause, take careful stock of where we are, where we have come from, and where we wish to go. A region as magnificently diverse, dynamic, and beautiful as this deserves no less and, in fact, deserves much more.

Notes

1. Donald J. Trump, "State of the Union Address" (February 4, 2020), https://www.whitehouse.gov/briefings-statements/remarks-president-trump-state-union-address-3/.

2. Patricia Nelson Limerick, "Limerick: Trump Drains the History of the American West of Dignity and Meaning," *Denver Post*, February 29, 2020, https://www.denverpost.com/2020/02/14/limerick-trump-drains-the-history-of-the-american-west-of-dignity-and-meaning/.

3. See Turner, "The Significance of the Frontier in American History."

4. Cronon, Miles, and Gitlin, "Becoming West: Toward a New Meaning for Western History," 3, 6.

5. For a brief sampling, see M. R. Montgomery, "Conquest and Paranoia in the American West," *Boston Globe*, July 9, 1987, 79; T. R. Reid, "Shootout in Academia over History of U.S. West: New Generation Confronts Frontier Tradition," *Washington Post*, October 10, 1989, A03; Larry McMurtry, "How the West Was Won or Lost," *New Republic*, October 22, 1990, 32–38; Richard Bernstein, "Unsettling the Old West: Now Historians Are Bad-Mouthing the American Frontier," *New York Times*, March 18, 1990, SM34; Associated Press, "Historians Object to Glorification of Settlers in West / Pioneers Exploited the Land," *Colorado Springs Gazette*, September 16, 1990, B8; B. K., "Revisionist Historian Lassos the Mythic West," *Christian Science Monitor*, December 18, 1990, 13; Ann Poore, "Patricia Limerick Wants the West Taken Seriously," *Salt Lake Tribune*, May 5, 1991, E1; Page Stegner, "How the West Was Unsettled," *Los Angeles Times*, January 5, 1992, 2; Richard E. Nicholls, "True West: A Reading List," *New York Times*, September 20, 1992, BR26; Janny Scott, "We're Wild about the West Again," *Los Angeles Times*, May 5, 1993, 1; Janny Scott, "Rival Old West Historians Try to Put Own Brand on Frontier," *Los Angeles Times*, May 18, 1993, 5; Timothy Egan, "Offspring of Indians and Settlers Edit Histories of the West of Old," *New York Times*, May 31, 1993, 1; Stephen Foehr, "Historian Believes Western Frontier Never Closed," *Las Vegas Review–Journal*, July 6, 1993, 1C; and Victor Greto, "Historians Quash Many Western Myths," *Colorado Springs Gazette*, June 5, 1994, F8.

6. For a contemporary sampling of the more contemplative or outright critical scholarly response to the New Western History movement, see August, "The Future of Western History"; Brinkley, "The Western Historians"; Gressley, "Whither Western American History"; Faragher, "The Frontier Trail"; Goetzmann, "Crisis of the New—West?"; Gordon-McCutchan, "Revising the Revisionists"; Klein, "Reclaiming the 'F' Word"; Nugent, "Where Is the American West?"; Paul and Malone, "Tradition and Challenge in Western Historiography"; Wunder, "What's Old about the New Western History: Part 1"; Wunder, "What's Old about the New Western History? Part 2."

7. Western historians have won the Bancroft Prize, viewed by many as the most prestigious academic book prize in American history, with increasing frequency since the 1980s. Winning authors of western topics include Donald Worster (1980), William Cronon (1992), Linda Gordon (2000), Susan Lee Johnson (2001), James F. Brooks (2003), Pekka Hämäläinen (2009), Thomas G. Andrews (2009), Margaret D. Jacobs (2010), Anne F. Hyde (2012), Ari Kelman (2014), Andrés Reséndez (2017), and Louis S. Warren (2018). Western authors who have been finalists for the Pulitzer Prize since 1980 include John B. Unruh (1980), Francis Paul Prucha (1985), Richard White (1992 and 2012), William Cronon (1992), J. Anthony Lukas (1998), Paula Mitchell Marks (1999), and Anne F. Hyde (2012). Winners of the Pulitzer include Elizabeth A. Fenn (2015) and T. J. Stiles (2016). Western winners or finalists of the National Book Award in nonfiction since 1980 include Peter J. Powell (1982), Richard Slotkin (1993), Timothy Egan (2006), Domingo Martinez (2012), Andrés Reséndez (2016), David Grann (2017), and David Treuer (2019). These numbers are even larger when including colonial or Early Republic "frontier" topics located farther east.

8. McGerr, "Is There a Twentieth-Century West?," 239.

9. Limerick, *Something in the Soil*, 18–19.

10. Limerick, *Something in the Soil*, 95.

11. Nash, *The American West in the Twentieth Century*, 1.

12. Nash, *The American West in the Twentieth Century*, 2.

13. Nash, *The American West in the Twentieth Century*, 296.

14. "Regional histories such as this one may well be guideposts to the future in the writing of history," opined Roderick Nash. Nash's "insights should be a starting point for future serious scholarship on the subject," wrote Thomas G. Alexander. "Nash's volume is likely to be a point of departure for a rash of books to come," predicted Moses Rischin. Leonard Arrington termed it "a splendid synthesis . . . as lively as it is informative." Lawrence E. Ziewcz praised the text, hoping Nash would follow it with more in-depth works, the results of which "could be even more spectacular." Others were more mixed in their estimations. Earl Pomeroy forecasted it would be "influential" but was riddled with errors. Others criticized its scope, tone, and conclusions. At the far end of the spectrum, Bert Fireman expressed great resentment with Nash's critical tone—a harbinger of the many negative reactions to the "New Western History" to follow a decade later. See Nash, *Arizona and the West*, 273; Alexander, *The Western Historical Quarterly*, 196–97; Arrington, *The Journal of American History*, 233–34; Ziewcz, *The History Teacher*, 129–30; Pomeroy, *The Pacific Northwest Quarterly*, 35; Wright, *Reviews in American History*, 43–47; Rischin, *California Historical Quarterly*, 85; Garlid, *Minnesota History*, 313; Wickens, *Pacific Historical Review*, 281–82; Fireman, *The Journal of Arizona History*, 185–86.

15. Etulain, "Gerald D. Nash and the Twentieth-Century American West," 190.

16. Hints of Nash's skepticism toward the New Western History can be sensed in a 1986 piece, "Where's the West?," and in his closing remarks on historiographic critiques of Turner's "Frontier Thesis" in his 1991 book *Creating the West*. By 1993, however, he articulated a full-throated denunciation of New Western historians, calling their work "propaganda" and "proselytization for what in essence are totalitarian ideologies." According to Nash, the evolving field was full of "pessimism" and "new stereotypes" that lionized ethnic and racial minorities and demonized "Anglo white males." It was "destructive" and sought to "undermine democracy." See Nash, "Where's the West?"; Nash, *Creating the West*, 89–99; Nash, "Point of View," 3–4.

17. Limerick, *The Legacy of Conquest*, 20.

18. Lewis, "The WHA at Fifty," 287–369.

19. See Billington, *Westward Expansion: A History of the American Frontier*.

20. See Milner, *Major Problems in the History of the American West* and Milner, Butler, and Lewis, *Major Problems in the History of the American West*.

21. See Anderson and Chamberlain, *Power and Promise*; Butler and Lansing, *The American West*; Higham and Katerberg, *Conquests and Consequences*; Hine and Faragher, *The American West*; Milner, *A New Significance*; Milner, O'Connor, and Sandweiss, *The Oxford History of the American West*; Nugent, *Into the West*; Nugent and Ridge, *American West*; White, *A New History of the American West*. More recently in 2018, Anne F. Hyde and William Deverell published *Shaped by the West*, a two-volume document reader that views broader American history through a western lens. See Deverell and Hyde, *Shaped by the West*.

22. See Athearn, *The Mythic West in Twentieth-Century America*; Etulain and Morton, *The American West in 2000*; Etulain, *Re-Imagining the Modern American West*; Johnson, *New Westers*; Malone and Etulain, *The American West*; Nash, *A Brief History of the American West Since 1945*; Nash and Etulain, *The Twentieth-Century West*; Wrobel and Steiner, *Many Wests*.

23. See Etulain and Malone, *The American West* and Hine, Faragher, and Coleman, *The American West*.
24. Higham and Katerberg, *Conquests and Consequences*, 397–98.
25. Higham and Katerberg, *Conquests and Consequences*, 431.
26. Anderson and Chamberlain, *Power and Promise*, 354.
27. Hine, Faragher, and Coleman, *The American West*, 453.
28. See Pyne, *The Pyrocene*.
29. Bergon, *Two-Buck Chuck and the Marlboro Man*, 8.
30. Limerick, *The Legacy of Conquest*, 26–28; Limerick, *Something in the Soil*, 18–21.

Bibliography

Alexander, Thomas G. Review of *The American West in the Twentieth Century*, by Gerald D. Nash. *The Western Historical Quarterly* 5, no. 2 (1974): 196–97.

Anderson, Gary C., and Kathleen P. Chamberlain. *Power and Promise: The Changing American West*. New York: Pearson, 2007.

Arrington, Leonard J. Review of *The American West in the Twentieth Century*, by Gerald D. Nash. *The Journal of American History* 61, no. 1 (1974): 233–34.

Athearn, Robert G. *The Mythic West in Twentieth-Century America*. Lawrence: University Press of Kansas, 1986.

August, Jack L. "The Future of Western History: The First Wave." *The Journal of Arizona History* 27, no. 2 (1986): 229–44.

Bergon, Frank. *Two-Buck Chuck and the Marlboro Man: The New Old West*. Reno: University of Nevada Press, 2019.

Billington, Ray Allen. *Westward Expansion: A History of the American Frontier*. New York: The Macmillan Company, 1949.

Brinkley, Alan. "The Western Historians: Don't Fence Them In." *New York Times Book Review* (September 20, 1992): 7:1.

Butler, Anne M., and Michael J. Lansing. *The American West: A Concise History*. New York: Wiley-Blackwell, 2007.

Cronon, William, George Miles, and Jay Gitlin. "Becoming West: Toward a New Meaning for Western History." In *Under an Open Sky: Rethinking America's Western Past*, edited by William Cronon, George Miles, and Jay Gitlin, 3–27. New York: W. W. Norton & Company, 1992.

Deverell, William F., and Anne F. Hyde. *Shaped by the West: A History of North America*. 2 vols. Berkeley: University of California Press, 2018.

Etulain, Richard W. "Gerald D. Nash and the Twentieth-Century American West." In *The American West in 2000: Essays in Honor of Gerald D. Nash*, edited by Richard W. Etulain and Ferenc Morton Szasz, 186–98. Albuquerque: University of New Mexico Press, 2003.

Etulain, Richard W. *Re-Imagining the Modern American West: A Century of Fiction, History, and Art*. Tucson: University of Arizona Press, 1996.

Etulain, Richard W., and Ferenc Morton, eds. *The American West in 2000: Essays in Honor of Gerald D. Nash*. Albuquerque: University New Mexico Press, 2003.

Etulain, Richard W., and Michael P. Malone. *The American West: A Modern History, 1900 to the Present*. 2nd ed. Lincoln: University of Nebraska Press, 2007.

Faragher, John Mack. "The Frontier Trail: Rethinking Turner and Reimagining the American West." *American Historical Review* 98, no. 1 (February 1993): 106–17.

Fireman, Bert M. Review of *The American West in the Twentieth Century*, by Gerald D. Nash. *The Journal of Arizona History* 15, no. 2 (1974): 185–86.

Garlid, George W. Review of *The American West in the Twentieth Century*, by Gerald D. Nash. *Minnesota History* 43, no. 8 (1973): 313.

Goetzmann, William H. "Crisis of the New—West?" *Continuity* 17 (Fall 1993): 17–29.

Gordon-McCutchan, R. C. "Revising the Revisionists: Manifesto of the Realist Western Historians." *Journal of the West* 33 (July 1994): 3–7.

Gressley, Gene M. "Whither Western American History? Speculations on a Direction." *Pacific Historical Review* 53, no. 4 (1984): 493–501.

Higham, Carol L., and William H. Katerberg. *Conquests and Consequences: The American West from Frontier to Region*. 3rd ed. New York: Wiley-Blackwell, 2009.

Hine, Robert V., and John Mack Faragher. *The American West: A New Interpretive History*. New Haven CT: Yale University Press, 2000.

Hine, Robert V., John Mack Faragher, and Jon T. Coleman. *The American West: A New Interpretive History*. 2nd ed. New Haven CT: Yale University Press, 2017.

Johnson, Michael L. *New Westers: The West in Contemporary American Culture*. Lawrence: University Press of Kansas, 1996.

Klein, Kerwin Lee. "Reclaiming the 'F' Word, or Being and Becoming Postwestern." *Pacific Historical Review* 65, no. 2 (1996): 179–215.

Lewis, David Rich, ed. "The WHA at Fifty: Essays on the State of Western History Scholarship: A Commemoration." *Western Historical Quarterly* 42, no. 3 (Autumn 2011): 287–369.

Limerick, Patricia Nelson. *The Legacy of Conquest: The Unbroken Past of the American West*. New York: W. W. Norton, 1987.

Limerick, Patricia Nelson. *Something in the Soil: Legacies and Reckonings in the New West*. New York: W. W. Norton & Company, 2000.

Malone, Michael P., and Richard W. Etulain. *The American West: A Twentieth-Century History*. Lincoln: University of Nebraska Press, 1989.

McGerr, Michael. "Is There a Twentieth-Century West?" In *Under an Open Sky: Rethinking America's Western Past*, edited by William Cronon, George Miles, and Jay Gitlin, 239–56. New York: W. W. Norton & Company, 1992.

Milner, Clyde A., II, ed. *Major Problems in the History of the American West: Documents and Essays*. Lexington MA: D. C. Heath & Co, 1989.

Milner, Clyde A., II. *A New Significance: Re-Envisioning the History of the American West*. New York: Oxford University Press, 1996.

Milner, Clyde A., II, Anne M. Butler, and David Rich Lewis, eds. *Major Problems in the History of the American West*. 2nd ed. Boston MA: Cengage Learning, 1997.

Milner, Clyde A., II, Carol A. O'Connor, and Martha A. Sandweiss, eds. *The Oxford History of the American West*. Rev. ed. New York: Oxford University Press, 1996.

Nash, Gerald D. *The American West in the Twentieth Century: A Short History of an Urban Oasis*. Englewood Cliffs NJ: Prentice-Hall, 1973.

Nash, Gerald D. *A Brief History of the American West Since 1945*. New York: Harcourt College Publishers, 2000.

Nash, Gerald D. *Creating the West: Historical Interpretations, 1890–1990*. Albuquerque: University of New Mexico Press, 1991.

Nash, Gerald D. "Point of View: One Hundred Years of Western History." *Journal of the West* 32, no. 1 (January 1993): 3–4.

Nash, Gerald D. "Where's the West?" *The Historian* 49 (November 1986): 1–9.

Nash, Gerald D., and Richard W. Etulain, eds. *The Twentieth-Century West: Historical Interpretations*. Albuquerque: University of New Mexico Press, 1989.

Nash, Roderick. Review of *The American West in the Twentieth Century*, by Gerald D. Nash. *Arizona and the West* 16, no. 3 (1974): 273.

Nugent, Walter. *Into the West: The Story of Its People*. New York: Knopf, 1999.

Nugent, Walter. "Where Is the American West? Report on a Survey." *Montana: The Magazine of Western History* 42, no. 3 (Summer 1992): 2–23.

Nugent, Walter, and Martin Ridge. *American West: The Reader*. Bloomington: Indiana University Press, 1999.

Paul, Rodman W., and Michael P. Malone. "Tradition and Challenge in Western Historiography." *The Western Historical Quarterly* 16, no. 1 (1985): 27–53.

Pomeroy, Earl. Review of *The American West in the Twentieth Century*, by Gerald D. Nash. *The Pacific Northwest Quarterly* 66, no. 1 (1975): 35.

Pyne, Stephen J. *The Pyrocene: How We Created an Age of Fire, and What Happens Next*. Berkeley: University of California Press, 2021.

Rischin, Moses. Review of *The American West in the Twentieth Century*, by Gerald D. Nash. *California Historical Quarterly* 54, no. 1 (1975): 85.

Turner, Frederick Jackson. "The Significance of the Frontier in American History." *Annual Report of the American Historical Association* (1893): 197–227.

White, Richard. *A New History of the American West: "It's Your Misfortune and None of My Own."* Norman: University of Oklahoma Press, 1991.

Wickens, James. Review of *The American West in the Twentieth Century*, by Gerald D. Nash. *Pacific Historical Review* 43, no. 2 (1974): 281–82.

Wright, James. Review of *The American West in the Twentieth Century*, by Gerald D. Nash. *Reviews in American History* 2, no. 1 (1974): 43–47.

Wrobel, David M., and Michael C. Steiner, eds. *Many Wests: Place, Culture, and Regional Identity*. Lawrence: University Press of Kansas, 1997.

Wunder, John R. "What's Old about the New Western History: Race and Gender, Part 1." *The Pacific Northwest Quarterly* 85, no. 2 (1994): 50–58.

Wunder, John R. "What's Old about the New Western History? Part 2: Environment and Economy." *The Pacific Northwest Quarterly* 89, no. 2 (1998): 84–96.

Ziewcz, Lawrence E. Review of *The American West in the Twentieth Century*, by Gerald D. Nash. *The History Teacher* 7, no. 1 (1973): 129–30.

THE NORTH AMERICAN WEST IN THE TWENTY-FIRST CENTURY

PART 1

Environmental Reckonings

1

Poisoned Wilderness

Superfund and Libby, Montana

JENNIFER DUNN

Located in the remote northwestern corner of Montana, the town of Libby sits in the natural splendor of the Kootenai National Forest and the Rocky Mountains (see fig. 1). Mountain ranges border the community of 2,600 residents, and the Kootenai River flows lazily past Libby's downtown district. As county seat of Lincoln County, Libby enjoyed a strong economy buoyed by resource-extractive industries for most of the twentieth century. Libby residents prized living in a beautiful place with limitless outdoor activities and good paying jobs. In the last decades of the century this seemingly idyllic small Montana town faced a number of challenges. Logging and mining industries suffered downturns starting in the 1980s, and the population dropped more than 20 percent over the following decades as people left in search of employment.[1] Then in 1999 news broke nationally about toxic asbestos found in the homes, yards, and bodies of Libby's residents. Asbestos fibers, released through decades of local vermiculite mining and processing, had infiltrated the lungs of Libby residents since the mid-twentieth century and caused thousands to sicken and hundreds to die.

To address the dire environmental and public health issues, the Environmental Protection Agency (EPA) designated Libby as a "Superfund" site, which provided federal funds for environmental remediation and medical assistance. The federal Superfund program, created in 1980, manages the cleanup of the nation's most hazardous and polluted waste sites. Superfund sites are places of extreme environmental degradation. In many cases the toxic contaminants

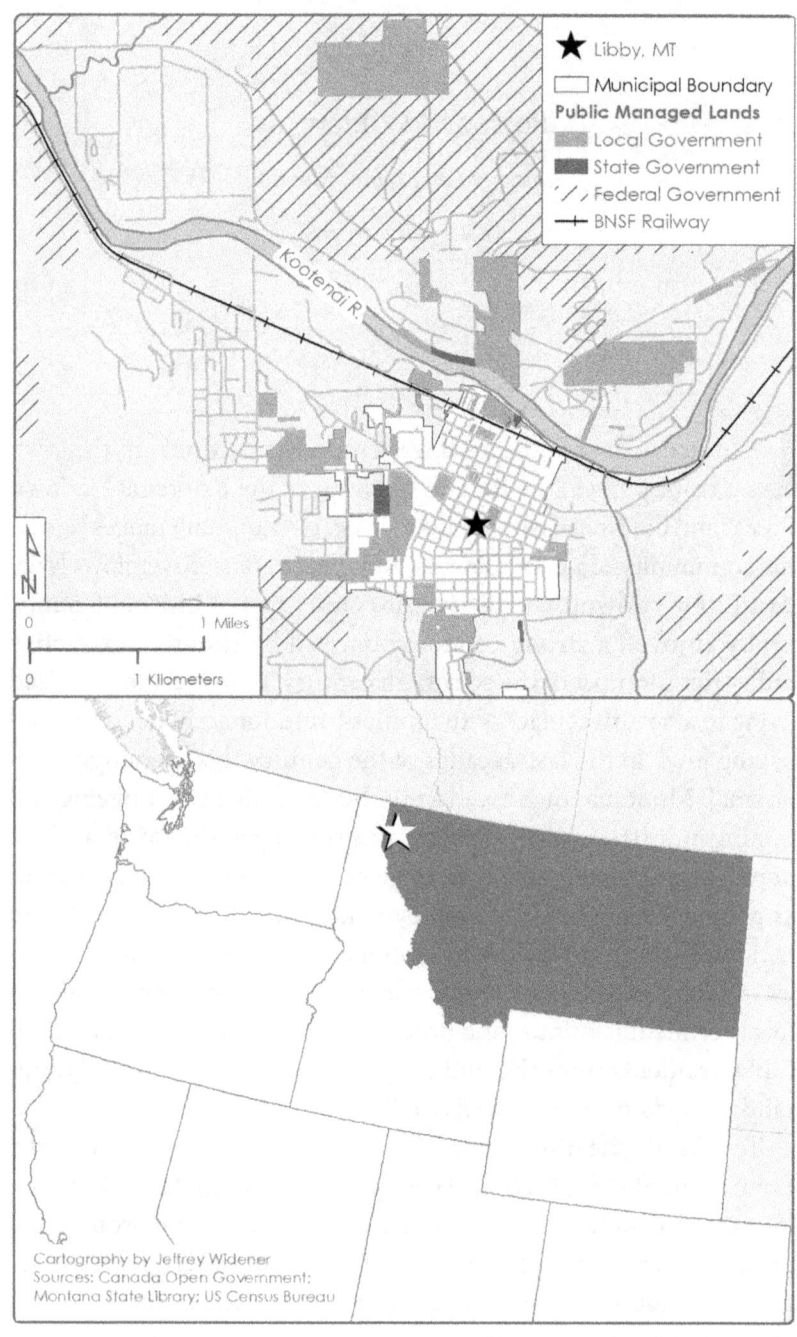

FIG. 1. Map of Libby, Montana. Map by Jeffrey M. Widener.

and pollutants found in Superfund communities resulted from a variety of twentieth-century extractive industries. Miners left their mark on the western landscape starting in the mid-1800s and continued mining throughout the next century and into the twenty-first. Immense wealth was harvested from underground, but vast damages to the environment and human health have been barely addressed through the Superfund program. The mine in Libby, closed by W. R. Grace in 1990, joined a legion of former mining sites: the EPA estimates there are more than half a million abandoned mines across the United States.[2] In the American West tens of thousands of former hard rock mines and smelter sites contain toxic chemicals and metals. Pollution is not the only challenge for residents in mining towns. Superfund communities often see their local industries close or slow down at the same time they are dealing with environmental and health problems. In situations such as these, communities often do not have the funds necessary for remediation, so the federal monies supplied by Superfund designation facilitate cleanup.

The story of Libby's contamination and resultant cleanup reflects a larger narrative of corporate malfeasance and government intervention found in many towns reliant on resource-extractive industries in the twentieth century. Libby also illustrates a larger process occurring in the American West where communities erase aspects of their past to benefit economically from tourism. Libby is not the only town disregarding aspects of their unpleasant history. Western communities often leave the violence of their past out of promotional literature, particularly the violence perpetuated by their ancestors against Native Americans. A different sort of violence occurred in Libby, and its lethal consequences still affect residents today. Mining employed many and supported the local economy, but it also poisoned Libby residents and their environment for most of the twentieth century. For decades their sicknesses remained unknown to others in the state and the nation as well as many in their hometown.

Other communities in the American West have also dealt with the environmental and health consequences caused by local industries. When resource-extractive economies slowed or shut down in the late-twentieth century, many towns turned to tourism, sometimes reluctantly, as a way to attract money and jobs. Libby manifested a tension found in such communities going through economic and social transition. How do locales clean the environment while resisting the stigma caused by a toxic landscape? After all being labeled a Superfund site might have a deleterious effect on tourism.

When Libby's poisoned environment became a public story, residents and governmental officials deliberated how to address their environmental and health concerns. This chapter examines the ways the community strove to reinvent itself during and after the asbestos cleanup. Not all Libby residents responded uniformly to the town's environmental and economic challenges, especially early on in the cleanup process. Analyzing local newspaper accounts reveals that when the cleanup process began residents held contradictory views on federal cleanup. Some, particularly local business interests concerned about the economic ramifications of a toxic legacy, resisted federal intervention, while others petitioned the EPA for Superfund designation to clean up their environment. Letters to the editor and stories in the paper reveal that most community misgivings about federal involvement in Libby disappeared as the scope of the asbestos contamination became apparent, and the town accepted the need for a government-funded cleanup. As the EPA finished its work in Lincoln County, and the town moved off the Superfund list in 2020, Libby residents faced decisions on how to market Libby for the future. Some Superfund sites retain physical markers of their industrial past: large open pit mines, for example, remain permanent tributes to mining and its environmental consequences. In contrast Libby's toxic legacy of mining resided in the bodies of its residents. While asbestos still permeates the homes, environment, and lungs of many residents, the town has few environmental scars from a century of mining. With no visible reminder of mining on the landscape, Libby residents weighed the acknowledgement of their extractive and deadly past against their desire to promote the community as a clean and healthy tourist destination. While asbestos contamination is unique to Libby's experience, many western mining towns share the same struggles in leaving behind their twentieth-century industrial past for an uncertain future.

From Gold Rush to Vermiculite Ore

Libby's early mining experiences mirrored the rest of Montana and much of the West. Following the 1864 discovery of gold at Alder Gulch, Montana's gold rush began, and, for a short time, the state was second only to California for gold production.[3] Libby's gold mining started soon after, and although the area never rivaled other communities in Montana with ore production, the legacies of hard rock mining remain: nearly three hundred abandoned or inactive mill and mine sites punctuate the 2.2 million acres of Kootenai National Forest surrounding Libby.[4] After the initial gold rush, technological and economic changes made other metals and minerals viable resources and sparked new mining industries. Prospectors found vermiculite, a unique non-metallic mineral, during Libby's early gold rush years but did not recognize its potential value.[5] In 1919 E. N. Alley, a part-time miner and owner of the Libby Hotel, bought mining claims on Rainy Creek near Libby.[6] Alley found vermiculite and observed its unique property of expanding with air pockets into a lightweight nonflammable material when heated.[7] With the mineral termed Zonolite, mining began in earnest six miles from Libby in the 1920s. The mine produced up to one hundred tons per day, processed locally and then shipped across the nation.[8] After processing, vermiculite does not burn or corrode. These properties made it popular for loose insulation used in the walls and attics of homes. In addition its puffy, spongy nature also aids in water and nutrition retention, so it was often used in gardening.[9]

Vermiculite itself is not harmful to human health, but the Libby vermiculite contains highly toxic asbestos fibers that, once airborne, infiltrate the lungs.[10] The asbestos fibers, shaped like needles, accumulate in the human body. Damage occurs to the lung membrane and tissues where the accumulating fibers cause hardening. Exposure to asbestos leads to a variety of health issues, including a lung disease called asbestosis or, in worse cases, lung cancer or a particularly aggressive form of malignant cancer called mesothelioma. All three diseases share common symptoms that can take up to forty years to develop after initial exposure: shortness of breath, persistent cough, and chest pain.[11] One graphic description of the impact of asbestos on the lungs describes how "the tissue changes from the elasticity and thickness of a balloon to that of a thick orange peel," making it impossible to take a deep breath.[12]

The Poisoning of a Montana Community

In 1963 W. R. Grace acquired the mine and continued to mine, mill, and distribute Libby vermiculite for almost thirty years. Still popular for home insulation and soil conditioners, Grace developed a spray-on insulation from Libby vermiculite that could be used in industrial and residential buildings, particularly skyscrapers.[13] As the asbestos-laden dust from the mine drifted down on the community below, Grace mined and processed nearly two hundred thousand tons of vermiculite each year until ceasing operations in 1990.[14] For miners exposure to asbestos first occurred as they dug vermiculite from the ground. Mills in Libby further crushed the ore, releasing asbestos-laden dust throughout the community. In addition Grace subsidized town improvements by donating vermiculite to build a new Little League baseball field and as a base for the high school track.[15] The company also gave free leftover vermiculite to town residents as ground cover and soil conditioner in their gardens. Citizens used vermiculite to repair public areas, such as boat ramps, parks, and schoolyards.[16] The ubiquitous vermiculite dust in Libby meant that citizens breathed in asbestos throughout their day. For the miners the cancer that developed in their lungs may have been an unwelcome but accepted result for high paying jobs. They likely felt different, however, when their families sickened and, in many cases, died. For the last decades of the twentieth century exposure to asbestos increased the mortality rate in Libby no matter the underlying diagnosis.[17]

Horrified by illnesses and deaths, some in Libby rallied to hold Grace responsible. By the time that the mine closed, residents had brought more than 140 lawsuits against Grace.[18] Yet people outside of Libby, as well as many living in town, generally did not appreciate the wide-reaching impact of asbestos on Libby residents. Some Montana newspapers briefly documented Libby lawsuits but sporadic articles did not add up to a damning indictment. Eventually the tally of victims of asbestos exposure grew too large to be dismissed, and federal and state governments took action, but Libby's toxic environment had remained largely unknown to those outside of Lincoln County for decades.

The first known case of asbestosis was diagnosed in Libby in the 1950s.[19] Numbers grew over the following decades with sicknesses and deaths. The legacy of Grace's malfeasance finally became a national story in November 1999 when *Seattle Post-Intelligencer* reporter Andrew Schneider published a series on W. R. Grace and Libby's asbestos titled, "Uncivil Action: A Town Left to Die." The articles focused on W. R. Grace, the state of Montana, and the federal government, all of whom Schneider accused as complicit in the asbestos contamination of Libby residents.

Libby's newspaper, the *Montanian*, responded to Schneider's exposé with a front-page article titled, "EPA to Help State Evaluate Asbestos in Libby." While recounting how the *Seattle Post-Intelligencer* stories provoked EPA administrators to explore the possible health threat in Libby, the *Montanian* challenged the "anecdotal and highly speculative interviews" cited by the *Seattle Post-Intelligencer*. According to the Libby newspaper, "There is no scientific evidence to support [the health concerns], and that no local, state or federal health agency can produce records to suggest that any health hazard remains."[20] Over the next six months the *Montanian* downplayed asbestos concerns. The *Seattle Post-Intelligencer*'s numbers of 192 deaths and 375 asbestos-related fatal illnesses were refuted in Libby's paper by Montana medical doctor Michael Spence. According to Spence the number of asbestos-related deaths was much lower than reported: fewer than one hundred deaths in the entire state over the last ten years.[21] In addition to challenging the higher casualty numbers, the *Montanian* contested the stories of widespread asbestos contamination. According to Libby's newspaper in the first few months of EPA testing only two local properties had asbestos fibers at levels that caused concern.

After the story broke many Libby residents had greater fears about how their community was characterized locally and nationally than the potential health risks from asbestos. Frustration mounted that

Libby was misrepresented as a valley of death, and a number of local citizens expressed anger at the media for its perceived unfair portrayal of the community. In January 2000 Tony Berget, Libby's mayor, wrote a letter to the *Montanian* defending himself against criticisms that his concerns for Libby only focused on the economic well-being rather than the public health of the town. Berget stated that the negative news coverage had damaged Libby's economy when, in fact, the preliminary findings from the EPA reassured him that asbestos was not a problem.[22] Montana Sen. Conrad Burns followed the next week with an editorial criticizing the "exaggerated" asbestos claims that had "impacts on tourism, real estate, and the economy of Libby."[23] Accusations against the media and its coverage of the asbestos issues came to a head in February 2000 when a *Montanian* editorial defended the freedom of the press and denounced the local community advisory committee whose members had reservations about media coverage and considered excluding the media from informational meetings between the EPA and the community. The *Montanian* criticized the committee's attempt to control public information on Libby's asbestos problem and noted that the consistent lone voice advocating freedom of speech came from the EPA on-site coordinator, Paul Peronard. Peronard had defended the press and its reporting by reiterating several times, "This is America," when faced with arguments against media coverage. The newspaper's final words on the importance of a free press were clear: "And stop blaming the media. The media didn't invent the asbestos problem. But they did make it possible for everyone to know about it."[24]

As the scope of the asbestos hazard in Libby grew, increasing numbers of residents advocated for federal cleanup. In July 2000 the EPA suggested all who lived in Libby before 1991 had probably been exposed to asbestos and should receive medical screenings to assess their risk of asbestos-related diseases.[25] After documenting the results from asbestos sampling and resident health screenings, the EPA declared that a "public health emergency" existed in Libby. This gave Libby the dubious distinction of being the first and only place to receive this designation, and Libby was described as "the worst case of industrial poisoning of a whole community in American history."[26] By early 2001 the EPA declared that it would be easier to list who was unaffected by asbestos in Libby than to count all those who were affected. Of those residents who had been screened for health issues, 30 percent showed a potential for lung disease. According to Peronard the percentage of affected citizens was "much worse than anyone thought." The EPA expected that 10 to 15 percent of those tested would have lung abnormalities. While the percentage of miners screened with lung scarring was not very surprising at 50 percent, the EPA expressed shock that 25 percent of residents who had not worked at the mine had lung health issues.[27]

In 2000 W. R. Grace announced the "Libby Medical Plan" to pay "asbestos-related medical bills and prescription drug costs for its former Libby employees, their families, and any present or past area residents who lived within a twenty-mile radius of the Libby mine or mill."[28] Critics of Grace pointed out, contrary to Grace's publicity, that the plan failed to cover 100 percent of many victims' medical bills.[29] The medical plan controversy aside, at first no monies from Grace went to environmental cleanup in Libby. In early discussions between the company and the EPA, Grace refused to participate in a consensual cleanup agreement but agreed to defer to an administrative order in which the EPA determined the cleanup plan and Grace paid for it. Grace's generosity to Libby proved to have limits. Through the administrative order W. R. Grace retained the right to sue if the company felt the cleanup costs were excessive.[30] In addition, even as the company touted its medical assistance, Grace closed the mine site and other related properties to the federal government, effectively delaying the remediation process.[31] The community encouraged Grace to reopen the mine site so cleanup could continue, and more than ninety residents petitioned Grace to work with the EPA as soon as possible.[32] Over the next few months Grace went on the defensive and at one point wrote the EPA offices in Washington DC to complain about local EPA officials. In their letter published in the *Montanian* Grace argued the local officials "encourage[d] a high level of anxiety and fear in the community," and Grace made a number of questionable assertions that were refuted by the editor and other letter writers.[33]

Superfund Comes to Libby

The EPA sued Grace and in March 2001 won full access to the mine and related properties for the cleanup.[34] Within two months the EPA recommended Superfund status as the best way to clean up Libby's asbestos contamination. This advice came soon after W. R. Grace filed for bankruptcy citing "a preponderance of asbestos-related lawsuits that have sent the company's stock plummeting and depleted the company's cash reserves."[35] The EPA counseled Libby residents to advocate for Superfund designation because of assumed future remediation costs and the challenges to petitioning a bankrupt Grace for funds. The early stages of cleanup in Libby had been done under an EPA program with limited funds, and the scope of the asbestos contamination necessitated funding only available under Superfund designation.[36]

Superfund designation cannot be arbitrarily imposed by the federal government but instead requires community support and a request from the state governor. Gov. Judy Martz had lived in Butte, Montana, and remained critical of the EPA's slow cleanup process there. Because of her concerns about Butte, Martz would not commit to asking for Superfund designation. The governor also expressed concerns about the state's share of Superfund costs estimated to be $5 million to $10 million.[37] Earlier that summer some residents had questioned the possible effects of Superfund designation on Libby's economy.[38] In response EPA representatives acknowledged that negative publicity and economic consequences often did accompany Superfund designations but reminded residents that the public already knew of Libby's toxic environment and that federal cleanup could only improve the situation.[39] Paul Peronard, an EPA official, admitted that he prioritized the health of Libby's residents over Libby's economic interests. When challenged in a public meeting about this decision, Peronard responded, "If I think I need to do a cleanup because there's a risk to people, that outweighs all other considerations. If that means I get eaten up by the local folks [for affecting Libby's economy], then I'll take my beating."[40] Residents also accused W. R. Grace of inciting an anti-Superfund attitude when

Grace argued the federal program would cause economic harm to Libby. One sarcastic response from a letter to the editor in the *Montanian* revealed how some in town viewed Grace's opinion: "Well, W. R. Grace, our community is already hurting, but thanks for the free advice!"[41] The letter writer pleaded with fellow citizens to support Superfund designation: "Governments on all levels failed to protect us. One government has acknowledged that failure and that is our federal government. Uncle Sam is reaching out a hand to a drowning community and we need to take hold."[42]

In August 2001 Martz's attorney general, Mike McGrath, recommended Superfund designation after W. R. Grace declared Chapter 11 bankruptcy, and their ability to fund a cleanup came into doubt.[43] By this time most people in Libby supported designation. Almost three hundred residents, local officials, and members of the press met with Governor Martz to present a unified front against cleanup by W. R. Grace, arguing that Libby needed Superfund designation and asking Martz to fast-track the cleanup process.[44] At this meeting Martz remained uncommitted to Superfund designation, and in a later visit to Libby Martz "flatly rejected a request by Lincoln County commissioners to put Libby's potential Superfund designation on a fast track."[45] However, in late December Martz surprised residents by formally requesting that the EPA fast-track the Superfund process for Libby.[46] This request shortened, by a year, the process of Superfund designation and did not allow opponents to slow or stop the process.[47] With the designation Libby became "one of the nation's top one hundred cleanup sites in spending and attention priority."[48] Martz's announcement prompted tears and a standing ovation from grateful residents, and cleanup began in earnest in Libby in 2002.[49]

Superfund sites are places so toxic and contaminated that the EPA recommends (and often funds) their cleanup. Nineteenth-century American industry operated with little governmental regulation, particularly in regard to pollution and waste. In the mid-twentieth century a growing public awareness of the ramifications of unregulated capitalism paired with the nascent environmental movement led to a new understanding: industry-caused environmental damages could only be fixed through science, technology, and massive governmental funding. In response to numerous air, water, and soil pollution catastrophes after World War II, the EPA created the Superfund program in 1980 to clean up the nation's most contaminated waste sites. This massive government program exists in every state, from dense urban areas to remote rural settings. According to Superfund reports, 16 percent of the U.S. population, or fifty-three million people, live within three miles of a Superfund site.[50] The EPA tracks more than 530,000 contaminated sites, covering an area the size of Indiana. The agency prioritizes its funding on the most dangerous and toxic places for cleanup.[51] More than 1,700 Superfund sites have been prioritized for cleanup by the EPA, including Libby, Montana.

The Future of Libby After Superfund

Libby's cleanup spanned more than fifteen years, required the investigation of 7,500 properties with a resulting cleanup of 2,400 properties, and cost more than $600 million (of that W. R. Grace paid for $250 million).[52] The extreme health and environmental crises found in town explained the relative speed of the cleanup and lack of controversy compared to other Superfund listings. During its seventeen-year cleanup in Libby, the EPA removed more than one million cubic yards of toxic soil and thirty thousand cubic yards of contaminated building materials.[53] In November 2015, more than a decade after cleanup started, the EPA released a health risk assessment for Libby that asserted that "the amount of [asbestos] in the air in downtown Libby is now nearly 100,000 times lower than when the vermiculite mine and mill were operating."[54] According to the EPA the successful cleanup resulted in asbestos levels in the ambient air consistent with other communities in Montana and the nation.[55]

Even with the removal of vast amounts of hazardous waste, questions and concerns persisted about lingering asbestos in the area. The EPA did not inspect almost seven hundred properties in and around Libby as owners either refused to participate in the cleanup or could not be contacted.[56] The asbestos levels at these properties, therefore, could not be determined by the EPA. In addition, inspected homes rarely had the asbestos removed. To streamline its cleanup efforts the EPA decided to seal asbestos into the walls of homes rather than removing it from all properties. While the EPA assured homeowners this remediation plan presented minimal risk to their health, residents expressed concerns about asbestos exposure from future home renovations and remodeling projects.[57] Structures with asbestos insulation were not the only sources of possible contamination. Although vast amounts of soil were removed from residential and commercial properties, the EPA acknowledged that asbestos contamination often exceeded the three-feet depth excavation requirement used for remediation.[58] Officials from the EPA explained that asbestos would remain in Libby: "If there's exposure [from asbestos] we'll remove it. But if it's in the soil at depth, we will not remove it. If it's contained in a wall of a commercial or residential building, we will not remove it."[59]

Asbestos contamination spread beyond the city limits. Scientific studies assessing the possible exposure to asbestos from tree bark warned that the forests surrounding Libby were "reservoirs" for fibers released during seventy years of vermiculite mining and processing.[60] These fibers could be released back into the air if the tree bark were disturbed, most commonly through logging or a forest fire. Future exposure to asbestos worried many city residents, but many might already have been exposed and did not yet have symptoms. With a thirty-to-forty-year dormancy period, future victims are expected to succumb to cancer in coming decades. Asbestos still remains in the environment, homes, and bodies of Libby residents even as the EPA ends its cleanup there.

While long-time residents struggle for breath, Libby looks for a way to survive and thrive in the twenty-first century. As the EPA touted the cleanup's success and removed Libby from the Superfund list—thereby moving the administration and monitoring responsibilities of the site to the Montana Department of Environmental Quality—the community looked to craft a new identity, leaving behind a toxic landscape and health concerns. As they entered a new century, Libby hoped to revitalize its stagnant economy. To this end Libby needed investment in multiple economic areas: from encouraging the development of new businesses to touting the recreational opportunities and scenic beauty of the region to tourists.[61]

Economic Revitalization in Libby

Communities in the twentieth-century American West often saw tourism as their best option to revitalize stagnant or declining extractive economies. As a panacea for economic ills, tourism induced a number of irrevocable changes for the residents and the towns.[62] The negative consequences of tourism have been documented, but amenity dollars remain important for many regional and local economies. Tourism created jobs for locals, and the scenic mountain areas had great tourist potential.[63] Most communities hoped for an economic boom from promoting their scenery and heritage to visitors and new residents. Libby has not been immune to the lure of these dollars. Similar to other economically downtrodden communities that have lost their resource-dependent economic base, Libby residents marketed the town as a place to visit and vacation after the local industries shuttered and the economy slowed.

Located far from Interstate 90 in a remote corner of the state, Libby officials worked to encourage and welcome visitors and new residents. Specific aspects of Libby were highlighted to portray the town's heritage. Festivals like Logger Days celebrated Libby's past and, in the process, shaped Libby's heritage. According to the Logger Days' website, the festival continued even through population declines and economic downturns: "Libby still identifies itself with its logging industry and heritage."[64] Long after local sawmills closed, Logger Days commemorated Libby's logging past as logging companies demonstrated machinery and techniques. Heritage is not a direct study of the past but rather a selection of meanings, memories, and traditions that are used to represent a past that those in the present day have deemed worth remembering.[65] Libby residents created celebrations and representations of Libby's past with the goal to craft heritage. They were not alone in this process. Both small and large western communities have celebrated their heritage through festivals and other events, creating a narrative of their town's past.[66] These types of events did not just fill hotel rooms with tourists but also revealed how residents displayed community pride and viewed their town's identity.

Logger Days presented Libby's heritage as one of a timber town. The mine and the miners who worked there to provide the majority of the world's supply of vermiculite for more than seventy years received no acknowledgment in Libby's public persona: no events represented mining work, no statues or monuments remembered the glory days of the W. R. Grace mine, and little mention existed about vermiculite's role in building America's skyscrapers. The Libby Chamber of Commerce website, one of the few Libby websites that mentioned asbestos mining and the subsequent Superfund remediation process, described the town's optimistic future: "After 15 years of intensive cleanup, Libby continues full speed ahead without the lulls of past transitions—just a few too many souls know how good this place is for it to be abandoned now."[67] Presumably these "lulls" were the downturns inherent in resource-extractive communities or the challenges to local economies when a town became contaminated by hazardous materials. The chamber included a webpage addressing the issues of asbestos contamination and Superfund: "In Libby we tend to be pretty frank people, so we're not going to sugarcoat this: Libby has had a widely publicized issue with asbestos."[68] After this admission the chamber quickly moved to alleviate concern and asserted that Libby was asbestos free: "In all truth, we've moved past it and day-to-day it has no impact on life here."[69] The community was ready to move past its Superfund designation and shed its toxic history. As the chamber website concluded optimistically, "The economy is already transforming with budding infrastructure and a drastic influx of technology. New businesses are growing and Libby's economy is diversifying like never before. *Libby's future is starting now.*"[70]

Libby hoped to rise from asbestos ashes, but rebirth was neither quick nor easy. Tourist dollars may have declined after initial Superfund designation, which was a concern for Libby businesspeople in the early days of EPA interaction. With reduced logging opportunities and the Grace mine closed, many residents found themselves out of work in a county where the average unemployment rate was twice the state's rate of 3.9 percent in 2017.[71] This was particularly concerning since Montana's economy had performed well overall: its employment rate increased by 20 percent in the first fifteen years of the century.[72] Lincoln County residents, on the other hand, struggled economically. Some welcomed the opportunity to earn good wages from the then largest employer in town: the EPA.[73] Others worked to craft a narrative that served the interests of tourism, economic growth, and continued existence in the twenty-first century. While Libby's chamber website acknowledged Libby's toxic past as the EPA left town, one wonders how long Superfund will remain in the community's social memory. Many other western communities cannot erase their resource-extractive pasts because of their landscape's environmental degradation. Covering 675 acres, Butte's Berkeley Pit, for example, will forever remain a memento to Butte's industrial past that shaped its people and their environment. Other communities with less visible environmental damage may have the ability to leave behind their toxic pasts and move forward with a new, outdoors-focused narrative. Dealing with a legacy of lead contamination, the EPA has spent thirty-five years and $900 million in Kellogg, Idaho, on cleanup. Through this process the town rebranded itself as a four-season outdoor playground, or as the chamber's website called it, "an outdoor recreationalist's paradise."[74] Similar to Kellogg, few physical aspects of Libby's vermiculite mining past remain. Even though more cases of lung disease and cancer will develop in Libby, the community has the ability to ignore the town's toxic legacy and Superfund past.

The desire to minimize Superfund and asbestos contamination started in the early years of cleanup. Soon after the asbestos news broke, some wanted to lessen the emphasis on the town's poisonous past. Howard McDonald, the executive director of the Libby Chamber of Commerce, penned a letter to the local newspaper encouraging readers not to dwell on the negative side of Libby's situation. McDonald argued that while residents had sickened and died, Libby was still a desirable place to live and visit. At the end of his letter he encouraged focusing on the positives in Libby: "Toxic dust is not blowing in the street. The grass is green, the air is clean and we do not feel we should publicize or amplify a problem that is mainly in the past tense, and where it is not, the problem is being addressed."[75]

Many western towns, like Libby, suffered a triple blow since the mid-twentieth century. First, these communities lost their resource-extractive economies, in many cases based in logging or mining. In the case of Libby both industries fell into severe decline by the time Superfund was implemented. Secondly, before leaving town industry had poisoned local landscapes and bodies. Finally, in Libby's case the town was then nationally labeled toxic and was designated a Superfund site that limited its ability to move on from its industrial, pollutive past. Libby is not alone in dealing with economic decline and environmental contamination. Other communities are also trying to reinvent themselves in the twenty-first century as they move away from their damaged pasts.

Remembering Superfund ... or Not

Where did this leave Libby as Superfund left town? Logging and mining opportunities were touted as ways to revive the local economy. Logging reached its peak output in Montana in the 1960s and 1970s with Libby as one of the main centers for commercial logging. In the last decades of the twentieth century, local sawmills closed and logging jobs disappeared. Timber resources dwindled in the area, and the last mill closed its doors in 2002.[76] Bringing back the timber industry in Libby proved challenging as the nearest mill sat ninety minutes away in northern Idaho.[77] The Hecla Mining Company wanted to revive silver and copper mining in the area with the Montanore Mine located eighteen miles from Libby. Hecla asserted that operations would last up to twenty years and would employ 450 people at full production.[78] Hecla and supporters of the mine argued that mining jobs would greatly improve the economic situation in Lincoln County.[79] Multiple environmental groups, however, countered that the mine could endanger protected species and surface water in the area and filed lawsuits to stop the mine.[80]

Population growth was, and continues to be, essential in Libby as younger residents moved away for employment opportunities elsewhere. Between 1990 and 2005 the number of young adults aged twenty-five to thirty-four declined 33 percent in Libby. An increase in older residents offset some of the population decline; much of the projected growth over the next few decades was expected in retirees.[81] The legacy of asbestos contamination and the resultant public health emergency provided Libby with superior access to healthcare compared to most towns its size—an attractive factor for older residents.[82] Libby, however, could not merely rely on retirees to boost the town's population. Younger residents and entrepreneurs were needed to reenergize and resurrect the town. In 2015 the city of Libby hired PartnersCreative, a Missoula-based marketing company, to rebrand its image and erase the connection between Libby and asbestos. In its report the marketing company asserted that many small towns in the West hoped to reestablish their economic wellbeing through tourism after local industries left.[83] To this end the rebranding effort suggested touting Libby's outdoor amenities, recreation, and remoteness as selling points to tourists and new residents.[84] In the early decades of the twenty-first century the opportunity to leave behind its toxic mining past and portray the town's economy and environment as clean, healthy, and bright proved to be attractive to many in Libby.

Not all Libby residents, however, wanted to forget the asbestos contamination and its victims. In spring 2001 many struggled to comprehend the news that hundreds of their neighbors and friends had been poisoned. In early April a memorial was suggested as a way to commemorate those who had died from asbestos-related diseases. A planning committee reached out to the community at-large to compile as many names of the deceased as they could, both miners and family members. In early May they had accumulated one hundred names and had developed a plan to display wooden crosses with names painted on them.[85] By Memorial Day 2001 171 crosses with names of victims were displayed, and eighty people attended the remembrance ceremony.[86] During the memorial, state Rep. Eileen Carney spoke and compared the asbestos victims to soldiers: while the military fallen gave their lives on the battlefield, Libby's victims were sacrificed by corporate America.[87] In her speech Carney discussed how many in Libby wished the asbestos problem would just go away. Carney, however, viewed the memorial as both a reminder of the lives lost and proof of Libby's resiliency and community spirit: "These crosses represent the people who have died. But they also serve to remind us that by pulling together we can tackle anything . . . we need to heal the town and to bring it together."[88] While the crosses did not become a permanent fixture in Libby, the Community Asbestos Memorial Project (CAMP) Committee worked to have a memorial site that "told the story of Libby, but also presented a vision of hope and symbol of the community moving forward."[89] For the memorial site the committee chose the former loading dock at the processing plant, a place found to have extremely high levels of asbestos during cleanup. In 2008 the memorial became the Fred Brown Pavilion, the center of a riverfront park dedicated to the long-time Libby mayor.[90] A metal sign, hanging at the entrance to the pavilion, commemorated the CAMP. The rows of stark, white crosses no longer existed to remind residents of individual victims of asbestos poisoning. The pavilion, however, stood commemorating Libby's past. Perhaps more importantly, it also celebrated Libby's survival of economic hardship and environmental tragedy as it moved into a hopeful future.

Notes

1. U.S. Department of Commerce, *1990 Census of Population and Housing*, 13.
2. CLU-IN, "Mining Sites."
3. Malone, *The Battle for Butte*, 6.
4. Hargrave et al., "Abandoned-Inactive Mines."
5. "W. R. Grace File Review Summary: Chronological Order of Events (CVID #3726)," Montana Department of Environmental Quality.
6. King, "Libby," Mesothelioma Center.
7. "Vermiculite," mindat.org.
8. "W. R. Grace File Review Summary."
9. Mason, "The Homeowners Column," University of Illinois Extension.
10. "OSH Answers Fact Sheets: Vermiculite Insulation Containing Asbestos," Canadian Centre for Occupational Health and Safety.
11. "Mesothelioma vs. Asbestos," Mesothelioma Guide.
12. Andrew Schneider, "Uncivil Action: A Town Left to Die," *Seattle Post-Intelligencer*, November 18, 1999, A10.
13. See King, "History of Asbestos," Mesothelioma Center.
14. "W. R. Grace," Mesothelioma Fund.
15. Mark Matthews, "Libby's Dark Secret," *High Country News*, March 13, 2000, 12.

16. "Asbestos: Vermiculite and Libby," Lincoln County Asbestos Resource Program.

17. U.S. Department of Health and Human Services, *Health Consultation: Mortality in Libby, Montana (1979–1998)*, August 8, 2002, 1. This study looked at death certificates in Libby from 1979 to 1998 to determine the following: the asbestosis mortality rate was forty to eighty times higher than expected, and the lung cancer rate was 20 to 30 percent higher. While mesothelioma is extremely rare and national mortality rates are not published, the mortality rates for this cancer increased in Libby as well.

18. Matthews, "Libby's Dark Secret," *High Country News*, March 13, 2000.

19. Schneider, "Uncivil Action," *Seattle Post-Intelligencer*, November 18, 1999.

20. "EPA to Help State Evaluate Asbestos in Libby," *Montanian*, November 24, 1999, 1.

21. "Governor Addresses Asbestos Concerns," *Montanian*, December 22, 1999, 1.

22. Tony Berget, "Libby Still Alive Despite News Reports," *Montanian*, January 19, 2000, 8.

23. Conrad Burns, "Asbestos Bill Meant to Help People," *Montanian*, January 26, 2000, 2.

24. "Speech Is Still Free," *Montanian*, February 9, 2000, 2.

25. "Total Exposure: EPA Says All Libby Residents Breathed Asbestos Before 1991," *Montanian*, July 19, 2000, 1.

26. U.S. Department of Labor, "Asbestos Awareness Lesson Plan: Libby Montana," 1.

27. David F. Latham, "Screening Finds Widespread Asbestos Exposure," *Montanian*, February 28, 2001, 1.

28. "Grace Unveils First-of-Its-Kind Medical Coverage," *Montanian*, April 19, 2000, 1.

29. David F. Latham, "Grace Medical Plan: First Payments Leave Asbestos Victims with Unpaid Hospital Bills," *Montanian*, October 11, 2000, 1.

30. "Grace Rejects EPA Asbestos Cleanup Plan," *Montanian*, April 26, 2000, 1.

31. David F. Latham, "Cleanup Could Be Delayed at Least One Year," *Montanian*, October 4, 2000, 1.

32. Latham, "Cleanup Could Be Delayed," *Montanian*, October 4, 2000.

33. "Grace Official Attacks Libby Clean-up Effort," *Montanian*, March 7, 2001, 2. One such claim by Grace was that prior to 1999 Grace had "no reason to believe that there was a continuing environmental problem in the community." Both the *Montanian* editor and other letter writers noted that former employees had admitted that Grace previously established a fund to pay off Libby asbestos victims.

34. "EPA Wins Lawsuit Against Grace," *Montanian*, March 14, 2001, 1.

35. David F. Latham, "W. R. Grace Files for Bankruptcy," *Montanian*, April 4, 2001, 1.

36. Clinton Maynard, "Dear Gov. Martz: Please Listen and Consider Our Concerns," *Montanian*, November 21, 2001, 8.

37. "Martz Nixes 'Silver Bullet' Option for Libby," *Montanian*, October 17, 2001, 1.

38. "Libby Community Advisory Group Meeting Summary," University of Montana, June 14, 2001.

39. "Libby Community Advisory Group Meeting Summary," University of Montana, May 17, 2001.

40. "Citizens Group Discusses Expanding Its Authority," *Montanian*, March 1, 2000, 8.

41. Clinton Maynard, "Libby Must Unify to Solve Asbestos Problem," *Montanian*, May 16, 2001, 2.

42. Maynard, "Libby Must Unify," *Montanian*, May 16, 2001.

43. "Attorney General Recommends Superfund Cleanup for Libby," *Montanian*, August 22, 2001, 1.

44. "Libby Presents Unified Front to Governor," *Montanian*, August 15, 2001, 1.

45. "Martz Nixes," *Montanian*, October 17, 2001.

46. "'Merry Christmas,' Gov. Martz Fires 'Silver Bullet' for Libby; Asbestos Cleanup Now Guaranteed," *Montanian*, December 26, 2001, 1.

47. "Merry Christmas," *Montanian*, December 26, 2001.

48. "Superfund Status Becomes Official," *Montanian*, March 6, 2002, 1.

49. Kathleen McLaughlin, "Martz Puts Libby Cleanup on Fast Track," *Billings Gazette*, December 21, 2001, 9A.

50. U.S. Environmental Protection Agency, "Population Surrounding 1,836 Superfund Remedial Sites," 1.

51. U.S. Environmental Protection Agency, "Measuring Progress in EPA's Land Cleanup Programs," 1.

52. Matthew Brown, "Montana Set to Take Over Deadly Asbestos Cleanup Site," *Business Insider*, September 21, 2017, https://www.businessinsider.com/ap-montana-set-to-take-over-deadly-asbestos-cleanup-site-2017-9.

53. U.S Environmental Protection Agency, "Libby Asbestos Site, Libby, MT," October 23, 2018, https://cumulis.epa.gov/supercpad/SiteProfiles/index.cfm?fuseaction=second.Cleanup&id=0801744#bkground.

54. U.S. Environmental Protection Agency, "Libby Asbestos Site."

55. U.S. Environmental Protection Agency, "Site-Wide Human Health Risk Assessment, Executive Summary: Libby Asbestos Superfund Site, Libby, Montana," by CDM Smith, 5.

56. Tim Povtak, "Bittersweet Ending to Asbestos Cleanup in Libby, Montana," Mesothelioma Center.

57. Matthew Brown, "U.S. Cleanup Would Leave Some Asbestos in Contaminated Libby, Montana," *St. Louis Post-Dispatch*, May 5, 2015, https://www.stltoday.com/business/local/u-s-cleanup-would-leave-some-asbestos-in-contaminated-libby/article_886cad8a-9e3f-57cc-b3a2-0e1503c748b8.html.

58. U.S. Environmental Protection Agency, "Libby Asbestos Superfund Site the Former Stimson Lumber Mill, Operable Unit 5 Lincoln County, Montana: Final Remedial Action Report," 3–1.

59. Rob Chaney, "Libby Residents Worried About EPA Plan to Leave Some Asbestos in Homes," *Missoulian*, May 5, 2015, https://missoulian.com/news/local/libby-residents-worried-about-epa-plan-to-leave-some-asbestos-in-homes/article_854497be-c7d8-5ef4-9acc-1b5523167de1.html.

60. Ward et al., "Amphibole Asbestos in Tree Bark," 395.

61. Corbin Cates-Carney, "Libby, Lincoln County Plan Beyond Superfund," *Montana Public Radio*, November 18, 2015, https://www.mtpr.org/post/libby-lincoln-county-plan-beyond-superfund.

62. See Rothman, *Devil's Bargains* and Childers, *Colorado Powder Keg*.

63. Hall and Lew, *Understanding and Managing Tourism Impacts*, 109.

64. "Libby Logger Days History," Logger Days.

65. Graham, "Heritage as Knowledge: Capital or Culture?," 1004.

66. Christensen, *Red Lodge and the Mythic West*, 128.

67. "Heritage," Libby Chamber of Commerce.
68. "Cleanup," Libby Chamber of Commerce.
69. "Cleanup," Libby Chamber of Commerce.
70. "Heritage," Libby Chamber of Commerce. Emphasis mine.
71. FRED Economic Data, "Unemployment Rate in Lincoln County, MT" and U.S. Department of Labor, "Montana Economy at a Glance."
72. Ray Rasker, "Montana's Economy, Public Lands, and Competitive Advantage," Headwaters Economics.
73. "Heritage," Libby Chamber of Commerce.
74. "Adventure Time," Silver Valley Chamber of Commerce.
75. Howard McDonald, "Asbestos Didn't Ruin Libby; the Future Remains Bright," *Montanian*, June 20, 2001, 2.
76. Kim Briggeman, "Cruel Story of Libby's Lost Logging Heritage," *Missoulian*, May 9, 2009, https://missoulian.com/news/local/cruel-story-of-libby-s-lost-logging-heritage/article_c89e44d9-8138-5d15-87b6-f6f5c37625b3.html.
77. Taylor Rose, "The Tragic Tale of Montana Logging," Selous Foundation for Public Policy Research.
78. Eve Byron, "Enviro Groups Tout 'Big Win' in Montanore Mining Lawsuit," *Missoulian*, July 29, 2019, https://missoulian.com/news/local/enviro-groups-tout-big-win-in-montanore-mining-lawsuit/article_5af7a94a-8f77-54df-bf21-d8138bc54433.html.
79. "Digging Deeper: Creating High-Paying Jobs and Protecting the Environment," Friends of Hecla Montana.
80. Tom James, "Judge Blocks Montana Mine Over Environmental Concerns," *Reuters*, May 31, 2017, https://www.reuters.com/article/us-montana-mine/judge-blocks-montana-mine-over-environmental-concerns-iduskbn18r3d2.
81. "City of Libby Growth Policy: A Revision to the 1972 Comprehensive Plan," City of Libby.
82. Jacob Baynham, "So You Want to Be a Dream Town?," *Outside*, August 31, 2016, https://www.outsideonline.com/2106801/so-you-want-be-dream-town.
83. John Blodgett, "Libby, Montana, Tries to Shake Its 'Superfund Stigma,'" *High Country News*, January 18, 2018, https://www.hcn.org/articles/the-montana-gap-libby-tries-to-shake-its-superfund-stigma.
84. Baynham, "So You Want to Be a Dream Town?," *Outside*.
85. "Asbestos-Victim Memorial Planned," *Montanian*, May 2, 2001, 1.
86. "Asbestos Memorial Dedicated May 30," *Montanian*, June 6, 2001, 8.
87. Eileen Carney, "People Can Heal Libby's Sorrow," *Montanian*, June 13, 2001, 2.
88. Carney, "People Can Heal," *Montanian*, June 13, 2001.
89. "CAMP: Community Asbestos Memorial Project," Asbestos Disease Awareness Organization.
90. U.S. Environmental Protection Agency, "Out of the Dust: Recreational Reuse After Vermiculite, the Libby Asbestos Superfund Site in Libby, Montana."

Bibliography

Asbestos Disease Awareness Organization. "CAMP: Community Asbestos Memorial Project." Accessed July 31, 2019. https://www.asbestosdiseaseawareness.org/tributes/camp.html.

Canadian Centre for Occupational Health and Safety. "OSH Answers Fact Sheets: Vermiculite Insulation Containing Asbestos." Last modified February 23, 2019. https://www.ccohs.ca/oshanswers/diseases/vermiculite.html.

Childers, Michael W. *Colorado Powder Keg: Ski Resorts and the Environmental Movement.* Lawrence: University Press of Kansas, 2012.

Christensen, Bonnie. *Red Lodge and the Mythic West: Coal Miners to Cowboys.* Lawrence: University Press of Kansas, 2002.

City of Libby. "City of Libby Growth Policy: A Revision to the 1972 Comprehensive Plan." November 1, 2010. https://cityoflibby.com/wpcontent/uploads/2018/06/LibbyGrowthPolicy__Final_110110.pdf.

CLU-IN. "Mining Sites: Characterization, Cleanup, and Revitalization of Mining Sites." Accessed January 8, 2021. https://clu-in.org/issues/default.focus/sec/Characterization,_Cleanup,_and_Revitalization_of_Mining_Sites/cat/Types_of_Mining_Sites/.

FRED Economic Data. "Unemployment Rate in Lincoln County, MT." Updated August 1, 2019. https://fred.stlouisfed.org/series/mtlinc3urn.

Friends of Hecla Montana. "Digging Deeper: Creating High-Paying Jobs and Protecting the Environment." Accessed July 31, 2019. https://friendsofhecla.com/about-hecla/.

Graham, Brian. "Heritage as Knowledge: Capital or Culture?" *Urban Studies* 39, nos. 5–6 (May 1, 2002): 1003–17. https://doi.org/10.1080.00420980220128426.

Hall, C. Michael, and Alan A. Lew. *Understanding and Managing Tourism Impacts: An Integrated Approach.* London: Routledge, 2009.

Hargrave, Phyllis A., Alan R. English, Mike D. Kerschen, Geno W. Liva, Jeffrey D. Lonn, James P. Madison, John J. Metesh, and Robert Wintergerst. "Abandoned-Inactive Mines of the Kootenai National Forest-Administered Land." Montana Bureau of Mines and Geology. December 1999. http://mbmg.mtech.edu/pdf-open-files/mbmg395_Kootenai.pdf.

King, Daniel. "History of Asbestos." Mesothelioma Center. Last modified December 19, 2018. https://www.asbestos.com/asbestos/history/.

———. "Libby." Mesothelioma Center. Last modified December 20, 2018. https://www.asbestos.com/jobsites/libby/.

Libby Chamber of Commerce. "Cleanup." Accessed March 20, 2018. http://www.libbychamber.org/live-work/cleanup/.

———. "Heritage." Accessed February 27, 2019. http://www.libbychamber.org/live-work/history/.

Lincoln County Asbestos Resource Program. "Asbestos: Vermiculite and Libby." Accessed April 15, 2019. http://lcarp.org/index.php/education/vermiculite-libby.

Logger Days. "Libby Logger Days History." Accessed January 27, 2019. https://www.loggerdays.org/history.php.

Malone, Michael P. *The Battle for Butte: Mining and Politics on the Northern Frontier, 1864–1906.* Seattle: University of Washington Press, 1981.

Mason, Sandra. "The Homeowners Column: Mixing Soils for Containers." University of Illinois Extension. https://web.extension.illinois.edu/cfiv/homeowners/000429.html.

Mesothelioma Fund. "W. R. Grace." Last modified March 26, 2018. https://www.mesotheliomafund.com/asbestos-trusts/w-r-grace/.

Mesothelioma Guide. "Mesothelioma vs. Asbestos." Accessed May 4, 2019. https://www.mesotheliomaguide.com/mesothelioma/diagnosis/mesothelioma-vs-asbestosis/.

Mindat.org. "Vermiculite." Accessed February 23, 2019. https://www.mindat.org/min-4170.html.

Montana Department of Environmental Quality. "W. R. Grace File Review Summary: Chronological Order of Events (CVID #3726)." Accessed March 8, 2019. http://deq.mt.gov/deqadmin/dir/libby/wrgracetimeline3113099.

Povtak, Tim. "Bittersweet Ending to Asbestos Cleanup in Libby, Montana." Mesothelioma Center. December 11, 2018. https://www.asbestos.com/news/2018/12/11/asbestos-cleanup-libby-ends/.

Rasker, Ray. "Montana's Economy, Public Lands, and Competitive Advantage." Headwaters Economics. August 2017. https://headwaterseconomics.org/economic-development/trends-performance/montanas-economy-and-protected-lands/.

Rose, Taylor. "The Tragic Tale of Montana Logging." Selous Foundation for Public Policy Research. October 20, 2015. http://sfppr.org/2015/10/the-tragic-tale-of-montana-logging/.

Rothman, Hal K. *Devil's Bargains: Tourism in the Twentieth-Century American West*. Lawrence: University Press of Kansas, 1998.

Silver Valley Chamber of Commerce. "Adventure Time." Accessed May 4, 2019. https://www.silvervalleychamber.com/visiting-the-silver-valley.html.

University of Montana. "Libby Community Advisory Group Meeting Summary." June 14, 2001. http://www.umt.edu/bioethics/libbyhealth/introduction/meetingpages/01jun14.aspx.

———. "Libby Community Advisory Group Meeting Summary." May 17, 2001. http://www.umt.edu/bioethics/libbyhealth/introduction/meetingpages/01may17.aspx.

U.S. Department of Commerce. *1990 Census of Population and Housing: Population and Housing Unit Costs, Montana*. Washington DC: GPO. https://www.census.gov/prod/cen1990/cph2/cph-2-28.pdf.

U.S. Department of Health and Human Services. *Health Consultation: Mortality in Libby, Montana (1979–1998)*. December 2002. https://www.atsdr.cdc.gov/hac/pha/LibbyAsbestosSite/mt_LibbyhcmortalityRev8-8-2002_508.pdf.

U.S. Department of Labor. "Asbestos Awareness Lesson Plan: Libby Montana." Accessed April 2, 2019. https://www.osha.gov/sites/default/files/2018-12/fy11_sh-22297-11_Asbestos-LibbyMontana.pdf.

———. "Montana Economy at a Glance." Accessed August 1, 2019. https://data.bls.gov/timeseries/lasst300000000000004?amp%253bdata_tool=xgtable&output_view=data&include_graphs=true.

U.S. Environmental Protection Agency. "Libby Asbestos Site, Libby, MT." October 23, 2018. https://cumulis.epa.gov/supercpad/SiteProfiles/index.cfm?fuseaction=second.Cleanup&id=0801744#bkground.

———. "Libby Asbestos Superfund Site the Former Stimson Lumber Mill, Operable Unit 5 Lincoln County, Montana: Final Remedial Action Report." September 28, 2016. https://semspub.epa.gov/work/08/1833450.pdf.

———. "Measuring Progress in EPA's Land Cleanup Programs." January 19, 2017. https://19january2017snapshot.epa.gov/sites/production/files/2014-09/documents/measuring-impact-of-progress-092314.pdf.

———. "Out of the Dust: Recreational Reuse After Vermiculite, the Libby Asbestos Superfund Site in Libby, Montana." May 2014. https://semspub.epa.gov/work/08/1570746.pdf.

———. "Population Surrounding 1,836 Superfund Remedial Sites." October 2017. https://www.epa.gov/sites/production/files/2015-09/documents/webpopulationrsuperfundsites9.28.15.pdf.

———. "Site-Wide Human Health Risk Assessment, Executive Summary: Libby Asbestos Superfund Site, Libby, Montana." By CDM Smith. November 2015. https://semspub.epa.gov/work/08/1562964.pdf.

Ward, Tony J., Terry M. Spear, Julie F. Hart, James S. Webber, and Mohamed I. Elashheb. "Amphibole Asbestos in Tree Bark—A Review of Findings for This Inhalational Exposure Source in Libby, Montana." *Journal of Occupational and Environmental Hygiene* 9, no. 6 (June 2012): 387–97.

2

Vulnerable Harvests

Agricultural Risk and Environmental Hazard in the Modern Great Plains West

DAVID D. VAIL

The modern Great Plains West is a region at risk. In the first two decades of the twenty-first century, states such as Nebraska, Kansas, and Colorado experienced some of their most substantial droughts, floods, fires, blizzards, and severe storms on record.[1] Many plains communities in these states have followed similar crisis response strategies. Local volunteers join emergency response personnel to address the immediate threats to their towns, fields, and irrigation systems. Next, city officials work with state coordination teams to help storm victims, offering emergency services, shelter, and counseling. Then federal agencies such as the Federal Emergency Management Agency team up with the National Oceanic and Atmospheric Administration (NOAA) to coordinate with state agencies to offer various kinds of assistance, from storm data and live updates on conditions, to building rescue shelters and providing food for displaced peoples. This kind of local, state, and federal collaboration in response to environmental hazards also relies upon volunteers. Often local to the disaster and affected themselves, members of nonprofit agencies, religious groups, and larger organizations such as the Red Cross serve as direct managers on the ground. This emergency response system has become fundamental to life in the modern Great Plains West.[2] A cursory survey of recent years offers striking examples about the environmental reckoning in store for the modern West.

In 2017 portions of the South Central Plains (from Texas to Kansas) caught fire with little hope of control. Fire is not new to the plains West or the greater West, but 2017's hazardous conditions revealed how the scale of risk and vulnerability had intensified in ways that community members and professionals did not anticipate. "For weeks," as author Ian Frazier describes it, "the National Weather Service out of Norman, Oklahoma, Amarillo, Texas, and Dodge City, Kansas, had been sending alerts. The conditions were perfect for wildfires. There had been almost no precipitation for six months; before that, however, a lot of rain had fallen, and now the plentiful prairie grasses stood up tall and tinder-dry. On some days, like this one, the winds blew at fifty-plus miles an hour, while the humidity dipped down into the single digits. An ice storm in January had damaged scores of power lines, making them more vulnerable."[3]

What ultimately became known as the Starbuck Fire (named after the fire chief of Ashland, Kansas) burned nearly two million acres. At least seven people died, and thousands of cattle perished. Although emergency operations centers, local volunteer fire fighting units, and state emergency personnel found success in saving rural towns and keeping most residents and livestock safe, the intensity as well as the ferocity of the flames devastated much of the production ground these communities rely upon for their identity and their pocketbooks.[4] Year after year these dangerous environmental conditions placed fields and towns at increased risk for fires that burned with greater frequency and intensity.[5] "That's how we get back to climate," explained NOAA scientist Deke Arndt. "When the climate situation intensifies fire danger conditions deeper into spring, the fire season mingles even more with dry line season. On the day pictured above, on the east side of a dry line, winds were strong from the south. After the dry line passed, winds howled out of the southwest. It was the first of two wind shifts that day. The cold front seen above, brought more westerly winds a short time later."[6]

Similar conditions contributed to intensified winter storms and spring flooding in 2018 and 2019 on the plains. In Nebraska a series of devastating blizzards, severe thunderstorms, and spring flooding set records throughout the year. In some cases flooding literally remade fertile croplands into sandbars.[7] Tornadoes devastated rural communities such as McCook and Farnam in spring of 2018. Winter storms started early in fall, with record-setting rain/snow mixtures.

Then a series of blizzard storms rolled through with hurricane-force winds. By March and April 2019 blizzards and ice turned to flooding. Ice sheets along the Platte River measured up to twenty feet in height. As rivers rearranged their banks, farmers lost existing crops. As sands replaced fertile soils, many delayed planting or accepted that some fields were permanently lost. As late as July 2019 communities such as Lexington, Kearney, and Gibbon experienced yet another round of devastating floods as a common summer thunderstorm overloaded an already high-water table along the Platte River.[8]

Environmental risk and vulnerability will continue to make and remake the twenty-first century American West. The modern Great Plains are a key case study for understanding vulnerability in western environments. Historians are only now coming to terms with the significance of vulnerability and risk. Many scholars define "vulnerability" as a "story that is created twice: the first time when the hazard occurs, and the second time when it leaves its cultural and social imprint upon people's recollection."[9] There is a third instance where the others meet: agricultural production landscapes. As extreme temperatures swing wildly and snowfall and heat index records are frequently broken—all while the economic tab rises to combat the aftermath—the recent history of the Great Plains can steer us toward solutions in developing energy alternatives, rethinking natural resource economies, and planning for frequent disasters. The historical roles of risk, hazard, and vulnerability from the region's recent past are all central to understanding how these forces in the Great Plains will continue to define the twenty-first-century West. "The centrality of nature in the western economy is at once a benefit and a detriment," according to historian David Danbom, "because that economy continues to be vulnerable to business cycles, environmental degradation, depletion of finite resources, and government regulation. And, looming over everything is the growing scarcity of water and the unknowable, but ominous, effects of climate change."[10]

Old Risks Become New Again

Historian Donald Worster remarked in his 2013 Western History Association presidential address that the twenty-first-century Amer-

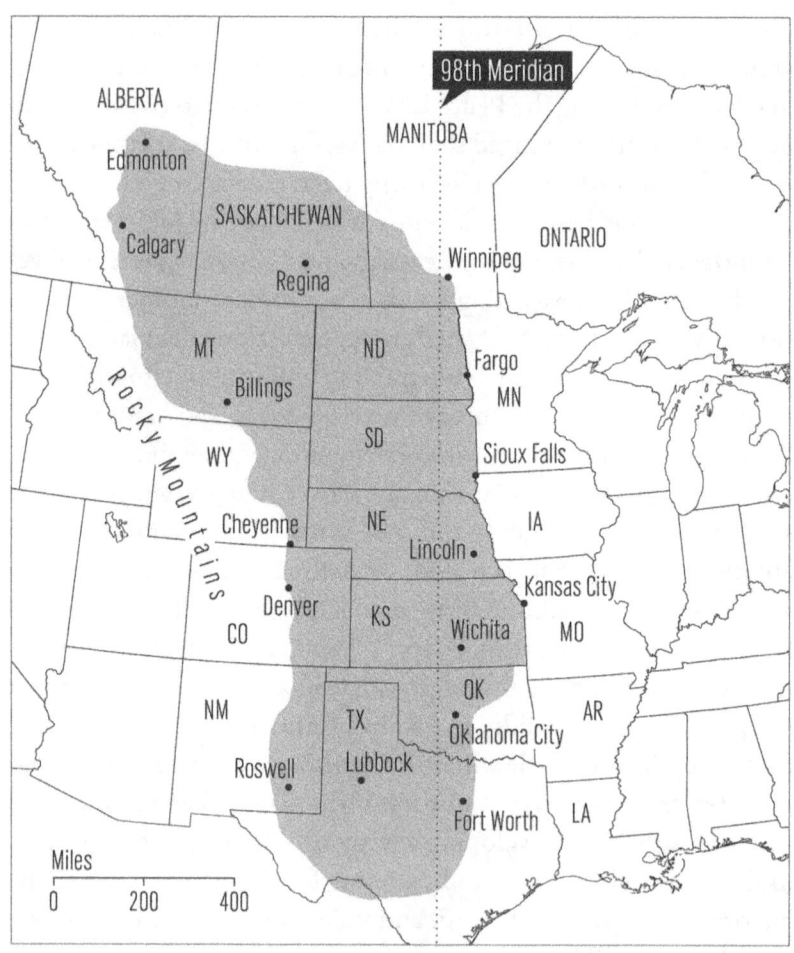

FIG. 2. Map of the Great Plains West. Courtesy Center for Great Plains Studies, University of Nebraska–Lincoln, 2019.

ican West was suffering from a "heightened sense of vulnerability." This region, "once almost immune to a tragic sensibility, now feels its vulnerability and fears what may come."[11] For the Great Plains environmental extremes are not new, but their frequency and intensity do highlight larger climatic changes that place the region at greater risk. As Colorado State University climatologist Russ Schumacher reports, "For researchers like me, this region is a fascinating, and sometimes frustrating place to study weather and climate. It's no accident that places like Colorado and Oklahoma are among the world's hubs for atmospheric science."[12] But Russ warns that the plains West is increasingly becoming an epicenter of the worst effects of climatic changes. As "big weather" continues to bash the Great Plains, intensity, severity, and record events are becoming commonplace to the tune of "billions of dollars in losses and damage."[13]

Although questions about water, aridity, drought, flooding, severe weather, and the numerous political, technical, and scientific alternatives have a long and distinguished legacy here, twenty-first-century westerners (in the Great Plains and elsewhere) find themselves facing more intense versions of these hazards' former selves. Those changes compound the risks already felt daily by farmers and ranchers. Economic systems increasingly favor large farming schemes. At the same time large-scale agribusinesses have advantages in weathering environmental or economic risk because they are "financed, marketed, transported, distributed, processed, manufactured, and sold agricultural products and equipment, gradually integrated into the national and international economies" that small farmers struggle to match.[14] Agricultural chemical applications (ground as well as aerial) might offer an ever-new system of reliable "operating procedures, computer software development, and other technological improvements" to protect crops against invasive insects or weeds as well as from chemical drift. But to produce in the Great Plains West means "constantly managing environmental change wrought by pesticides and navigating the social and political responses to them.... Unpredictable weather patterns, mistaken chemical mixtures, and missed targets [continue] to increase the risks."[15] The region continues to suffer from debilitating fires, droughts, flooding, blizzards, soil loss, and invasive weeds and insects that have long defined the plains West, but their intensity and destructive power seem to grow exponentially.[16]

In this way the distant West informs the modern twenty-first-century West, beginning with explorer and scientist John Wesley Powell and his studies of the Colorado River Basin. His warnings remain key to understanding the tensions around community development, conservation of natural resources, and climatic relationships.[17] For his part Powell offered two central conclusions in his *Report on the*

Arid Lands of the United States that troubled his contemporaries and continue to trouble ours. As historian William deBuys explains, in many ways Powell could be considered America's first "bio-regional thinker and the lessons he taught are lessons we still are at pains to learn."[18] The first controversy was that "the lands of the West were not an empty stage that westering Americans could people and build on as they wished."[19] Powell saw a region of limits—climatic, environmental, and agricultural—that irrigation, farming, or ranching could not easily overcome. Many "westerners and would-be westerners, from homesteaders to senators," according to deBuys, "did not like that kind of talk. It sounded too negative for what seemed to be a boundless American future, a future in which the West as everybody knew, would play a central role."[20] These ecological, environmental, and agricultural tensions continue into the twenty-first-century American West, especially in the Great Plains region.

Powell's second conclusion was even more problematic for federal policymakers. The *Report* insisted that developing land and using natural resources needed to work in "accordance with the climatic, hydrological, and geological congestions of the land."[21] To accomplish this goal meant a regional approach that considered watersheds, weather patterns, and climatic relationships, not just economic opportunity. Powell's central argument, as deBuys suggests, rebuked "the way which people settled the West would have irremediable consequences. Provide the wrong institutions, the wrong systems for survey and land tenure, the wrong bias in law for holding water rights, and the results would be suffering, betrayed ideals, loss of wealth, and the erosion of democracy . . . the West was too dry to support the kind of agriculture that had provided a foundation for settlement of the East."[22]

The role of risk and vulnerability as key concepts in understanding Powell's early warnings, and a failure to heed them, make risk and vulnerability key ideas to connect modern and historic Wests. The "modern West" concept first emerges with historians who considered similar relationships within specific regions such as in Walter Prescott Webb's *The Great Plains* (1931) with Webb placing the arid-humid divide at the ninety-eighth meridian.[23] Other modern

West scholars such as Wallace Stegner and his *Beyond the Hundredth Meridian: The Exploration of the Grand Canyon and the Second Opening of the West* (1953) blended story, science, history, and community to give the one-hundredth a timeless significance within the American West canon.[24] Historian W. Eugene Hollon reassessed both Powell and Webb in *The Great American Desert: Then and Now* (1966) by investigating the concept of aridity through his own experience with the 1930s drought and its return in the 1950s. A crucial line in Hollon's work resonates forward to the limitations that westerners seem to rediscover often to their own peril: "Man inevitably remains the trespasser in the Great American Desert, but he cannot abandon it for the simple reason that he long has no other place to go."[25]

Although written in the formalizing years of the environmental movement and long before the modern scientific constructs of climate change, both Stegner and Hollon serve as a scholarly bridge to new western historians' work: Patricia Limerick's *Legacy of Conquest: The Unbroken Past of the American West* (1987), Donald Worster's *Rivers of Empire: Water, Aridity, and the Growth of the American West* (1985), and Richard White's *It's Your Misfortune and None of My Own: A New History of the American West* (1991). In addition we look to a key group of scholars in Clyde Milner II, Anne Hyde, Susan Lee Johnson, David Rich Lewis, and Susan Rhoades Neel, who met at Utah State University in 1992 to develop new interpretations of the people and places within the West. Their anthology *A New Significance: Re-Envisioning the History of the American West* (1992) attempted to reconcile a central problem in the growing field—that "despite a century of arguing about the 'who,' 'what,' and 'where,' we have a lot of work to do."[26] The hope of those authors (as with this chapter) is that these new perspectives inspire a "renewed sense of the West as a region that is as significant as it is complex." And "accepting complexity and approaching it with new tools will create a new West—which, like the old West, will demand our redoubled attentions."[27] When it comes to the study of risk and vulnerability, the Great Plains West is a key region of environmental reckoning. The attempts to investigate, mitigate, and even ignore these forces bring into focus some of the central tensions that will persist in the twenty-first century. One historical vignette is in the form of the Great Plains Agricultural Council (GPAC). Through its story we can trace the evolution of the emergency response systems now vital to the region and the longer discussions about renewable resources, alternative production practices, and the policies that recognize the consequences of intensifying environmental conditions with expanding pursuits of profit.

The Great Plains Agricultural Council Studies

Although long expressed in scientific studies, rural farm diaries, and industrial journals, risk and vulnerability came to define the Great Plains in the 1930s in a way that reshaped local and national perceptions for future decades. Members of the GPAC led this effort by conducting numerous interdisciplinary experiments to protect harvests for the preservation and health of production land. Their regional risk perceptions drew on a combination of expert scientific analysis as well as practitioner knowledge. The GPAC work also developed a form of "rescue science" that allowed farmers, agricultural scientists, and policymakers to have the kind of immediate information to act on pending environmental emergencies. Yet as GPAC members tried to offer short-term disaster relief plans for rural agricultural communities, they also pursued longer studies on climate, waterways, crop diseases, and pesticide toxicity that would help construct a farm-based conservation for the region in the twenty-first century.

The GPAC originated in Pres. Franklin Roosevelt's 1930s "Great Plains Consortium" plan to organize an interstate and cross-discipline group that possessed experience in farming, science, education, and politics to address the growing environmental problems of the dust bowl. These early meetings connected scientists from regional land-grant institutions, various state agencies in the region, and federal efforts in Washington DC. The GPAC developed subcommittees that spearheaded soil reclamation experiments and arranged conservation districts for "land retirement zones."[28] Other committees focused on the declines in land prices and rural disjuncture.[29] In these various committees, scientists, farmers, and policymakers collaborated to offer immediate solutions to drought and the dust storms.

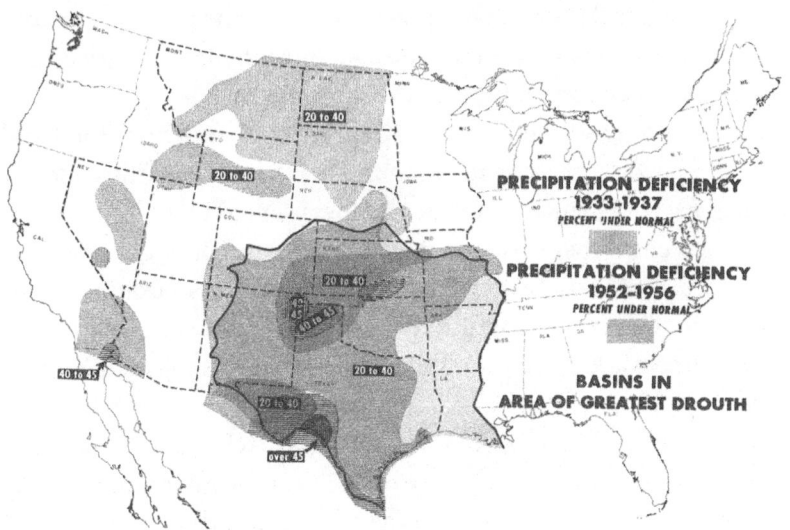

FIG. 3. 1950s drought map of the Great Plains West, including 1930s and 1950s data for President Eisenhower's Drought Tour. Courtesy Dwight D. Eisenhower Presidential Library, Abilene, Kansas.

The GPAC's longer focus on vulnerable agricultural environments continued throughout the Cold War era. Based on their efforts during the 1930s, the council established additional protocols that specialized in regional environmental threats. Members serving on the Insect Committee, for example, worked with entomologists and extension personnel in their respective regions (northern and southern) to study ecological relationships between crop production and pest invasions. Other committees included Plains Research (which pursued climate studies), Soil Stabilization, and Water Resources, to name a few. The council continued to expand its work on agricultural vulnerability by conducting studies that could alleviate environmental hazards, but many members also hoped to pursue preventative measures—solving a regional crisis before it hit.[30]

Farmers, with GPAC support, learned new "regenerating" strategies such as planting erosion-resistant crops to keep agricultural environments healthy. GPAC also conducted weather experiments to begin mapping relationships between variations in current drought trends and longer-term changes in climate. These kinds of scientific experiments and professional-practitioner collaborations in the late 1940s and early 1950s extended the council's influence in agricultural science and policymaking over the next few decades.[31]

The ongoing studies conducted by GPAC throughout the Cold War and beyond gave rise to organizations that built on the council's efforts. Of course many council members served in multiple expert roles that cut across various scientific, environmental, and agricultural specializations. A central focus of GPAC scientists from the 1930s had to do with severe conditions such as wind erosion. With input from farmers and agricultural scientists, GPAC established "hazard zones," or farms that required emergency treatment since the land was entirely devoid of vegetation. The GPAC scientists warned that "unless these areas are taken care of, in fall and winter months, they will probably begin to blow with the first wind in the spring and will spread and damage other areas surrounding them very quickly."[32] Farmers and scientists observed that GPAC-sponsored wind-erosion experiments had long-term significance in planning land use and not just as a rescue tactic to preserve soil health.[33] The GPAC scientists encouraged comprehensive grassland reclamation practices in an effort to convert hazard zones back into healthy ones.

Water scarcity represented another perennial risk on the Great Plains. Many GPAC studies focused on drought, providing a framework of agricultural science management that continued into the early 2000s. Again the council's early purpose to study the disasters of dust and drought in the 1930s remained in the cultural memories of most GPAC members in the late 1950s when the region was at severe risk again. Pres. Dwight Eisenhower's urgent message to the 85th Congress in spring of 1957 describes the precarity of Great Plains residents and their fields: "The prolonged drought in a number of the Great Plains and Southwestern States has long since reached disaster proportions. The Federal Government has, for several years, carried forward an active and varied program of emergency aid in those States.... The Federal Government should insure that appropriate and effective measures are taken to assist State and local governments in alleviating emergency conditions brought about by prolonged drought and other severe natural disasters."[34] By March of that year President Eisenhower and his staff openly worried that the severe conditions plaguing the Great Plains West could be a return to dust bowl conditions.

Eisenhower relied on local and regional experts from the GPAC to help forge a series of agricultural-environmental rescue plans to immediately assist farming communities. An earlier council report in 1956 included a series of longer-term environmental studies that endorsed a sustainable plan that insisted on a balance between production and protection. President Eisenhower incorporated the council's findings when he traveled throughout the region on his "Drought Tour." At every stop the president spoke to rural communities and met with scientists, farmers, and policymakers to ask for short-term mitigation strategies and long-term conservation ideas—solutions that linked the health of the land with its capability to produce.[35]

Eisenhower returned to Wichita, Kansas, before departing to Washington to check in on council proceedings of the Drought Conference held there. More than 190 conference participants discussed current drought research for immediate relief. Farmers and ranchers presided over panels on protecting pastures and croplands from soil erosion and dust storms. Numerous local, state, and federal representatives joined council members in the planning of a "program for the Great plains to assist farmers and ranchers to develop for themselves a land-use program . . . [that] rests on the foundation blocks of further conservation, wise use and management of the area's soil and water resources. It recognizes that if the agriculture of the region is to be stable certain portions ought to be permanently in grasses."[36]

Eisenhower's tour expanded climate and soil research to emphasize a "great need for determining the incidence and range of weather variation and its relationships to crop yields and the mapping of climatic patterns by major climatic and soil areas of the Plains as a means of clarifying weather risk."[37] His plan called for a new cultural view that linked healthy production fields with healthy environments: "The goal is a more stable agriculture. . . . To achieve this goal, there must be widespread use of the good soil management

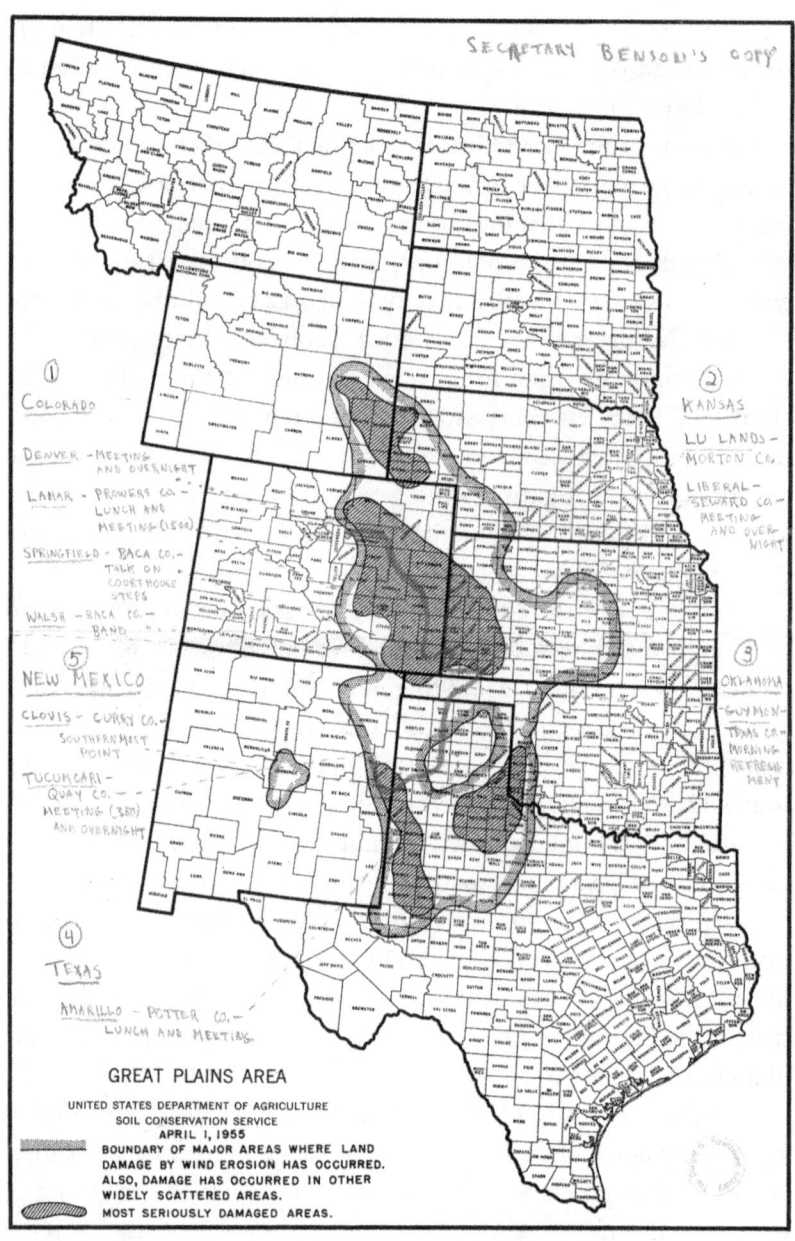

FIG. 4. Secretary of Agriculture Ezra Taft Benson's drought tour map, including proposed stops for President Eisenhower. Courtesy Dwight D. Eisenhower Presidential Library, Abilene, Kansas.

and water conservation practices and adjustments in sizes and types of farms which will enable farmers and ranchers to effectively cope with the climatic hazards of the region. There must also be a complete understanding of the objective and coordinated teamwork on the part of all concerned, farmers, landowners, civic and agricultural groups, private industry, local, State and Federal agencies and governments."[38]

A third risk came in pesticides—a technology that was supposed to protect fields and pocketbooks. Many landowners in the Great Plains West discovered that what helped their fields produce could also harm them. From the 1940s to the 1990s organizations such as GPAC and other regional councils that it inspired—such as the North Central Weed Control Conference (NCWCC) in 1944 or Great Plains Tree Pest Council (GPTPC) in 1990—explored specialized studies of risk and vulnerability related to pests and chemicals. Farmers and ranchers looked to these groups for recommendations on chemical treatments, toxicology, or the latest scientific studies on weeds.[39] The central message of GPAC and others in the plains West was a type of farm-based conservation—that a change of thinking about the land "was a first step in addressing many farmers' and agriculturalists' concerns over the rapidly growing use of new chemicals ... pesticides' potency followed its own path apart from user intentions or company specifications."[40] Production agriculture could not accomplish sustained harvests unless "agriculturalists, farmers, and aerial applicators followed the toxicology of pesticides and the biology of pests, not simply the economic goals they set for their fields."[41]

In the 1980s GPAC scientists moved beyond the threats of agricultural chemicals to farm soils or surface streams to aquifers underground. Charles S. Helling, a soil scientist for the Agricultural Research Service, told the Fort Collins, Colorado, audience at the 1987 council meeting that one of the ongoing dangers according to agricultural science had to do with point-source pollution—but not where they might expect. Pesticides began turning up in groundwater supplies, contaminating the surrounding fields as well as threatening potable water. Helling reported that most pesticides posed risks to humans, crops, and wildlife in rural communities, reaching groundwater "through direct well contamination, for example, by back-siphoning from a spray tank or channeling from surface to groundwater along an improperly cased well."[42] Since pesticides traveled through a series of ecological processes, such as leaching, degradation, runoff, and absorption, prevention required producers to be scientists as well as conservationists. Applicators needed to study "pesticides characteristics, soil, climate, hydrogeology, and agronomic management," as all are "factors that potentially influence pesticide movement."[43] Many other speakers offered additional recommendations for Great Plains residents to balance the agricultural health of their fields and the health of ecological relationships between production lands and wildlife or themselves. These prescriptions for prevention guided regional policies and individual practices over the next forty years. Some statutes included farmers and ranchers only hiring certified ground sprayers and aerial applicators, or creating freshwater "buffer zones" to keep drift swaths (especially from aerial deployments) at a safe distance from water sources. Also plains states pursued legislation to prohibit chemical use "in areas where groundwater monitoring [had] established the presence of the pesticide in concentrations above a specified level."[44]

Alternative Agriculture for Energy, Conservation, and Wildlife

A key GPAC approach to address these environmental and agricultural risks came through expanding farm-based conservation. Due in part to the increasing risks of the economic crisis plaguing Great Plains states throughout the 1980s, many council members arrived in Garden City, Kansas, for the 1981 annual meeting worried about the region's environmental-economic challenges. Instability in farm prices and trade embargoes on certain agricultural commodities such as grain placed many rural communities in peril.[45]

In addition unfavorable weather conditions and a combination of federal policies contributed to declining land values that "rippled through the rural economy, and in 1987 three hundred agricultural banks failed, more than in any year since the Great Depression."[46] In the early months of 1981 the council planned a rescue. North Dakota Department of Agriculture scientist Claude Schmidt opened the meeting in Garden City, Kansas, with a tone of urgency. States in the Great Plains West had to pursue alternatives in energy for agriculture immediately. With the ongoing oil embargo "there has been great interest in alternative sources of energy on ways to decrease our dependency on oil.... Many government agencies have been involved in this effort... setting the stage [for the GPAC] workshop on alternative sources of energy for agriculture."[47]

Keynote speaker M. O. Bagby followed, exploring how alternative agriculture could work in the region. Central to Bagby's plan was for GPAC to continue working with land-grant universities to develop centers of specialized study that could work toward energy independence. Farmers, ranchers, and agricultural scientists had "to discover, develop, and demonstrate technology which will permit agriculture to be energy self-sufficient by 1990 under conditions of sustained production of food, feed, and fiber.... [Plans must] envision that technology developed from farm-generated energy will carry into other sectors of the American economy."[48] Bagby concluded with a charge that resonated well into the early 2000s: "Although much knowledge still must be gained before technologies based on these renewable resources can be established, the potential for technical feasibility is very encouraging. The future of these alternatives, of course, will be determined through need and economics. And, although no renewable energy crop is likely to resolve our energy problems, such crops can certainly play a part in the solution."[49]

The need for securing future harvests for the Great Plains West was due to the region's ongoing environmental and economic risks as well as its growing connections to international markets. Making food production stable increasingly meant the council had to embrace "alternative sources" for agriculture to "more adroitly face the environmental and economic risks."[50] Other members attending the 1981 meeting presented on wind and solar power experiments. R. Nolan Clark, director for the Agricultural Wind Energy Research Laboratory as well as the United States Department of Agriculture (USDA) Conservation and Production Research Laboratory in Texas, reported on the latest advancements for both forms of renewable energy. For Clark the Great Plains was a key region to study alternative agriculture, which, he argued, would be less novel to rural communities striving for practical solutions.[51]

Another panel led by Mylo A. Hellickson from South Dakota State University argued for the expansion of solar energy applications in Great Plains agriculture to make rural communities more profitable as well as fields more secure.[52] To address these socioeconomic-environmental tensions, Hellickson insisted that a cross-disciplinary approach, linking local field knowledge with scientific expertise, was the best way to explore these alternative technologies: "Although achievement of parity among these renewable and conventional characteristics [of production lands] is a necessary and first step, it must also be recognized that all actions taken with respect to energy resources influence a wide segment of society . . . recognizing that the structure of the Great Plains Agricultural Council and similar regional organizations lends itself very well to addressing the other interrelationships that are vital to the acceptance and utilization of renewable energy resources."[53]

The themes of risk, agricultural vulnerability, and food security continued to blend throughout the following year's conference in North Platte, Nebraska. Landowners, agriculturalists, and policymakers continued exploring additional alternatives for agricultural production lands as the 1980s farm crisis continued to grow. The GPAC committees studied ecofallow as an approach that prioritized farmland conservation as a solution to environmental and economic risks. As an early version of no-till farming, GPAC scientists encouraged attendees to employ the tilling technique in a section of their fields to reduce weeds and insects while also limiting the need for pricey agricultural chemicals. For University of Nebraska agronomist D. G. Hanway, ecofallow represented a kind of alternative agriculture that could redefine farming systems throughout the Great Plains that followed ecological relationships instead of production schedules.

Like Powell's warnings almost a century before, Hanway argued that research priorities had to address the region's limits:

The "Dirty Thirties" sensitized the people of the Great Plains to problems of land protection and improving efficiency of use of limited rainfall. That conservation tillage workshop in 1976 was just one in a series of conferences in the Great Plains through the years addressing this general problem. Looking back, the concerns represented by that workshop and the efforts to bring new technologies to bear on regional problems has proved prophetic of a growing national and international concern on losses of land productivity due to erosion in a world where growing populations represent an ever-increasing need for food production.[54]

Hanway explained that conservation production systems were the way forward in the Great Plains West because ecofallow and other no-till practices considered the health of the soil and crops in ways traditional production ignored:

> I think it has become very clear from the changes that are being adopted across the Great Plains that the concepts of conservation and of production are complementary in application rather than being in opposition. In this area of limited rainfall there will continue to be added emphasis on increasing the efficiency of getting that rainfall into the root zone of the crops we wish to grow and then of managing those crops so that we maximize their productivity. We find that we do this by maintaining adequate residues and that we protect the land at the same time.[55]

Gail Wicks, another agricultural scientist working at the University of Nebraska–Lincoln North Platte Station, expanded on Hanway's results and held the same concerns about the application of agricultural chemicals to fields, making them more vulnerable to invasive weeds and insects as well as exposing them to misapplied toxic dusts and sprays. These more traditional methods needed to change, he insisted, since "after a couple years it was apparent that reliance on atrazine [popular herbicide of the period] alone was inadequate. Such things as row spacing, date of planting, variety, seeding rate of winter wheat and amount of straw produced affected density and vigor. These factors greatly influenced the degree of weed control from field to field."[56]

Instead, the North Platte Station developed a more comprehensive ecofallow farming-conservation system that Wick called "eco-farming," which he defined as "a system of controlling weeds and managing crop residues throughout a crop rotation with minimum use of tillage so as to reduce soil erosion and production costs while increasing weed control, water infiltration, moisture conservation and crop yields."[57] Farmers in attendance also spoke in support of this new system. Roger Schroeder from Holbrook, Nebraska, explained that ecofallow conservation protected his farmlands from flooding in the spring and harnessed water during the scarce summer months. Typical topsoil loss due to wind erosion and flooding offered his cropland multiple protections that, in the end, made his fields more productive.[58] Ecofarming also seemed promising in protecting wildlife habitats. As Nebraska wildlife biologist George Nason reported, this system of conservation could help wildlife living in production landscapes: "Considering the many benefits of ecofallow in terms of reduced wind and water erosion, reduced fuel costs and labor time, the practice should become permanently established as a farm technique. Ground nesting wildlife should prosper from a safer, more abundant nesting environment."[59] However, the potential of this kind of farm-based conservation came with risks, too. Ecofarming worked well when water was abundant and rainfall was normal. But a few dry spells combined with a few severe windstorms could make croplands vulnerable.[60]

Throughout the mid-1980s and 1990s GPAC met in other parts of the Great Plains to debate policies, discuss experiments, and hear from local community members. Drought and scarcity remained high on the list of concerns of rural communities, especially the depletion of Ogallala Aquifer.[61] GPAC meetings in places such as Laramie, Wyoming (1984), Lubbock, Texas (1989), Wichita, Kansas (1991), and Bismarck, North Dakota (1994), honed discussions on how new digital technologies could anticipate the factors of returning environmental and agricultural risks. Council studies such as William Easterling's "The Impact of Climate Change on Agriculture in the Great Plains" (1991) or Terry Messmer's "Endangered Species and Pesticide Protection: Executive Summary and Recommendations" (1994) offered a strong framework for regional farm-based conservation for the year 2000 and in the years since.[62] Although the council ultimately disbanded in the late 1990s due to funding

GREAT PLAINS AGRICULTURAL COUNCIL
Activities and Accomplishments
May 1990   Volume 1

1991 Annual Meeting
At its June 1989 meeting, the Executive Committee accepted an invitation from Kansas State University to host the 1991 Annual Meeting of the Council. The meeting will be held in Wichita, June 4-6, 1991.

APHIS New GPAC Member

The Animal and Plant Health Inspection Service (APHIS) is the most recent USDA agency to join the GPAC. APHIS joins seven other USDA member agencies (AMS, ARS, CSRS, ERS, ES, FS, and SCS) on the Council.

50 Years (±) for the GPAC

Depending on when you begin to count, the GPAC (or its predecessor organizations) have been around for 50 years.

In 1939 and again in 1940 the Regional Agricultural Council of the Southern Great Plains and the Regional Agricultural Council of the Northern Great Plains met jointly. The two Councils grew out of USDA - Land Grant University initiated efforts to assist farmers and rural communities combat the drought of the 1930s. Formal merger of the two Councils occurred in 1946.

The initial seeds for the GPAC can be traced to a 1934 meeting of the Administrator of the Federal Extension Service and the Presidents of the Land Grant Universities in the Southern Great Plains. Presently, nine Land Grant Universities and eight USDA agencies are active members of the GPAC.

The mission of APHIS is to provide leadership in ensuring the health and care of animals and plants, to improve agricultural productivity and competitiveness, and to contribute to the national economy. APHIS' contributions include: excluding exotic agricultural pests and diseases; detecting, monitoring and managing agricultural pests and diseases; providing scientific and technical services; facilitating agricultural exports; protecting the welfare of animals; protecting endangered species; and collecting, analyzing and disseminating information.

The agency Administrator is Dr. James W. Glosser. Even before becoming official members of the GPAC some APHIS personnel have contributed to GPAC activities; for example, APHIS personnel have made important contributions to the Wildlife Committee and the Leafy Spurge Task Force. With the increased emphasis on trade, environmental, animal care and food safety issues, the contributions of APHIS personnel to GPAC programs are welcomed.

GPAC Award

At its October 1989 meeting, the Executive Committee initiated the GPAC Outstanding Service Award. The Award will recognize those individuals whose contributions can be directly linked to activities which further the stated purposes and objectives of the Great Plains Agricultural Council.

Nominations are due August 1 and may be made by any Standing Committee or any GPAC member agency. The first award will be presented at the 1991 Annual Meeting.

FIG. 5. Great Plains Agricultural Council activities and accomplishments. Newsletter, May 1990. Records of the Great Plains Agricultural Council, Agricultural and Natural Resources Archive, Colorado State University.

reductions at land-grant universities and the expansion of privatized crop consulting services, the GPAC established an infrastructure that the Great Plains West relied upon well into the first two decades of the twenty-first century.

Conclusion: An At-Risk Future West

Climate scientists warned in 2018 that the one hundredth meridian continues to move east. The storied line that naturalist-explorer John Wesley Powell described as the significant boundary is expanding, bringing familiar risks and new vulnerabilities to the Great Plains states: "From east to west across this belt a wonderful transformation is observed. On the east a luxuriant growth of brass is seen, and the gaudy flowers of the order *Compositae* make the prairie landscape beautiful. Passing westward, species after species of luxuriant grass and brilliant flowering plants disappear; the ground gradually becomes naked, with bunch grasses here and there; now and then a thorny cactus is seen, and yucca plant thrusts out its sharp bayonets."[63] As the Earth Institute reported, the eastward advancement of this line carries real climatic implications: "That the divide has turned out to be real as reflected by population and agriculture on opposite sides," and due to climate change, "it will probably continue shifting in coming decades, expanding the arid climate of the west into what we think as the Midwest [or more precisely the Great Plains region]."[64]

Drought, wind erosion, reduced soil health, toxic miss-sprays by chemical applicators, and depletion of the Ogallala Aquifer are constant headlines of these decades. Farm-based conservation is on the rise as a means to compensate, with plains states committing large acreages to no-till farming.[65] Experiment stations and scientific collaborations such as University of Nebraska's Drought Monitoring Institute continue the council's charge to explore the intersections between production ecosystems and the environmental as well as economic risks that persist within current agricultural production models.[66]

The history of the GPAC in the five decades after World War II offers many insights about the risks and vulnerabilities that continue to challenge the Great Plains West today and the modern American West tomorrow. A central legacy of the council is its pursuit of interdisciplinary approaches and constituencies in studying the hazards increasingly common in the modern West. At the same time GPAC experienced growing tensions between practitioner knowledge and scientific expertise as its members tried to pursue farm-based conservation goals with larger production pressures and environmental realities in mind—a dilemma central to the twenty-first-century West. And as the council's efforts show, analyzing risk is a highly interconnected process. The recent history of the GPAC suggests that these kinds of collaborations that were once possible need to be rediscovered and expanded upon in the decades to come. To mitigate risk means more than short-term reductions or solutions. Producers, policy makers, and agriculturalists must reconsider their larger agricultural production environments as contributors to disasters, not apart from them. The future of the Great Plains West will require just this kind of reckoning that blends the historical with the contemporary in an effort to address the longer health and welfare of communities—rural, urban, and ecological. So "seeing this history anew," to return to Worster, may just be "our ace in the hole." For a while now "we have been learning about living in arid places, and surely that knowledge will be useful in the future. . . . Whether or not such hope is realistic in the new and changed age of vulnerability, we will need to know the history of the American West—and every other place—better than ever."[67] Certainly the modern West continues to be a vulnerable and hazardous one. The GPAC's collaborative pursuits offer an important model for the risks ahead.

Notes

1. Russ Schumacher, "Why the Great Plains Has Such Epic Weather," *Conversation*, April 12, 2019, http://theconversation.com/why-the-great-plains-has-such-epic-weather-115209; Shannon Van Sant, "The Midwest Battles Historic Floods in the Aftermath of the 'Bomb Cyclone,'" National Public Radio, March 16, 2019, https://www.npr.org/2019/03/16/704130300/the-midwest-battles-historic-floods-in-the-aftermath-of-bomb-cyclone; Bill Chappell, "A 2nd Bomb Cyclone: Colorado Predicted to Go from 80 Degrees to a Blizzard," High Plains Public Radio, April 9, 2019, https://www.hppr.org/post/second-bomb-cyclone-colorado-predicted-go-80-degrees-blizzard. See also, Dewey, *Great Plains Weather*.

2. Examples of national, state, and local agencies abound (scientific and emergency services) in Dewey, *Great Plains Weather*. See also Mills, *Operation Snowbound*.

3. Ian Frazier, "The Day the Great Plains Burned," *New Yorker*, November 5, 2017, https://www.newyorker.com/magazine/2018/11/05/the-day-the-great-plains-burned.

4. Oliver Morrison, "Kansas' Biggest Fire Ever Was Named After Chief from Town of 8 People," *Wichita Eagle*, March 25, 2017, https://www-1.kansas.com/news/local/article140618998.html; Chris Mooney, "Wildfires Used to Be Rare in the Great Plains. They've More than Tripled in 30 Years," *Washington Post*, June 16, 2017, https://www.washingtonpost.com/news/energy-environment/wp/2017/06/16/scientists-find-a-400-percent-increase-in-wildfire-destruction-in-the-great-plains/.

5. Donovan, Wonkka, and Twidwell, "Surging Wildfire Activity in a Grassland Biome," 5986–93; Joyce et al., "Native and Agricultural Forests at Risk," 59–74; Clabo, "Contemporary Pyrogeography," 1–14; see also Frazier, "The Day the Great Plains Burned," *New Yorker*.

6. Arndt, "Prairie Fires on the Southern Plains."

7. Marjie Ducey, "'Mountain of Sand' Covers Some Nebraska Farms After Floods, Adding Pains to Planting Season," *Omaha World Herald*, May 3, 2019, https://www.omaha.com/money/mountain-of-sand-covers-some-nebraska-farms-after-floods-adding/article_022a7ada-cb81-5b7c-b90f-07770aa7ba11.html; Mitch Smith, Jack Healy, and Timothy Williams, "'It's Probably Over for Us': Record Flooding Pummels Midwest When Farms Can Least Afford It," *New York Times*, March 18, 2019, https://www.nytimes.com/2019/03/18/us/nebraska-floods.html; Allison Mollenkamp, "Farm Flooding Losses Likely at Least One Billion Dollars," *NET News*, March 19, 2019, http://netnebraska.org/article/news/1167271/farm-flooding-losses-likely-least-one-billion-dollars; Mihir Zaveri, "Record-High Floods in Nebraska Breach Levees and Isolate Towns," *New York Times*, March 16, 2019, https://www.nytimes.com/2019/03/16/us/nebraska-flooding.html.

8. Erika Pritchard, "Kearney Area Battling Floodwaters Tuesday; Buildings Flooded, Water Rescues Needed," *Kearney Hub*, July 9, 2019, https://www.kearneyhub.com/news/local/kearney-area-battling-floodwaters-tuesday-buildings-flooded-water-rescues-needed/article_e4b26d5c-a266-11e9-8c69-7f5bdc3d5f74.html.

9. Hommels, Mesman, and Bijker, *Vulnerability in Technological Cultures*, 13. For recent studies on risk and vulnerability, see Carr Childers, *The Size of the Risk*; Pietruska, *Looking Forward*; Oden, *Harvest of Hazards*.

10. Danbom, "Introduction," 3.

11. Worster, "The American West," 5–16.

12. Schumacher, "Why the Great Plains Has Such Epic Weather," *Conversation*.

13. Schumacher, "Why the Great Plains Has Such Epic Weather," *Conversation*.

14. McDean, "Agribusiness in the American West," 213.

15. Vail, *Chemical Lands*, 134.

16. See West, *The Contested Plains* and Courtwright, *Prairie Fire*. For recent works on flood and blizzards of the Great Plains West, see Mills, *Operation Snowbound*; Kerstetter, *Flood on the Tracks*.

17. See Ross, *The Promise of the Grand Canyon*; Robert Glennon, "Observations: John Wesley Powell, Great Explorer of the American West, He Was the First to Survey the Colorado River, 150 Years Ago—and His Ideas About Water Resources in that Arid Region

Were Prescient," *Scientific American*, June 26, 2019, https://blogs.scientificamerican.com/observations/john-wesley-powell-great-explorer-of-the-american-west/. See also Worster, *A River Running West*.

18. deBuys, *Seeing Things Whole*, 1.

19. deBuys, *Seeing Things Whole*, 1. See also Vetter, *Field Life*.

20. deBuys, *Seeing Things Whole*, 1, 139–208; Sweeney, *Prelude to the Dust Bowl*, 3–18.

21. deBuys, *Seeing Things Whole*, 1.

22. deBuys, *Seeing Things Whole*, 1. For a sense of Powell's detractors see Smythe, *The Conquest of Arid America*, 19, 32, 24, 30, 43–48.

23. Webb, *The Great Plains*, 8–9.

24. See Stegner, *Beyond the Hundredth Meridian*.

25. Hollon, *The Great American Desert*, 253. See also Webb, "The American West: Perpetual Mirage," 25–31.

26. Milner, *A New Significance*, 305.

27. Milner, *A New Significance*, 305. See also Sherow, *A Sense of the American West*; West, "Thinking West," 25–52; Flores, "Societies to Match the Scenery," 256–70.

28. Tomasek, "The Great Plains Agricultural Council," 45; Eisenhower Presidential Library, "Drought Conference," 1–10. See also Marcus, *Service as Mandate*; Gilbert, *Planning Democracy*.

29. See Shover, *First Majority—Last Minority*.

30. Ottoson and Hildreth, "The Great Plains Agricultural Council," 1–19.

31. Ottoson and Hildreth, "The Great Plains Agricultural Council," 1–4.

32. Tomasek, "The Great Plains Agricultural Council," 48–49.

33. Eisenhower Presidential Library, "Drought Conference," 1–2

34. Eisenhower, "Message from the President," 166–67.

35. Eisenhower, "Message from the President," 166–67. See also Tomasek, "The Great Plains Agricultural Council."

36. Great Plains Agricultural Council, *Program for the Great Plains*, 3.

37. Great Plains Agricultural Council, *Program for the Great Plains*, 1–11.

38. Ottoson and Hildreth, "The Great Plains Agricultural Council," 10; Tomasek, "The Great Plains Agricultural Council," 53.

39. Hanson, "Past, Present, and Future," 12. See also Larson, "Habits and Characteristics of Weeds," 66–67; Coulter, "From Test Tube to Airplane Operators," 42. For a larger historical survey on the NCWCC and its role in the Great Plains West, see Vail, *Chemical Lands*, chapter 2. For GPTPC work, see "Minutes of the First Meeting of the Great Plains Tree Pest Workshop," 1–18; Johnson, "Risk Assessment Maps," 7; Harrell and Stepanek, "Report to Great Plains Tree Pest Council," 3–4.

40. Vail, *Chemical Lands*, 26. See also Coupland, "Life History Studies of Weeds," 35–38; Klingman and McCarty, *Interrelations of Methods of Weed Control*, 1–47.

41. Vail, *Chemical Lands*, 26.

42. Helling, "Movement of Agricultural Chemicals," 57.

43. Helling, "Movement of Agricultural Chemicals," 57.

44. Hellling, "Movement of Agricultural Chemicals," 67; Cantor, Blair, and Zahm, "Agricultural Chemicals," 73–88; Amsden, "Progress and Problems," 89–96.

45. Devine and Vail, "Sustaining the Conversation," 2.

46. Devine and Vail, "Sustaining the Conversation," 2. See also Hanson, "Beyond the Farm Debt Crisis," 33; John R. Campbell, "Modern Farm Aid to Ease Crisis," *New York Times*, September 25, 1985, A19. See also Dudley, *Debt and Dispossession* and Harl, *The Farm Debt Crisis of the 1980s*.

47. Schmidt, "Alternative Sources of Energy," 1. See also Johnson and Bouzaher, *Conservation of Great Plains Ecosystems*, 211–27.

48. Bagby, "Energy," 3.

49. Bagby, "Energy," 9.

50. Bagby, "Energy," 9

51. Clark, "Agricultural Applications," 72–73.

52. Hellickson, "Solar Energy," 81.

53. Hellickson, "Solar Energy," 81–82.

54. Hanway, "Enroute to Conservation," 49.

55. Hanway, "Enroute to Conservation," 52.

56. Wicks, "Update on Ecofallow," 53; Hergert, "Fertilizer Programs," 63–72.

57. Wicks, "Update on Ecofallow," 54.

58. Schroeder, "Why EcoFallow," 59; Schroeder, "Value of Residue," 60–61.

59. Nason, "Ecofallow and Wildlife in Nebraska," 14.

60. Fenster, "Potential and Problems," 55–58.

61. Gessaman and Erickson, "Water Resource Conditions," 1–14; Carlson, "High Plains-Ogallala Aquifer," 15–48. See also Opie, "The Drought of 1988," 261–90.

62. Armold and Amend, "Grazing Land Simulator," 49–60; Rice, "Computer Models," 61–70; Geiger, "Software Packages," 75–78; Johnsrud, "An Overview," 1–6; Vanderholm, "Development of Farming Systems," 81–92; Easterling, "The Impact of Climate Change," 155–61; Messmer, "Endangered Species," 67–72.

63. See Powell, *Report*.

64. Seager et al., "Whither the 100th Meridian?," 2–3; Fergen et al., "Out Where the West Begins," 155–72. See also Watson, Zinyowera, and Moss, *The Regional Impacts of Climate Change*.

65. USDA, "Conservation Producers Protect or Improve Millions of Acres of Agricultural Land," 1–2.

66. A recent example is the Daugherty Water for Food Global Institute at the University of Nebraska, "2019 Water for Food Global Conference: Water for a Hungry World: Innovation in Water and Food Security," April 29–30, 2019.

67. Worster, "The American West," 16.

Bibliography

Archival Sources

Eisenhower Presidential Library and Boyhood Home. Abilene, Kansas
    Eisenhower, David D. "Drought Conference and Great Plains Plan." Cabinet Minutes, February 1–March 29, 1957 (3) (Cabinet meetings of February 27 and 28).

Hale Library, Kansas State University, Manhattan, Kansas
    Coulter, L. L. "From Test Tube to Airplane Operators." In NCWCC *Proceedings*, 42. 1949.

Coupland, Robert T. "Life History Studies of Weeds." In NCWCC *Proceedings*, 35–38. 1952.

Hanson, Noel. "Past, Present, and Future in the North Central Weed Control Conference." In NCWCC *Proceedings*, 8–12. 1947.

Larson, A. H. "Habits and Characteristics of Weeds." In NCWCC *Proceedings*, 66–69. 1944.

North Dakota State University Special Collections and Archives, Fargo, North Dakota

Harrell, Mark, and Laurie Stepanek. "Report to Great Plains Tree Pest Council." In GPTPC *Proceedings*, 1–4. 2003.

Johnson, Dave. "Risk Assessment Maps." In GPTPC *Proceedings*, 7. 2000.

"Minutes of the First Meeting of the Great Plains Tree Pest Workshop." In GPTPW *Proceedings*, 1–18. 1993.

University of Nebraska–Lincoln Libraries, Lincoln, Nebraska

Amsden, Timothy L. "Progress and Problems in Developing and Implementing a Groundwater Protection Strategy." In GPAC *Proceedings*, 89–96. 1987.

Armold, Anita A., and John Amend. "Grazing Land Simulator: An Education/Extension Computerized Tool for the General Public." In GPAC *Proceedings*, 49–60. 1984.

Bagby, M. O. "Energy: Alternative Sources for Agriculture." In GPAC *Proceedings*, 3–10. 1981.

Cantor, Kenneth P., Aaron Blair, and Shelia Hoar Zahm. "Agricultural Chemicals, Drinking Water, and Public Health: An Epidemiologic Overview." In GPAC *Proceedings*, 73–88. 1987.

Carlson, David L. "High Plains-Ogallala Aquifer." In GPAC *Proceedings*, 15–48. 1983.

Clark, R. Nolan. "Agricultural Applications for Wind Energy." In GPAC *Proceedings*, 71–79. 1981.

Easterling, William E. "The Impact of Climate Change on Agriculture in the Great Plains." In GPAC *Proceedings*, 155–61. 1984.

Fenster, C. R. "Potential and Problems of Ecofarming in Drier Environments." In GPAC *Proceedings*, 55–58. 1981.

Geiger, Betty. "Software Packages from the Private Sector of the Range Livestock Industry—Their Use and Availability." In GPAC *Proceedings*, 75–78. 1984.

Gessaman, Paul H., and Merlin W. Erickson. "Water Resource Conditions in the Great Plains." In GPAC *Proceedings*, 1–14. 1983.

Hanway, D. G. "Enroute to Conservation Production Farming Systems." In GPAC *Proceedings*, 49–52. 1982.

Hellickson, Mylo A. "Solar Energy for Agriculture-Crop Drying and Livestock Building Heating." In GPAC *Proceedings*, 81–100. 1981.

Helling, Charles S. "Movement of Agricultural Chemicals into and within Underground Aquifers." In GPAC *Proceedings*, 57–71. 1987.

Hergert, Gary W. "Fertilizer Programs for Ecofarming Conditions." In GPAC *Proceedings*, 63–72. 1981.

Johnsrud, Myron D. "An Overview of Environmental Issues and Great Plains Agriculture." In GPAC *Proceedings*, 1–6. 1989.

Messmer, Terry A. "Endangered Species and Pesticide Protection: Executive Summary and Recommendations." In GPAC Proceedings, 67–72. 1994.

Nason, George W. "Ecofallow and Wildlife in Nebraska." In GPAC Proceedings, 13–14. 1982.

Ottoson, Howard W., and R. J. Hildreth. "The Great Plains Agricultural Council: The First 50 Years, and the Second." In GPAC Proceedings, 1–19. 1985.

Rice, R. W. "Computer Models as Rangelands Research Tools: SPUR." In GPAC Proceedings, 61–70. 1984.

Schmidt, Claude. "Alternative Sources of Energy for Agriculture in the Great Plains." In GPAC Proceedings, 1–2. 1981.

Schroeder, Roger. "Why EcoFallow—Soil and Water Conservation." In GPAC Proceedings, 59–61. 1982.

Vanderholm, Dale H. "Development of Farming Systems to Reduce Adverse Effects on the Environment." In GPAC Proceedings, 81–92. 1989.

Wicks, Gail A. "Update on Ecofallow in the Winter Wheat-Sorghum-Fallow Rotation." In GPAC Proceedings, 53–54. 1982.

Published Works

Arndt, Deke. "Prairie Fires on the Southern Plains." *NOAA Climate.org: Beyond the Data*, April 21, 2016, https://www.climate.gov/news-features/blogs/beyond-data/prairie-fires-southern-plains.

Carr Childers, Leisl. *The Size of the Risk: Histories of Multiple Use in the Great Basin*. Norman: University of Oklahoma Press, 2015.

Clabo, Darren. "Contemporary Pyrogeography and Wildfire-Climate Relationships of South Dakota." *Atmosphere* 9 (May 2018): 1–14.

Courtwright, Julie. *Prairie Fire: A Great Plains History*. Lawrence: University Press of Kansas, 2011.

Danbom, David. "Introduction." In *Bridging the Distance: Common Issues of the Rural West*, edited by David Danbom, 1–4. Salt Lake City: University of Utah Press, 2015.

deBuys, William. *Seeing Things Whole: The Essential John Wesley Powell*. New York: Island, 2001.

Devine, Jenny Barker, and David D. Vail. "Sustaining the Conversation: The Farm Crisis in the Midwest." *Middle West Review* 2 (Fall 2015): 1–10.

Dewey, Kenneth F. *Great Plains Weather*. Lincoln: University of Nebraska Press, 2019.

Donovan, Victoria M., Carissa L. Wonkka, and Dirac Twidwell. "Surging Wildfire Activity in a Grassland Biome." *Geophysical Research Letters* 44 (June 2017): 5986–93.

Dudley, Kathryn Marie. *Debt and Dispossession: Farm Loss in America's Heartland*. Chicago: University of Chicago Press, 2000.

Eisenhower, Dwight D. "Message from the President of the United States Relative to Alleviating Emergency Conditions Brought about by Prolonged Drought and Other Severe Natural Disasters, March 5, 1957." Washington DC: Office of the Federal Register, National Archives and Records Service, General Services Administration, 1958. 166–70.

Fergen, Joshua T., Jeffrey B. Jacquet, Bishal Kasu, Matthew Barnett, Anne Junod, and Sandeep Kumar. "Out Where the West Begins: Measuring Land-Use Preferences and Environmental Attitudes Across the Great Plains Transition Zone." *Great Plains Research* 28 (Fall 2018): 155–72.

Flores, Dan. "Societies to Match the Scenery: Twentieth-Century Environmental History in the American West." In *The Blackwell Companion to the American West*, edited by William Deverell, 256–70. Malden MA: Blackwell, 2007.

Gilbert, Jess. *Planning Democracy: Agrarian Intellectuals and the Intended New Deal*. New Haven: Yale University Press, 2015.

Great Plains Agricultural Council. *Program for the Great Plains*. Washington DC: GPO, 1956.

Hanson, Greg. "Beyond the Farm Debt Crisis." *Choices: The Magazine of Food, Farm and Resource* 5, no. 4 (1990): 33.

Harl, Neil E. *The Farm Debt Crisis of the 1980s*. Ames: Iowa State University Press, 1990.

Hollon, W. Eugene. *The Great American Desert: Then and Now*. New York: Oxford University Press, 1966.

Hommels, Anique, Jessia Mesman, and Wiebe E. Bijker. *Vulnerability in Technological Cultures: New Directions in Research and Governance*. Cambridge MA: MIT Press, 2014.

Johnson, S. R., and Aziz Bouzaher. *Conservation of Great Plains Ecosystems: Current Science, Future Options*. Dordrecht, Netherlands: Kluwer Academic, 1995.

Joyce, Linda A., Gary Bentrup, Antony S. Cheng, Peter Kolb, Michele Schoeneberger, and Justin Derner. "Native and Agricultural Forests at Risk to a Changing Climate in the Northern Plains." *Climatic Change* 146 (January 2018): 59–74.

Kerstetter, Todd M. *Flood on the Tracks: Living, Dying, and the Nature of Disaster in the Elkhorn River Basin*. Lubbock: Texas Tech University, 2018.

Klingman, Dayton L., and M. K. McCarty. *Interrelations of Methods of Weed Control and Pasture Management at Lincoln, Nebraska, 1949–1955*. Washington DC: GPO, 1958.

Marcus, Alan I. *Service as Mandate: How American Land-Grant Universities Shaped the Modern World, 1920–2015*. Tuscaloosa: University of Alabama Press, 2015.

McDean, Harry C. "Agribusiness in the American West." In *The Rural West Since World War II*, edited by R. Douglas Hurt, 213–48. Lawrence: University Press of Kansas, 1998.

Mills, David W. *Operation Snowbound: Life Behind the Blizzards of 1949*. Fargo: University of North Dakota Press, 2018.

Milner, Clyde A., II, ed. *A New Significance: Re-envisioning the History of the American West*. New York: Oxford University Press, 1996.

Oden, Derek S. *Harvest of Hazards: Family Farming, Accidents, and Expertise in the Corn Belt, 1940–1975*. Iowa City: University of Iowa Press, 2017.

Opie, John. "The Drought of 1988, the Global Warming Experiment, and Its Challenge to Irrigation in the Old Dust Bowl Region." *A Sense of the American West: An Anthology of Environmental History*, edited by James E. Sherow, 261–90. Albuquerque: University of New Mexico Press, 1998.

Pietruska, Jamie. *Looking Forward: Prediction and Uncertainty in Modern America*. Chicago: University of Chicago Press, 2017.

Powell, John Wesley. *Report on the Arid Region of the United States, with a More Detailed Account of the Lands of Utah*. Washington DC: GPO, 1897.

Ross, John F. *The Promise of the Grand Canyon: John Wesley Powell's Perilous Journey and His Vision for the American West*. New York: Viking Press, 2018.

Schroeder, Roger. "Value of Residue." Paper presented at GPAC Proceedings, Garden City, Kansas, 1981.

Seager, Richard, Nathan Lis, Jamie Feldman, Mingfang Ting, A. Park Williams, Jennifer Nakamura, Haibo Liu, and Naomi Henderson. "Whither the 100th Meridian? The Once and Future Physical and Human Geography of America's Arid-Humid Divide. Part 1: The Story So far." *Earth Interactions* 22, no. 5 (2018): 1–22.

Sherow, James E. *A Sense of the American West: An Anthology of Environmental History.* Albuquerque: University of New Mexico Press, 1998.

Shover, John L. *First Majority—Last Minority: The Transforming of Rural Life in America.* DeKalb: Northern Illinois University Press, 1976.

Smythe, William E. *The Conquest of Arid America.* New York: Harper & Brothers, 1900.

Stegner, Wallace. *Beyond the Hundredth Meridian: The Exploration of the Grand Canyon and the Second Opening of the West.* Boston: Houghton Mifflin, 1953.

Sweeney, Kevin Z. *Prelude to the Dust Bowl: Drought in the Nineteenth-Century Southern Plains.* Norman: University of Oklahoma Press, 2016.

Tomasek, Henry John. "The Great Plains Agricultural Council." PhD diss., University of Chicago, 1959.

USDA. "Conservation Producers Protect or Improve Millions of Acres of Agricultural Land." *Highlights* 12, no. 6 (July 2014): 1–2.

Vail, David D. *Chemical Lands: Pesticides, Aerial Spraying, and Health in North America's Grasslands Since 1945.* Tuscaloosa: University of Alabama Press, 2018.

Vetter, Jeremy. *Field Life: Science in the American West during the Railroad Era.* Pittsburgh: University of Pittsburgh Press, 2016.

Watson, Robert T., Marufu C. Zinyowera, and Richard H. Moss. *The Regional Impacts of Climate Change: An Assessment of Vulnerability.* Cambridge, UK: Cambridge University Press, 1998.

Webb, Walter Prescott. "The American West: Perpetual Mirage." *Harper's Magazine* (May 1957): 25–31.

Webb, Walter Prescott. *The Great Plains.* Boston: Ginn, 1931.

West, Elliott. *The Contested Plains: Indians, Goldseekers, and the Rush to Colorado.* Lawrence: University Press of Kansas, 1998.

West, Elliott. "Thinking West." In *The Blackwell Companion to the American West*, edited by William Deverell, 25–52. Malden MA: Blackwell, 2007.

Worster, Donald. "The American West in an Age of Vulnerability." *Western Historical Quarterly* 45 (Spring 2014): 5–16.

Worster, Donald. *A River Running West: The Life of John Wesley Powell.* New York: Oxford University Press, 2001.

PART 2

Indigenous Lands and Sovereignty

3

Sacred Space and Identity

The Fight for Chi'chil Biłdagoteel (Oak Flat) and the History of the San Carlos Apachean Peoples

MARCUS C. MACKTIMA

In the twenty-first century the Indigenous peoples of the United States endure some of the same struggles faced by their ancestors centuries ago. They speak out against those who threaten Indigenous traditional homelands with destruction for the sake of profit. At Standing Rock Indigenous peoples joined together through the #NoDAPL movement to resist the construction of a pipeline that threatens the people's access to clean water. In Utah the Indigenous peoples at Bears Ears, a land that is significant to many Indigenous peoples, declare that the removal of government protections for this place leaves the monument vulnerable to mining prospects, vandalism, and grave robbing. In the views of the nonindigenous, land is only worthy of protection if there is a distinct problem for the colonizing whole. Relevance of place is important as well, however: "Places are appreciated primarily for their historical significance and do not provide the sense of permanency and rootedness that the Indian sacred places represent."[1] Efforts to protect land significant to Indigenous peoples transcend the need for environmental protections. Land is an intrinsic and necessary facet of the Indigenous worldview and is foundational to various concepts of Indigenous identity. Nick Estes, a member of the Lower Brule Sioux tribe, stated, in relation to #NoDAPL, "Every act on our part to recover and reclaim our lives and land and to resist elimination is an attempt to recuperate that lost humanity—a humanity this settler state refuses and denies even to its own."[2] Chi'chil Biłdagoteel (Oak Flat) fits well within this discussion, but there is something more.

In the early 1990s the San Carlos Apache tribe fought to secure environmental protections for Dził Nchaa Si An (Mount Graham) to save their spiritual heritage when the University of Arizona, in collusion with the Vatican, attempted to construct a telescope on the sacred mountain. Despite the tribe's efforts, the telescope was constructed on the mountain, ignoring its sacredness to the Apache peoples. In the early twenty-first century, the Rio Tinto group attempted, and secured, a land exchange that included a sacred Apache site that, at the time of this writing, is threatened with potential ruination from underground mining. The San Carlos Apache tribe articulated their position through testimonies to various governmental bodies and opposed any construction or mining at both these places based on the spiritual and physical significances of the land. The official position was clear at Dził Nchaa Si An and Chi'chil Biłdagoteel, but dissenters from the tribe expressed a different perspective. Of course these voices were used and manipulated by outside entities in an attempt to demonstrate Indigenous support for their cause, but one question must be asked: why is there dissent?

The question of "sacredness," specifically in relation to Chi'chil Biłdagoteel, is rooted in historical trauma and identity. Forced removals relocated many Indigenous peoples to the San Carlos Indian Reservation in the nineteenth century, and the Indian Reorganization Act (or, Indian New Deal) required Indigenous nations to conform to a purely Western form of governance resulting in a consolidated reservation identity. Consequently, the "dissenting voice" is a result of this altered perspective of identity, and what is considered "sacred" for the San Carlos Apache peoples, specifically the affirmation of Chi'chil Biłdagoteel, is dependent upon the individual tribal member whose family was, and still is, impacted by these historical traumas.

On Thursday, November 1, 2007, then San Carlos Apache Nation chairman Wendsler Nosie represented his people and testified in the U.S. House of Representatives to express the concerns of the people regarding Chi'chil Biłdagoteel. He stated, "Oak Flat is a place where a blessed gift was given to the people about morals and ethics and how to maintain the Earth."[3] The legislative hearing was in regard to H. R. 3301, the "Southeast Arizona Land Exchange and Conservation Act of 2007," discussed in the House Subcommittee on National Parks, Forests, and Public Lands of the Committee on Natural Resources. In this single statement Nosie affirmed the concerns of the Apache people and encompassed the entirety of the Apachean relationship to the land at Chi'chil Biłdagoteel, a place that the Apache people occupied for centuries before European invasion. His acknowledgement of this place is multifaceted and speaks to the complexities of the Apachean lifeways. The culture is rooted in place, and it is in that place that much of the religious iconography, relationships, and understandings of identity were revealed to the people. The Apachean relationship to land goes beyond the common misconceptions of the ecological Indian, a cultural trope often associated with Indigenous peoples when discussing land issues; as land, or place, is incredibly significant to the Apaches' "peoplehood."[4]

Chi'chil Biłdagoteel and Apache Leap Mountain, situated in the mountainous southern boundaries of the Tonto National Forest in eastern Arizona near the small town of Superior, received a considerable amount of attention from politicians, corporations, and numerous Indigenous communities surrounding the area during the mid- to late 2000s and 2010s. The location itself holds an abundance of life-sustaining properties that make it a veritable oasis within a desert landscape—spiritual for the Indigenous and materialistic for the nonindigenous. It attracts many outdoor enthusiasts, environmentalists, and communities who rely upon the mountain spring water. Its abundance of earthly material also drew the attention of Resolution Copper, a subsidiary of Rio Tinto.

Resolution Copper currently operates a mine atop Apache Leap Mountain, and in the past, mining was not an issue. The problem is the proposed underground mining technique. Extracting the copper lying beneath Chi'chil Biłdagoteel will cause surface subsidence, which "occurs as the material above the ore body gradually moves downward to replace the ore that has been mined," leading to Chi'chil Biłdagoteel's destruction.[5] As a result of this clear intention to destroy a sacred site and contaminate life-giving ground-

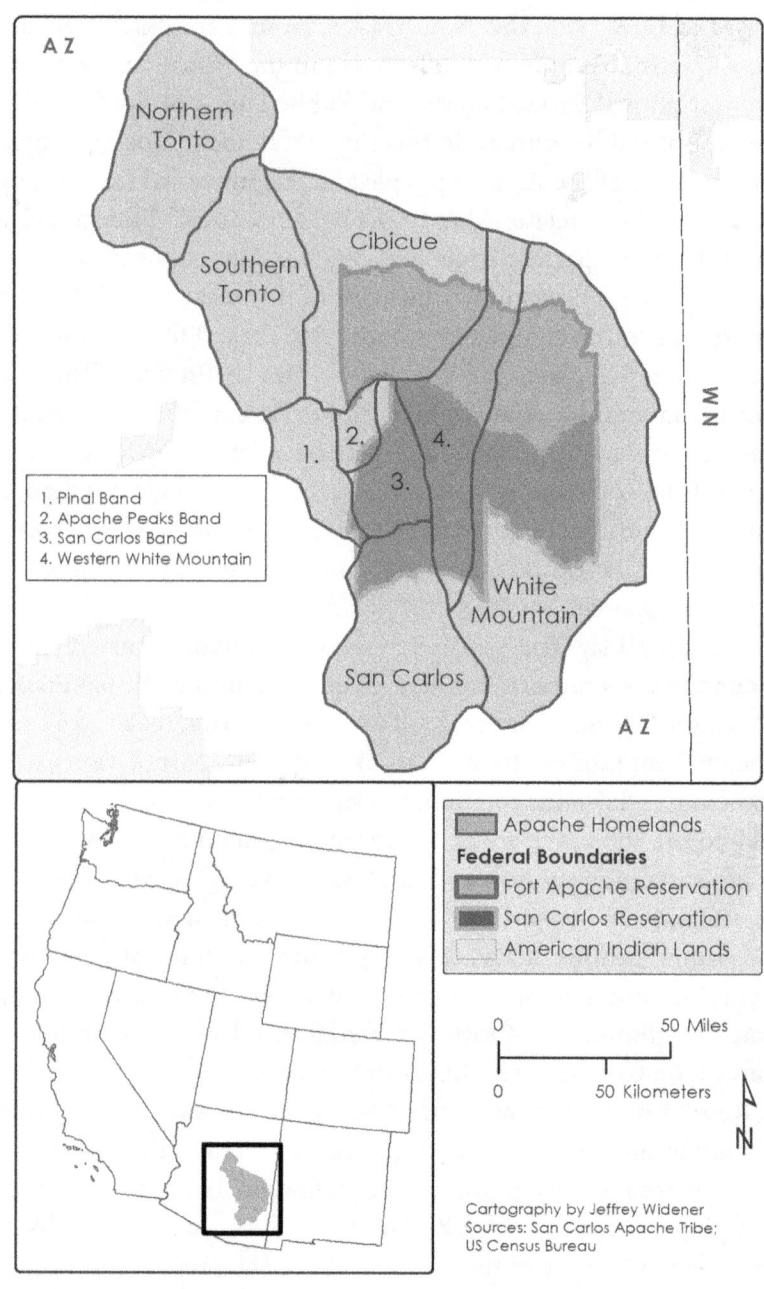

FIG. 6. Map of Apachean homelands. Map by Jeffrey M. Widener.

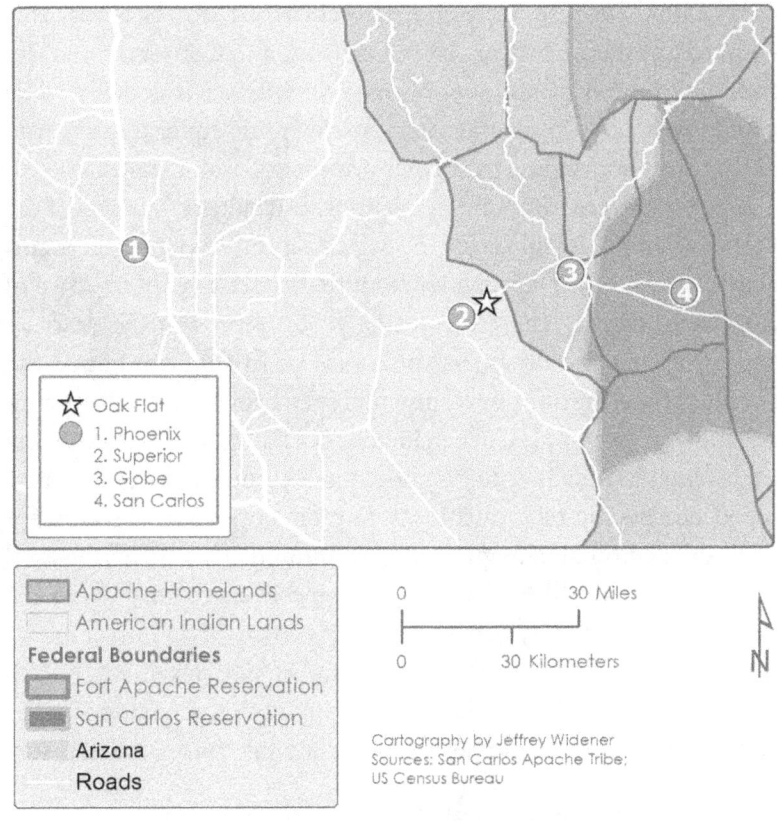

FIG. 7. Map of Chi'chil Biłdagoteel (Oak Flat) and surrounding region. Map by Jeffrey M. Widener.

water with exposed rock waste, the San Carlos Apache peoples, in conjunction with other tribal governments, are fighting to preserve the site and stop the construction of a mine in a place considered sacred to many Indigenous peoples.

Irrespective of the land's sacredness, the mining subsidiary pursued a land exchange with the federal government to acquire the land, protected by executive order, at Chi'chil Biłdagoteel. Starting in 2005 the first attempts to secure the land for the company were brought by Arizona Sen. Jon Kyl and Sen. John McCain as standalone bills. The efforts arranged by the Arizona politicians resulted in continuous failures, but on December 19, 2014, Congress passed the National Defense Authorization Act (NDAA) for fiscal year 2015 with the Southeast Arizona Land Exchange and Conservation rider added by John McCain hours before the bill was scheduled to be voted upon.[6] The "must-pass" measure was subsequently approved in Congress and signed by former president Barak Obama.

Despite the environmental, religious, and cultural impacts of the proposed mine, Resolution Copper and its allies persisted, incorporating dissenting Apache voices into its narrative. In the case of Apachean identity, these dissenting voices represent the destructive nature of the cultural and historical trauma inflicted upon the people through various governmental measures intended to assimilate Indigenous peoples, which includes previous land disputes. The traditional Apache identity is rooted in a complex social structure based on specific relationships, while the contemporary concept relies on a colonial perception of nationhood. To fully understand the issue at Chi'chil Biłdagoteel, it is necessary to go beyond the initial reports made by tribal members who do, or do not, consider Chi'chil Biłdagoteel to be a sacred site and, instead, examine the cultural and historical precedent, beginning with the creation of the San Carlos Apache Reservation, to explain the cause of dissention.

Apache Political Identity and Its Problems

A map of silver mines created after the Gadsden Purchase in 1859 displays the location of the "San Carlos River."[7] This name was applied to the reservation and its people, with the town of San Carlos placed at the intersection of the San Carlos River and Gila River.[8] It has no bearing on the people and is not of Apachean origin, but on December 14, 1872, Pres. Ulysses S. Grant signed an executive order that formally established the San Carlos Division of the White Mountain Indian Reservation, later renamed the San Carlos Indian Reservation.[9] The executive order was signed one year after the Indian Appropriations Act of 1871, which ended Indian treaty making in the United States. The formation of the reservation and its development into a political entity explains the change in Apache identity in the twenty-first century, specifically in relation to the dispute at Chi'chil Biłdagoteel.

After the establishment of the reserve in 1872, a conglomeration of Indigenous peoples, each with their own distinct traditional identities, was forced onto the reservation at gun point by the U.S. Army, with other Apachean groups arriving first. In the aftermath of the Camp Grant Massacre in April 1871, where more than one hundred Pinal and Aravaipa Apache were killed by Anglos, Mexicans, and Tohono O'odham warriors, an influx of Apachean Indigenous groups were forced onto the reservation.[10] In 1932 Grenville Goodwin interviewed Bija Gush Kaiyé, a member of a band not present at the time of the massacre, who stated that "the agent said we would all move to San Carlos and that he wanted all the Indians to come to that place."[11] High-level officials in Washington established a concentration policy that deactivated other Arizona reservations—an inherent danger of the discontinuation of treaty making—and removed many peoples to the San Carlos reservation.

The policy first removed "1,500 Yavapai and Walapai [sic] peoples from Camp Verde to San Carlos."[12] Concurrently, President Grant issued several executive orders that placed pieces of the reservation back into the public domain between 1873 and 1877, and subsequent presidents followed suit in 1877, 1902, and 1912.[13] The reservation contained portions of traditional lands that belonged to the Aravaipa Apaches, who resided in the southwestern regions of the reservation. In 1896 a mineral strip was considered by the federal government for reincorporation into the public domain and required a public hearing with the San Carlos tribal council, which included members from other Indigenous groups. The issue was of great concern for the Aravaipa, but the land was of no consequence to the Yavapai and White Mountain Apaches who were included in the decision. Ultimately the measure passed with 56 percent agreeing to reincorporation in exchange for $12,433 per year.[14] The forced accumulation of Indigenous peoples onto a single reservation had resonating effects that are felt well into the twentieth and twenty-first centuries.

Decades later in 1934 the Indian Reorganization Act formally solidified political identities for Indigenous peoples as they were forced to assimilate into the American body politic and construct governments that mirrored the American system. It was presented as a measure to provide self-determination and self-governance; but in reality it was self-determination as decreed by the federal government. On January 17, 1936, the constitution and bylaws of the San Carlos Apache tribe were approved, and the San Carlos Apache Nation was politically recognized.[15] The formal recognition of the San Carlos Apache Nation created a political identity that labeled itself as "Apache" but disassociates itself from the history of forced removals and the distinct nature of Apachean society. Within this name is an imprisoning feature that chains the individual member to the higher American authority. As a result the people are forced to associate themselves with the designation of "San Carlos Apache" or as a resident of the "San Carlos Apache Reservation."

An identity tied to reservation borders was perpetuated for generations, and land disputes exemplify the problems this identity caused. The conflict at Dził Nchaa Si An during the late twentieth century was, and continues to be, a great concern for the San Carlos Apache peoples. The similarities between Dził Nchaa Si An and Chi'chil Biłdagoteel are significant; however, the focus is on the land itself. While many nonindigenous groups discussed the issue of land use, the larger conversation in this matter is the question of *cultural* identity and the negative repercussions of the *political* identity established in the mid-twentieth century by the federal government. The problems at Dził Nchaa Si An were many, but dissenting voices within the tribe demonstrate the tendency of members to conform to the singular Apachean identity that is perpetuated by the continued use of the San Carlos moniker. At both Dził Nchaa Si An and Chi'chil Biłdagoteel, this point, coupled with the established environmental and spiritual concerns, only exacerbated the issue.

One of the first attempts to undermine significant laws and protections for sacred Dził Nchaa Si An came when John McCain attached a "midnight rider" to the 1988 NDAA that stipulated an exemption from environmental regulations for the University of Arizona's Mount Graham International Observatory, a tactic that was repeated in the dispute over Chi'chil Biłdagoteel in 2015 for Resolution Copper.[16] The following year, in a letter dated December 27, 1989, the University of Arizona's Office of Coordinator of Indian Programs sent a letter to the chairman of the San Carlos Apache Nation, Buck Kitcheyan. The greeting to the highest office of the Apache Nation begins with "Dear Buck," as opposed to "Dear Mr. Chairman," or "Dear Mr. Kitcheyan." The letter extended an invitation to a meeting between representatives of the university and prominent Apache leaders to discuss the university's intention to construct a multimillion-dollar telescope, in partnership with the Roman Catholic Church, atop Dził Nchaa Si An in southeastern Arizona. University officials stated their willingness to respect the religious beliefs and practices of the San Carlos Apache people and discuss the impact of the construction of the Mount Graham International Observatory. As a standalone document this represented the University of Arizona's readiness to address the concerns of the tribe regarding the intended construction of an observatory on non-reservation Apache territory. However, the tone of the document exuded a kind of authority that was "granted" to the university by non-Apaches over lands deemed significant to the Apache people, a people who have resided on or near this mountain for centuries.[17]

During the late 1980s and early 1990s the San Carlos Apache tribe asserted its sovereignty over the contested site at Dzil Nchaa Si An. On July 10, 1990, the tribe executed a resolution that formally established a political stance against the construction of the telescope.[18] Tribal leaders also insisted that both government and university officials provide the necessary documentation and consultations required by law before construction on sensitive sites commenced. The demand came as a result of the apparent oversight by these organizations to initiate any government-to-government communications. Chairman Kitcheyan complained to United States Department of Agriculture Forest Service Southwestern Region forester David Jolly that they subverted federal law and failed to conduct the appropriate actions required to ensure the protection of Indigenous sacred sites.[19] The tribe continued to press the Forest Service on the issue and stated on June 4, 1991, that the government agency unlawfully allowed the issuance of a permit for construction and subverted the National Historic Preservation Act, which stipulates a requirement for consultation and cultural impact studies on culturally sensitive sites.[20]

This project was a joint endeavor with the Roman Catholic Church, and, as such, efforts were made by the tribe to contact and appeal to Pope John Paul II at the Vatican and inform him of the religious nature of the site in relation to the Apache people's traditional customs. A delegation of San Carlos Apache representatives traveled to Europe on a tour that attempted to garner support for the movement from those countries that intended to invest in the telescope and also requested a meeting with the pope, which he denied due to scheduling conflicts.[21] Many attempts were made by San Carlos Apache tribal representatives throughout the 1990s to protect Dził Nchaa Si An, but they were not without dissenters.

The tribal government consistently passed official resolutions that affirmed the position of the tribe, continuously stating that the mountain is indeed sacred and that they were opposed to the construction of the telescope. As the discussion continued throughout the 1990s members who initially supported the tribe shifted to become supporters of the university. Former chairman Harrison Talgo, in an effort to undermine the work of the Apache Survival Coalition—a nonprofit founded by tribal member Ola Cassadore of Bylas, Arizona—stated in a letter to Jack Thomas, then chief of the Forest Service, that their meeting with the coalition was unofficial and did not reflect the position of the tribe. Cassadore's organization worked tirelessly during the 1990s to halt construction of the telescope, and the movement experienced a setback with the opposition of the former chairman. Talgo later lost his reelection bid eleven months later and became a University of Arizona construction engineer at Dził Nchaa Si An as well as a public relations consultant for the university.[22] The tribe maintained its position, but the chairman and others spoke out against Dził Nchaa Si An's significance.

Willliam Belvado, an elected official who served on the San Carlos Apache tribal council at the time, asserted his dissenting position on Dził Nchaa Si An to congressmen Sidney Yates (D-IL) and Jim Kolbe (R-AZ), both congressional representatives investigating the issue. In his letter to the congressmen he stated, "It is not, and never has been, an issue of concern for the San Carlos Apache people" and affirmed the fact that the mountain does not reside on "reservation" territory.²³ Both Talgo and Belvado relied upon a colonial conception of space and determined that Indigenous space can only exist within "reservation boundaries," or imaginary lines created by the settler-colonial authority. Indigenous peoples do not define sacred space in such terms but understand the significance of space through relationship and inherent unexplained power.²⁴

Despite the connections Indigenous people possess with their traditional homelands, they have consistently been removed or ignored to make way for whatever "technological achievement" or "advancement" that nonindigenous corporations and individuals deem worthy, leading to the occupation or replacement of Indigenous spaces, as it is currently at Bear's Ears and #NoDAPL. Though in the case of the San Carlos Apache peoples, there is not a traditional singular whole that is able to conceptualize the apparent discrepancies between members. Within the people's history are the rudimentary underpinnings of a foreign entity's attempt to eliminate the traditional Indigenous identities in favor of a westernized perspective of citizenry.

Governmental Precedence at Chi'chil Biłdagoteel

In 1955 President Eisenhower signed Public Order 1229, ordering that Oak Flat Picnic and Campground be "withdrawn from all forms of appropriation under the public land laws, including the mining but not mineral-leasing laws, and reserved for use of the Forest Service, Department of Agriculture, as campgrounds, recreation areas, or for the public purposes as indicated."²⁵ Since that time the location has been under the protection of the federal government. The stipulations within the order limit the mining prospects and were designed with the mindset that this land be set aside for the benefit of the people, free from contamination. Despite these intentions, since 2005 Resolution Copper, under the guise of Rio Tinto, attempted to acquire the land, but with the protection order signed by Eisenhower, obtaining the land to mine was impossible without congressional approval. Despite the efforts of the San Carlos Apache people, outdoor enthusiasts, and environmentalists to maintain the protections, this changed in 2014 with the inclusion of a midnight rider in the 2015 defense bill submitted by Senator McCain hours before it was sent to the floor.[26]

The first attempts to exchange sacred Chi'chil Biłdagoteel came in the form of Senate Bill S.1122 and House Bill H. R. 2618 on May 25, 2005. The bills "would have conveyed 3,025 acres of national forest land to Resolution in exchange for approximately 4,814 acres owned by Resolution."[27] Both failed in Congress and were reintroduced five more times: in 2006, 2007, 2008, 2010, and 2013. Each time it was defeated with the help of strong opposition from the collective forces of various anti-mining entities, including the San Carlos Apache Nation. The bills introduced in 2005 did not provide protections or considerations for Indigenous peoples, and each submission after was changed slightly, with one bill title altered to reflect the significance on the economy, aptly named the Copper Basin Jobs Act.[28]

The first congressional hearings began in 2007, and in an effort to garner support for the bill, the *Arizona Capital Times* featured an article that detailed the intentions of the company. In the article Resolution Copper explained the prospect of adding a new park for the benefit of climbers and campers, a move intended to pander to outdoor enthusiasts, but they also expected individuals to pay to use the new facilities. Throughout the article the Apache people are mentioned only once at the beginning and only in passing. Nevertheless, the proposal received much scrutiny from the San Carlos Apache Nation and others in Congress.

In November 2007 the legislative hearings before the Subcommittee on National Parks, Forests, and Public Lands included discussions between Rep. Raúl Grijalva, Sen. Jeff Flake, and representatives from the Yavapai Nation, San Carlos Apache Nation, and Resolution Copper. Statements provided by nonindigenous groups briefly mentioned the cultural significance of Chi'chil Biłdogoteel to Indigenous peoples but failed to recognize the implications of the land to the people and their identity. Testimonies given by the Yavapai and San Carlos Apache defended their anti-mining position from an Indigenous perspective as both detailed the significance of the place in relation to their religious and cultural practices. Pro-mining nonindigenous attendees provided testimony that only acknowledged the land's cultural significance with acorn picking, a seasonal food gathering done since time immemorial but hardly of equal significance to the more complex cultural implications of the site to Indigenous identity and tradition.[29]

A second hearing was initiated in 2008 in the Current Public Lands and Forests Legislation in the Subcommittee on Public Lands and Forests on Senate Bill S. 3157, the Southeast Arizona Land Exchange and Conservation Act of 2008. Statements related to the mining at Chi'chil Biłdogoteel were heard, and each new testimony affirmed the economic benefits to the state. The testimonies of Sen. Jon Kyl and Joel Holtrop, deputy chief of the National Forest System, never mentioned Apache concerns, and statements issued by Resolution Copper stated the intention of the company to welcome consultations with tribal governments but did not determine who would initiate the conversation. Indigenous concerns to the proposed mine were not acknowledged or mentioned by any of the attendees until the testimony of Shan Lewis, president of the Inter-Tribal Council of Arizona. Representing the interests of both Chairman Nosie and President Bear of the Yavapai Nation, Lewis commented, "The Federal Agencies involved have failed to consult with us on a government-to-government basis on this matter. In this regard, this hearing is quite premature. No consultation has occurred."[30] The bill did not receive support in Congress, and the measure failed.

The following year a bill with the same designation as previous bills went into a similar committee hearing where Senators McCain and Kyl, Joel Holtrop of the Forest Service, and David Salisbury, president of Resolution Copper, again spoke of the financial benefits of the mine. In this hearing, however, Holtrop confirmed one of the suspicions held by tribal governments regarding the follow-through of public law:

> The bill requires the agency to conduct an environmental impact statement after the agency no longer owns the property on which the mine would be located. The purpose of the National Environmental Policy Act (NEPA) is to inform the decision maker about potential impacts prior to making a decision. Given the current language, we

would assume that we would only be analyzing impacts from mining activities on the surrounding National Forest land, not the land to be conveyed. Consistent with Administration policy, NEPA should be done before moving forward on the land exchange.[31]

The language in this bill passed the burden of a NEPA study into Resolution Copper, a measure specifically put in place to prevent adverse effects from land disturbances and ensure adherence to federal laws. By passing this on to the company, the Forest Service subverted the governmental oversight created to keep potentially dangerous material from contaminating the surrounding environment. This bill did not make it to the floor but Resolution Copper continued their efforts for another eight years until the infamous rider in 2014, which included this same section of the bill.

The last major attempt by Resolution Copper and the Arizona senators to initiate the much sought-after land swap came in 2013. The issue garnered international attention and was heavily focused on tribal sovereignty, Indigenous rights, and religious freedom for Indigenous peoples. The new chairman of the San Carlos Apache Nation, Terry Rambler, continued the fight for Chi'chil Biłdogoteel and testified before the House Natural Resources Subcommittee on Energy and Minerals, and the Senate Subcommittee on Public Lands, Forests, and Mining. In his address he reaffirmed the tribe's opposition "because of the dangerous precedent that it would set in transferring a known tribal sacred area located on federal land to a foreign-owned mining company for activities that will ultimately destroy the area while circumventing meaningful government-to-government consultation between the U.S. and Indian tribes."[32] Chairman Rambler articulated the exact measures required to ensure the continued protection of the site and claimed these measures were circumvented in the proposed bills. He cited the negligence of the Forest Service and other federal agencies who failed to: 1) conduct the necessary environmental impact reports required by NEPA; 2) hold tribal consultations required by executive order 13175; and 3) heed the National Historic Preservation Act, which necessitates Section 106 cultural consultations when a site directly impacts tribal peoples. The cooperative and inclusive language written in laws related to a tribe's cultural integrity was intended to ensure the active involvement of Indigenous peoples in these affairs. These laws were ignored by those seeking to profit from the destruction of Indigenous claims, and the chairman succinctly explained the missteps taken by the federal government as well as the implications of their actions on both tribal sovereignty and cultural integrity. Just as it was with Dził Nchaa Si An, however, the tribe was not without dissenting voices, and these were certainly used to the greatest extent by Senator McCain and Resolution Copper.

Apache Cultural Integrity and Apache Nationalism

The *Arizona Republic* published an article on July 23, 2015, by San Carlos Apache tribal member Dale Miles entitled, "Oak Flat Is Sacred? It Never Was Before." In this op-ed piece he detailed his own personal reasons for why the site was not sacred and fell upon his own credentials as a former "Tribal Historian" by citing his book, *The History of the San Carlos Apache*, which was published by the tribe. He mentioned the mine shaft previously constructed by Resolution Copper in the 1970s and the lack of protest by the San Carlos Apache people.[33] Other members also spoke out against the tribe and the efforts of protestors occupying Chi'chil Biłdogoteel after the land-swap legislation in 2014. Tribal member Karen Kitcheyan Jones stated she agreed with the elders who said, "'Oak Flat is not sacred. There are no sacred songs or sacred prayers that say Oak Flat is a Holy Place.' These very elders also ask, 'Why is there a Holy Ground over there, why? That is not good.'"[34] Dissenting tribal members caused considerable damage to the efforts of well-meaning protestors, but as it was during the 1990s at Dził Nchaa Si An, the most damage came from that of tribal leaders.

In the 2011 testimonies, former tribal chairman Harrison Talgo, who also supported the Mount Graham International Observatory, voiced his support of H. R. 1904, the 2011 version of the Southeast Arizona Land Exchange and Conservation Act. He spoke positively of the job prospects and economic potential for the tribe stating, "This is about putting my people, a lot of people, to work. I believe economic development should be our leadership's top priority. I have previously testified before Congress in support of economic projects. I have done so in the face of oppositions from other leaders who have opposed these same opportunities on or near the reservation."[35] Collectively these opposing opinions are a hinderance and complication in the tribe's attempt to confirm and establish the traditional and historical presence of the people on contested territory. They undermine the creditability of the tribe within the Euro-American context, but taken out of that context, the perspective changes. Traditional Apachean views recognize the disparities between the opposing voices and other tribal members, and they are not a discredit to the efforts of those members attempting to save traditional sites. Within the Euro-American context, this is an issue of disunity and Apache nationalism where members associate themselves with a nation created by non-Apaches.

The land designations that are now the San Carlos Apache and White Mountain Apache Reservations are only a fraction of traditional Apachean homelands. Each of these reservations includes numerous Indigenous peoples who, prior to reservation life, possessed little to no association with the land they currently occupy. Even among other Apachean groups the variances between the peoples were wide, and the lands they occupied were distinct and relative to the people. In the case of the "Western Apache," Grenville Goodwin, an anthropologist who worked closely with the San Carlos Apachean peoples in the 1930s and 1940s, produced a manuscript detailing the distinctiveness of Apachean groups. He stated, "Whereas other divisions can be called 'tribes' in the sense that they formed a fairly unified people both politically and culturally, 'tribe' is not altogether applicable to the Western Apache."[36] Apachean groups in Arizona were not a cohesive group aligned with a central political identity. The people were split into bands, clans, and families based on a matrilineal system.

The identity of a "San Carlos Apache member" reflects that of an individual belonging to a singular people with one history and one heritage, when, traditionally, they are in fact an incredibly diverse group. The Elders Cultural Advisory Council meeting held in 2011 on the San Carlos Apache Reservation affirmed this concept when speaking of Chi'chil Biłdagoteel. In the published memorandum the council stated, "The ancestors of *some* of our Tribal members lived there and passed their knowledge to their descendants who are alive today."[37] The elders understood that the people who currently live on the reservation possessed specific stories passed to them from their ancestors. The tribal knowledge that many received included several generations' worth of oral traditions, each linked to a separate band, clan, and family group. Chairman Rambler substantiated these claims in his congressional testimony: "At least eight Apache clans and two Western Apache Bands have documented history in the area. Apache clans originated from this area and Apaches on the Reservation have ancestors who came from the Oak Flat area before being forced to Old San Carlos."[38] Grenville Goodwin's study of the Western Apache documented twenty distinct bands placed throughout eastern Arizona from the Catalina Mountains in the south near Tucson, up to the northern parts of Arizona near Flagstaff, encompassing much of the eastern half of the state near the current Arizona–New Mexico border. The documented sixty clans each had their own familial structures, chiefs, and sub chiefs. A map, illustrated by Goodwin, displays the approximate boundaries of the twenty bands and places the Southern Tonto local group, which includes seven of the twenty bands, and one clan from the San Carlos local group, a conglomeration of four distinct bands, near the vicinity of Chi'chil Biłdagoteel, for a total of eight bands.[39] Of those eight bands, it is difficult to say with western anthropological and historical evidence which two bands and eight clans claimed those lands.

Indigenous knowledge is rarely acknowledged as significant primary information by the academy and in legal proceedings to solidify historical fact, but in this instance, the understanding of traditions passed to the descendants of the clans is relevant. As such, dissenting voices from the federally recognized tribal whole are not relaying a concept of traditional knowledge that is unfounded; they are presenting knowledge passed to them from their own families, clans, and bands. The same is true for those who consider the region to be sacred. Their knowledge is no less important than those who claim otherwise. In this regard both are correct in saying that Chi'chil Biłdagoteel is sacred and not. To those who claim its sacredness, they are retelling the stories of their ancestors, and dissenters are doing the same. The corruption of the Apachean identity and failure to remember are central to this discussion. Apache nationalism was created as a byproduct of the San Carlos Apache political identity and fostered by the Constitution of the San Carlos Apache Tribe, a document that has controlled the power structures of the people for decades. It is the result of the 1934 Indian Reorganization Act created to manipulate the governing bodies of the Indigenous peoples in the country and fashion them into political entities recognizable to the settler-colonial worldview.[40] These constitutions were written as "cookie-cutter" documents that detailed who is permitted to be in power and how that power is distributed. It makes no mention of accommodations for traditional practices, the institution of the clan and band systems, familial practices, or the matrilineal hierarchies. Under this document, governance is filtered through the colonial authority of the United States and onto the subjugated Apache peoples, disallowing the acknowledgement of traditional Apachean lifeways. After nearly eighty years of this instituted practice, the people have accorded a concept of identity consumed by nationalistic tendencies consigned in a foreign political identity to subsequent generations. This ultimately results in a hostile reaction when those who oppose the established structure dare to remove themselves. In the case of Chi'chil Biłdagoteel, both the opposition and defenders placed themselves outside of this Euro-American nationalistic framework and into an Indigenous one bereft of its invasive settler-colonial manipulations on what is considered an appropriate interpretation of identity.

Conclusion

Since the founding of the San Carlos Apache Reservation in 1872 the people have been in constant danger of losing their traditional identities. Some Apachean perceptions of the world have been distorted, and many have been blinded by the prospect of financial or political gain. The tendency of tribal members to associate themselves with the collective whole sets a dangerous precedent when companies and politicians, such as Resolution Copper and supporters of the southeast Arizona land exchange, exploit these attitudes to promote their own agendas.

The forced removal of Apachean groups and other Indigenous peoples onto a single reservation was detrimental to the cultural practices of each of those peoples. Land disputes in the late nineteenth century saw the loss of Aravaipa homelands with the inclusion of non-Apachean Indigenous considerations for lands that were of little importance to those groups. Furthermore, the continued implementation of federal law and policy on the reservation perpetuated the continued destruction of traditional Apachean identities with the passage of the Indian Reorganization Act in 1934, where they were forced to institute a foreign constitutional concept to govern the people as a whole, regardless of the clan/band designations. The dispute at Dził Nchaa Si An in the late 1980s and early 1990s, an issue that continues into the twenty-first century, was an instance wherein the nationalistic tendencies of the newer generations of Apache were exemplified. The dissenting views on this particular issue foreshadowed the problems that were experienced at Chi'chil Biłdagoteel. Resolution Copper's move to acquire federally protected and culturally significant lands for the purpose of mining, which may result in the destruction of the land, was riddled with complications from the very beginning. It was only through the deceptive tactics of John McCain (with the inclusion of a rider in the final bill with no recognition of the change) that the acquisition was permitted.

To understand the complexity of the cultural implications at Chi'chil Biłdagoteel in regard to the reasons for dissention, it is necessary to explore the history of the people as it relates to their identity. The continued disassociation with traditional identities places the people in a position where the discrepancies between oral traditions and stories becomes a point of contention rather than a unifying characteristic of the culture. Each member possessed knowledge that was passed on by their ancestors. Attempts by the federal government to undermine the cultural practices of the people developed an Apache nationalism that was fostered through the construction of the San Carlos Apache Nation, where members dissent from a conceptualized whole. Those land disputes, both historical and current, experienced by the peoples of the San Carlos Apache Reservation, where members disagreed on a place's "sacredness," cement the fact that history and cultural traditions are relevant to the Apachean argument, both for and against. Identity is incredibly relevant to Apache history, as well as for many other Indigenous peoples. The sins of the country against Indigenous peoples continue into the modern day and manifest in this new Indigenous worldview rooted in Western concepts. How a people express identity and historically understand it must be considered in future works related to contemporary Indigenous issues.

Notes

1. Deloria, *God Is Red*, 66.
2. Estes, "Fighting for Our Lives," 116.
3. U.S. Congress, *Southeast Arizona Land Exchange and Conservation Act of 2007*, 17.
4. Thomas explains that peoplehood is established by reflecting upon four key areas of influence among a people: language, ceremony, land, and history. This foundational understanding permits the necessary acknowledgements of vastly different peoples, even within similar groups such as the Athabaskan, and further provides a means to understand identity. See Holm, Pearson, and Chavis, "Peoplehood," 7–24. The authors incorporated this approach to formulate a concept of sovereignty based on the "peoplehood model" and make necessary adjustments to Thomas's theory of peoplehood. The areas are rebranded for a better representation as sacred history, ceremonial cycle, language, and sacred space.
5. Resolution Copper, *General Plan of Operations*, 15.
6. Levin and Buck, *Mckeon National Defense*.
7. *Map of Arizona, or the Gadsden Purchase*, 1859. The Gadsden Purchase allowed for the purchase of the remaining sections of what is today known as Arizona and New Mexico. The purchase included the city of Tucson, Arizona, created new borders for the United States, and removed the boundary from the Gila River in Arizona to its current border just south of Nogales, Arizona. It also removed the Article 11 treaty obligation that required the United States to assist or repay Mexican citizens for any depredations experienced by raiding Apaches and Comanches. See Kiser, *Dragoons in Apacheland*.
8. Clum, *Apache Agent*, 94.
9. Grant, *Executive Orders*, 17.
10. The Camp Grant Massacre is an incident that occurred in April 1871 when a group of white Americans, Mexicans, and Tohono O'odham warriors attacked a peaceful group of Pinal and Aravaipa Apaches under the protection of Lieutenant Whitman, acting commander of Camp Grant. This attack resulted in the murders of 144 Apaches, mostly women and children. For more information about the Camp Grant Massacre see Colwell-Chanthaphonh, *Massacre at Camp Grant* and Jacoby, *Shadows at Dawn*.

11. Colwell-Chanthaphonh, *Massacre at Camp Grant*, 37.
12. Haley, *Apaches*, 306.
13. Grant, *Executive Orders*, 83–87.
14. Colwell-Chanthaphonh. *Massacre at Camp Grant*, 76.
15. U.S. Department of the Interior, *Constitution and By-Laws*.
16. James P. Jordan, "John McCain's 'Midnight Riders' Put Borderlands at Risk," *People's World*, September 15, 2015, https://www.peoplesworld.org/article/john-mccain-s-midnight-riders-put-borderlands-at-risk/.
17. Gordon V. Krutz, in a letter to Buck Kitcheyan, December 27, 1989.
18. San Carlos Apache Tribe, *San Carlos Apache Tribe Resolution No. 90–68* (1990).
19. Buck Kitcheyan, in a letter to David Jolly, August 31, 1990.
20. Buck Kitcheyan, in a letter to David Jolly, August 31, 1990.
21. "Apache Delegation Denied Audience with Pope," *San Carlos Apache Moccasin*, May 26, 1992.
22. Harrison Talgo, in a letter to Jack Thomas, December 14, 1993.
23. William Belvado, in a letter to Sidney Yates, December 5, 1995.
24. Deloria, *God Is Red*, 146.
25. Federal Register, PLO 1229 (October 1, 1955).
26. Jordan, "John McCain's 'Midnight Riders'," *People's World*, September 15, 2015.
27. Lovett, "Not All Land Exchanges Are Created Equal," 366.
28. U.S. Congress, House, *Copper Basin Jobs Act* (March 18, 2010).
29. U.S. Congress, *Southeast Arizona Land Exchange and Conservation Act of 2007*.
30. U.S. Congress, Senate, *Current Public Lands and Forests Legislation*, 47.
31. U.S. Congress, Senate, *Public Land and Forests Bills*, 5.
32. "Senate Energy and Natural Resources Subcommittee," *Congressional Documents and Publications* (November 20, 2013).
33. Dale Miles, "Oak Flat Is a Sacred Site? It Never Was Before," *AZCentral*, July 23, 2015, http://www.azcentral.com/story/opinion/op-ed/2015/07/23/oak-flatsacred/30587803/.
34. David F. Briggs, "Apaches Question Actions of their Leadership," *Arizona Daily Independent News Network*, July 8, 2015, https://arizonadailyindependent.com/2015/07/08/apaches-question-actions-of-their-leadership/.
35. U.S. Congress, House, *Legislative Hearing on H. R. 1904*, 68.
36. Goodwin, *Social Organization of the Western Apache*, 6.
37. San Carlos Apache Tribe, *Elders Council Memorandum*, 2 (emphasis added).
38. U.S. Congress, Senate, "Testimony by Terry Rambler," 3–4.
39. Goodwin, *Social Organization of the Western Apache*, 5
40. Dunbar-Ortiz, *An Indigenous Peoples' History*, 171–72.

Bibliography

Clum, Woodworth. *Apache Agent: The Story of John P. Clum*. Cambridge: Riverside, 1936.
Colwell-Chanthaphonh, Chip. *Massacre at Camp Grant: Forgetting and Remembering Apache History*. Tucson: University of Arizona Press, 2007.
Deloria, Vine, Jr. *God Is Red: A Native View of Religion*. Golden CO: Fulcrum, 2003.
Dunbar-Ortiz, Roxanne. *An Indigenous Peoples' History of the United States*. Boston: Beacon, 2014.

Estes, Nick. "Fighting for Our Lives: #NoDAPL in Historical Context." *Wicazo Sa Review* 32, no. 2 (2017): 115–22.

Federal Register. PLO 1229 (October 1, 1955).

Goodwin, Grenville. *Social Organization of the Western Apache*. Chicago: University of Chicago Press, 1942.

Grant, Ulysses S. *Executive Orders Relating to Indian Reserves from May 14, 1855 to July 1, 1902*. Washington DC: GPO, 1902.

Haley, James L. *Apaches: A History and Culture Portrait*. Garden City NY: Doubleday, 1981.

Holm, Tom, J. Diane Pearson, and Ben Chavis. "Peoplehood: A Model for the Extension of Sovereignty in American Indian Studies." *Wicazo Sa Review* 18, no. 1 (2003): 7–24.

Jacoby, Karl. *Shadows at Dawn: A Borderlands Massacre and the Violence of History*. New York: Penguin, 2010.

Kiser, William S. *Dragoons in Apacheland: Conquest and Resistance in Southern New Mexico, 1846–1861*. Norman: University of Oklahoma Press, 2012.

Levin, Carl A., and Howard P. Buck. *Mckeon National Defense Authorization Act for Fiscal Year 2015*. 113 P. L. 291, 128 Stat. 3292, 2014 Enacted H. R. 3979, 113 Enacted H. R. 3979. December 19, 2014.

Lovett, Katharine E. "Not All Land Exchanges Are Created Equal: A Case Study of the Oak Flat Land Exchange." *Colorado Natural Resources, Energy & Environmental Law Review* 28, no. 2 (2017): 355–86.

Map of Arizona, or the Gadsden Purchase, with the Position of Its Silver Mines as Now Worked. 1859. Graff Collection, Newberry Library, Chicago.

Resolution Copper. *General Plan of Operations*. May 9, 2016.

San Carlos Apache Tribe. *Elders Council Memorandum*, December 14, 2011.

———. *San Carlos Apache Tribe Resolution No. 90–68*, 1990.

Thomas, Robert K. "The Taproots of Peoplehood." *Americans Before Columbus* 10, no. 5 (1982).

U.S. Department of the Interior, Office of Indian Affairs. *Constitution and By-Laws of the San Carlos Apache Tribe*. 1936.

U.S. House of Representatives Subcommittee on National Parks, Forests, and Public Lands. *Southeast Arizona Land Exchange and Conservation Act of 2007*. 110th Cong., 1st sess. 2007.

———. *House Copper Basin Jobs Act*. H. R. 4880, 111th Cong., 2nd sess. Introduced March 18, 2010.

———. *Southeast Arizona Land Exchange and Conservation Act Of 2011*. H. R. 1904, 112th Cong., 1st sess. 2011.

U.S. Senate. "Senate Energy and Natural Resources Subcommittee on Public Lands, Forests and Mining Hearing; S. 339, to Facilitate the Efficient Extraction of Mineral Resources in Southeast Arizona by Authorizing and Directing an Exchange of Federal and Non-Federal land; Testimony by Terry Rambler, Chairman, San Carlos Apache Tribe, San Carlos AZ." Congressional Documents and Publications. November 20, 2013. https://advance-lexis.com.ezproxy.lib.ou.edu/api/document?collection=news&id=urn:contentItem:59WJ-C0K1-DYVR-P403-00000-00&context=1516831.1.

U.S. Senate Subcommittee on Public Lands and Forests. *Current Public Lands and Forests Legislation*. 110th Cong., 2nd sess. 2008.

———. *Public Land and Forests Bills*. 111th Cong., 1st sess. 2009.

4

Chess or Checkers?

Fracking in Greater Chaco

SONI GRANT

I awoke to an alarming email. A policy researcher with the Navajo Nation Tri-Chapter Council—composed of the three Navajo Nation Chapter governments of Counselor, Ojo Encino, and Torreon—had been sifting through data about recent oil production in the area on the New Mexico Oil Conservation Division (NMOCD) website when he happened upon an obscure mention of a substantial oil spill in Counselor Chapter.[1] He sees incidents like these in the data regularly—spills, tank fires, and blowouts of which the community is not notified. In this case the sheer volume of substances released compelled him to alert local leaders and a handful of outside collaborators like myself. The incident report was not easy to find, located more than halfway down the long NMOCD page for Enduring Resources' well 315H, itself buried in the bowels of the agency's website. Some 46,200 gallons of produced water and 12,600 gallons of oil were released onto the land where they quickly flowed along the path of an arroyo.[2] The spill had occurred several weeks back but was news to everyone getting this early morning email, including elected Chapter officials.

As I began plugging the well's GPS coordinates into Google Maps, I received a panicked call from Daniel Tso, a longtime Diné rights advocate, who had recently been elected as Council Delegate to represent several Chapters in Eastern Navajo Agency on the Navajo Nation Council. Daniel asked if I could dig into the online files for well 315H and obtain some information about its administrative history. But most of all Daniel wanted to know the status of the land where it is located.

Daniel audibly cringed, "Oh no," when I told him that the well is located on Indian allotment land, where it taps into a pool of oil that extends underground for some three thousand acres. This pool had recently been "unitized," or contractually merged among leaseholders, to form the North Escavada Unit, a subsurface space from which oil trapped tightly in the Mancos Shale can be extracted. Daniel then chuckled along with me when I specified that, according to the oil company's records at the time of unitization, most of the North Escavada Unit is owned by 909 Diné allottees. In this moment of shared humor, we laughed not at the environmental devastation but rather at the uncomfortable reality of fractionation of Diné land holdings in the region, whose complexity sometimes reaches a level of incredulity that it becomes—if only for the briefest of moments—almost funny. The mood quickly darkened as the urgency that had prompted Daniel's call sunk in once again.

Residents in the Tri-Chapter region often underscore land—and specifically "land status," or jurisdiction—when they talk about oil and gas. Land is not only the space where extraction takes place: land's status produces the conditions of possibility for its extraction and for the forms of regulation and accountability available. Land *status* is especially important in this part of Dinétah, on the eastern border of the Navajo Reservation, because across this checkerboard region, jurisdiction is so fragmented that even with an intimate knowledge of place, it is at times hard to know exactly where one is standing in relation to the law.[3]

This chapter sketches the making of a checkerboard in Dinétah in order to illustrate how land relations established over the course of colonial settlement shape contemporary experiences of extraction. In particular I show how settlement produces a generative ambiguity about the very terms by which jurisdictional claims in the region can be made. Situating the checkerboard within a history of its jurisdiction shifts the question of present-day land management from the difficult task of managing for multiple uses to a question about who has the authority to invoke authority on these lands.[4]

The making of the checkerboard is a story of territorial dispossession by means of the forced institutionalization of settler ways of being in relation with land, even as Diné people maintain their land relations with determination. As land in Dinétah was gradually parceled out into distinct categories of ownership, new ways of thinking about and relating with land were introduced. In its administration by federal and state actors, land was treated as a resource understood through two of its constitutive relations: Earth's surface and subsurface. Abstracted in such a way, the surface and subsurface became objects of property, a racialized commodity form.[5]

Property, both public and private, is a social relation whose existence depends on others' non-property.[6] A property right is not about the object of possession but is rather a claim enforced by the law and social conventions.[7] In her seminal piece "Whiteness as Property," Cheryl Harris shows how "property rights in the United States are rooted in racial domination."[8] The racial identities of Black and Indigenous peoples became the legal justifications for slavery (ownership of a person) and territorial dispossession (ownership of land), tethering the institutions of whiteness and property. Aileen Moreton-Robinson dissects the possessive logics through which white subjects come to "invest in reproducing and reaffirming the nation-state's ownership, control, and domination" over Indigenous lands and bodies.[9] Brenna Bhandar builds on Harris's and Moreton-Robinson's work to trace the emergence of "racial regimes of ownership," a juridical formation in settler colonial states in which racial identities and property law are produced through one another. Bhandar argues that the appropriation and commodification of land and labor produce a hierarchy of racial subjectivities that organizes modern property law around whiteness.[10]

While Harris, Moreton-Robinson, and Bhandar focus on the racialization of property in settler colonies, recent scholarship on territory and sovereignty has challenged topographical representations and concepts of terrain itself. Anthropologists, geographers, and architects have argued that the space of state sovereignty is, or at least aspires to be, volumetric.[11] In contrast to a two-dimensional cartographic view, attention to the spatiality of terrain across volumes allows scholars to track forms of power and knowledge that operate below, above, and in parallel to the surface of the Earth.

This chapter is indebted to these critical insights about race, property, and the multiple dimensions of territory, but my aims here are slightly different. I trace techniques of jurisdiction through which settler authority over Dinétah was claimed and is maintained, and practices through which it continues to be contested. On the checkerboard, where action is often strangled by tangled authorities, jurisdiction—rather than an abstract concept of settler sovereignty—comes into view as the conduit through which power is exercised.[12] Centering jurisdiction, I am less interested in pointing out when state power is exercised across multiple dimensions like the "surface" and "subsurface" but rather in examining how these elements of Dinétah come to be seen as separate parts to begin with and to what consequences.

In this sense, more relevant for my purposes than the burgeoning literature on voluminosity is a longstanding body of Indigenous studies scholarship and practice that conceptualize land, which is inclusive of but not reducible to Indigenous territory, as a *relation* encompassing the Earth's strata, its air, water, living beings, and storied places and Indigenous practices.[13] To speak of collective Diné self-governance—whether in the language of sovereignty or in Diné-specific terms[14]—is already to invoke a multi-dimensional relation. In what follows I briefly describe three imperial projects to advance the settlement of the American West—railroad construction, homesteading, and Indian allotment—that disrupted this relation by fragmenting land into components over which settler ownership was claimed. Combined, these projects unleashed a complex process of dispossession that continues to this day. While the checkerboard had no sole architect, and while its multiple progenitors quickly lost control of the process of fragmentation their actions set into motion, the resulting spatial and juridical arrangement has not ceased to serve the conjoined agendas of settlement and extraction.

Fracking in Greater Chaco

With approximately forty thousand active and abandoned oil and gas wells throughout the San Juan Basin of northwest New Mexico, Dinétah is no stranger to industrial energy production. Diné people living in the region have borne the brunt of a century of extraction, beginning with oil and gas, uranium, and coal.[15] Even as Indigenous opposition and shifting political economic conditions have, in the early twenty-first century, brought a definitive end to uranium mining and a phasing out of coal production on Diné lands, industrial capital has proven adept at transforming land into new sources of fossil energy.

Fracking, the technique used to extract oil from the Mancos Shale, is one such novel form of industrial development in both scale and scope.[16] Older wells drilled throughout the twentieth century tapped more permeable underground formations: layers of sandstone, coal, and limestone. These formations contain hydrocarbons in large quantities, the remnants of organic oceanic matter deposited when the Western Interior Seaway began to retreat some 70 million years ago.[17] Unlike the Mancos Shale, these hydrocarbons are, in industry speak, "conventional." This means that they can be extracted with the use of traditional vertical drilling techniques that harness the natural pressure of an underground reservoir to pump oil and gas up to the surface. In shale, however, hydrocarbons are tightly held in the rock's minuscule pores. The innovation of twenty-first-century fracking is to horizontally drill through the rock and open up its pores by injecting large volumes of water, sand, and chemicals through the drill bore at high pressures.[18] With fracking—a technique that was rapidly spreading across the country in places like Pennsylvania and North Dakota—the San Juan Basin's Mancos Shale, a previously untapped geological reservoir, became accessible for the first time around 2010. A new resource was made.

The Mancos Shale attracted the most investment in the southern San Juan Basin, a historically less densely drilled area where the shale formation happens to be richest in oil. With fracking, development moved quickly not only into several Diné communities, but also very close to Chaco Culture National Historical Park, a United Nations World Heritage Site that protects a place of critical cultural and spiritual importance for Diné and Pueblo peoples in the Southwest. The proximity of fracking to Chaco made it particularly controversial, not only for Indigenous peoples who were directly

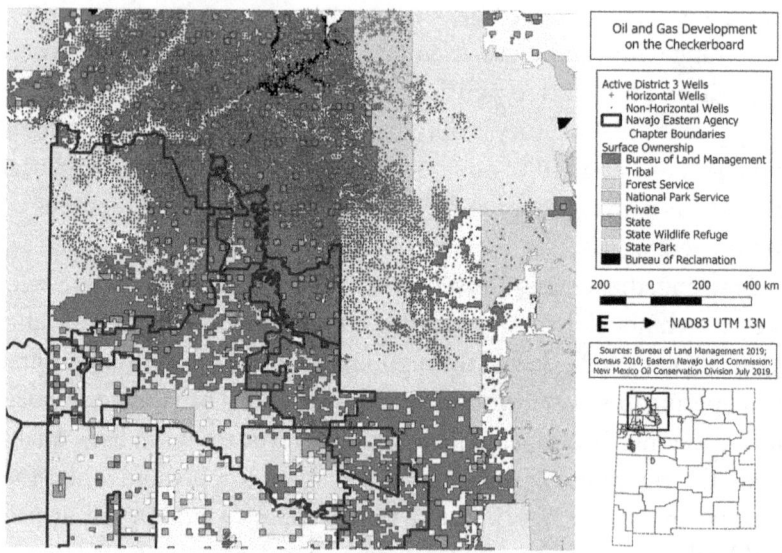

FIG. 8. Oil and gas extraction on the checkerboard. Map by Brandon Velivis.

impacted, but also for environmentalists and archaeologists across the country. Forming at times unlikely alliances, Diné and Pueblo peoples, tribal governments, small nonprofits, and big green groups came together around the place-name "Greater Chaco" in ongoing efforts to protect Chaco and the vast landscape that surrounds the park from extraction.

And yet despite formal opposition from the Navajo Nation, local Diné Chapters, the All Pueblo Council of Governors, the National Congress of American Indians, and environmental groups, the United States Bureau of Land Management (BLM) continued to permit drilling and to lease federally administered lands in close proximity to the park.[19] Leveraging solidarity from other Indigenous-led movements to protect sacred lands and waters across Turtle Island—such as the #NoDAPL movement led by the Standing Rock Sioux Nation, or intertribal efforts to protect Bears Ears—a broad-based coalition led by Diné and Pueblo peoples mobilized to oppose the expansion of extraction across the Greater Chaco landscape.[20] Living in the heart of the Mancos Shale boom, Daniel Tso and residents of the Tri-Chapter have been at the forefront of this movement.

Chess or Checkers?

Several months before the spill I tagged along with Daniel as he led a group of high school students from Santa Fe on his now famous "Fracking Is Fracking Reality Tour." As he had done countless times over the past several years with groups large and small, Daniel took the students through the backroads of nearby Diné communities to see the impacts of oil and gas development on the landscape. One of our stops that day happened to be Enduring Resources' well 315H, the same well that would, months later, release tens of thousands of gallons of petrochemicals into a tributary of the Escavada Wash. On that bright October day one of the wells on the pad was being actively fracked. A parade of trucks and tanks made for a vibrant display of color and noise. The harsh chemical odor wafting from the site was so strong that Daniel cut this stop short, ushering everyone back into vehicles to continue the tour.

Earlier that morning Daniel and I stood waiting in the gravel parking lot of Counselor Chapter House watching the oil trucks go by on Highway 550. By ten o'clock the autumn sun had turned the air from crisp to warm and was beginning to melt the frost on the sagebrush that covers the small field beneath Arrow Mesa, the rocky outcrop that shelters the Chapter House. When the students stumbled out of their vans bleary-eyed from a cold night camping at Chaco Canyon, Daniel asked them to form a circle in the parking lot. He positioned himself in the center and launched into a story of this place. He explained that Diné people have lived in this place for a *long* time—since time immemorial. Daniel's ancestors were here when the U.S. government rounded up the Diné on the devastating Long Walk to Hwéeldi in the early 1860s, and his ancestors returned to this area in 1868 upon the signing of the United States-Navajo Treaty.[21] Yet this part of Diné homelands never became reservation trust land. The Diné lived here along with settlers recently arrived in the area as the land was slowly alienated from them in the early twentieth century, leaving sections of surface land and minerals alternately controlled by federal, state, tribal, and private entities.

Several of the students were wearing plaid flannel shirts that day, just the right layer for autumn in the high desert. Daniel called attention to one shirt in particular worn by an attentive young woman, a checkered mix of browns, off-whites, and yellows. He asked the group to imagine the shirt as this land, with a neat tangle of authorities overlaying the landscape. He explained how each color represented a different jurisdiction, with the dominant brown being federal land, crisscrossed by many others. He concluded that in a way, this tightly woven jurisdictional configuration, known locally as "the checkerboard," transforms this place into a "no man's land." There are so many rules that it is hard to know which ones apply where or to pinpoint who has the authority to make decisions about land use.

"No man's land" struck me as a corollary to another metaphor Daniel often uses to explain the checkerboard to outsiders: "They call it the checkerboard, but they never tell us if we are playing chess or checkers." The "they" here is the set of agencies that authorize oil and gas extraction on federal and state lands on the checkerboard, and with whom Daniel and his colleagues in the Tri-Chapter are constantly engaged in a game that feels deeply rigged.

Checkering the Land

In a 1938 address to the Navajo Nation Tribal Council, vice chairman Howard Gorman, like Daniel eighty years later, used the term "No-Man's Land" to describe the checkerboard of northwestern New Mexico, where he said nine thousand Diné people were "struggling along on barest subsistences [sic]." At the time Gorman was advocating for the passage of the New Mexico Boundary Bill, a federal bill that would have consolidated Diné land holdings in the checkerboard area, which by then were severely fragmented. At stake in the consolidation of Diné land holdings was nothing less than "the salvation" of Diné people living on the land in question, Gorman emphasized.[22]

Congress would ultimately fail to ratify the New Mexico Boundary Bill. Albeit the most comprehensive, this bill would neither be the first nor the last effort by Diné and federal actors to attempt a remedy to what was then recognized as the *problem* of the checkerboard. The problem would only grow weedier over time as parties acquired legal title to parcels of land in the area, as fractionation of Indian allotments increased exponentially, and as people living in the region continued to forge attachments to land and place.

The United States-Navajo Treaty of 1868 granted the Diné a reservation that was but a small part of their former territory between the Six Sacred Mountains. During treaty discussions U.S. General W. T. Sherman told Diné people that they were to live upon a newly established reservation. Those who refused to do so could live on unoccupied land outside of reservation boundaries only if they consented to subject themselves to the laws of the United States.[23] To the dissatisfaction of white settlers who would soon arrive in Dinétah, many Diné people chose the latter option, returning from Hwéeldi to their former homes east of the newly established Navajo Reservation on what was now claimed as the public domain of the United States.[24]

Railroading

While Diné people were held prisoners at Hwéeldi, Congress chartered the Atlantic and Pacific Railroad Company in 1866 to build a railroad from Springfield, Missouri, to the California state line. For forty miles on either side of the planned line, the Atlantic and Pacific was granted alternate sections of 640 acres of surface land, while the federal government retained mineral rights below these tracts. These grants were made with the purpose of subsidizing railroad construction, providing the railroad company with leasable surface land along the line.[25] As a condition of the 1868 treaty, Diné people were to "make no opposition to the construction of the railroads now being built or hereafter to be built across the continent."[26]

Homesteading

Anglo-American settlement in the region was gradual. Some settlers leased sections of railroad lands whereas others applied for homesteading permits. The Homesteading Act of 1862 and other homesteading acts to follow encouraged American citizens to move west and settle on 160-acre plots of land. For a minimal application fee and five years of continual occupancy on the land, the male adult head of the family could gain title to the tract—provided that over the course of their stay they had made improvements to the land through cultivation and the construction of a home.[27]

Homesteading policies contained provisions that would have lasting consequences for twentieth- and twenty-first-century oil and gas development in the present-day checkerboard because they contributed not only to a patchwork pattern of surface jurisdiction but also to uneven ownership of subsurface mineral rights. The first Homesteading Act of 1862 conveyed mineral rights to homesteaders along with title to their plot. However by 1910 the federal government recognized differential values of surface and subsurface resources on the public domain and began allowing settlement on surface lands while reserving mineral rights to itself.[28]

By the late 1870s white settlers who had arrived in the area expressed considerable anxiety to government officials about Diné people living and grazing animals on the public domain. Diné people living east of the reservation became classified as "off-reservation," "nonreservation," or "public domain Navajos," a quasi-juridical categorization that bolstered anxieties about Native presence among settlers recently arrived in the area and facilitated state interventions to manage a people now "out of place."[29] For instance in 1877 148 individuals in present-day Farmington sent a petition to Indian agent Alexander Irvine complaining about "bands of Navajoe [sic] Indians scattered along the river," who were making it "very annoying to the settlers by means of threatening to drive them away and driving stock and scattering them." The petition stated that "some of the settlers are annoyed beyond endurance" and pleaded that something be done to mitigate trouble with the Indians.[30]

This expression of settler entitlement to property undisturbed by Native presence is an early sign of the tension and hostility over the control of the range that would only increase over the coming decades.[31] In light of this growing tension—and to provide enough land for Diné people living east of the reservation to subsist and water their flock—the reservation was extended in 1880, primarily to the north and east of the 1868 treaty reservation. To the east this extension brought the reservation line fifteen miles closer to Chaco Canyon.[32]

Allotment

A third and devastating process through which Dinétah was parceled into distinct pieces of land was through allotment. The General Allotment Act of 1887 had transformative effects east of the Navajo Reservation in the early twentieth century, and its legacy continues to be felt daily in Dinétah. As Judith Rosyter notes the General Allotment Act marked a shift in the federal Indian policy that preceded it. Whereas earlier nineteenth-century policy was "primarily oriented towards the separation of tribes and citizens" into discrete reservations, allotment was aimed at the assimilation of Indigenous peoples through the gradual replacement of communal land ownership with private property.[33]

The General Allotment Act allowed for tribal lands to be surveyed and divided into "allotments" of approximately 80 to 160 acres.[34] These small tracts of land were granted to individual tribal members, who became beneficial owners of allotments over which the federal government would act as trustee for twenty-five years. After this probationary period, or sooner if an allottee was proven as "competent and capable of managing his or her affairs," allottees would receive fee patents to the allotments.[35] Lands not allotted to Indigenous peoples were opened up for use by settlers. After allottees received patents on their allotments, many were allowed to sell their land to non-Indians. In these ways allotment resulted in extraordinary territorial dispossession—Indian land holdings in the United States decreased from 138 million acres to 48 million acres between 1887, when allotment began, and 1934, when it ended.[36]

Original allottees were denied the right to determine how allotments would be distributed upon death. Instead, allotments typically passed on through state intestacy laws, wherein each heir to the original allottee would inherit an undivided fractional interest in the allotment. As a result of this continued fractionation of ownership, many allotments on the checkerboard today—and throughout Indigenous lands in the United States—have hundreds and even thousands of co-owners.[37]

The allotment process on the public domain in Dinétah began

in 1906 and continued in fits and starts through the early 1930s.[38] Approximately 4,000 allotments were patented to Diné individuals, with about 3,900 of those tracts located in northwestern New Mexico and the rest in Arizona and Utah. These parcels cover more than 750,000 acres of land with more than 40,000 known co-owners.[39]

Land Buy-Back

Almost a century later in 2015 the Navajo Nation would launch the first phase of a buy-back program to purchase fractional interests in allotments from willing sellers. This program was carried out in partnership with the Department of the Interior's Land Buy-Back Program for Tribal Nations, initiated as part of the 2009 settlement agreement in *Cobell v. Salazar*.[40] First filed as a class action in 1996 by Eloise Cobell (Niitsítapi Blackfoot Confederacy) and four other plaintiffs representing all individual Indian trust beneficiaries (allottees and other trust interest holders), the suit charged the Department of the Interior and the Department of the Treasury with gross mismanagement of Native American trust funds. With thousands of filings over fourteen years of litigation, *Cobell* was one of the largest suits ever filed against the federal government. Through research and discovery the plaintiffs showed egregious misconduct on the part of the federal government, who simply could not provide an account of the money it currently held in trust in Individual Indian Money accounts, and who was found in civil contempt of court for failing to maintain, losing, and in some cases destroying physical records of trust assets.[41]

The landmark *Cobell* settlement agreement resulted in a $3.4 billion fund, of which $1.9 billion was set aside for the purchase of fractionated individual trust lands (interests in allotments).[42] On Navajo Nation more than eleven thousand people (or 43 percent of those who received offers) elected to sell their interests back to the tribe in the first phase of the buy-back, returning fractional percentages of 160-acre tracts and a handful of entire tracts to tribal jurisdiction.[43] Through the buy-back program, the checkerboard continues to shift, above and below ground, into the twenty-first century.

Reservation Additions and Subtractions

As competition over rangeland and water resources between white stockmen and Diné people grew, Pres. Theodore Roosevelt heeded to recommendations from allotting agents, commissioner of Indian Affairs, Francis E. Leupp, and calls from Diné people themselves to extend the reservation.[44] In November 1907 Roosevelt signed Executive Order 709, withdrawing from the public domain about one million acres in San Juan and McKinley Counties and annexing these acres to the Navajo Reservation.[45] Allotment of parcels to individual Diné inhabitants within the executive order addition continued, and allotting agents helped Diné applicants to secure parcels with springs and water holes so that they could sustain livestock and crops. But because the executive order addition did not affect existing rights in the area, white settlers continued to lease sections still owned by the railroad companies.[46]

Roosevelt soon succumbed to strong opposition to the reservation extension from settlers in the area. By December 1908 he restored twenty-six townships in the newly extended reservation to the public domain.[47] And by 1911 President Taft's administration deemed the allotment process to have been sufficiently completed within the entire reservation addition. Taft restored all of the land that Roosevelt had initially tacked onto the reservation to the public domain, leaving approximately 2,500 allotments—representing less than 50 percent of the Diné people eligible for allotments and covering less than half of the new extension—checkered throughout a sea of now federally and privately claimed land.[48]

A drama of jurisdiction continued to unfold through the 1920s and early 1930s as the reconfigurations of the landscape unleashed through railroad leases, homesteading, and allotment persisted. In the early 1920s the discovery of oil east of the reservation led the U.S. government to organize a Navajo Tribal Council for the sole purpose of approving oil leases.[49] While some Diné and federal actors waged an ultimately unsuccessful fight to consolidate Diné land holdings by using the tribe's recently acquired oil monies to purchase or trade sections of railroad and federal land, the newly appointed commissioner of Indian Affairs, John Collier, devised a violent livestock reduction program that he hoped would help solve the problem of erosion caused by what he perceived as decades of overgrazing in Navajo country. As Marsha Weisiger notes, while Collier blamed erosion on overgrazing, it was really a result of federal actors' decision to force Diné people onto an area too small to support their stock.[50] The 1934 passage of the Indian Reorganization Act and the Taylor Grazing Act brought an end to both allotment and homesteading as means for Indigenous people and settlers alike to claim title to land on the public domain.[51] The checkerboard area was now increasingly subject to administration by the Grazing Service and the General Land Office, which would merge in 1946 to become the Bureau of Land Management.[52]

It would not be long before Cold War-era booms in oil, gas, coal, and uranium would take off in Dinétah. As Diné scholar John Redhouse describes, the checkerboard pattern of land ownership that had formed over the previous century saw little change for nearly three decades after the implementation of the Taylor Grazing Act. But beginning in 1964 lands in Dinétah that had been withdrawn for Diné use were opened for mineral leasing. As the coal, oil, and gas potential of these lands was increasingly known, federal and private actors became concerned with Diné occupancy in the area.[53]

Unauthorized Occupants

In 1974 BLM published a report called "Navajo Occupancy on National Resource Lands in Northwest New Mexico," in which it found that nearly eight thousand Diné people were living on the public domain without authorization. The report outlined the problem as such: not only were Diné people illegally occupying federally managed lands, but more than two thousand of them lived on tracts that conflicted with mineral development, particularly coal, oil, and gas.[54] The agency had received letters and comments from energy companies requesting that "squatters" be removed from their leases, from conservation groups urging for the protection of public lands, and from Diné organizations asking that land be set aside for Diné use.[55] The report laid out a number of strategies for addressing unauthorized occupancy and ultimately recommended that existing unauthorized occupants be "given the opportunity to acquire the area occupied by exchanging land of equal value" in cases where the occupant did not interfere with mineral development.[56]

Between 1980 and 1987 the BLM Farmington Field Office legalized approximately five hundred homesites belonging to Diné families, who had previously lacked federal authority to dwell on the public domain.[57] The agency's broader approach to the problem of unauthorized occupancy took the form of programs for land exchanges, which have continued since the 1980s and have helped consolidate some land holdings.[58] In doing so land consolidation has also authorized some Diné occupancy in the area.[59] But the overall shape of the checkerboard—as a Navajo Nation Council resolution would describe it in 2012, "A crazy quilt of land titles and governmental jurisdiction, and lack of basic services and infrastructure taken for granted in non-Indian areas"—remains.[60]

On the checkerboard, land exchanges—no matter the size—are hard-won achievements, and while they may alleviate day-to-day difficulties of cohabitation on the range, they do not resolve longstanding claims to title and belonging. Moreover, while land exchanges have consolidated some surface holdings, they have not always had the same effect on the subsurface. As with the exchanges consummated in the 1980s under BLM's Navajo Occupancy Resolution Program, many land exchanges in the area only swap surface rights, further splitting surface and subsurface estates.[61]

That a people who have lived in a place since time immemorial could come to be seen as squatters on their ancestral territory reveals the tremendous capacity of the law to perpetuate a narrative spacetime that omits the conditions of its own authority.[62] This form of colonial unknowing shores up the federal government's leasing of the public domain for extraction even in the face of strong Diné opposition.[63]

Tangled Authorities

Several months after learning about the spill I joined community leaders from the Tri-Chapter as they accompanied staff from the New Mexico Environment Department and NMOCD to tour well sites in the area. The tour was held immediately after a public hearing at Counselor Chapter House regarding the state's efforts to develop new methane rules for the oil and gas industry. My colleagues from the Tri-Chapter wanted to make sure that the agencies saw and smelled firsthand some of the impacts of oil and gas. Weaving through bumpy dirt roads, our small caravan eventually pulled up next to well 315H. We disembarked from our vehicles and stood there, gazing back and forth from the well pad to the patches of disturbed ground where contaminated soil had been excavated. Not far in the distance we could make out the contours of the arroyo into which oil and wastewater had rushed.

After listening to community members' concerns about the spill, the agencies informed us that there was finally a remediation plan in place and that NMOCD would be overseeing it. However, they conceded, the process of arriving at this plan had not been easy. As it rushed through the arroyo, the oily mixture crossed multiple surface and subsurface jurisdictions in only a mile and a half, passing across surface areas, mineral deposits, and waters managed by various federal and state actors. Through further conversations with regulators and a review of the scant documentation about the incident that became available, I would discern that in the aftermath of the spill, six federal, state, and tribal agencies, along with Enduring Resources and its many contractors, grappled with what was required of them in the situation. An agreement had to be reached among all of the responsible parties about which laws applied where and who was responsible for enforcement. This took some time to negotiate. Meanwhile, oil seeped deeper into the ground. Eventually a sampling and remediation plan was devised. No one ever notified the allottees who co-own fractional interests in the land, held in trust for them by the federal government, or local leaders in Counselor Chapter. No fine or penalty was ever issued to the oil company.

In witnessing many interactions like this one between residents and the agencies that regulate the oil and gas industry, I have come to see the checkerboard as a formation that, at times, confounds not only people who live there but also the entities who are meant to introduce order in this fractured landscape. The spill at well 315H illustrates how the checkerboard's property regimes, institutionalized gradually over the course of colonial settlement in the region, break down when they are confronted with industrial pollution that spills over their boundaries. In its attempt to parcel out land's relations, settler jurisdiction fails to contain the effects of the actions it authorizes. But in moments of jurisdictional ambiguity and the crises of responsibility they engender, it is nevertheless Diné lands and people who bear the burdens of inaction.

In this light, Daniel's rhetorical question—is this a game of chess or checkers?—is not only an incisive critique of the checkerboard's legal geography. Foregrounding jurisdiction, or *land's status*, inverts commonplace notions of what is infrastructural to resource extraction—such as the pumpjacks, compressors, and pipelines that cover the San Juan Basin. This shift forces consideration of the tangled forms of authority that authorize extraction as equally important sites of critical analysis, political action, and reorganization. To call into question the rules of the game is also to challenge the legitimacy of that authority. It is to keep a determined gaze fixed on the problem of the checkerboard but with an eye toward a jurisdictional arrangement that would affirm both Diné presence and sovereignty.

Notes

1. Chapters are local units of Navajo Nation government. There are 110 chapters throughout Navajo Nation. See Rodgers, "Chapter Images."

2. LTE Environmental Inc., "Report of Final Sampling and Closure Request." "Produced water" is a combination of the water and chemicals used to drill a well and the toxins that come up from underground. It tends to be salty, muddy, and laced with chemicals and radionuclides.

3. Diné Bikéyah is a commonly used Diné term to describe traditional Diné homelands within the six Sacred Mountains. These homelands are much larger than the present-day reservation. Dinétah and Diné Bikéyah are sometimes used interchangeably, while in other instances Dinétah is used to describe a specific place in present-day Eastern Navajo Agency where Diné people came into the world. I use Dinétah to describe this space in Eastern Navajo Agency.

4. On jurisdiction as the authority to invoke authority, see Pasternak, *Grounded Authority*. "Multiple use" is the ethic that guides federal land management agencies like BLM. There is a similar ethos within the New Mexico State Land Office.

5. Meredith Palmer, "Rendering Settler Sovereign Landscapes," 793–810; see Pasternak, *Grounded Authority*.

6. See Blomley, "Law, Property" and Goldstein, "By Force of Expectation."

7. MacPherson, "The Meaning of Property," 1–14; see Tsosie, "Land, Culture, and Community."

8. Harris, "Whiteness as Property," 1716.

9. Moreton-Robinson, *The White Possessive*, xii.

10. See Bhandar, *The Colonial Lives of Property*.

11. See Billé, *Voluminous States*; Braun, "Producing Vertical Territory," 7–46; Elden, "Secure the Volume," 35–51; Sloterdijk, *Terror from the Air*; Zurita, Munro, and Houston, "Un-Earthing the Subterranean Anthropocene," 298–305; Weizman, "Introduction to the Politics of Verticality."

12. See Cormack, *A Power to Do Justice*; Dennison, "Entangled Sovereignties"; Ford, *Settler Sovereignty*; Pasternak, *Grounded Authority*; Richland, "Jurisdiction," 209–26; Simpson, *Mohawk Interruptus*.

13. See for instance Lee, "Land," 57–62; Murphy, "Some Keywords toward Decolonial Methods," 376–84; Rowe and Tuck, "Settler Colonialism and Cultural Studies," 3–13; Tuck and Yang, "Decolonization Is Not a Metaphor," 1–40; Watts, "Indigenous Place-Thought and Agency amongst Humans and Non-Humans," 20–34.

14. Emerson, "Diné Sovereign Action," 160–78.

15. See for instance Chamberlain, *Under Sacred Ground*; Curley, "T'aa'hwo Aji t'eego," 1–16; Masco, *The Nuclear Borderlands*; Montoya, "Yellow Water," 91–115; Pasternak, *Yellow Dirt*; Powell, *Landscapes of Power*; Yazzie, "Decolonizing Development in Diné Bikéyah," 25–39.

16. See Hu, "Imperial Metaphysics" and Wylie, *Fractivism*.

17. Fassett, "Oil and Gas Resources," 181–96.

18. For more on the technique of hydraulic fracturing, see Wylie, *Fractivism*.

19. Since at least 2017 the All Pueblo Council of Governors and the Navajo Nation have joined in calling for protection of the Greater Chaco landscape from oil and gas drilling. For example see All Pueblo Council of Governors, "Tribal Leaders Host Historic Summit" and Navajo Nation, "OPVP Protect Chaco Canyon Region."

20. See Baca, *Shash Jaa'*; Estes, *Our History Is the Future*; Keeler, *Edge of Morning*.

21. For more information about Kit Carson's devastating scorched-Earth campaign and Hwéeldi, see Denetdale Nez, *Reclaiming Diné History* and Iverson and Roessel, *Diné*. The collective memory of Carson's catastrophic campaign, the Long Walk, and the prison camps at Hwéeldi continue to shape Diné political and social belonging in critical ways. See Powell, *Landscapes of Power* and Yazzie, "Decolonizing Development."

22. Howard Gorman. "Howard Gorman's Boundary Data." Richard Young Papers, Proposed New Mexico Boundary Bill 1938. MSS 672, box 3, folder 2. University of New Mexico Center for Southwest Research, 1938.

23. See Brugge, *A History of the Chaco Navajos*.

24. The Mexican-American War of 1846–1848 ended with the signing of the 1848 Treaty of Guadalupe Hidalgo. The United States acquired from Mexico 55 percent of its territory (more than 525,0000 square miles), including parts or all of present-day Arizona, California, New Mexico, Texas, Colorado, Nevada, and Utah. See Treaty of Guadalupe-Hidalgo. With the Treaty of Guadalupe Hidalgo the Americans now staked a territorial claim to Diné homelands, but it would be nearly two decades before the Diné were forced to cede their lands.

25. Most of this grant was forfeited in 1886 after eastern portions of the rail line were built, but it remained valid between Albuquerque, New Mexico, and California. In 1876 the

St. Louis and San Francisco Railroad Company took over the Atlantic and Pacific, and in 1880 the Atchison, Topeka, and Santa Fe Railroad bought a half-interest share. Four years later in 1884 the Aztec Land and Cattle Company bought one million acres of the grant land. In 1894 when the Atlantic and Pacific Railroad Company was liquidated, the remaining grant was divided between two railroad companies. The Atchison, Topeka, and Santa Fe share went to an affiliate called the Santa Fe Pacific Railroad Company, while the St. Louis and San Francisco transferred its share to its subsidiary, the New Mexico and Arizona Land Company. See Mosk, *Land Tenure Problems*.

26. Kappler, *Indian Affairs*, 1016. On the concept of "railroad colonialism," see Karuka, *Empire's Tracks*.

27. See Brugge, *A History of the Chaco Navajos*.

28. *Amoco Production Company v. Southern Ute Indian Tribe*, No. 98–830, 526 U.S. 865 (10th Cir. 1999).

29. Smith, "A Report from the Commissioner of Indian Affairs Relation"; Samuel Stacher, "History of Crownpoint NM. 1910–1935: By Supt. S. F. Stacher During His Administration." Stacher Family Papers MSS 382, box 1, folder 4. University of New Mexico Center for Southwest Research and Special Collections; Stacher, "Letter to the Commissioner of Indian Affairs," November 1, 1926.

30. Brugge, *A History of the Chaco Navajos*, 71.

31. On how an expectation of property emerges out of economies of dispossession of Indigenous peoples in the United States see Goldstein, "By Force of Expectation" and Moreton-Robinson, *The White Possessive*.

32. Brugge, *A History of the Chaco Navajos*, 90. This extension was the second of seventeen executive order extensions and other formal additions of the Navajo Reservation between 1878 and 1933, including the 1882 creation of the Hopi Reservation. See Kelly, *The Navajo Indians and Federal Indian Policy*.

33. Royster, "The Legacy of Allotment," 8.

34. The size of allotments varied. Individual heads of household received 160 acres. Individual adults received eighty acres. Orphaned children often received less. See Royster, "The Legacy of Allotment."

35. The Burke Act of 1906 eliminated the twenty-five-year transition period and authorized earlier issuance of fee patents, "Burke Act," Pub. L. No. 59–149, 34 Stat. 182; see Royster, "The Legacy of Allotment."

36. See Guzman, "Give or Take an Acre."

37. In 2012 the average fractionated tract with undivided trust interests had thirty-one co-owners, but many tracts greatly exceed this average. See Shoemaker, "Complexity's Shadow." See also Guzman, "Give or Take an Acre"; Royster, "The Legacy of Allotment"; Ruppel, *Unearthing Indian Land*.

38. See Brugge, *A History of the Chaco Navajos* and Stacher, "History of Crownpoint N. M."

39. "Hearing Before the United States Congress Senate Committee on Indian Affairs: Indian Land Consolidation Act Amendments; and to Permit the Leasing of Oil and Gas Rights on Navajo Allotted Lands," United States Congress Senate Committee on Indian Affairs (1999). Jerry Degroat, in discussion with the author, March 25, 2019. Today the subsurface accrues to the surface on most allotments. However, Diné allotment owners of approximately 2,500 parcels had to fight for ownership rights of the subsurface, which the

federal government attempted to retain for itself upon patenting. New patents that included surface and subsurface rights were issued in 1996. See *Mescal v. United States* 1:83-cv-01408.

40. *Cobell v. Salazar* 573 F.3d 808 D.C. Cir. 2009.

41. See "Contempt at Interior," *New York Times*, September 19, 2002, https://www.nytimes.com/2002/09/19/opinion/contempt-at-interior.html. In Dinétah a class action lawsuit filed by Diné allottees affiliated itself with and lent support to the *Cobell* case. In *Shii Shi Keyah v. USA* (1991), an association of Diné allottees won a settlement that would force the federal government to disburse royalty payments on time and to establish the Federal Indian Mineral Office to assist allottees with the management of their mineral resources.

42. In addition $1.4 billion was disbursed among *Cobell* class plaintiffs, and an Indian Education Scholarship Fund of up to $60 million was created. The *Cobell* settlement was not celebrated by all individual Indian interest holders and their advocates. See Goldstein, "Finance and Foreclosure in the Colonial Present" for a representative critique.

43. Department of the Interior, "2016 Status Report."

44. See Kelly, *The Navajo Indians and Federal Indian Policy* and Mosk, *Land Tenure Problems*.

45. Shortly afterward, Executive Order 744 amended a typographical error in 709, which had the extension unintentionally encroach into the boundaries of the Jicarilla Apache Nation.

46. See Kelly, *The Navajo Indians and Federal Indian Policy*.

47. See Hagerman, *Navajo Indian Reservation*.

48. See Brugge, *A History of the Chaco Navajos*.

49. I do not elaborate on the history of the Navajo Tribal Council here, but for an excellent account see Chamberlain, *Under Sacred Ground*.

50. First soliciting the voluntary sale and then directing the outright slaughter of sheep and other livestock by the tens of thousands, Collier's livestock reduction program had devastating effects on Diné mutton and wool subsistence economies, reducing Diné herds by more than half. Given the central role that sheep play in Diné social and cultural life, the livestock reduction program had reverberating traumatic effects across generations. See Denetdale, *Reclaiming Diné History*; Iverson and Roessel, *Diné: A History of the Navajos*; Powell, *Landscapes of Power*; Yazzie, "Decolonizing Development."

51. The Taylor Grazing Act of 1934 authorized the secretary of the interior to create grazing districts in which the department would manage permits for grazing and infrastructure projects. While the passage of the act did not change ownership of surface or subsurface lands on the checkerboard, it did have an effect on land use. Each grazing district had an advisory board composed of local constituents that made recommendations to higher-ups on permits. But as most Diné could not read or write in English, they were ineligible to vote on the boards, and white stockmen tended to dominate recommendations for permits. Cognizant that the Diné were being choked off the range, in 1939 John Collier worked with Secretary Ickes to create a special grazing district—District 7—on the checkerboard, essentially encompassing the area that the New Mexico Boundary Bill would have added to the reservation. The advisory board for District 7 had additional members to represent "Indian interests," such as the Indian Office, the Soil Conservation Service, and the Forest Service. While effectively turning the administration of the area over to the Grazing Service (now the Bureau of Land Management), the creation of District

7 did ensure that Diné people secured most of the remaining grazing permits in the area, much to the protest of white stockmen. See Mosk, *Land Tenure Problems* and Weisiger, *Dreaming of Sheep in Navajo Country*.

52. See Weisiger, *Dreaming of Sheep in Navajo Country*.

53. See Redhouse, *The Leasing of Dinétah*.

54. Bureau of Land Management, "Navajo Occupancy on National Resource Lands," 1.

55. Many of the conservation groups who provided feedback to the BLM on the issue of unauthorized occupancy were not sympathetic to the needs of Diné families living on the public domain. While the conservationists were primarily concerned with halting unchecked resource development, they also felt that the problem of unauthorized occupancy should be handled immediately, primarily by land exchanges. For example the New Mexico Wildlife Federation wrote: "Steps to evict unauthorized occupants of Federal land should begin at once. Discrimination due to national origin or race in enforcement of trespass laws should be stopped. There will be instances where exceptions to the above policy may be necessary. If it is necessary or desirable to authorize this unauthorized occupancy, requirements should be made for an exchange of land rather than an outright gift or sale of the National Resource Land." The Sandia Mountain Wildlife and Conservation Association was even blunter: "We are concerned, even alarmed, at the amount of land being lost to Navajos by squatters. We would appreciate your thoughts on what we can do in order to halt this land grab." Bureau of Land Management, "Navajo Occupancy on National Resource Lands," appendix G.

56. Bureau of Land Management, "Navajo Occupancy on National Resource Lands," appendix 1.

57. Bureau of Land Management. "Farmington Resource Management Plan," 2–7.

58. First, a 1980 Public Land Order (5721) withdrew 6,700 acres of surface federal land in the San Juan Basin for exchange between the BLM and the Navajo Tribe. The exchange was finally authorized by the passage of a 1983 law, and once consummated the BLM worked with the tribe and the Bureau of Indian Affairs to identify other areas for potential exchanges. The BLM Farmington Field Office resource management plans for 1987 and 2003 both indicated hundreds of thousands of acres available for exchange with the Navajo Nation. See BLM 1988 & 2003.

59. The problem of unauthorized occupancy continued in the twenty-first century for the BLM. In 2012 the Associated Press reported, "Around 45 Navajo families are living on U.S. Bureau of Land Management near Bloomfield without permission." "Navajo Families Squatting on BLM Land," *Albuquerque Journal*, February 9, 2012, https://www.abqjournal.com/86555/45-navajo-families-on-blm-land-without-ok.html.

60. "Navajo Nation Council Resolution CO-47–12."

61. For example, in November 2018 the Navajo Nation and the New Mexico State Land Office celebrated a land exchange that was three decades in the making. The Navajo Nation gained some scattered 4,500 acres in the checkerboard area, while the state would receive from the Nation two large ranch parcels south of the reservation of approximately the same size and equally valued at $15 million. In the patents and deeds outlining the details of the exchange, both parties unequivocally reserved for themselves the mineral rights underlying the surface acreage they traded. The State Land Office's press release announcing the exchange said the deal would "remedy the inadvertent placement on Navajo dwellings and two Navajo cemeteries on State Trust Lands" and, by virtue of consolidating some check-

erboard lands, make management easier for both parties. "The Navajo people who have placed structures on state trust lands will be able to finally obtain much needed rights-of-ways for basic life-sustaining services, such as water, electricity & gas," the press release said. State Land Commissioner, "State Land Office," 2018.

62. See Cormack, *A Power to Do Justice* and Richland, "Jurisdiction."

63. See Vimalassery, Pegues, and Goldstein, "On Colonial Unknowing"; Vimalassery, Pegues, and Goldstein, "Colonial Unknowing."

Bibliography

All Pueblo Council of Governors. "Tribal Leaders Host Historic Summit to Support the Protection of the Greater Chaco Landscape," March 22, 2019. https://www.apcg.org/uncategorized/historic-joint-convening-between-the-all-pueblo-council-of-governors-and-navajo-nation-2019/.

"An Action Relation to the Resources and Development and Naabik'iyati' Committees." Navajo Nation Council Resolution CO-47-12, 2012.

Baca, Angelo. *Shash Jaa': Bears Ears*. New York University: Culture & Media Program, 2016.

Bhandar, Brenna. *The Colonial Lives of Property: Law, Land, and Racial Regimes of Ownership*. Durham NC: Duke University Press, 2018.

Billé, Franck, ed. *Voluminous States: Sovereignty, Materiality, and the Territorial Imagination*. Durham NC: Duke University Press, 2020.

Blomley, Nicholas. "Law, Property, and the Geography of Violence: The Frontier, the Survey, and the Grid." *Annals of the Association of American Geographers* 93, no. 1 (2003): 121–41.

Braun, Bruce. "Producing Vertical Territory." *Ecumen* no. 1 (2000): 7–46.

Brugge, David. *A History of the Chaco Navajos*. Reports of the Chaco Center, no. 4. Albuquerque NM: Division of Chaco Research, National Park Service, Department of the Interior, 1980.

Bureau of Land Management. "Farmington Resource Management Plan." Albuquerque NM: United States Department of the Interior Bureau of Land Management Albuquerque District Office Farmington Resource Area, 1988.

———. "Farmington Resource Management Plan with Record of Decision." Farmington NM: United States Department of the Interior Bureau of Land Management Farmington Field Office, 2003.

———. "Navajo Occupancy on National Resource Lands in Northwest New Mexico." Albuquerque NM: United States Department of the Interior Bureau of Land Management Albuquerque District Office, 1974.

Chamberlain, Kathleen. *Under Sacred Ground: A History of Navajo Oil, 1922–1982*. Albuquerque: University of New Mexico Press, 2000.

Cormack, Bradin. *A Power to Do Justice: Jurisdiction, English Literature, and the Rise of Common Law*. Chicago: University of Chicago Press, 2008.

Curley, Andrew. "T'aa'hwo Aji t'eego and the Moral Economy of Navajo Coal Workers." *Annals of the American Association of Geographers* (2018): 1–16.

Denetdale, Jennifer Nez. *Reclaiming Diné History: The Legacies of Navajo Chief Manuelito and Juanita*. Tucson: University of Arizona Press, 2007.

Dennison, Jean. "Entangled Sovereignties: The Osage Nation's Interconnections with Governmental and Corporate Authorities." *American Ethnologist* 44, no. 4 (2017): 684–96.

Elden, Stuart. "Secure the Volume: Vertical Geopolitics and the Depth of Power." *Political Geography* no. 34 (2013): 35–51.

Emerson, Larry. "Diné Sovereign Action: Rejection Colonial Sovereignty and Invoking Diné Peacemaking." In *Navajo Sovereignty: Understandings and Visions of the Diné People*, edited by Lloyd Lee, 160–78. Tucson: University of Arizona Press, 2017.

Estes, Nick. *Our History Is the Future: Standing Rock Versus the Dakota Access Pipeline, and the Long Tradition of Indigenous Resistance*. New York: Verso, 2019.

Fassett, James. "Oil and Gas Resources of the San Juan Basin: New Mexico and Colorado." In *New Mexico Geological Society Guidebook*, edited by James Fassett, Kate Zeilger, and Virgil Lueth, 181–96. New Mexico: 61st Field Conference, 2010.

Ford, Lisa. *Settler Sovereignty: Jurisdiction and Indigenous People in America and Australia, 1788–1836*. Cambridge: Harvard University Press, 2010.

Goeman, Mishuana. *Mark My Words: Native Women Mapping Our Nations*. Minneapolis: University of Minnesota Press, 2013.

Goldstein, Alyosha. "By Force of Expectation: Colonization, Public Lands, and the Property Relation." UCLA *Law Review Discourse* 65, no. 124 (2018): 124–40.

———. "Finance and Foreclosure in the Colonial Present." *Radical History Review* no. 118 (2014): 42–63.

Guzman, Kathleen. "Give or Take an Acre: Property Norms and the Indian Land Consolidation Act." *Iowa Law Review* 85 (2000): 595–662.

Hagerman, Herbert. "Navajo Indian Reservation." Washington DC: United States Senate, 1932.

Harris, Cheryl. "Whiteness as Property." *Harvard Law Review* 106, no. 8 (1993): 1707–91.

Hu, Cameron. "Imperial Metaphysics." PhD diss., University of Chicago, 2021.

Iverson, Peter, and Monty Roessel. *Diné: A History of the Navajos*. Albuquerque: University of New Mexico Press, 2002.

Kahn, Jeffrey. "Geographies of Discretion and the Jurisdictional Imagination." *PoLAR: Political and Legal Anthropology Review* 40, no. 1 (2017): 5–27.

Kappler, Charles, ed. *Indian Affairs: Laws and Treaties*. Washington DC: GPO, 1904.

Karuka, Manu. *Empire's Tracks: Indigenous Nations, Chinese Workers, and the Transcontinental Railroad*. Oakland: University of California Press, 2019.

Keeler, Jacqueline, ed. *Edge of Morning: Native Voices Speak for the Bears Ears*. Minneapolis: Birchbark, 2017.

Kelly, Lawrence. *The Navajo Indians and Federal Indian Policy 1900–1935*. Tucson: University of Arizona Press, 1970.

Lee, Lloyd. "Land: Nihi Keyah." In *Edge of Morning: Native Voices Speak for the Bears Ears*, edited by Jacqueline Keeler, 57–62. Salt Lake City UT: Torrey House, 2017.

LTE Environmental, INC. "Report of Final Sampling & Closure Request: NEU 315, Release Response API 30-043-21888, NMOCD Incident NCS1905249442, Sandoval County, New Mexico." 077919003. Prepared for Enduring Resources, 2019.

MacPherson, C. B. "The Meaning of Property." In *Property: Mainstream and Critical Positions*, edited by C. B. MacPherson, 1–14. Toronto: University of Toronto Press, 1978.

Masco, Joseph. *The Nuclear Borderlands: The Manhattan Project in Post-Cold War New Mexico*. Princeton NJ: Princeton University Press, 2006.

Montoya, Teresa. "Yellow Water: Rupture and Return One Year after the Gold King Mine Spill." *Anthropology Now* 9 (2016): 91–115.

Moreton-Robinson, Aileen. *The White Possessive: Property, Power, and Indigenous Sovereignty.* Durham NC: Duke University Press, 2015.

Mosk, Stanford. *Land Tenure Problems in the Santa Fe Railroad Grant Area.* Berkeley: University of California Press, 1944.

Murphy, Michelle. "Some Keywords toward Decolonial Methods: Studying Settler Colonial Histories and Environmental Violence from Tkaronto." *History and Theory* 59, no. 3 (2020): 376–84.

Navajo Nation. "OPVP Protect Chaco Canyon Region through Collaboration with All Pueblo Council of Governors." Office of the President and Vice President: February 24, 2017.

Palmer, Meredith. "Rendering Settler Sovereign Landscapes: Race and Property in the Empire State." *Environment and Planning D: Society and Space* 38, no. 5 (2020): 793–810. https://doi.org/10.1177/0263775820922233.

Pasternak, Judy. *Yellow Dirt: A Poisoned Land and the Betrayal of the Navajos.* New York: Free Press, 2010.

Pasternak, Shiri. *Grounded Authority: The Algonquins of Barrier Lake against the State.* Minneapolis: University of Minnesota Press, 2017.

Powell, Dana. *Landscapes of Power: Politics of Energy in the Navajo Nation.* Durham NC: Duke University Press, 2018.

Redhouse, John. *The Leasing of Dinétah: An Eastern Navajo Odyssey.* Roots of Navajo Relocation Series. Albuquerque NM: Redhouse/Wright Productions, 1984.

Richard Young Papers. University of New Mexico Center for Southwest Research, Albuquerque.

Richland, Justin. "Jurisdiction: Grounding Law in Language." *Annual Review of Anthropology* 42 (2013): 209–26.

Rodgers, Larry. *Chapter Images: Profiles of 110 Navajo Nation Chapters.* Window Rock AZ: Navajo Nation, 2004.

Rowe, Aimee Carrillo, and Eve Tuck. "Settler Colonialism and Cultural Studies: Ongoing Settlement, Cultural Production, and Resistance." *Cultural Studies, Critical Methodologies* 17, no. 1 (2017): 3–13.

Royster, Judith. "The Legacy of Allotment." *Arizona State Law Journal* 27 (1995): 2–78.

Ruppel, Kristin. *Unearthing Indian Land Living with the Legacies of Allotment.* Tucson: University of Arizona Press, 2008.

Shoemaker, Jessica. "Complexity's Shadow: American Indian Property, Sovereignty, and the Future." *Michigan Law Review* 115, no. 487 (2017): 487–552.

Simpson, Audra. *Mohawk Interruptus: Political Life across the Borders of Settler States.* Durham NC: Duke University Press, 2014.

Sloterdijk, Peter. *Terror from the Air.* Translated by Amy Patton and Steve Corcoran. Los Angeles CA: Semiotext(e), 2002.

Smith, Thomas. "A Report from the Commissioner of Indian Affairs Relation to a Treaty with the Navajo Indians." 54th Congress, 2nd sess., no. 310. February 23, 1897.

Stacher Family Papers. Center for Southwest Research and Special Collections, University of New Mexico, Albuquerque.

"Treaty of Guadalupe-Hidalgo." National Archives. February 2, 1848. https://www.archives.gov/historical-docs/todays-doc/index.html?dod-date=202.

Tsosie, Rebecca. "Land, Culture, and Community: Reflections on Native Sovereignty and Property in America." *Indiana Law Review* 34 (2001): 1291–312.

Tuck, Eve, and K. Wayne Yang. "Decolonization Is Not a Metaphor." *Decolonization: Indigeneity, Education & Society* 1, no. 1 (2012): 1–40.

U.S. Department of the Interior. "2016 Status Report: Land Buy-Back Program for Tribal Nations." 2016.

U.S. Senate Committee on Indian Affairs and Committee on Resources. *Indian Land Consolidation Act Amendments; and to Permit the Leasing of Oil and Gas Rights on Navajo Allotted Lands*. S. 1586 and S. 1315. 106th Congress. 1st sess.

Vimalassery, Manu, Juliana Pegues, and Alyosha Goldstein. "Colonial Unknowing and Relations of Study." *Theory & Event* 20, no. 4 (2017): 1042–54.

———. "On Colonial Unknowing." *Theory & Event* 4, no. 19 (2016): https://muse.jhu.edu/article/633283.

Voyles, Traci. *Wastelanding: Legacies of Uranium Mining in Navajo Country*. Minneapolis: University of Minnesota Press, 2015.

Watts, Vanessa. "Indigenous Place-Thought and Agency amongst Humans and Non-Humans (First Woman and Sky Woman Go on a European World Tour!)." *Decolonization: Indigeneity, Education & Society* 2, no. 1 (2013): 20–34.

Weisiger, Marsha. *Dreaming of Sheep in Navajo Country*. Seattle: University of Washington Press, 2009.

Weizman, Eyal. "Introduction to the Politics of Verticality." *Open Democracy*, 2002. https://www.opendemocracy.net/en/article_801jsp/.

Wylie, Sara. *Fractivism: Corporate Bodies and Chemical Bonds*. Durham NC: Duke University Press, 2018.

Yazzie, Melanie. "Decolonizing Development in Diné Bikéyah: Resource Extraction, Anti-Capitalism, and Relational Futures." *Environment and Society: Advances in Research* 9 (2018): 25–39.

Zurita, Maria de Lourdes Melo, Paul Munro, and Donna Houston. "Un-Earthing the Subterranean Anthropocene." AREA 50 (2018): 298–305.

PART 3

Urban and Rural Transformations

5

Westworld

Life on the High-Tech Frontier

STUART W. LESLIE AND LAYNE R. KARAFANTIS

The recent HBO remake of Michael Crichton's fictional *Westworld* brilliantly reimagines the original film in light of advances in haptic androids, virtual reality, artificial intelligence, and real-time surveillance that scarcely seem science fiction nowadays. *Westworld* came to life in the Los Angeles production studios of HBO, the anchor of Ivy Station, a $300-million complex of offices, upscale apartments, and retail space in Culver City. Boosters pitch this sprawling, live-where-you-work community to a workforce where no one seems over thirty and every day is casual Friday. Dubbed Silicon Beach by its real estate developers, an increasing number of high-tech companies have clustered on the west side of Los Angeles County, roughly from the city of Santa Monica south to Los Angeles International Airport (LAX). The neighborhood of Playa Vista alone hosts the Los Angeles branches of Google, YouTube, Facebook, and other tech giants on a campus (and in some of the same buildings) that once housed Hughes Aircraft. At the height of the Cold War twenty thousand Hughes defense workers designed and built radar systems, guided missiles, and other highly classified technologies in these spaces. Their successors now design proprietary software for streaming video, social media, and targeted internet marketing. Perhaps no single place so perfectly embodies the fundamental shift in the economic geography of the New West, a late twentieth-century industrial regime driven by Cold War defense spending, now eclipsed by early twenty-first-century, high-tech consumer companies competing in the global digital market.

Along the new far western frontier—in places such as Seattle, Silicon Valley, Los Angeles, and San Diego—the creative class has been busy inventing a future that delivers many of the promises and perils of its fictional *Westworld* counterpart: the ultimate gated community and a "place of unlimited possibilities" open only to the tech savvy and the extremely wealthy, with its own rules and corporate overlords who can appear as soulless as their robots. A new generation of high-tech workers drawn to Amazon, Google, SpaceX, and Biotech Beach have brought with them a self-consciously hipster workstyle/lifestyle that has remade the West Coast's high-tech hubs in their own image. They are younger, ethnically diverse, politically liberal, and more mobile than the "suburban warriors" of the Cold War.[1] These now-iconic companies have (re)energized regional economies and amassed enormous wealth for the favored few. The enclaves of privilege in which employees work and live have reinforced regional patterns of socially stratified and racially segregated communities, increased the economic exploitation of a contractor underclass, heightened gender disparities, and furthered the divide between the haves and have-nots, who struggle to find or keep their places in this distinctly twenty-first-century economic landscape.[2]

After the end of the Cold War, as economic historian Gavin Wright explains, the "knowledge-economy clusters" in these four cities belonged more to the western Pacific Rim than to the American West as conventionally demarcated, and more to the emerging twenty-first century than to the post–World War II era that spawned them.[3] Their signature companies—Amazon (1994), Apple (1976, relaunched in 1997 with the return of Steve Jobs as CEO), Google (1998), Facebook (2004), SpaceX (2002), and the Sanford Consortium for Regenerative Medicine (2006)—face more west than east, with supply chains, manufacturing facilities, and research and development centers extending into South, Southeast, and East Asia, despite some well-publicized disputes with the Chinese government. Indian, Chinese, and Taiwanese computer programmers and software designers, many U.S.-educated, have been a major presence in Silicon Valley (and increasingly in Seattle and Los Angeles as well) since the turn of the century, part of a global "brain circulation" as important for the West Coast's future as the ocean currents of the Pacific itself.[4] East Asian tech giants meanwhile have established beachheads in U.S. technology hubs. China's Alibaba has engineering centers in Silicon Valley and Seattle. Takeda, Japan's largest pharmaceutical company, opened a Global Research Center in San Diego in 2019 to leverage its fifteen-year investment there.

The New Western History appeared at the very end of the Cold War, a moment, at least in retrospect, as salient as Turner's frontier thesis had been a century before. What did regional history mean in the "flat" (if lumpy) world of post-Cold War globalization, where the defining themes of the New Western History—continuity, convergence, conquest, and complexity—still matter but have a very different resonance on a global scale? Politically and economically it is as if the Pacific coast fell to one side of the fault lines running from Washington State to the Mexican border, and the rest of the American West fell to the other, one embracing neo-liberalism, the other a neo-nationalism. On either side of that rift, and within the urban dynamos of the knowledge cities themselves, the challenge now and for the future, as Richard White suggests, is "rising inequality" that globalization has only exacerbated.[5]

"Work Hard. Have Fun. Make History."

Before Microsoft and Amazon, Boeing defined high-tech Seattle. From modest beginnings in 1916 as a regional maker of seaplanes and transport aircraft, Boeing weathered the booms and busts of wartime and depression to become an industry leader in both commercial and military aviation.[6] During World War II Boeing opened Plant 2, a huge new facility south of downtown for building B-17 and B-24 bombers, then built another in nearby Renton and hired forty thousand additional workers for its Seattle facilities.[7] Lacking skilled, unionized workers to meet burgeoning demand, Boeing engineers redesigned planes so they could be built with assembly-line methods by semi-skilled workers—more than half of whom were women by the war's end. Seattle's defense industries, including its shipyards, attracted thousands of African Americans from the South, as did other western companies, though only token numbers of African Americans found work at Boeing during the war (just 285 women and 44 men).[8] Cold War contracts for missiles, air defense, and long-range nuclear bombers turned Boeing into Seattle's largest employer by far with one hundred thousand workers, accounting for half of the region's manufacturing jobs.

Boeing's white-collar workers—young, male, and married with children—sought a suburban lifestyle in bedroom communities like Lake Hills, which was racially and ethnically homogeneous, politically conservative, and harbored little tolerance for anyone other than organization men. Lake Hills—adjoining Bellevue and within easy commute of Boeing's plants to the south, north, and west—opened in 1955 as the largest community of its kind in the Northwest, with four thousand houses and seventeen thousand residents, "a self-contained city in a country atmosphere."[9] An estimated three-quarters of Lake Hills residents worked at Boeing as engineers, scientists, and middle managers, and often called their new town Boeing Plant 3.[10] Proud of their employer and its contributions to national defense, Lake Hills homeowners consistently voted Republican, supported building a fallout shelter under the elementary school playground, and flocked to displays of Boeing missiles at the local shopping mall.

Boeing's longstanding reputation as a corporate "family" never recovered from its merger with McDonnell-Douglas in 1996 and the relocation of its corporate headquarters to Chicago in 2001. Boeing's new president, the former CEO at McDonnell-Douglas, sent a shockwave through the company when he told employees to "quit behaving like a family and become more like a team."[11] At best Boeing remained a staunchly traditional family where women made up 80 percent of the clerical staff, 10 percent of managers, and just 5 percent of the engineers.[12] With seventy-eight thousand workers in Seattle—more than Microsoft and Amazon combined—Boeing remains the region's largest single employer but has lost the high-tech luster it once enjoyed.

Amazon never had the Seattle connections of Boeing or Microsoft, yet it profited as its location allowed the company to reduce the sales tax it would have to collect from its out-of-state customers.

Jeff Bezos, a former Wall Street fund manager, launched the company in a Bellevue garage in 1994, then moved it to rented space south of downtown Seattle in an effort to create an urban vibe. Bezos insisted that Amazon was a high-tech startup, not an online retailer. In his earliest job posting he sought software designers and computer engineers with "experience designing and building large and complex (yet maintainable) systems, and you should be able to do so in about one-third the time that most competent people think possible."[13] Amazon Web Services (AWS), the cloud computing subsidiary hidden behind an acronym and a trademarked smile, demonstrated that Amazon could beat Microsoft, Google, and IBM at their own game; Amazon now has a larger share of the cloud platform market than all of the others combined.

Instead of building a traditional corporate campus—as every other tech giant had done, including Microsoft in suburban Redmond—Bezos decided "that by staying in the urban core, Amazon would attract members of the hip creative class," leading to the redevelopment and transformation of entire neighborhoods.[14] In 2007 Amazon began acquiring property in South Lake Union, a declining working-class community north of downtown. In place of a single headquarters, it leased space in a dozen different buildings within a few blocks of each other, often giving them quirky, insider names (such as Wainwright, in honor of the first person to order an Amazon book), and it soon had opened enough office space for six thousand employees. In the decade since, the company has leased or built another twenty-nine buildings, expanding the "campus" south into the Denny Regrade neighborhood, anchored by its Day 1 and Doppler (the corporate code name for its Alexa smart speaker) office towers.[15] The recently opened Spheres enclose a carefully curated urban jungle, a literal think tank where eight hundred employees at a time can trade their cubicles for a unique workspace designed to replenish their creative juices.

South Lake Union accounts for forty-five thousand Amazonians spread across eight million square feet of prime urban real estate, and its continued growth has become the new model of a company town. Amazon already owns or occupies a fifth of the entire city's

FIG. 9. The Amazon Spheres with Amazon headquarters building rising behind it. Unlike other high-tech giants, Amazon deliberately chose an urban campus that has now turned Seattle into a twenty-first-century version of the company town. Wikipedia, https://commons.wikimedia.org/wiki/File:Amazon_Spheres_from_6th_Avenue,_April_2020.jpg.

office space—by far the biggest corporate footprint of any company in any American city. In place of old warehouses and acres of parking, some $4 billion in new real estate investments now stand. Modest apartment complexes have given way to upscale condominiums, and much of South Lake Union is unrecognizable to long-term residents, who consider it an "artificial neighborhood."

Where an earlier generation of Boeing engineers looked to build equity in their suburban homes, young Amazon engineers hope to build equity in their company. Stock-based compensation, the rule for newly hired senior engineers, is generous—about twice what Microsoft offers comparable employees—but these startup packages are heavily weighted toward years three and four, so that employees who leave early lose most of the benefits.[16] And yet Amazon still has one of the highest turnover rates even among other high-tech companies, as much a matter of ruthless weeding out as having new hires leave for greener pastures.[17] Few of Amazon's new employees buy houses or condos because not many of them expect to stay that long, in contrast to the lifetime residencies of Boeing engineers before them. The vast majority of South Lake Union's eighteen thousand residents rent rather than own (83 versus 17 percent). The community as a whole earns an A+ rating, with high marks for just about everything its young employees care about: diversity, nightlife, commute time, health and fitness, and public schools. For cost of living, on the other hand, South Lake Union earns a C and for housing just a C+, as rents have risen 63 percent since 2010, and even two-bedroom condos now run $800,000 and up.[18]

Like Silicon Valley, Seattle now has a tech culture so entrenched that Amazon filmed a "Life in Seattle" recruiting video to counter the stereotypes of geek culture, high housing prices, rainy weather, and stressful jobs. A "United Colors of Benetton" cast of millennials offers an upbeat commentary favorably comparing Seattle to Southern California and New York. Understandably it instantly spawned some spot-on YouTube parodies with new voice-overs asserting, "I really like the neighborhoods of Seattle and how we've been able to keep the poor people segregated from the rest of us," or, "You have your web designers, your database administrators, your application developers; there are so many different kinds of people types here."[19] Indeed Amazon is far less diverse than its public face suggests. Its professional workforce and upper-level management are still heavily male and white (just two women among Bezos's thirty-seven direct reports), with African Americans and Hispanics noticeably missing in action. Despite its stated commitment to gender equity, Amazon has a poor track record of hiring, promoting, and paying women, even compared with Facebook.[20] To the company's public embarrassment, its own recruiting algorithm, designed to increase diversity, turned out to be riddled with sexist assumptions. In trying to "train" their software by feeding it résumés from proven computer engineers, its designers unintentionally built a strong gender bias into the system.[21]

Amazon may not yet employ as many workers in the region as Boeing, but it is gaining fast, and its current market value, about $1 trillion, is four times that of the aerospace giant. Seattle and Amazon have placed an enormous wager on one another, with the deck stacked in Amazon's favor. Amazon continues to push for corporate welfare in its hometown. The company received $54 million in tax breaks for its campus alone, plus successively lobbied for massive infrastructure improvements. The company then threatened to halt future expansion if the city passed a proposed corporate "head tax" to pay for affordable housing and other city priorities. Seattle has every reason to be wary. Washington State offered Boeing an $8.7-billion tax subsidy in 2013, only to see Boeing cut twenty thousand jobs in the Puget Sound region over the next five years.[22] For Boeing and its young engineers moving into Lake Hills in 1955, even the sky did not seem to be the limit. Yet as every high-tech company and community has learned the hard way, booms never last forever, and when they falter, corporations can downsize or relocate or outsource in ways that cities cannot.

"Don't Be Evil" Becomes "Do the Right Thing"

Silicon Valley has become a brand name as recognizable as any of its most famous companies—Apple, Google, and Facebook—and serves as shorthand for high-tech industry and a new knowledge economy that other places can only hope to replicate or emulate. Its corporate leaders—Steve Jobs, Larry Page and Sergey Brin, Mark Zuckerberg—have become the secular saints of the cyberworld and their gleaming headquarters—Apple Park by Norman Foster, Googleplex by Bjarke Ingels, Facebook by Frank Gehry—its cathedrals. Silicon Valley mythology presents the region as a booming industrial utopia where talented people work themselves to the bone in exchange for outsized salaries and stock options. In reality the region suffers from myriad detriments including environmental pollution, traffic congestion, inadequate housing, and extreme forms of inequality.[23] Despite the slogans of its many tech companies that preach disruption and talk of saving the world, it is "increasingly impossible to believe that tech firms are working disinterestedly in service of some larger social good." High tech in Silicon Valley and the larger Bay Area unabashedly embraces neo-liberal capitalism.[24]

Silicon Valley has a short memory. The current generation has forgotten how the Valley of Heart's Delight became Silicon Valley in the 1960s and 1970s and grew to become the epicenter of an international high-tech behemoth.[25] During its origins as the Stanford Industrial Park in the 1950s, Cold War spending played a decisive role in the region's rapid growth. Its largest companies—Lockheed Missiles and Space, Ford Aerospace, Intel, and Varian Associates—depended as heavily on defense contracts as on Stanford University.[26] Only in the 1990s with the rise of the internet did Silicon Valley begin attracting massive amounts of private venture capital. Its boundaries moved south to San Jose, the self-proclaimed "capital of Silicon Valley," and north to San Francisco along the 101 and the aptly named El Camino Real, a royal road to wealth.[27]

As tech wealth poured into the Bay Area, economic benefits did not spread equally. The region's middle class has stagnated as income inequality has skyrocketed.[28] Low-income and homeless residents go through city trash in the hopes of finding discarded valuables—including items from the bins outside of Mark Zuckerberg's opulent residence in San Francisco.[29] Homeownership in Silicon Valley is far out of the reach of many residents. Modest houses often cost more than $1 million, and the rent on small apartments is easily between $2,500 and $3,500 per month.[30] The influx of tech workers into less affluent districts has systematically removed people of color from long-standing communities, pushing them far into the peripheries of a much larger Bay Area, which some claim now includes places like Sacramento and Gilroy, cities inland and three hours to the north and south, respectively. Indeed "as space-age architecture edges closer to streets where homeless people sleep in their cars, the concept of two Americas is becoming painfully visible."[31]

Contracting has changed the nature of tech employment in the Bay Area. Silicon Valley in the twenty-first century has an established pool of skilled workers—from coders to seed investors to attorneys—which makes it an easy place to recruit talent. The cost of office space and the need to offer competitive salaries, however, initiated a relatively recent movement toward remote hiring and contracting.[32] Hiring contractors—also known as temporary or contingent workers, or even by the euphemistic "flexible talent"—has been increasingly implemented as the solution to keeping costs down, leading to the proliferation of this exploitative form of employment.[33] A new class of workers exists within tech—a "shadow workforce"—and their concerns are far more fragile than their counterparts' concerns, for the latter are operating with obscene salaries and benefits packages.[34] Contingent workers serve meals, drive buses, and clean facilities at tech campuses; they also provide skilled labor such as devising circuit boards, developing and testing software, and managing marketing departments.[35] These workers do not have job security and frequently are not given standard benefits, such as healthcare, paid vacation or sick leave, or retirement investment options. With few exceptions these "temps" are viewed by management and company-employed workers alike as "mercenar[ies] whose allegiance to the company, and thus to the job, is actively suspect."[36] This ignores the reality that contractors would give anything to work as direct employees, and the closest many can get to these firms is via a contracting opportunity.

In 2016 the average yearly pay for tech employees was six figures, while blue-collar workers were not even making $20,000 per year and living far below the poverty line in the Bay Area. Notably Black and Hispanic employees made up almost 60 percent of that workforce. White-collar contractors suffered little better, averaging only half the annual incomes of their counterparts at the same companies.[37] These types of income disparities have deepened the chasm between rich and poor in Silicon Valley, creating a massive class dubbed the Working Poor, while simultaneously catalyzing an increase in homelessness in the region.

Google's unofficial motto since the early 2000s was "Don't Be Evil." This changed to "Do the Right Thing" when the company was acquired by Alphabet Inc. in 2018.[38] Later that year, when Google employees believed that their employer was not adhering to either slogan, they staged a walkout. The protest was catalyzed by the company's response to allegations of sexual harassment, in which Google provided an offender with a $90-million exit package. Many Google contractors, however, did not learn about the protest and did not participate because they did not have access to internal mailing lists; in another instance, contractors were not alerted to the presence of an active shooter on a tech campus. In response temporary workers, vendors, and contractors (known collectively as TVCS) penned an open letter to Google CEO Sundar Pichai. They accused the company of creating a segregated workforce in which TVCS are paid less and receive fewer benefits than others performing the same tasks, and they demanded a more equitable workplace. Google now requires that some of its contracting firms provide basic benefits to its workers, such as paid time off and healthcare.[39] Facing similar demands Apple dismissively addressed its use of temporary workers as "both a predictable evolution and the future."[40] To Apple, at least, chronic job insecurity is but a sign of the times.

Newly hired contractors at Apple do not find themselves working at the inspiring and amenity-filled Cupertino campus but instead at a bland building six miles away on Hammerwood Avenue (see fig. 10). Officially employees of Apex Systems, contracting for Apple, they live under constant threat of termination. A former contractor admitted, "It was made pretty plain to us that we were at-will employees and they would fire us at any time."[41] Day-to-day work reinforces a status of inferiority, as badges are marked so that employees can be quickly identified as contractors, further evidence of a dehumanizing caste system. Contractors hoping that they might at least put the Apple name on their résumés soon discovered they were limited to listing that they had worked for a "Major Tech Company Via Apex Systems."

In 2018 contract workers outnumbered direct employees for the first time in Google's twenty-year history. As the number of contract workers has increased, the average tenure of full-time employees has declined, and wages have decreased over the last twenty years for older employees of all types, despite rising costs of living.[42] In Silicon Valley "gone are the days when steady employment at one company was seen as a good thing" (at least, to human resource departments). Some hiring managers even view longer tenures with a company as a red flag indicating that a prospective worker cannot find a job anywhere else. "Permanent employment—there's no such thing anymore. The line will get blurrier and blurrier," said tech-hiring firm

FIG. 10. Google walkout at its Mountain View, California, headquarters on November 1, 2018. Google workers across the globe joined the protest against sexual harassment and gender inequities in the workplace. A year later protesters took to the streets to call out Google for "displacement and poverty, surveillance and repression, and misogyny and inequality.... Google is Evil." Reuters/Alamy.

Beeline's Hoffmeyer.[43] Contingent workers are left wondering why prosperity has been so inequitably distributed.[44]

Workers are not the only ones frustrated by the financial costs that have made life in the Bay Area tenuous. Startups are facing issues with recruiting talent due to salary expectations driven by the Bay Area's soaring cost of living as well as by competition from larger companies like Google and Facebook, who can afford to pay living wages. "As we've been looking to hire, we're running into the same issue that everyone else is running into—in that the Bay Area is broken," said Michael Dougherty, co-founder and CEO of a San Mateo-based advertising tech startup.[45] Glenna Matthews, author of *Silicon Valley, Women, and the California Dream*, asked, "Of course, no region could generate the kind of wealth produced by Silicon Valley without some portion of its inhabitants benefiting from it. But who, how much, and at what cost?"[46]

Revolts against tech from the disenfranchised underscore the state of the Valley. Protesters smashed the windows of a Google commuter bus in Oakland in 2013; the National Security Agency has used "backdoors" at the data centers of tech giants, posing a threat to privacy and instigating outcry; and surge pricing done by ride-share services such as Uber—compounded by its gig economy practices—has received enormous derision.[47] Sen. Elizabeth Warren (D-MA) recently called attention to the authoritarianism of large technology companies in American society: "Today's big tech companies have too much power—too much power over our economy, our society, and our democracy.... They've bulldozed competition, used our private information for profit, and tilted the playing field against everyone else. And in the process, they have hurt small businesses and stifled innovation."[48] Predatory tech companies in Silicon Valley are hypocritically destroying the type of garage-built entrepreneurial spirit that built the region in the first place and might be initiating its demise.

"Los Angeles, America's Future Spaceport"

SpaceX, the private space vehicle manufacturer founded by billionaire-entrepreneur Elon Musk in 2002, set up shop on a site left vacant by Northrop Corporation in the community of Hawthorne, where legendary engineer Jack Northrop designed and built the first flying wings and where his successors manufactured military fighters and missiles throughout the Cold War. Musk, who earned his early fortune as the co-founder of PayPal, founded SpaceX with the ultimate ambition of producing hardware that might send humans to Mars.[49] SpaceX facilities in Hawthorne, located in South Los Angeles, have been described as "very Silicon Valley only way cooler" due to an open-office working environment with democratic access to the company's "Mission Control" housed within a sprawling industrial plant.[50] SpaceX represents one-fourth of the valuation of the region's high-tech agglomeration known as Silicon Beach and serves as a notable outlier in a cluster largely dominated by streaming services and social media.[51] This single venture has successfully repurposed preexisting infrastructure and revived aerospace manufacturing in Southern California.

FIG. 11. SpaceX headquarters in Hawthorne, California. SpaceX repurposed Northrop Corporation's former headquarters for a new corporate space race. Mixed-use real estate developments in Hawthorne offer every amenity SpaceX's millennial employees could want. Where will long-time Hawthorne residents, a majority of them African American and Hispanic and below the poverty line, live and work as their community is increasingly gentrified? trekandshoot/Alamy.

During the Cold War Los Angeles exemplified the military-industrial complex. The aerospace industry and associated research institutions and federally funded think tanks swarmed the region, spurred by the prevalence of aviation companies dating back to the early twentieth century. During World War II two million Angelenos worked in the aviation industry, and the region housed almost 70 percent of the nation's aerospace workers.[52] Veterans flocked to local universities, and many pursued degrees in the burgeoning field of aerospace engineering. By the 1980s fifteen of the nation's largest aerospace firms were headquartered in Southern California, including Lockheed, Northrop, TRW Automotive, Hughes Aircraft, and North American Aviation. When the aerospace industry precipitously declined in the 1990s, many firms folded, merged, or otherwise relocated from the region. Yet the military-based manufacturing past of the city provided the foundation for future ventures as well as contributed to an economic upturn in the twenty-first century.

In the last twenty years jobs related to space vehicles and missiles have climbed by more than 60 percent, with a quarter of those jobs located in Southern California.[53]

The Hawthorne Municipal Airport was in sorry shape in 2005, with leaking roofs and missing doors. Kearny Real Estate purchased this site—the future headquarters for SpaceX—and modernized some buildings while demolishing others, resulting in a twenty-one-building industrial park. Kearny sold its first building to SpaceX in 2007. Soon after, the company leased the majority of commercial space (to pursue commercial space) in this development and now occupies ten buildings in Hawthorne after significantly expanding between 2014 and 2016 due in part to a $2.6-billion contract with the National Aeronautics and Space Administration to build an astronaut transport capsule.[54] SpaceX's headquarters in Hawthorne put it right in the middle of aerospace alley, a place ripe for recruiting aeronautical engineers. "More important than anything is quality of people," according to Greg Autry, director of the Southern California Commercial Spaceflight Initiative at the University of Southern California Marshall School of Business.[55] While SpaceX has a stronghold in Los Angeles, it is not the largest regional employer in aerospace by quite a margin. That distinction goes to Northrop Grumman, which relocated its headquarters to Virginia in 2011 (ostensibly to be closer to its government customers) but still employs approximately 16,600 workers in Los Angeles County. The long-standing presence of aerospace in Los Angeles by firms such as Northrop Grumman has made the locale attractive to newer aerospace companies.

According to Los Angeles mayor Eric Garcetti, "Businesses like SpaceX can't afford to not be in Los Angeles.... The pipeline for the workforce... [and] access to an incredible supply chain and geography really almost demand that Los Angeles would be the top of anyone's list."[56] And SpaceX is contributing opportunities for both white- and blue-collar work, including jobs in supply chain management and vehicle engineering.[57] SpaceX has also played a role in motivating other businesses to locate their headquarters in Hawthorne, which had previously been considered an affordable yet undesirable place due to noise and air pollution from neighboring LAX and nearby freeways. New businesses in Hawthorne include an organic coffee and tea chain, a brewery, and a high-end motorcycle manufacturer. Amazon jumped in the fray and announced plans to relocate its Ring doorbell security enterprise from Santa Monica to Hawthorne in 2018. The presence of additional tech businesses signals to some that the area is transforming its reputation as a "nose-down industrial city to something, well, cool."[58] The addition of mixed-use projects, such as Steinberg Hart's plan for a 2.53-acre development neighboring SpaceX and the Hawthorne Municipal Airport along Crenshaw Boulevard, showcases how the city is changing to accommodate high-tech businesses and their workers.[59]

Companies setting up shop in old warehouses that formerly served the aerospace industry have been drawn to Hawthorne by the cachet of SpaceX and Musk's Tesla Design Center, also located in town. Adjacent ancillary industries, including aerospace vendors and subcontractors, are providing an increasing market for retail businesses that serve the needs of workers, such as restaurants and bars. The neighboring $2.6-billion Inglewood stadium being built for the Rams and the Chargers National Football League teams is another factor leading to the development of this area of the county, which includes plans to build hotels to accommodate visitors. Unfortunately longtime residents feel threatened by these developments. "Inglewood is the 'City of Champions,' and like all good champions, Inglewood is rising again," said Daniel Tabor, former Los Angeles mayor and councilman. "But it has been a missed opportunity for economic participation by the residents and local businesses."[60] Ballooning rents and evictions without cause have displaced entire families from this long-standing African American enclave.

Musk's latest Hawthorne-based venture, The Boring Company, underscores changes happening in the community that residents feel they are powerless to control. The entrepreneur wants to "revolutionize boring technology" to alleviate traffic congestion and noise pollution in Los Angeles. His effort began when he purchased a dilapidated home in Hawthorne (also known as the Boring House) near his SpaceX campus; he then began digging a fourteen-feet-wide, mile-long tunnel in which he hoped to eventually whisk cars and "pods" from one area of Los Angeles to another. Musk was able to initiate this project quickly as Hawthorne is still home to many low-income residents—many of whom are people of color—who do not have the time or money to attend community meetings and file lawsuits essential in practicing Not-in-My-Backyard-ism. "They have so much money, so much capital, to make things happen, that your vote wouldn't mean anything," according to Fred Lopez, who lives down the street from the Boring House. During the planning-commission hearing in which the company's plans were discussed, resident Sammy Andrade said that he was worried about whether the digging would make his home sink into the ground eventually. "But I'm a nobody," said Andrade, "And I know there's a lot of political money involved with this big project for the city." Gaining exemptions from the California Environmental Quality Act (CEQA), which requires an Environmental Impact Report, enabled Musk's boring project to begin with an otherwise unthinkable quickness. Less than a month after the initial contract was submitted, the city council approved construction of the tunnel in August 2017. When Musk attempted to create another tunnel under the west side of Los Angeles, in contrast, wealthy homeowners hastily filed a lawsuit to prevent its construction. According to Juan Matute, the deputy director of the University of California, Los Angeles Institute of Transportation Studies, "The Hawthorne tunnel did happen pretty quickly, and it doesn't seem like anybody regionally was paying attention when that approval happened. This is typical with CEQA—a community that's more disadvantaged and not as politically engaged doesn't have the capacity to file lawsuits." Indeed Hawthorne residents living below or near the poverty line, often working two jobs, simply did not have the time to share their concerns about the impact of the tunnel on their community.[61]

Due to the increased prevalence of SpaceX and its suppliers, the rent for warehouses in Hawthorne has tripled. The Hawthorne Arts Complex, for example, received such high demand for its artist studios that almost half of them were leased before they were even built. Since the arrival of SpaceX in 2007 home prices have steadily increased, and the demand for rental units sparked controversy when a SpaceX representative euphemistically told the Hawthorne City Council that a 230-unit, low-income apartment complex would not be "correct for this space."[62] Income inequality and the collapse of the middle class have become extremely real and contentious issues in Los Angeles. The criminalization of prevalent informal economies, including those of street vendors, day laborers, and domestic workers, has been a subject of recent discussion strongly tied to nativism and institutionalized racism. Many workers are the same ones who have been excluded from their communities due to rising rents—in large part due to gentrification brought on by an influx of higher-income residents who work in the technology sector. As previously "unattractive" neighborhoods are now being labeled "comeback cities," many long-time residents have been displaced, labeled impediments to progress. The irony is that many of these neighborhoods were viewed as desirable by new tech workers because of their distinctiveness and cultural character, which they destroyed by their arrival.[63] After twenty years of new tech in Los Angeles, we are only beginning to learn how these changes might ultimately alter the region's landscape and quality of life for its inhabitants.

"Let's Make San Diego the Scientific Capital of the World"

San Diego, following a deliberate strategy of luring and nurturing "eds and meds"—research universities, hospitals, and biomedical research institutes—reinvented itself from a premier example of a Cold War "metropolitan-military complex" into Biotech Beach and California's second-most-populous county.[64] San Diego's biotechnology cluster has subsequently spun off hundreds of startups, attracted significant investments from big pharmaceutical companies, and grown into the second largest biotech hub in the country.

Long home port for the Pacific Fleet, San Diego became a major center for military aircraft manufacturing during World War II when Consolidated Aircraft (later Convair) dramatically expanded its facilities there, increasing its workforce from 3,170 in 1939 to 44,423 (40 percent of them women).[65] To keep Convair from moving to Long Beach, San Diego gave the company twenty acres of prime real estate adjoining the airport for a nominal rent and invested heavily in infrastructure—water, sewer, rail line extensions—for its new factories.⁶⁶ San Diego's massive naval base and booming aircraft factories drew far more workers than the city could possibly accommodate. When trailers and boarding houses could no longer handle the sheer numbers, the federal government stepped in, building Linda Vista, a planned community for thirteen thousand people on an isolated mesa north of town. The first and largest defense housing project funded by the Lanham Defense Housing Act, Linda Vista went up in less than a year.⁶⁷ Navy contracts for jet fighters kept Convair's aircraft assembly lines humming through the 1950s and 1960s, pushing its employment back up to 38,710.⁶⁸

The Atlas missile put Convair into the space business and San Diego into the space race. As prime contractor for America's first intercontinental ballistic missile, Convair constructed a $20-million self-contained missile facility, Convair Astronautics, ten miles northeast of its airport plants. It eventually grew to forty-seven thousand employees, the vast majority of them ethnically white, and white rather than blue collar.⁶⁹ Convair's parent company, General Dynamics, invested another $10 million in a campus for its General Atomics division on 320 acres in La Jolla donated by the city. Its scientists and engineers, like their counterparts at Convair Astronautics, chose new suburban developments north of Linda Vista and other older working-class neighborhoods.

Convair did not survive the end of the Cold War and neither did its high-paying jobs. General Dynamics closed or sold off its divisions one by one to other aerospace firms and tore down its aircraft and missile plants in the 1990s. General Atomics, a privately-held company since 1986, remains a major defense contractor specializing in drones, lasers, and nuclear fusion, with fifteen thousand employees. Convair's high-tech legacy also lives on in companies such as Linkabit, which relocated to San Diego in 1985, and in its dozens of spinoffs, many of them heavily dependent on defense contracts in their early years, including telecommunications giant Qualcomm, with 9,400 employees in San Diego and 34,000 worldwide.

As defense contracts wound down San Diego increasingly staked its future on biomedicine and biotechnology. Roger Revelle, director of the Scripps Institution of Oceanography in La Jolla, had long envisioned a San Diego campus of the University of California, a small, research-intensive, graduate institution specializing in science and engineering, a "public Cal Tech," he liked to call it. The consummate cold warrior, Revelle had built postwar Scripps into a world center of physical oceanography with classified Navy contracts. His idea for a new kind of Cold War think tank had strong support from local defense contractors. General Dynamics pledged $1 million for the new university, seeing it as a natural partner for General Atomics. To sweeten the pot San Diego voters approved a proposition donating five hundred acres of land just north of General Atomics for the new campus. Under pressure from the state regents, University of California, San Diego (UCSD) broadened its mission to become a full-service university, though one with notable strengths in the physical and natural sciences. Its graduate division opened in 1960 with a faculty boasting Nobel laureates Harold Urey and Marie Goeppert-Mayer, and the School of Science and Engineering followed three years later.[70] UCSD's medical school, launched in 1966 on the MD/PhD model pioneered by Johns Hopkins, emphasized biomedical research and close ties to the university's basic science departments and institutes such as the Center for Molecular Genetics. In two decades it grew into one of the nation's top public medical schools, accounting for a third of UCSD's total research funding.

With UCSD as an anchor, San Diego attracted biomedical institutes that might not otherwise have considered moving there. In 1960, to lure Jonas Salk from the University of Pittsburgh, San Diego's mayor—himself a polio survivor—offered twenty-seven breathtaking acres on Torrey Pines Mesa in La Jolla, where Salk and his architect Louis Kahn built the Salk Institute, an architectural gem that would attract and nurture a dozen Nobel laureates.[71] Renowned immunologist Frank Dixon, Salk's colleague at the University of Pittsburgh School of Medicine, relocated to San Diego in 1961 with four of his colleagues to reinvigorate Scripps Research Institute. Scripps got thirty-five acres of city land just north of the Salk Institute, overlooking the famous Torrey Pines Golf Course. Under Dixon's leadership Scripps grew into one of the best nonprofit biomedical research organizations anywhere, with a "faculty" of 265 (including three Nobel prizewinners) and a staff of 2,700 specializing in immunology, metabolic disease, and molecular and cellular neuroscience. *Nature* recently ranked it first in the world for the quality and impact of its research.[72] William and Lillian Fishman retired from the Tufts University School of Medicine in 1975 and moved to La Jolla to found the Burnham Institute for Medical Research, a cancer center with 850 scientists and a North Torrey Pines Road address that ranks in the top five nationally in National Institutes of Health (NIH) funding. Kimishige and Teruko Ishizaka, another husband-and-wife team, left the Johns Hopkins School of Medicine to found the La Jolla Institute for Allergy and Immunology in 1988. Nobel laureate Gerald Edelman moved his Neurosciences Institute from Rockefeller University in New York City to La Jolla in 1993, where it later became part of Scripps.[73] By offering researchers at these institutes adjunct or joint appointments, UCSD gave its faculty an enormous boost in prestige and rankings.

Younger and more entrepreneurial than other University of California campuses, UCSD and its medical school attracted faculty interested in consulting with local research institutes and in starting their own companies, and who trained graduate students ready to work in them. Hybritech, founded in 1978 by a faculty member seeking to commercialize research in monoclonal antibodies, became UCSD's first and still most successful biotech spinoff. Begun in rented space at the Burnham Institute, Hybritech spun off a half-dozen other companies before being acquired by Eli Lilly for $480 million in 1986. More than fifty San Diego biotech startups can trace their origins to Hybritech. Similarly in 1999 Warner-Lambert (later part of Pfizer) paid $2.1 billion to acquire Agouron Pharmaceuticals, the first San Diego startup to develop and market its own therapeutic drug, a protease inhibitor. UCSD, Salk, and Scripps among them have spun out 112 biotech companies, and most of them have stayed close to campus in the "Golden Triangle" just east of La Jolla. In a field where 85 percent of PhD graduates go on to academic positions, 95 percent of the PhDs trained in biomedical fields at UCSD and at San Diego State University take jobs in private industry, most with local companies.[74]

FIG. 12. The Sanford Consortium, overlooking the Torrey Pines Golf Course and the Pacific Ocean, is the latest architectural and scientific star in the La Jolla constellation. Unless these young scientists have equity shares in a successful biotech startup, they will face a long commute to affordable housing. Courtesy Jason Knowles for Fentress Architects.

After losing to San Francisco in the competition to host California's Stem Cell Agency—a $3-billion state proposition to fund stem cell research and related therapies—San Diego created its own "collaboratory," drawing together five of La Jolla's leading laboratories plus UCSD in 2006. The university provided the land—7.5 acres of prime oceanfront property just north of the Salk Institute—and state and private donors contributed $140 million in initial funding. The Sanford Consortium for Regenerative Medicine complex, completed in 2011, had added yet another star to the local constellation of biotech research institutes.

By 2010 San Diego's biotech cluster, with fourteen thousand employees and nearly two hundred companies, had already pulled ahead of its major rivals, Boston and Silicon Valley, when adjusted for population. Novartis, Lilly, Johnson and Johnson, and Pfizer have all placed research and development divisions there.[75] With biotech research jobs paying an average salary of $136,000, San Diego has a demographic any city would envy. That prosperity, however, has been heavily concentrated in La Jolla and adjoining suburbs north of the city, enclaves of white (and increasingly Asian) male privilege, with some of the highest housing prices in the country. Female scientists face considerable discrimination, with less lab space and lower salaries than their male counterparts, even though women now earn more PhDs in the biomedical sciences than men.[76] San Diego meanwhile ranks second in the nation for the "intensity of gentrification," most notably in once-Hispanic neighborhoods, and fourth in homeless population among major U.S. cities, not adjusted for population.[77]

Conclusion

Just as "the rise of the gunbelt" during the Cold War shifted the epicenter of U.S. high-tech industry from the older industrial corridors of the Northeast and Midwest to the emerging centers of aerospace and defense electronics on the West Coast, so "the crash of blue-sky California" and its defense industry at the end of the Cold War marked the great divide between the New West of the late twentieth century and its successor.[78] In the 1990s California gained 340,000 workers in computer systems, software, and information technology, while losing 210,000 in aerospace. The state's aerospace industry, with 92,000 workers in 2017 (far below its Cold War employment peak of 250,000), has been dwarfed by the exponential growth of the new information economy and its high-tech sector. A generation of high-paying, blue-collar manufacturing jobs disappeared with the decline of the military-industrial complex, drastically increasing the wage gap between the working class and the creative class, the latter's lifestyle dependent on "willful blindness towards the other—much less positive—features of life on the West Coast: racism, poverty, and environmental degradation."[79]

In some respects the new New West more closely resembles the nineteenth century than the mid-twentieth century. This century's digital robber barons believe just as passionately in American exceptionalism and Manifest Destiny as their Gilded Age predecessors and have the same faith in unfettered, entrepreneurial capitalism, the same reverence for disruptive innovation, the same distrust of government regulation, the same reliance on leveraged financing done largely with other people's money, and the same assurance that what is good for their companies is good for America. "Will the Internet get railroaded?" their lawyers wonder, asserting that "regulation designed for monopoly railroads of yesteryear threatens the essential pace of technological change and innovation that has been critical to Internet investment and innovation and along with it U.S. global broadband leadership."[80] In an ironic twist on Richard White's exposé of the transcontinental railroads, these new captains of industry worry that the public—through the Federal Communications Commission or other federal agencies—will "railroad" them.[81] They have forgotten, or simply ignored, how much their firms have benefitted from enormous public subsidies. Before the internet was the Advanced Research Projects Agency Network, courtesy of the Department of Defense, and before that, billions of dollars of government investment in research and development made possible the high-performance chips, fiber optics, data storage, and the other building blocks of the internet. Similarly NIH grants to the biotech industry vastly exceed venture capital investment.

Free enterprise is never free, its costs and benefits never spread equitably, and little attention is paid to the human balance sheet. Would-be Silicon Glens, Fens, Forests, Prairies, Mountains, and Slopes should bear that lesson in mind.[82] Despite the growth of high-tech jobs in the rest of the West—Salt Lake City, Boise, Denver, Austin—jobs in the digital services industry (a reasonable proxy for high tech) have become more rather than less concentrated in recent years, with Seattle, San Francisco, San Jose, and Los Angeles actually increasing their relative as well as absolute lead.[83] The industry's executives and their lobbyists fear "high-tech populism" for a reason, preferring to talk about "high-tech progressivism." What they seek is a second "triumph of conservatism" that would capture potential regulators and preserve the neo-conservative status quo.[84] They subscribe to their own version of the Turner thesis (Fred's and not Frederick Jackson's) with cyberspace as the new frontier.[85] That utopian aspiration seems at best a distant dream or self-delusion. As one longtime Silicon Valley watcher sagely remarked, "No, the internet is not so much the wild, wild West anymore. Increasingly, it's more like Westworld. And we're the androids."[86]

Notes

1. See McGirr, *Suburban Warriors*.
2. Walker, *Pictures of a Gone City*, 42, 98, 348.
3. Wright, "World War II, the Cold War, and the Knowledge Economies," 74–99. Wright independently "traces the institutional and economic evolution of four Pacific Coast knowledge-economy clusters from wartime to Cold War to commercialization: Los Angeles, San Francisco Bay Area, Seattle, and San Diego," with a focus on aerospace and computers and electronics, stressing how some clusters (Silicon Valley and Seattle) "civilianized" high tech better than others (Los Angeles and San Diego).
4. See Saxenian, *The New Argonauts*.
5. White, "Afterward," 183.
6. Kirkendall, "The Boeing Company," 137–49.
7. Markusen, *The Rise of the Gunbelt*, 148–55.
8. Myers, *Capitalist Family Values*, 81.
9. McConaghy, "No Ordinary Place," 259.
10. McConaghy, "No Ordinary Place," 287–98.
11. Grunberg and Moore, *Emerging from Turbulence*, 3.
12. Greenberg et al., *Turbulence*, 128.
13. Stone, *The Everything Store*, 30.
14. Mike Rosenberg and Angel Gonzalez, "Thanks to Amazon, Seattle Is Now America's Biggest Company Town," *Seattle Times*, August 23, 2017, https://www.seattletimes.com/business/amazon/thanks-to-amazon-seattle-is-now-americas-biggest-company-town/.
15. Mike Rosenberg, "Watch Amazon's Seattle Campus Quadruple in Size in a Decade," *Seattle Times*, November 30, 2017, https://www.seattletimes.com/business/real-estate/watch-amazons-seattle-campus-quadruple-in-size-in-a-decade/.
16. "Amazon Stock Compensation: Great for Employees but a Liability," Real Finance Guy, September 1, 2018, https://www.realfinanceguy.com/home/2018/9/1/amazon-stock-compensation.
17. Tim Johnson, "The Real Trouble with Tech Professionals: High Turnover," *Forbes*, June 29, 2018, https://www.forbes.com/sites/forbesbusinessdevelopmentcouncil/2018/06/29/the-real-problem-with-tech-professionals-high-turnover/#7b8aa6d42014.
18. "South Lake Union," Niche, accessed April 17, 2019, https://www.niche.com/places-to-live/n/south-lake-union-seattle-wa.
19. Mark Byrnes, "Brutal Parodies of Amazon's 'Life in Seattle' Recruitment Video," Citylab, May 14, 2015, https://www.citylab.com/equity/2015/05/seattle-pokes-fun-at-amazon-recruiting-video-life-in-seattle/393251.
20. "Amazon's Unfair Deal of the Day: Undercutting Women, and Their Wages," Free and Fair Markets Initiative, accessed June 10, 2019, https://freeandfairmarketsinitiative.org/ffmi-reports/report-amazons-unfair-deal-of-the-day.
21. Jeffrey Dasin, "Amazon Scraps Secret AI Recruiting Tool that Showed Bias against Women," *Reuters*, October 9, 2018, https://www.reuters.com/article/us-amazon-com-jobs-automation-insight/amazon-scraps-secret-ai-recruiting-tool-that-showed-bias-against-women-iduskcn1mk08g.
22. Danny Westneat, "Subsidy Arms Race for Amazon? We of All People Should Know How This Turns Out," *Seattle Times*, October 6, 2017, https://www.seattletimes.com/seattle

-news/politics/we-of-all-people-should-know-how-this-subsidy-arms-race-for-amazon-turns-out/.

23. Tom Standage, "Why Start-ups Are Leaving Silicon Valley," *Economist*, August 30, 2018, https://www.economist.com/leaders/2018/08/30/why-startups-are-leaving-silicon-valley.

24. Kate Losse, "The False Promise of Silicon Valley's Quest to Save the World," *New Republic*, February 7, 2019, https://newrepublic.com/article/153034/false-promise-silicon-valleys-quest-save-world.

25. Hall and Markusen, *Silicon Landscapes*, 45; Hayes, *Behind the Silicon Curtain*, 11.

26. Leslie, *The Cold War and American Science*, 241–56; Pellow and Park, *The Silicon Valley of Dreams*, 60–61.

27. Rogers and Larsen, *Silicon Valley Fever*, 231–34; see also Siegel and Markoff, *The High Cost of High Tech*; Walker, *Pictures*, 33; Barry Jaruzelski, "Why Silicon Valley's Success Is So Hard to Replicate," *Scientific American*, March 4, 2014, https://www.scientificamerican.com/article/why-silicon-valleys-success-is-so-hard-to-replicate.

28. For a fuller picture of the impact of high tech on housing equity in San Francisco see Walker, *Pictures*; Spencer, *A People's History of Silicon Valley*, 10–11; Michael Smerklo, "What the *Economist* Got Wrong About the Decline of Silicon Valley," *Forbes*, September 18, 2018, https://www.forbes.com/sites/mikesmerklo/2018/09/18/what-the-economist-got-wrong-about-the-decline-of-silicon-valley/#6bf7f4aa203d.

29. Thomas Fuller, "In San Francisco, Making a Living from Your Billionaire Neighbor's Trash," *New York Times*, April 7, 2019, https://www.nytimes.com/2019/04/07/us/trash-pickers-san-francisco-zuckerberg.html.

30. Ryan Nakashima, "'Silicon Beach' Brings Tech Boom to Los Angeles," *Phys Org*, October 22, 2014, https://phys.org/news/2014-10-silicon-beach-tech-boom-los.html.

31. Richard Waters, "The Great Silicon Valley Land Grab," *Financial Times*, August 26, 2017, https://www.ft.com/content/82bc282e-8790-11e7-bf50-e1c239b45787.

32. Sissi Cao, "Silicon Valley's Astronomical Housing Price Creates Problem for Start-ups," *Observer*, April 9, 2018, https://observer.com/2018/04/silicon-valley-housing-prices-create-startup-problem.

33. Ellen Shang, "Silicon Valley's Dirty Secret: Using a Shadow Workforce of Contract Employees to Drive Profits," CNBC, October 22, 2018, https://www.cnbc.com/2018/10/22/silicon-valley-using-contract-employees-to-drive-profits.html.

34. Mark Bergen and Josh Eidelson, "Inside Google's Shadow Workforce," *Bloomberg*, July 25, 2018, https://www.bloomberg.com/news/articles/2018-07-25/inside-google-s-shadow-workforce.

35. Joshua Brustein, "'Black Site' a Black Eye?," *Los Angeles Times*, February 18, 2019, https://www.pressreader.com/usa/los-angeles-times/20190218/281530817294139.

36. Hayes, *Behind the Silicon Curtain*, 52.

37. Rick Morgan, "SurveyMonkey Defies Silicon Valley Labor Caste System, Offering Contract Workers Full Benefits," CNBC, April 19, 2018, https://www.cnbc.com/2018/04/19/surveymonkey-breaks-with-silicon-valley-over-contract-worker-benefits.html.

38. Kate Conger, "Google Removes 'Don't Be Evil' Clause From Its Code of Conduct," *Gizmodo*, May 18, 2018, https://gizmodo.com/google-removes-nearly-all-mentions-of-dont-be-evil-from-1826153393.

39. TVCs at Google: "Invisible No Longer: Google's Shadow Workforce Speaks Up," *Medium*, December 5, 2018, https://medium.com/@GoogleWalkout/invisible-no-longer-googles-shadow-workforce-speaks-up-9ea04b7bcc41; Julia Carrie Wong, "Google Staff Condemn Treatment of Temp Workers in 'Historic' Show of Solidarity," *Guardian*, April 2, 2019, https://www.theguardian.com/technology/2019/apr/02/google-workers-sign-letter-temp-contractors-protest; Alexia Fernández Campbell, "Google Will Extend Some Benefits to Contract Workers after Internal Protest," *Vox*, April 4, 2019, https://www.vox.com/2019/4/4/18293900/google-contractors-benefits-policy.

40. Brustein, "'Black Site' a Black Eye?," *Los Angeles Times*, February 18, 2019.

41. Brustein, "'Black Site' a Black Eye?," *Los Angeles Times*, February 18, 2019.

42. Nate Swanner, "VC Funding Fueled 20-Year Silicon Valley Wage Decline: Study," *Dice*, November 27, 2018, https://insights.dice.com/2018/11/27/20-year-silicon-valley-wage-decline.

43. Shang, "Silicon Valley's Dirty Secret," CNBC, October 22, 2018.

44. Matthews, *Silicon Valley*, 9–11.

45. "'The Bay Area Is Broken': Why Silicon Valley Startups Are Hiring Elsewhere," *Daily Republic*, April 29, 2018, https://www.dailyrepublic.com/all-dr-news/wires/business/the-bay-area-is-broken-why-silicon-valley-startups-are-hiring-elsewhere.

46. Matthews, *Silicon Valley*, 1; Daniel Harris, "What Silicon Valley Doesn't Get About People," *Citylab*, September 14, 2017, https://www.citylab.com/design/2017/09/what-silicon-valley-doesnt-get-about-people/539799.

47. Margot Roosevelt, "Uber, Lyft Say Making Driver Employees Would 'Pose a Risk to Our Businesses,'" *Los Angeles Times*, June 12, 2019, https://www.latimes.com/business/la-fi-tn-uber-lyft-contractor-drivers-20190612-story.html; Johana Buiyan, "Treat Workers as Employees? Uber, Lyft and Others Are Scrambling for a Compromise," *Los Angeles Times*, June 23, 2019, https://www.latimes.com/business/technology/la-fi-tn-dynamex-contractors-ab5-20190623-story.html; Margot Roosevelt, "Are You an Employee or a Contractor? Carpenters, Strippers and Dog Walkers Now Face that Question," *Los Angeles Times*, February 23, 2019, https://www.latimes.com/business/la-fi-dynamex-contractors-20190223-story.html.

48. Evan Halpar, "No Longer a Political Winner: Silicon Valley Is a Minefield for 2020 Hopefuls," *Los Angeles Times*, March 28, 2019, https://www.latimes.com/politics/la-na-pol-silicon-valley-presidential-politics-20190328-story.html.

49. "SpaceX Company History," Where Is Roadster?, accessed December 24, 2018, https://www.whereisroadster.com/spacex; Jeffrey Kluger, "10 Things to Know about SpaceX," *Time*, accessed December 24, 2018, http://time.com/space-x-ten-things-to-know.

50. Kluger, "10 Things to Know about SpaceX," *Time*, accessed December 24, 2018; Geoff Manaugh, "Los Angeles, America's Future Spaceport," *Atlantic*, May 17, 2018, https://www.theatlantic.com/technology/archive/2018/05/los-angeles-americas-future-spaceport/560420.

51. Jacob Wolinsky and Rochelle Bailis, "Silicon Beach Is Worth $155 Billion in Valuation," *Value Walk*, October 10, 2018, https://www.valuewalk.com/2018/10/silicon-beach-155-billion-valuation.

52. Katharine Gammon, "The Launch Pad: USC Alumni and Researchers Build on the Region's Legacy in Aerospace Aviation to Push the Next Generation of Spaceflight," *USC Trojan*, August 2018, 33–36.

53. Gammon, "The Launch Pad," *USC Trojan*, August 2018.

54. Samantha Masunaga, "Why Does SpaceX Stay in the Costly Los Angeles Area? It's Where the Talent Is," *Los Angeles Times*, October 17, 2018, https://www.latimes.com/business/la-fi-spacex-los-angeles-20181017-story.html.

55. Masunaga, "Why Does SpaceX Stay," *Los Angeles Times*, October 17, 2018.

56. Masunaga, "Why Does SpaceX Stay," *Los Angeles Times*, October 17, 2018.

57. Joshua Fruhlinger, "SpaceX Production Hiring Up 24 Percent Since September with a Focus on Hawthorne Facility," *Thinknum*, accessed July 2, 2019, https://media.thinknum.com/articles/spacex-bumps-up-hiring-efforts-hawthorne-october-2018.

58. Samantha Masunaga, "With the Rise of SpaceX and Rams Stadium, Hawthorne's Industrial Areas Are Becoming Hip," *Los Angeles Times*, December 15, 2017, https://www.latimes.com/business/la-fi-hawthorne-real-estate-20171215-story.html.

59. Joseph Pimentel, "SpaceX's New Neighbor in Hawthorne Will Be Amazon's Ring," *Bisnow*, May 17, 2018, https://www.bisnow.com/los-angeles/news/office/ding-dong-spacexs-new-neighbor-in-hawthorne-will-be-amazons-ring-88547; Steven Sharp, "First Look at Hawthorne's SpaceX-Adjacent Multi-Use Development," *Urbanize Los Angeles*, March 2, 2018, https://urbanize.la/post/first-look-hawthornes-spacex-adjacent-mixed-use-development.

60. Angel Jennings, "One of California's Last Black Enclaves Threatened by Inglewood's Stadium Deal," *Los Angeles Times*, April 10, 2019, https://www.latimes.com/local/lanow/la-me-inglewood-gentrification-rent-crenshaw-rams-stadium-20190410-htmlstory.html.

61. Alana Semuels, "When Elon Musk Tunnels Under Your Home," *Atlantic*, November 15, 2018, https://www.theatlantic.com/technology/archive/2018/11/los-angeles-elon-musk-tunnels-under-neighborhood/575725.

62. Masunaga, "With the Rise of SpaceX And Rams Stadium," *Los Angeles Times*, December 15, 2017.

63. "City Rising," KCET, accessed June 15, 2019, http://www.kcet.org/shows/city-rising.

64. Lotchin, *Fortress California*, 297–318.

65. Yenne, *Into the Sunset*, 22–25.

66. John Lawrence, "General Dynamics, Once a San Diego Mainstay, Now Dearly Departed," *San Diego Free Press*, July 16, 1916, https://sandiegofreepress.org/2016/07/general-dynamics-san-diego/#.XQJSp3t7lsM.

67. Taschner, "Boomerang Boom" and Killory, "Temporary Suburbs" offer critical appraisals of Linda Vista.

68. Yenne, *Into the Sunset*, 44–58.

69. Leslie, "William Pereira's Aerospace Modernism," 127–58.

70. Anderson, *An Improbable Venture*, 131–51.

71. Bourgeois, *Genesis of the Salk Institute*, 107–19.

72. Bradley Fikes, "The Scripps Research Institute Ranked First Worldwide in Science," *San Diego Union Tribune*, August 10, 2017, https://www.sandiegouniontribune.com/business/biotech/sd-me-scripps-science-20170810-story.html.

73. Coleman, *Utopias and Architecture*, 257–79.

74. DeVol et al., *America's Biotech*, 13–25.

75. The United States Centre at the University of Sydney, *Biotechnology Cluster Project: San Diego Analysis*, 15–16.

76. Mallory Pickett, "'I Want What My Male Colleague Has, and that Will Cost a Few Million Dollars,'" *New York Times*, April 18, 2019, https://www.nytimes.com/2019/04/18/magazine/salk-institute-discrimination-science.html.

77. See Richardson, Mitchell, and Franco, "Shifting Neighborhoods: Gentrification and Cultural Displacement in American Cities."

78. Markusen, *The Rise of the Gunbelt*, 82–117; see Beers, *Blue Sky Dream*.

79. Sarah Jones, "The Year Silicon Valley Went Morally Bankrupt," *New Republic*, December 8, 2018, https://newrepublic.com/article/139147/year-silicon-valley-went-morally-bankrupt. Florida's *Cities and the Creative Class*, like his *Rise of the Creative Class*, downplays class conflict and community displacement.

80. Drexel, "Net Neutrality: Will the Internet Get Railroaded?," 6–8.

81. White, in *Railroaded*, is well aware of these parallels.

82. "Silicon Glen: The Miracle that Just Melted Away," *Scotsman*, November 8, 2007, https://www.scotsman.com/news-2-15012/silicon-glen-the-miracle-that-just-melted-away-1-698782; see Dobbs and Wollner, *Silicon Forest*; see Hwang and Horowitt, *The Rainforest*, which characteristically promises to reveal the elusive recipe.

83. Mark Muro and Jacob Whiton, "Tech Is (Still) Concentrating in the Bay Area: An Update on America's Winner-Take-Most Economic Phenomenon," *Brookings Institution*, December 18, 2018, https://www.brookings.edu/blog/the-avenue/2018/12/17/tech-is-still-concentrating-in-the-bay-area-an-update-on-americas-winner-take-most-economic-phenomenon.

84. See Aitkinsen, Castro, and McQuinn, "How Tech Populism Is Undermining Innovation"; see Kolko, *The Triumph of Conservatism*.

85. See Turner, *From Counterculture to Cyberculture*.

86. Steven Levy, "The Internet Isn't the Wild West Anymore. It's *Westworld*," *Wired*, April 1, 2017, https://www.wired.com/2017/04/the-internet-isnt-the-wild-wild-west-anymore-its-westworld.

Selected Bibliography

Aitkinsen, Robert, Daniel Castro, and Alan McQuinn. "How Tech Populism Is Undermining Innovation." Information Technology and Innovation Foundation, April 2015. www2.itif.org/2015-tech-populism.pdf.

Anderson, Nancy. *An Improbable Venture: A History of the University of California, San Diego*. La Jolla: University of California, San Diego, 1993.

Beers, David. *Blue Sky Dream: A Memoir of America's Fall from Grace*. New York: Random House, 1996.

Bourgeois, Suzanne. *Genesis of the Salk Institute*. Berkeley: University of California Press, 2013.

Coleman, Nathaniel. *Utopias and Architecture*. London: Routledge, 2005.

DeVol, Ross, Perry Wong, Junghoon Ki, Armen Bedroussian, and Rob Koepp. *America's Biotech and Life Science Clusters*. Santa Monica CA: Milken Institute, June 2004.

Dobbs, Gordon, and Craig Wollner. *Silicon Forest: High-Tech in the Portland Area, 1945–1986*. Portland OR: Portland Historical Society, 1990.

Drexel, William R. "Net Neutrality: Will the Internet Get Railroaded?" *Infrastructure* 54 (Summer 2015): 6–8.

Florida, Richard. *Cities and the Creative Class*. London: Routledge, 2005.

———. *Rise of the Creative Class: And How It's Transforming Work, Leisure, Community, and Everyday Life*. New York: Basic, 2004.

Greenberg, Edward, Leon Grunberg, Sarah Moore, and Patricia Sikora. *Turbulence: Boeing and the State of American Workers and Managers*. New Haven CT: Yale University Press, 2010.

Grunberg, Leon, and Sarah Moore. *Emerging from Turbulence: Boeing and Stories of the American Workplace Today*. New York: Rowman & Littlefield, 2016.

Hall, Peter, and Ann Markusen, eds. *Silicon Landscapes*. Boston: Allen & Unwin, 1985.

Hayes, Dennis. *Behind the Silicon Curtain: The Seductions of Work in a Lonely Era*. Boston: South End, 1989.

Hwang, Victor, and Greg Horowitt. *The Rainforest: The Secret to Building the Next Silicon Valley*. Los Altos CA: Regenwald, 2012.

Killory, Christine. "Temporary Suburbs: The Lost Opportunity of San Diego's National Defense Housing Projects." *Journal of San Diego History* (Spring 1993). https://sandiegohistory.org/journal/1993/january/suburbs/.

Kirkendall, Richard. "The Boeing Company and the Military-Metropolitan-Industrial Complex, 1945–1953." *Pacific Northwest Quarterly* 85 (October 1994): 137–49.

Kolko, Gabriel. *The Triumph of Conservatism: A Reinterpretation of American History, 1900–1916*. New York: Free Press, 1963.

Leslie, Stuart W. *The Cold War and American Science: The Military-Industrial-Academic Complex at MIT and Stanford*. New York: Columbia University Press, 1994.

———. "William Pereira's Aerospace Modernism." In *Blue Sky Metropolis: The Aerospace Century in Southern California*, edited by Peter Westwick, 127–58. Berkeley: University of California Press, 2012.

Lotchin, Roger. *Fortress California, 1910–1961: From Warfare to Welfare*. New York: Oxford University Press, 1992.

Markusen, Ann, Scott Campbell, Peter Hall, and Sabina Deitrick. *The Rise of the Gunbelt: The Military Remapping of Industrial America*. New York: Oxford University Press, 1991.

Matthews, Glenna. *Silicon Valley, Women, and the California Dream*. Palo Alto CA: Stanford University Press, 2003.

McConaghy, Lorraine. *No Ordinary Place: Three Postwar Suburbs and Their Critics*. PhD diss., University of Washington, 1993.

McGirr, Lisa. *Suburban Warriors: The Origins of the New American Right*. Princeton NJ: Princeton University Press, 2001.

Myers, Polly Reed. *Capitalist Family Values: Gender, Work, and Corporate Culture at Boeing*. Lincoln: University of Nebraska Press, 2015.

Pellow, David N., and Lisa Sun-Hee Park. *The Silicon Valley of Dreams: Environmental Justice, Immigrant Workers, and the High-Tech Global Economy*. New York: New York University Press, 2002.

Richardson, Jason, Bruce Mitchell, and Juan Franco. "Shifting Neighborhoods: Gentrification and Cultural Displacement in American Cities." *National Community Reinvestment Coalition*. March 19, 2019. https://ncrc.org/gentrification.

Rogers, Everett M., and Judith K. Larsen. *Silicon Valley Fever: Growth of High-Technology Culture*. New York: Basic, 1984.

Saxenian, AnnaLee. *The New Argonauts: Regional Advantage in a Global Economy*. Cambridge: Harvard University Press, 2006.

Siegel, Lenny, and John Markoff. *The High Cost of High Tech: The Dark Side of the Chip*. New York: Harper & Row, 1985.

Spencer, Keith A. *A People's History of Silicon Valley: How the Tech Industry Exploits Workers, Erodes Privacy, and Undermines Democracy*. London: Eyewear, 2018.

Stone, Brad. *The Everything Store: Jeff Bezos and the Age of Amazon*. New York: Little Brown, 2013.

Taschner, Mary. "Boomerang Boom: San Diego, 1941–1942." *Journal of San Diego History* (Winter 1982). https://sandiegohistory.org/journal/1982/january/boom/.

Turner, Fred. *From Counterculture to Cyberculture: Stewart Brand, the Whole Earth Network, and the Rise of Digital Utopianism*. Chicago: University of Chicago Press, 2006.

U.S. Centre at the University of Sydney. *Biotechnology Cluster Project: San Diego Analysis*. April 2010, 15–16. https://extension.ucsd.edu/UCSDExtension/media/UCSDExtensionsMedia/community-and-research/center-for-research-and-evaluation/Biotechnology-Cluster-Project-San-Diego-Analysis.pdf.

Walker, Richard A. *Pictures of a Gone City: Tech and the Dark Side of Prosperity in the San Francisco Bay Area*. Oakland CA: PM, 2018.

White, Richard. "Afterward." In *World War II and the West It Wrought*, edited by Mark Brilliant and David Kennedy, 179–84. Redwood City CA: Stanford University Press, 2020.

———. *Railroaded: The Transcontinentals and the Making of Modern America*. New York: Norton, 2011.

Wright, Gavin. "World War II, the Cold War, and the Knowledge Economies of the Pacific Coast." In *World War II and the West It Wrought*, edited by Mark Brilliant and David Kennedy, 74–99. Redwood City CA: Stanford University Press, 2020.

Yenne, Bill. *Into the Sunset: The Convair Story*. Lyme CT: Greenwich, 1995.

6

Our Mission, No Eviction

Resisting Gentrification in San Francisco

LINDSEY PASSENGER WIECK

In 1970 René Yañez and Ralph Maradiaga opened Galería de la Raza, an art gallery on Twenty-Fourth Street in the Mission District of San Francisco. In 1972 they curated a show with original drawings by the all-star Mexican artists Diego Rivera, José Clemente Orozco, and David Alfaro Siqueiros, a notable show for a gallery only in its second year. But no one came. And so Yañez and Maradiaga moved the show for a single day to Balmy Alley, a nearby street that would eventually become a hub of Latinx mural art.[1] Taking the art to the streets attracted the neighborhood's working-class residents as they had hoped.

René Yañez filled his life with creative, out-of-the-box thinking like this. He created spaces for artists to make and share their art, fostering Latino culture and community in the Mission District. Yañez's efforts provided a place for diverse residents to laugh, resist, mourn, and create. But during his nearly fifty years there—from the late 1960s through the late 2010s—the neighborhood shifted from a predominantly Latino space to one infiltrated by gentrifiers, Google buses, and farm-to-table organic eateries. Boundaries between new and old residents blurred. Hip coffee shops replaced longtime local businesses, and Latinos, artists, and other working-class residents faced eviction as the Mission gentrified. As the neighborhood transformed, Yañez used art and culture to resist these changes and offer social commentary on inequities in the Mission and beyond. In the years before his 2018 death, Yañez too would face eviction from his home of more than thirty years. Yañez's story reveals a

FIG. 13. An altar in front of the SOMArts Cultural Center remembered Yañez after his death in 2018. Courtesy Alicia Cruz.

central irony in the history of the Mission and of other gentrifying neighborhoods—people like Yañez, who cultivated culturally rich communities that appealed to gentrifiers, are often kicked out when the real estate prices skyrocket.

Yañez's life in the Mission allows us to trace how the neighborhood changed from the late 1960s to the late 2010s. The demographic, economic, and cultural changes of a gentrifying neighborhood had real and tangible impacts on the people who lived there. Simultaneously the people who lived there resisted these larger structural changes. This chapter uses Yañez's art and activism to understand how residents cultivated community in the Mission even as the neighborhood transformed around them. Yañez founded Galería de la Raza, fostered the growth of local Día de los Muertos rituals, and protested evictions in the neighborhood. These efforts brought local Latinos together, making the Mission visible as a Latino space. These same spaces also offered Mission Latinos opportunities to critique and question the sociopolitical conditions of the neighborhood and beyond. As the tech boom and mounting costs of living crowded out Mission Latinos, the artistic and cultural spaces created by Yañez and others in the 1970s and 1980s provided residents with cultural mechanisms to resist gentrification and economic changes in the 1990s through the 2010s.

Bringing Día de los Muertos to the Mission

René Yañez arrived in the Bay Area in 1967, moving to the Mission District shortly thereafter. The Mission District, a neighborhood just south of downtown San Francisco, has long housed working-class peoples. After World War II upwardly mobile Irish and Italian immigrants moved out, leaving behind affordable housing and jobs in nearby factories and warehouses. In the post-war decades Latinos, ranging from longtime U.S. residents to recent Latin American migrants, filled the neighborhood.[2] By 1976 the Mission population was 60 percent Latino. These new residents faced problems including poor quality schools, inadequate health care, rising crime rates, police brutality, deteriorating housing structures, and racial discrimination. By the time Yañez arrived in the neighborhood local activists had begun organizing Mission Latinos to fight for safer, more equitable local spaces. Simultaneously in the late 1960s and early 1970s residents worked to build a community by articulating a shared identity based on a broadly defined Latino heritage. They did this, in part, by making a place for Latino residents' diverse cultural endeavors, including displaying the art they made.[3]

Soon after arriving Yañez contributed to these efforts to cultivate a Mission Latino community by creating spaces for Latino residents to share their art. In July 1970 he and artist Ralph Maradiaga opened Galería de la Raza, a community art gallery in the Mission.[4] At a time when many artists of color lacked opportunities to display their art in mainstream museums and galleries, the Galería opened new doors. Decolonizing the city's art spaces the Galería welcomed Latino artists to share their art with local residents in a more inclusive space.[5]

Yañez and Maradiaga's radical inclusivity helped make the Galería a unique artistic space.[6] They enlarged the Latino artistic community by including women, queer people, and new artists. Also the Galería's founders used the term "Raza" in the gallery's name to break with European high art. In the mid- to late-twentieth century Latinos in the United States understood La Raza to refer to "the people" or "the community," a concept that broadly included the culture and problems shared by Latin Americans throughout the Western Hemisphere.[7] By using Raza in its name the Galería showcased the Mission Latino community's diversity and connected its identity to Third World politics and activism.[8] As Tomás Ybarra-Frausto explains, Bay Area cultural activists "were searching for a point of unity among the diverse Latino communities living [in] the barrios of the Mission District," and so Raza communicates shared connections "defined by a shared historical identity and destiny."[9] Along with other local institutions and sites of political activism, the Galería provided a space for artists and residents to develop and affirm a collective identity rooted in pan-Latino and Third World global connections.

The Galería, with its commitment to inclusivity and a broadly defined Latinidad, enabled artists to share their work largely free from discrimination. Ybarra-Frausto calls the Galería a "zone of refuge"

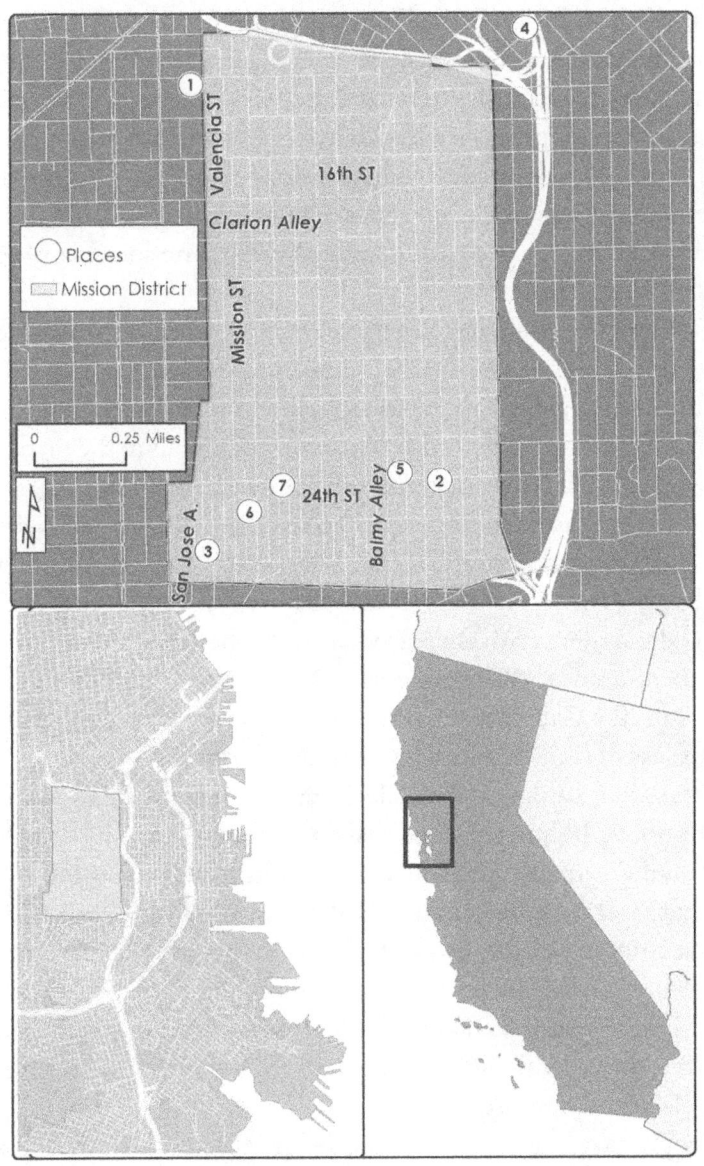

FIG. 14. Map of San Francisco Mission District. Map by Jeffrey M. Widener. *Legend*: 1: Galería de la Raza (1970–72), 425 Fourteenth Street; 2: Galería de la Raza (1972–2018), 2851 Twenty-Fourth Street; 3: Galería de la Raza, temporary location (2018–), 1470 Valencia St.; 4: SOMArts Cultural Center, 934 Brannan Street; 5: El Tecolote, 2958 Twenty-Fourth Street; 6: Mission Cultural Center, 2868 Mission Street; 7: La Victoria Bakery, 3249 Twenty-Fourth Street.

because it was "a site for nurturing and protecting Chicana/o artists and for promoting and safe-keeping their work."[10] This feeling of safety encouraged artists to reflect on topics central to Latino identity, culture, and politics in the United States and in Latin America. At a time when the mainstream art world maintained its exclusivity by privileging the perspectives of elite white artists, the Galería empowered its diverse artists to critically reflect on society by breaking from the mainstream.[11]

Not only did the Galería revolutionize who could make and display art in the city, it also transformed who had access to art. Residents increasingly encountered art in the Mission with the creation of other local arts centers and the painting of murals in the 1970s and beyond. As residents engaged with art nearby their homes, many experienced pride and a sense of connection to the Mission's developing Latino community.[12] The Galería also printed and distributed *calendarios* (calendars) from 1973 to 1977. With its *calendarios* the Galería inexpensively placed art onto the walls of community members' homes.[13] By making art and culture more available to local residents, the Galería asserted that everyone deserved access to art, regardless of racial identity or economic status.[14]

By sharing Latino art the Galería transformed the Mission neighborhood by helping people visualize how culture linked them together. For many residents art and culture resided at the center of what it meant to be a Latino in the Mission. In addition to cultivating community locally, the Galería also helped popularize public celebrations of Día de los Muertos throughout the United States. For Mission Latinos Día de los Muertos fostered community and allowed for critical engagement with sociopolitical issues in San Francisco and Latin America.

People have long celebrated Día de los Muertos throughout Latin America. However prior to the 1970s Latinos in the United States did not widely participate in Día de los Muertos rituals until Chicanos like Yañez popularized its public observance.[15] In 1972 Yañez introduced Día de los Muertos to the Mission through altar installations at the Galería de la Raza.[16] That same year Self Help Graphics, an arts center in Los Angeles, sponsored a Day of the Dead street procession in which "people dressed as skeletons and walked to a nearby cemetery."[17] Few really knew what they were doing at this point. The Galería's first exhibit consisted only of a table with a candle, a picture, and flowers set on top. But this simple altar resonated with people, and so Yañez, Maradiaga, and the Galería continued sponsoring and expanding its Día de los Muertos rituals.[18] These early celebrations produced new traditions and rituals within the Mission Latino community.[19] In part because of Yañez and the Galería, Día de los Muertos grew in importance and visibility throughout the late twentieth and early twenty-first centuries in the United States.

In Latin America Día de los Muertos is typically steeped in Catholicism. In the United States, by contrast, Día de los Muertos largely became a secular ritual. Spiritual components, however, do remain. While seeking to break from the Catholic Church's colonialism, many Chicanos still used Catholic symbols such as rosary beads and pictures of Jesus and the Virgen de Guadalupe, mixing them with Indigenous symbols like Aztec calendars and figurines of Aztec and Mayan deities. Chicano artists also integrated popular cultural icons ranging from Frida Kahlo and Cesar Chavez to comic book superheroes.[20]

The variety of items, or *ofrendas* (harvest offerings), on the altars created throughout the United States today demonstrates the cultural hybridity of Día de los Muertos. *Ofrendas* often contain items that represent these different cultures including sugar skulls, marigolds, copal incense, salt, corn, tamales, and *pan de muerto*. Just as the Galería's Latino art cultivated cultural affirmation for residents, Día de los Muertos similarly fostered cultural identity and pride by blending symbols from Latin America with those from U.S. Latino culture.[21] This blending helped residents realize that this cultural hybridity mirrored community-building efforts and cultural mixing that were happening simultaneously in the Mission.

In 1981 Yañez expanded the reach of Día de los Muertos in San Francisco by organizing a small procession of about twenty-five people. Holding candles, participants walked around the block. These first processions in the early 1980s were quiet and spiritual.[22] Quickly word spread, and this procession grew each year. Thousands of visitors came from throughout the region as this procession became known as one of the Mission's most colorful events.[23] The procession's shift from a localized ritual to an event joined by thousands of outsiders paralleled the development of the public rituals of Día de los Muertos celebrated across the United States today.

As Latino residents enacted these hybrid cultural identities in public spaces, a Latino community began to coalesce in the Mission: "As shared cultural practices, public rituals of altar making, walking together in street processions, and holding candlelight vigils and related activities can stimulate feelings of empathy and solidarity among diverse Latinos, creating a sense of 'imagined community' or 'horizontal comradeship among people who have never met.'"[24] As residents visited the Galería, artists developed art for display in the Mission and beyond. Residents joined together in Día de los Muertos rituals, bonding over shared commonalities and bridging their diverse backgrounds to make the Mission a Latino space.[25] With the work of Yañez and other artists and activists, Latinidad thrived in the Mission as art and culture filled the streets. Residents fiercely articulated notions of pan-Latino power and rights just as the city approached a major demographic and economic shift.

The Mission's New Migration

In the 1980s and 1990s young urban professionals (yuppies) inundated San Francisco's high-rise offices downtown, and many moved to the Mission to live. Breaking from the suburban lifestyle of their parents and peers, yuppies chose to live in urban spaces near where they worked. This "new gentry" included people such as "childless flight attendants, unmarried computer programmers and upscale young professionals."[26] The Mission's sunshine and Victorian homes attracted these newcomers, as did the rich culture and community that Yañez and his fellow artists helped create. These new yuppie residents wanted to live in a space filled with ethnic culture and old homes. By immersing themselves in the Mission's Latino community and its spaces, these newcomers sought to consume an authentic neighborhood feel that had been lost in the suburbs. But ultimately these desires would bring this community turmoil.

This yuppie migration had consequences for those living in the Mission. The cost of living rose as did evictions and the displacement of previous residents. In 1978 *El Tecolote*, a local bilingual newspaper, detailed the plight of Mission residents Natalia and Juan after their landlord sold the apartment building where they lived. The new owner raised rent by seventy-five dollars a month, and later by fifteen dollars more, which was prohibitively expensive for many residents. Juan and Natalia exemplified the thousands of families displaced by gentrification through this yuppie migration. By then more than one hundred families each month were already having to move.[27]

These displacements frayed the neighborhood's social fabric. Before this yuppie migration residents like Juan and Natalia had felt secure within the growing Latino Mission community. *El Tecolote* describes how Latino residents felt a "sense of responsibility" for each other.[28] However rising rent costs and evictions threatened this community support system as many residents had to leave the city to find cheaper housing. While Yañez, the Galería de la Raza, and other arts institutions developed and strengthened this community by fostering shared cultural bonds, economic and demographic changes strained these fledgling connections. These early waves of gentrifiers in the late 1970s through the 1990s fundamentally changed the demographic and cultural identity of the Mission.

The neighborhood's transformation persisted as new waves of gentrifiers flooded the Mission during the "Dot-Com Boom" of the late 1990s and early 2000s and again in the 2010s with "Tech Boom 2.0." We could visualize these decades as layers of gentrification stacking up in the neighborhood, a concept Loretta Lees coined as "super-gentrification." With super-gentrification Lee describes that "many first-stage (sweat equity) gentrifiers have sold their property to new (very well-off gentrifiers), who are regentrifying property in the neighborhood."[29] In the case of the Mission we see early yuppie gentrifiers displaced by increasingly brash waves of tech workers, hipsters, and other upwardly mobile folks, all while Mission Latinos tried to protect their residential and commercial spaces, their culture, and their social and political rights.

In the late 1990s the rise of the internet and venture capital fueled an economic boom in Silicon Valley and San Francisco. Tech workers and venture capitalists funneled into the city looking for culturally vibrant places to live and spend their wealth. Even though the dot-com bubble burst in 2001, waves of gentrification and displacement continued throughout the 2000s and 2010s. In the mid-2000s, for example, Google attracted many new workers to the area, and in 2011 Mayor Ed Lee fueled tech growth in the city by granting a tax break for Twitter, Dropbox, and other tech companies who set up shop in San Francisco. By 2014 Angel List, a networking site for investors, listed "5,249 tech startups in San Francisco, each worth $4.6 [million] on average and offering an average salary of $105,000."[30] These waves of investment and economic growth led Silicon Valley and San Francisco tech workers, as well as hipsters and other gentrifiers, to move into the Mission and the neighborhoods surrounding it.

These waves of gentrifiers changed the neighborhood in several ways. First, these wealthy new residents sought to spend their money in the city. Their desire for artisanal coffee shops, farm-to-table restaurants, and quirky stores near their residences spurred the closure of local Latino businesses. These closures often happen when landlords raise the rental price for storefronts, pushing local business owners out. Others close because business owners cannot keep up with the rising costs of doing business in an increasingly affluent city.[31] Second, racial divides between wealthy, white tech workers and Latino residents became visible on the neighborhood's landscape. Many of these luxury businesses reside on Valencia Street, one of the Mission's main corridors. There, one scholar describes, "white bodies are wandering, buying, relaxing, or bicycling."[32] In contrast on Mission Street, a parallel corridor fifty meters away, the Latino Mission dominates. Here "one enters the Latino Mission with its taquerias, its murals glorifying the community's struggles for social justice, its Latino community centers, and most importantly its dwellers' brown bodies."[33] While this oversimplifies the neighborhood's racial divides, residents' wealth, privilege, and race often map onto the neighborhood's landscapes. Today amenities for the wealthy line both Mission and Twenty-Fourth Streets, two of the neighborhood's most significant Latino strongholds.

FIG. 15. Eviction mural with offerings laid in front of it at Twenty-Fourth and Bryant in the Mission, 2013. The mural recognizes neighborhood changes by depicting the death of "La Mision" (The Mission). Courtesy Naomi Fiss.

Gentrification in the Mission has also transformed the neighborhood's culture. Guillermo Gómez-Peña, an artist and cultural commentator, reflects on these changes: "I see them every day, the hordes of iPad and iPhone texting zombies, oblivious to us and our lives, our inspirations and tribulations.... I see them in my building and on the street, invading the city with an attitude of unchecked entitlement, taking over every square inch and squeezing out the last drops of otherness."[34] Tech workers' obliviousness to a shared sense of community in the Latino Mission has created a cultural clash. New generations' reliance on technology and their desire to consume authentic experiences have led them to rely on apps for finding a sense of community and locating social services. Who needs a bus when you can take an Uber? Why do you need local cultural amenities when you use an app to get anywhere in the city? Late twentieth- and early twenty-first-century Mission Latinos fought to build a community to provide local systems of support, but gentrifiers became less and less reliant on these older systems of community.

These patterns of gentrification and urban change can be witnessed throughout the West in the late twentieth and early twenty-first centuries. The tech industry has shaped gentrification in the West starting as early as the 1980s and 1990s.[35] Since then tech workers' high wages have driven up the cost of living around them, and skyrocketing rent prices have led to displacement. Tech workers' entitlement and desire for luxury amenities have fueled tensions among neighborhood residents in the Mission, in addition to other western cities, including Seattle and Austin.[36] Gentrification, however, looks very different in each of these cities. The Mission stands out from other gentrification narratives because its Latino and working-class populations have not abandoned the neighborhood. In fact the fight has continued there for more than forty years now. Comparative histories that explore the relationship between gentrification and the tech industry in the West could reveal variations in displacement and wealth as well as in the racial animosity that gentrification creates.

Racial difference is not the case in all neighborhoods facing gentrification. In some areas, like Boyle Heights in Los Angeles, residents face *gentefication* (a playful mashup of *gente*, or people, and gentrification that originated in 2007). Boyle Heights, a traditionally working-class Latino neighborhood, has recently faced gentrification by Generation X and millennial Latinos. *Gentefiers*, often college-educated, middle-class Latinos who grew up in this neighborhood, have returned to open businesses and revitalize the community. Like gentrification this economic shift can displace longtime residents. Despite negative consequences, *gentefiers* often have positive motives of neighborhood improvement and community engagement. One source notes, "Just up the block from Self Help Graphics [the other initial organizer of Day of the Dead processions in the United States] is Mr. Romero's coffee shop, its name meaning First Cup in Spanish, selling $4 lattes. Next door is Eastside Luv, a sleek bar that attracts younger patrons whom some call *Chipsters*, for Chicano hipsters."[37] These types of businesses are tailored to younger Latino residents. *Gentefication* is a complicated process that was first seen in western cities but has since spread to other Latino neighborhoods in the United States—like Chicago's Pilsen neighborhood—and is a process deserving of further study.

Our Mission, No Eviction: Protesting Displacement

From the late 1990s to the 2010s the Mission changed more quickly than ever as gentrification intensified evictions and displacements. Median home values in the Mission climbed from $223,800 in April 1996 to $962,200 in February 2014.[38] Rent rates also rose exponentially. Over this same period the Mission's Latino population shrunk from 54 percent of the total neighborhood population in 1990 to 39 percent in 2012.[39] The neighborhood was changing in ways that benefited the more affluent newcomers while pushing out those in rent-controlled and affordable housing.

In 2013 these changes reached Yañez and his family when he and his partner, Cynthia Wallis, received an eviction notice. At the time both Yañez and Wallis faced terminal cancer diagnoses. The owner planned to take the rental off the market, and so everyone in the building received eviction notices, including Yañez's ex-wife, Yolanda López, and their son, Rio, who also lived there. After their divorce in the early 1980s Yañez and López had raised their son together from separate units of this historic San Jose Avenue building.[40] As they all faced eviction in 2013 an irony emerged. Yañez, López, and others who had created the Latino Mission would be forced to leave it. The number of artists and creatives in the Mission dwindled. Yañez had counted almost two hundred artists living in the Mission in 1970 when the Galería first opened. By 2013 he could not even count twenty artists who remained.[41]

Evicting the artists who produced the neighborhood's colorful walls and vibrant culture had consequences. As Guillermo Gómez-Peña explained, "They are not only expelling the homeless and the gangbangers.... They are also expelling the performance artists, the poets, the muralists, the activists, the working-class families—all these wonderful urban tribes that made this neighborhood a very special neighborhood for decades." He continued, "One day ... they will wake up to an extremely unbearable ocean of sameness."[42] Yolanda López elaborated on the consequences of these evictions: "There's always been a flavor, a little bit of, a touch of rebellion in San Francisco, and that little beauty is going to be lost."[43]

Evictions to apartments under rent control, like that of Yañez and his family, forced longtime residents out of the neighborhood and the city. Yañez was paying about $450 in rent per month when he received his eviction notice. In a city with one of the highest costs of living in the country, he and his family would not be able to relocate nearby.[44] The loss of rent-controlled housing resulted in the process Gómez-Peña described, one in which the city lost its diversity, as well as its teachers and its garbage collectors, its artists and its cultural workers.

Many Latino residents have relied on rent control to remain in the Mission. Rent control in San Francisco protects tenants living in buildings built before 1980. With rent control policies rent prices can rise only minimally to reflect annual inflation. These policies allow sixteen "just cause" types of eviction.[45] Rent control is important to the Mission's artists and activists. Rio Yañez explained, "Rent control is what afforded my parents with the opportunity to live in this city and make art. Being an artist means they have no savings, no retirement, no health care. They live check to check. For their dedication to art, that's where they are. With elderly people like them, with limited income, this essentially makes them homeless."[46] Sergio Iantorno, the landlord of the building in which they lived, offered Yañez and López each between $11,000 and $13,000 for relocation. Rio Yañez explained, "There's nowhere they could go for that amount of money in San Francisco, and certainly not in the Mission.... They aren't looking for a huge buyout so that they can start a new life. They are in their seventies."[47] Like many, Yañez, Wallis, and López had few options for finding a new place to live in the Mission because of the high rent costs. Rent control was supposed to protect residents like them.

In contrast landlords and building owners despise rent control because it limits a building's profitability. With the Ellis Act, a 1985 state law, landlords could evict tenants in rent-controlled apartments by "going out of business," selling the building, or converting rental units into condos or Tenancies in Common.[48] Increasingly landlords have used the Ellis Act in rising real estate markets to dump unprofitable rent-controlled apartments by selling buildings to developers, converting multi-unit buildings into single-unit homes, or even re-renting units for higher rent despite prohibitions against re-rentals. Many Ellis Act evictions have taken place under new ownership of these buildings, and, because there are no limits to the number of buildings that one can take off the rental market, development companies continue to buy up old buildings, evict the residents, and convert the buildings into more profitable units for sale.[49] The Ellis Act enables real estate speculation while slashing rent control and tenant protections.

When buildings are "Ellised," or taken off the rental market, the city limits what owners can do with them. If owners convert units into rentals within five years of the evictions, the Ellis Act mandates that owners must rent at the same price the previous tenants paid. If they rent the units again within a ten-year period, previous tenants must receive an opportunity to return.[50] Despite these regulations the city's enforcement has been lax, and tenants have reported that building owners have ignored these restrictions, for example, by reopening before ten years have elapsed without offering former tenants rental units. Even if an owner follows these mandates, typically residents have found a new residence by the time that they would be offered a rental in their old location.[51] Overall San Francisco and other California cities lack the means for diligent enforcement of the Ellis Act beyond initial evictions. There is little evidence as to whether this lack of enforcement is due to financial and personnel limitations or a conscious choice to promote real estate development. However without accountability through enforcement too often landlords re-rent units earlier or more expensively than permitted or convert units into Airbnbs in violation of the Ellis Act.[52]

The Ellis Act provides some limited protections to those being evicted. Landlords cannot do partial Ellis Act evictions—they must evict all residents of a building. The Ellis Act requires owners to provide evicted tenants with 120 days' notice to locate other housing arrangements and a year for seniors and disabled residents.[53] Landlords must also offer evicted tenants with funds for relocation. However many San Franciscans who have been Ellised note these inadequate accommodations prevent them from finding new rental accommodations within the city. For many losing rent-controlled apartments forces them to leave the city. Many have moved to Oakland or further into the East Bay, wherever they could locate affordable housing.[54]

Most Ellis Act evictions cannot be stopped because the law leaves little room for subjectivity in appealing whether evictions meet the conditions specified by this law.[55] Although resistance is often futile, Yañez fought back. The neighborhood was changing, Yañez explained: "A lot of those artists in Clarion Alley that tourists come to see, no longer live in the Mission. It's cultural eviction." He argued, "Being a Latino artist, you have certain responsibilities to activism."[56] Committed to fighting cultural eviction, Yañez publicly expressed his discontent: "It's a matter of resistance. Techies have a different view of culture. It's a different phenomenon that is coming into San Francisco, and it's redefining culture and contribution."[57] René Yañez, along with his son, Rio, and Rio's mother, Yolanda López, made their plight visible through their art and activism, which provided them a platform to resist change in the neighborhood.

Yolanda López protested the inhumane process of eviction by creating art. Author Adriana Camarena joined López in March 2014 to make a collaborative installation, "Eviction Scene Investigation," using the paperwork of eviction.[58] López continued this style of activism in May 2014, when she and her son, Rio, held a "garage sale" at the Galería de la Raza, using art to protest eviction. Camarena noted, "Probably the most valuable piece in the Garage Sale . . . is the price sticker that reminds people that this is the eviction of two lifelong Mission artists: 'Yolanda López and Rio Yañez's Eviction Garage Sale.'"[59] This garage sale took place at the Galería, which was fitting because this place had served as a starting point and a hub for the artistic expression of this family and the larger Latino community of the Mission.[60]

Protest also extended to Día de los Muertos. Its rituals have long offered Mission residents spaces to reflect on issues from Central American political repression to AIDS in San Francisco. As Día de los Muertos grew in the 1990s, it also increasingly offered a space to comment on cultural, social, and demographic shifts in the Mission. Yañez curated "Rooms for the Dead" exhibits each year, starting in 1990 at the Mission Cultural Center. He divided the top floor into "a maze of twenty-nine private eight-by-eight-foot rooms, 'each containing a universe of creations, memories and reflections on life and death.'"[61] A different person curated each room with a different topic, theme, or vibe. These altars increasingly became, as Cordova describes, "more experimental, more multicultural, more installation-like, and more dramatic."[62]

By the 1990s the size of the procession grew from a few hundred to thousands. Regina Marchi, a scholar who has studied Día de los Muertos celebrations throughout the United States, notes the Mission hosts the nation's largest Día de los Muertos procession. With an estimated twenty thousand participants by the early 2000s, the celebration now includes "Aztec blessing rituals and danza groups, colorful banners, sidewalk altars, chalk art, giant skeleton puppets, Cuban Santería practitioners, and a Jamaican steel drum band on wheels."[63] During these years the procession changed as lines blurred between Halloween and Día de los Muertos, and the procession became more of a carnivalesque spectacle.

As it grew it lost its local intimacy. Marchi did extensive oral interviews with Latinos in San Francisco and beyond about their experiences with Día de los Muertos. She details these changes residents experienced:

> About half of the San Francisco Latinos I interviewed share the feelings of the following Chicana artist: "When René started the processions at Galería de la Raza, they were real. It was somber, sad, and beautiful, like the processions that happen in Mexico.... But in San Francisco, everyone who wasn't part of the tradition jumped in with their drums, jumped in with their caricatures, cartoons, skates, and puppets that have no meaning to the procession. So it turned into a kind of carnival. It has no meaning. Not in a real sense.... It's just cool and popular to be there."[64]

She quotes another Chicana artist: "People come [to the procession] from all over the Bay Area, which is a good thing, but... perhaps unintentionally when people like something, they begin to change the very essence of what it is. Something becomes very popular and very hip, but there is a way we can appreciate the essence without changing it."[65] With this growth Día de los Muertos in San Francisco transformed into an event with a large regional following. Efforts to protest eviction and displacement at the procession, however, marked an effort to reclaim Día de los Muertos as an event for a particular segment of the community.

The rise of the Mission's Día de los Muertos procession offered an extremely visible forum for residents to express their dissatisfaction with economic, social, and political changes in the neighborhood in the 2010s. Together the community fought for Yañez and others facing eviction during Día de los Muertos. On November 2, 2013, the group Our Mission No Eviction organized hundreds of Latino residents to march in the Día de los Muertos parade. They carried "a 7-foot lit-up *calavera* (skull) with the words 'Aqui estamos y no nos vamos' (We're here and we're not leaving)."[66] For years some Mission Latino residents had avoided Día de los Muertos in the Mission, frustrated it had become "a Bohemian Halloween parade."[67] However these protests brought some residents back in 2013. After avoiding the event for about fifteen years, Valencia Street resident Nancy Obregon returned because of "the muerte of our barrio."[68] While remembering and honoring loved ones who had passed, participants also mourned the cultural death of the Mission.

This Día de los Muertos protest followed Our Mission No Eviction's inaugural rally on October 12, 2013, where more than four hundred people marched down Twenty-Fourth Street. Robert Hernandez, a longtime Mission activist and cultural worker, Erick Arguello, president of the Lower Twenty-Fourth Street Merchants and Neighbors Association, and Jose Carrasco, a youth services manager at the Good Samaritan Family Resource Center, founded Our Mission No Eviction in 2013 in response to rising concerns about displacement in the neighborhood.[69] During this rally approximately twenty speakers argued for affordable housing, better protections for tenants' rights, and more sensitivity to racial relations.[70]

From their earliest years both the Galería de la Raza and Día de los Muertos have offered Mission residents a platform to reflect on

FIG. 16. René Yañez and his son, Rio, at the November 2, 2013, Day of the Dead procession. Courtesy Shane Menez and El Tecolote.

political issues in the United States and Latin America.[71] Altars have long provided a platform for political and social commentary on death and social inequities including gang violence, border crossing deaths, pesticide poisoning in farm workers, and police violence.[72] Within this framework of using art and culture to resist, it makes sense that the 2013 and 2014 Día de los Muertos events focused on issues of eviction, gentrification, and safety within the Mission community.

In a 2017 interview René Yañez explains that part of the appeal of Día de los Muertos is its potential as a platform for political commentary and resistance: "You can make fun of politicians and current events."[73] This satiric tradition goes back to José Guadalupe Posada, a Mexican printmaker, political cartoonist, and satirist, who is most known for La Catrina, a skeleton image that has become an icon of Día de los Muertos. La Catrina, Mexican museum curator David de la Torre explained, reminds us, "Death brings this neutralizing force; everyone is equal in the end. Sometimes people have to be reminded."[74] Death, from remembering the dead to reflecting on la muerte de la Mision, remains a constant in these Día de los Muertos rituals.

In 2014 René and Rio Yañez co-curated their ninth Día de los Muertos exhibit at SOMArts's Cultural Center. The exhibit, "Visions at Twilight," blended culture and politics to celebrate death and creatively "spark dialogue about controversial issues within their community."[75] The exhibit tackled difficult issues including displacement by gentrification and evictions and institutionalized police violence, featuring an exhibit dedicated to Alejandro Nieto, a twenty-eight-year-old Latino killed by the San Francisco Police Department in 2014. But the father-son pair saw hope in mourning the loss of their culture, their homes, and their community, as Rio explained, "Some [of these pieces] are very mournful, but it's also the reason why we are presenting this, the reason we are pushing back is because there is some form of hope that we can make a change here."[76] Opening space for conversation and pushing against social and political boundaries is typical of the work of both René and Rio.

Beyond their curated Rooms of the Dead, other 2014 Día de Los Muertos events in the neighborhood mourned the changing Mission. From protests to Día de los Muertos exhibits, residents tried to come to terms with the changes taking place. Martina Ayala curated an exhibit entitled "La Llorona: Llanto de vida y muerte en el Distrito de la Misión" (La Llorona: Weeping for the Life and Death of the Mission District), which featured work by more than seventy local artists in forty-two altars. Ayala believed "people needed a public place where they could come and mourn for the death of their community, and we are using the celebration to celebrate life and death and to reclaim our culture."[77] Some artists paired activism and art clearly in their work. Local artist Luis Vasquez Gomez's altar, Mad Zillion, showed the impacts of gentrification on residents. In this interactive piece visitors could write letters to the mayor and planning commission about the impact of gentrification.[78] While not everyone connected Día de los Muertos and the tense sociopolitical situation in the Mission, the ritual's artistic forms provided cultural spaces for resisting change and reflecting on loss.

This in some ways is a truly western story. Yañez and the Mission echo Wests of the past as displacement has removed people selectively, boom and bust cycles have produced explosions of wealth, and racial and economic disparities have resulted in dramatic inequalities throughout the region. In addition Hal Rothman's West resounds throughout these spaces. Rothman showed how economic growth and consumption led to the displacement of longtime residents throughout the West.[79] Gentrifiers' obsession with authentic spaces similarly has raised the cost of living, forcing locals out. Just as service workers could not live where they worked in ski resorts and tourist spaces of the West, so too were artists, activists, and laborers pushed out of the Mission. While initially places like San Francisco and Park City, Utah, may not look much alike, they share problems created when places cultivate amenities for the wealthy without protecting low-cost housing for residents who preceded the economic boom. Further research into tech booms and the gentrification that often follows in western cities will enable rich points of comparison between contemporary examples of tech booms and gentrification. Also such studies will show connections between contemporary examples and eighteenth- through twentieth-century examples of boom and bust, economic investment and speculation, and the creation of amenity systems for the wealthy. Because these twenty-first-century narratives of gentrification and displacement are not new but rather echo Wests long gone, further study merits attention from scholars and community members alike.

The Fight Rages On

Despite efforts to advocate against Ellis Act evictions and protect the Mission's Latinidad, death and eviction won out this time. Cynthia Wallis, Yañez's partner, died in 2016. After producing several final provocative art exhibitions in 2017 and 2018, Yañez died in May 2018.[80] Rio Yañez moved from the neighborhood as well. Ultimately none of this activism changed the family's story, but it did make the problems of gentrification and displacement more visible at local, regional, and national levels. As of 2019 residents continue to fight evictions in the neighborhood, and the Anti-Eviction Mapping Project combines with other efforts to record and publicize the injustices faced by local residents. Advocacy efforts to fight Ellis Act evictions along with calls to change the Ellis Act and better monitor its imple-

FIG. 17. Community members built an altar in front of the SOMArts Cultural Center to remember Yañez after his death in 2018. Courtesy Alicia Cruz.

mentation continue as well. This fight between gentrifiers, Latino and working-class residents, and real estate moguls has been neither short nor tidy. It still rages on.

In June 2018 the Galería de la Raza learned that they too faced eviction after their property owner announced a rent increase from $3,127 a month to $6,200 a month, despite the Galería's forty-six-year tenancy in this two-storefront gallery space. Even with the Galería's attempts to compromise—paying a higher rent and contributing to building renovations—they could not protect the Galería's tenancy on Twenty-Fourth Street. Rio Yañez mourned the loss of this space:

> I've been struggling with so many intense emotions about Galería de la Raza being forced from its home of almost five decades. The Galería was my dad's first child, my big brother whose floors I learned to walk on, whose walls helped form my identity, and whose community has supported myself and other artists for generations. I am devastated that within months of my dad's passing that this space he helped create is being taken from a community that needs it now more than ever. This loss is so personal to me but I know it is for so many others as well.[81]

As of December 2018 the Galería found a temporary home on Valencia Street, with plans to move into the ground floor of an affordable housing complex being built by the Mission Economic Development Agency. The Galería's displacement followed in the wake of several evictions of longtime Mission Latino businesses, including the sixty-seven-year-old La Victoria bakery, also on Twenty-Fourth Street.[82] As of 2019 evictions in the neighborhood, even on Twenty-Fourth Street in the heart of the Mission, do not slow as the cost of living and this speculative real estate market continue to grow. Although the tech industry, gentrifiers, and real estate speculators refuse to back down, resistance against these exploitative changes continues. As Ani Rivera, director of the Galería, proclaimed, "Whatever happens, Galería de la Raza will not go away. . . . Be bold, be creative, and above all, be fabulous."[83] Through it all, the Galería, the Yañez family, and many others have maintained hope for the continuance of a Latino Mission, and the art and culture that help define it, through continued adaptation by the community. After all, change, like death, is inevitable.

Notes

1. Julian Mark and Lydia Chavez, "A Tribute to René Yañez, an Artist Who Never Got Old," *Mission Local*, July 4, 2018, https://missionlocal.org/2018/07/a-tribute-to-rene-yanez-an-artist-who-never-got-old/.

2. Godfrey, *Neighborhoods in Transition*, 113.

3. See Wieck, "Contesting the Mission."

4. Although between fifteen to twenty-five men founded the Galería, Yañez and Maradiaga became the two responsible for running it. Cordova, *The Heart of the Mission*, 83, 85.

5. Ryan Kost, "How Galería Founder René Yañez Helped Give the Mission Its Artistic Soul," SF*Chronicle*, January 28, 2018, https://www.sfchronicle.com/art/article/Gal-ria-founder-Ren-Ya-ez-still-watching-his-12531407.php.

6. Kost, "How Galería Founder René Yañez Helped," SF*Chronicle*, January 28, 2018.

7. "Defining La Raza," *Atlantic*, May 29, 2009, https://www.theatlantic.com/daily-dish/archive/2009/05/defining-la-raza/201238/. See Oboler, *Ethnic Labels, Latino Lives*, for more on Latino-related terminology.

8. Cordova, *The Heart of the Mission*, 86–87.

9. Ybarra-Frausto, "The Legacy," 2.

10. Ybarra-Frausto, "The Legacy," 1.

11. At this time most art museums and galleries celebrated traditional art produced in particular styles rather than seeking out diverse artists and art forms. Cordova, *The Heart of the Mission*, 85; "About Galería de la Raza," Galería de la Raza, accessed March 11, 2019, http://www.galeriadelaraza.org/eng/about/index.php.

12. Kost, "How Galería Founder René Yañez Helped," SF*Chronicle*, January 28, 2018.

13. Ybarra-Frausto, "The Legacy," 4.

14. Cordova, *The Heart of the Mission*, 90.

15. Marchi, "Hybridity and Authenticity," 272.

16. Laura Waxmann, "Day of the Dead: Local Artists Mourn Loss of Life, Culture," *El Tecolote*, October 22, 2014, http://eltecolote.org/content/en/features/day-of-dead-exhibit-blend-tradition-with-current-events/. Despite Casa Hispana de Bellas Artes earlier hosting small, private Día de los Muertos celebrations, Cary Cordova posits that this has been largely forgotten because the Galería's events were so much more visible. Cordova, *The Heart of the Mission*, 209, 213.

17. Marchi, "Hybridity and Authenticity," 281.

18. "René Yañez on Day of the Dead," Shaping San Francisco, Internet Archive, 2017, http://archive.org/details/ReneYanezOnDayOfTheDead.

19. Cordova, *The Heart of the Mission*, 207; "René Yañez on Day of the Dead," Shaping San Francisco.

20. Marchi, "Hybridity and Authenticity," 280.

21. Marchi, "Hybridity and Authenticity," 279; Marchi, *Day of the Dead*, 39–50.

22. Marchi, "Hybridity and Authenticity," 282.

23. Waxmann, "Day of the Dead: Local Artists Mourn," *El Tecolote*, October 22, 2014.

24. Marchi, "Hybridity and Authenticity," 278.

25. See Wieck, "Contesting the Mission"; Cordova, *The Heart of the Mission*; Marchi, *Day of the Dead*.

26. Lynn Ludlow and Mireya Navarro, "Changes Simmer in an Old Potpourri," *San Francisco Examiner*, October 23, 1981, *San Francisco Examiner* clippings, San Francisco Public Library.

27. "Anglo Professionals Move In," *El Tecolote*, July 1978, 4–5. *El Tecolote* (The Owl) began as a four-page, biweekly, bilingual publication produced in a La Raza Journalism class at San Francisco State in 1970. It later moved to the Mission and produced one to two issues per month. Wieck, "Contesting the Mission," 29–126.

28. "Anglo Professionals Move In," *El Tecolote*, July 1978.

29. Lees, "A Reappraisal of Gentrification," 398.

30. Zoë Corbyn, "Is San Francisco Losing Its Soul?," *Observer*, February 23, 2014, https://www.theguardian.com/world/2014/feb/23/is-san-francisco-losing-its-soul.

31. Janelle Bitker, "Mission Pie Becomes the Latest Closure to Break San Francisco's Heart," *San Francisco Chronicle*, June 19, 2019, https://www.sfchronicle.com/food/article/Mission-Pie-becomes-the-latest-closure-to-break-14008400.php; J. K. Dineen, "Longtime Mission Cultural Spot Galería de la Raza in Danger of Losing Space," *San Francisco Chronicle*, October 29, 2018, https://www.sfchronicle.com/realestate/article/Longtime-Mission-cultural-spot-Galer-a-de-la-13346029.php?.

32. Opillard, "Resisting the Politics of Displacement," 7.

33. Opillard, "Resisting the Politics of Displacement," 7.

34. Peter Hernandez, "Protest against Gentrification Erupts in the Mission," *El Tecolote*, October 15, 2013, http://eltecolote.org/content/news/protest-against-gentrification-erupts-in-the-mission/.

35. See Leslie and Karafantis chapter herein, "Westworld: Life on the High-Tech Frontier."

36. For example, see Leanna Garfield, "Photos Show How Seattle's Favorite Businesses Vanished after Amazon Showed Up," *Business Insider*, February 20, 2018, https://www.businessinsider.com/amazon-hq2-vanishing-seattle-shows-how-the-city-is-gentrifying-2018-2; Richard Reed, "Seattle Takes a Small Step against Gentrification," *Los Angeles Times*, April 16, 2019, https://www.latimes.com/nation/la-na-seattle-housing-gentrification-tech-boom-20190416-story.html; Nicole Karlis, "Apple's Plans for $1 Billion Austin Campus May Throw Gas on a Gentrification Fire," *Salon*, December 13, 2018, https://www.salon.com/2018/12/13/apples-plans-for-1-billion-austin-campus-may-throw-gas-on-a-gentrification-fire/; Brandon Formby, "Report Says Gentrification Threatens to Displace Austin's Low-Income Residents, Communities of Color," *Texas Tribune*, September 18, 2018, https://www.texastribune.org/2018/09/18/gentrification-threatens-austins-low-income-residents-and-communities-/.

37. Ludwig Hurtado, "What Happens When Latinx People Gentrify Latinx Communities," *Vice* (blog), January 31, 2019, https://www.vice.com/en_us/article/mbynkq/what-happens-when-latinx-people-gentrify-latinx-communities. See also Gustavo Arellano, "Can 'Chipsters' and Barrio Activists Find Common Ground?," *Los Angeles Times*, May 16, 2018, https://www.latimes.com/opinion/op-ed/la-oe-arellano-gentefication-20180516-story.html; Dianne Solis, "To Ease Gentrification Pain, Some Latinos Embrace 'Gentefication' to Preserve Culture," *Chicago Tribune*, accessed August 1, 2019, https://www.chicagotribune

.com/voice-it/ct-hoy-to-ease-gentrification-pain-some-latinos-embrace-gentefication-to-preserve-culture-20180214-story.html; Natalie Delgadillo, "Defining 'Gentefication' in Latino Neighborhoods," *CityLab*, August 15, 2016, http://www.citylab.com/housing/2016/08/defining-gentefication-in-latino-neighborhoods/495923/.

38. Statistics based on Zillow, reported in Suzanne Espinosa Solis, "Meet the Monarch of the Mission Who's Fighting Gentrification," sFGate, April 25, 2014, https://www.sfgate.com/news/article/Meet-the-monarch-of-the-Mission-who-s-fighting-5428478.php.

39. Solis, "Meet the Monarch," sFGate, April 25, 2014.

40. Heather Mack, "'Royalty' of the Mission Art Scene Faces Eviction," *Mission Local*, October 2, 2013, https://missionlocal.org/2013/10/royalty-of-the-mission-art-scene-faces-eviction/.

41. Janina Glasov, "No Room Left in San Francisco for an Artist Who Helped Make the Mission What [It] Is," *San Francisco Bay Guardian*, October 11, 2013, http://sfbgarchive.48hills.org/sfbgarchive/2013/10/11/no-room-left-san-francisco-artist-who-helped-make-mission-what/.

42. Erica Goode and Claire Cain Miller, "Backlash by the Bay: Tech Riches Alter a City," *New York Times*, October 19, 2018, https://www.nytimes.com/2013/11/25/us/backlash-by-the-bay-tech-riches-alter-a-city.html.

43. Goode and Miller, "Backlash by the Bay," *New York Times*, October 19, 2018.

44. Mack, "'Royalty' of the Mission," *Mission Local*, October 2, 2013.

45. "Rent Control," San Francisco Tenants Union, accessed June 1, 2019, https://www.sftu.org/rentcontrol/; Jessica Placzek, "Is Rent Control Working and Should We Have More or Less of It?," KQED, June 28, 2018, https://www.kqed.org/news/11677380/is-rent-control-working-and-should-we-have-more-or-less-of-it. On historic debates over rent control, see Randy Shaw, "1980–1991: Rent Control Wars," *FoundSF*, accessed March 10, 2019, http://www.foundsf.org/index.php?title=1980-1991:_RENT_CONTROL_WARS.

46. Mack, "'Royalty' of the Mission," *Mission Local*, October 2, 2013.

47. Mack, "'Royalty' of the Mission," *Mission Local*, October 2, 2013.

48. Ted Gullickson, "New Study Calls for Ellis Act Reform," *Beyond Chron*, February 17, 2005, http://beyondchron.org/new-study-calls-for-ellis-act-reform/.

49. Gullickson, "New Study Calls," *Beyond Chron*, February 17, 2005; Cynthia Fong, "The Ellis Act Does Not Make Sense," *San Francisco Examiner*, September 15, 2017, http://www.sfexaminer.com/ellis-act-not-make-sense/.

50. "Ellis Act Evictions," San Francisco Tenants Union, accessed March 8, 2019, https://www.sftu.org/ellis/.

51. Fong, "The Ellis Act Does Not Make Sense," *San Francisco Examiner*, September 15, 2017; Emily Alpert Reyes, "Tenants Got a Rare Chance to Come Back after Being Evicted—but Most Didn't," *Los Angeles Times*, September 17, 2018, https://www.latimes.com/local/lanow/la-me-ln-right-to-return-20180917-story.html.

52. Fong, "The Ellis Act Does Not Make Sense," *San Francisco Examiner*, September 15, 2017; Sean Lubbers, "The Ellis Act—Landlord Rights or Tenant Abuse?," *Foundations of Law and Society* (blog), December 7, 2016, https://foundationsoflawandsociety.wordpress.com/2016/12/07/the-ellis-act-landlord-rights-or-tenant-abuse/; Bridgette Webb, "Evicted Residents Vow to Keep Eye on Building," *Los Feliz Ledger*, May 14, 2015, http://www.losfelizledger.com/article/evicted-residents-vow-to-keep-eye-on-building/.

53. "Ellis Act Evictions," San Francisco Tenants Union.

54. Verma, Rinzler, and Zuk, "Rising House Costs and Re-Segregation in San Francisco."

55. Rarely do tenants succeed in appealing Ellis Act evictions and then usually only with the help of local legal aid organizations. Randy Shaw, "Ellis Eviction of Latino Seniors Stopped in SF's Mission's District," *Beyond Chron*, March 11, 2014, http://beyondchron.org/ellis-eviction-of-latino-seniors-stopped-in-sfs-missions-district/; Dominic Fracassa, "Noe Valley Woman 1st to Beat Ellis Act Eviction through Trial," *SFGate*, November 12, 2017, https://www.sfgate.com/bayarea/article/Noe-Valley-woman-1st-to-beat-Ellis-Act-eviction-12349346.php; Marivic Cabural, "San Francisco Reaches Deal to Stop Evictions at Mid-Market Street Building," *SFist*, February 19, 2019, https://sfist.com/2019/02/19/san-francisco-reaches-deal-to-stop-ellis-act-evictions-in-mid-market-street/.

56. "Benefit for Mission Artists Attracts Latino All Stars," *Mission Local*, October 26, 2013, https://missionlocal.org/2013/10/benefit-for-chicano-mission-artists-attracts-latino-all-stars/.

57. Waxmann, "Day of the Dead: Local Artists Mourn," *El Tecolote*, October 22, 2014.

58. Claire Weissbluth, "Artist Turns 'Paper Intimidation' of Eviction into Art," *Mission Local*, March 29, 2014, https://missionlocal.org/2014/03/artist-yolanda-lopez-turns-eviction-into-art/.

59. Lydia Chavez, "Eviction, Garage Sale, a Sense of Place," *Mission Local*, May 4, 2014, https://missionlocal.org/2014/05/eviction-garage-sale-a-sense-of-place/.

60. Chavez, "Eviction, Garage Sale, A Sense of Place," *Mission Local*, May 4, 2014.

61. Cordova, *The Heart of the Mission*, 227.

62. Cordova, *The Heart of the Mission*, 230.

63. Marchi, "Hybridity and Authenticity," 282.

64. Marchi, *Day of the Dead*, 107.

65. Marchi, *Day of the Dead*, 107.

66. Solis, "Meet the Monarch," *SFGate*, April 25, 2014.

67. Solis, "Meet the Monarch," *SFGate*, April 25, 2014.

68. Solis, "Meet the Monarch," *SFGate*, April 25, 2014.

69. Solis, "Meet the Monarch," *SFGate*, April 25, 2014.

70. Hernandez, "Protest against Gentrification Erupts in the Mission," *El Tecolote*, October 15, 2013.

71. Cordova, *The Heart of the Mission*, 88. The Galería de la Raza Archives at the University of California, Santa Barbara's California Ethnic and Multicultural Archives also reflect this commitment to featuring art that provided social and political commentary.

72. Marchi, "Hybridity and Authenticity," 283.

73. "René Yañez on Day of the Dead," Shaping San Francisco.

74. Christine Delsol, "La Catrina: Mexico's Grande Dame of Death," *SFGate*, October 25, 2011, https://www.sfgate.com/mexico/mexicomix/article/La-Catrina-Mexico-s-grande-dame-of-death-2318009.php.

75. Waxmann, "Day of the Dead: Local Artists Mourn," *El Tecolote*, October 22, 2014.

76. Waxmann, "Day of the Dead: Local Artists Mourn," *El Tecolote*, October 22, 2014.

77. Angélica Ekeke, "Community Honors Life and Death through Tradition," *El Tecolote*, October 26, 2013, http://eltecolote.org/content/arts_culture/community-honors-life-and-death-through-tradition/.

78. Ekeke, "Community Honors Life and Death through Tradition," *El Tecolote*, October 26, 2013.

79. See Rothman, *Devil's Bargains*.

80. Mark and Chavez, "A Tribute to René Yañez," *Mission Local*, July 4, 2018.

81. Rio Yañez, Facebook, October 29, 2018, https://www.facebook.com/photo.php?fbid=10157362609687573&set=a.54219552572&type=3&theater.

82. Dineen, "Longtime Mission Cultural Spot," *San Francisco Chronicle*, October 29, 2018; Julian Mark, "Evicted Galería de la Raza Lands on Valencia Street," *Mission Local*, December 21, 2018, https://missionlocal.org/2018/12/evicted-galeria-de-la-raza-lands-on-valencia-street/.

83. Ida Mojadad, "Galería de la Raza Faces Imminent Eviction after Failed Negotiations," sf *Weekly*, October 29, 2018, http://www.sfweekly.com/news/galeria-de-la-raza-faces-imminent-eviction-after-failed-negotiations/.

Bibliography

Cordova, Cary. *The Heart of the Mission: Latino Art and Politics in San Francisco*. Philadelphia: University of Pennsylvania Press, 2017.

Godfrey, Brian J. *Neighborhoods in Transition: The Making of San Francisco's Ethnic and Nonconformist Communities*. Berkeley: University of California Press, 1988.

Goldman, Alexandra. "The 'Google Shuttle Effect': Gentrification and San Francisco's Dot Com Boom 2.0." MA thesis, University of California, Berkeley, 2013.

Lees, Loretta. "A Reappraisal of Gentrification: Towards a 'Geography of Gentrification.'" *Progress in Human Geography* 24, no. 3 (2000): 389–408.

Leslie, Stuart W., and Layne R. Karafantis. "Westworld: Life on the High-Tech Frontier," in *The North American West in the Twenty-First Century*, edited by Brenden W. Rensink, herein. Lincoln: University of Nebraska Press, 2022.

Marchi, Regina M. *Day of the Dead in the USA: The Migration and Transformation of a Cultural Phenomenon*. New Brunswick NJ: Rutgers University Press, 2009.

Marchi, Regina M. "Hybridity and Authenticity in U.S. Day of the Dead Celebrations." *The Journal of American Folklore* 126, no. 501 (Summer 2013): 272–301.

Oboler, Suzanne. *Ethnic Labels, Latino Lives: Identity and the Politics of (Re)Presentation in the United States*. Minneapolis: University of Minnesota Press, 1995.

Opillard, Florian. "Resisting the Politics of Displacement in the San Francisco Bay Area: Anti-Gentrification Activism in the Tech Boom 2.0." *European Journal of American Studies* 10, no. 3 (2015).

Rothman, Hal K. *Devil's Bargains: Tourism in the Twentieth-Century American West*. Lawrence: University Press of Kansas, 2000.

Verma, Philip, Dan Rinzler, and Miriam Zuk. "Rising House Costs and Re-Segregation in San Francisco." University of California, Berkeley, Urban Displacement Project and the California Housing Partnership, n.d. http://www.urbandisplacement.org/sites/default/files/images/sf_final.pdf.

Wieck, Lindsey Passenger. "Contesting the Mission: The Cultural Politics of Gentrification in Postwar San Francisco." PhD diss., University of Notre Dame, 2016.

Ybarra-Frausto, Tomás. "The Legacy of La Galería de la Raza/Studio 24." Unpublished manuscript, n.d. International Center for the Arts of the Americas at the Museum of Fine Arts, Houston.

7

Agritourism as Land-Saving Action in the New West

JEFFREY M. WIDENER

In the *American West as Living Space*, Wallace Stegner wrote about the rapid urban expansion occurring throughout the region and the growth that included extensive encroachment onto farmlands. Stegner found western sentiment in the region at the time to be "what matters is here, now, the seizable opportunity," which he illustrated with a statement from a Silicon Valley executive: "We don't need any history.... What we need is more attention to our computers and the moves of the competition." Stegner wrote, "Habits persist. The hard, aggressive, single-minded energy that according to politicians made America great is demonstrated every day in resource raids and leveraged takeovers by entrepreneurs; and along with that competitive individualism and ruthlessness goes a rejection of any controlling past or tradition." There appeared to be no interest among conglomerates, Stegner noted, in talking to farmers in the Silicon Valley to determine ways the two opposing worlds might work together to preserve the places and lifeways in what was once the "fruit bowl of the world."[1]

As technology conglomerates, developers, and amenity migrants move into over-tapped regions, associated development typically sprawls across farmland. The competition for land and water resources, inequitable land-use policies that often do little to protect farmers, and an insatiable thirst for amenities that satisfy the desires of people not affiliated with agricultural industries are nothing new for the twenty-first-century American West. Environmental change, globalizing economies, technological improvements in natural resource extraction, and continued rapid urban development dominate nearly every corner of this quixotic region. Perhaps, however, they are even more paramount now than ever.[2]

Agriculture has played an imperative role in the shaping of the Euro-American settled American West and cannot be overlooked. How, then, might farmers navigate their industry as a sea of development takes place on their doorsteps? Those new and old to the agricultural industry, and especially those who operate on a smaller, industrial scale, must grapple with this question. In other words, how might they assure themselves that they will not go the way of the Silicon Valley? Recent growth of agritourism in Colorado's Grand Valley provides an intriguing case study on these very issues, and it offers potential answers to crises faced by agriculturists across the West.

Colorado's Grand Valley is a roughly thirty-mile stretch of prime farmland, made possible through several water reclamation projects in the Colorado River Valley on the state's Western Slope (see fig. 18). The region serves as a microcosm of the changes that are taking place in a rapidly growing twenty-first-century West. In this valley—especially its eastern end—agritourism is a leitmotif-in-action, aiding in the perseveration of the agricultural industry and its landscapes. Agritourism offers a unique opportunity in the Grand Valley. It provides educational experiences to participants conveying the value of local agriculture, the need to conserve water, and the importance of preserving prime agricultural land from development. Agritourism is also a boom for small-town economic development via its festivals and other traditional and innovative agritourism activities, providing an added amenity for tourists. But many local growers in the upper Grand Valley regard this inherent feature—education—as the most important element for ensuring the sustainability and preservation of their industry and the place and lifeway that they hold dear. While there is some contention among developers, local residents, community planners, and government officials, the survival of agriculture here looks promising compared to similar places in the American West. This chapter will showcase how local farmers, community members, and visitors in Colorado's Grand Valley are

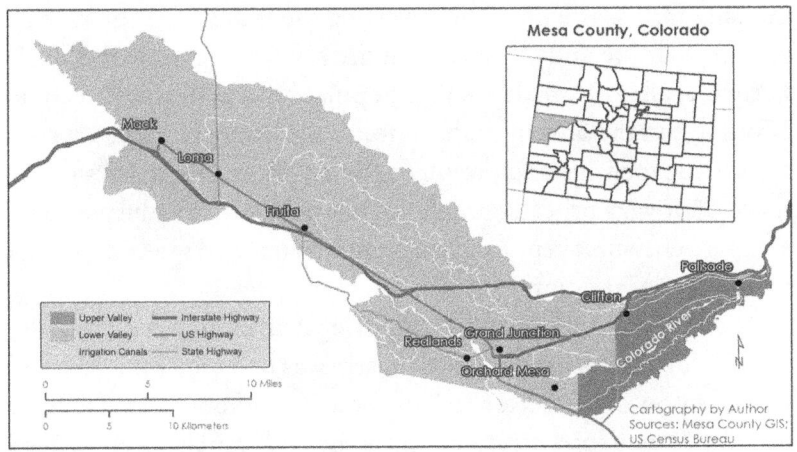

FIG. 18. Map of the Grand Valley marked by its lower and upper regions. Map by Jeffrey M. Widener.

maximizing the potential of the agricultural industry that is unique to the heritage of this precious region.

Agritourism in Colorado and the Grand Valley

Agritourism is a relatively new term for an old-fashioned activity: connecting travelers with agriculture in an "authentic" way, allowing them to discover "geographically distinctive food, drink and experience."[3] In 1872 a Colorado Springs newspaper reported, "There is a growing tendency to make Agricultural Fairs attractive to large crowds of sight-seers rather than instructive to farmers, and their success is measured by the number who are admitted to the grounds instead of by the actual effect which they have upon the cultivation of the soil or the improvement of stock."[4] In 1885 another eastern Colorado newspaper stated, "Your true tourist always likes to test the local specialties in food and drink, for without them he feels as if he had hardly known the country. Travelers always enjoy with an especial relish the antelope steak served at railway eating-houses in Colorado and western Kansas on this account."[5] In 1904 the publication *All About Grand Junction* noted that the town's "various Peach days and other festival occasions" helped "advertise the valley," and that the Grand Valley Fruit Fair Association provided "amusements . . .

in many forms, as a means of diverting the mind from the routine of every-day life and as a rest from the cares of regular vocations."[6] Early on railroads made visiting popular among those who could afford it, but the advent of the automobile began to make tourism a more inexpensive and popular activity.[7] The modern versions of these discovery processes include how agritourism educates people on twenty-first-century issues centered on food safety and water and land conservation.

According to a 2001 United States Department of Agriculture survey, the top reason people visited a farm was to "enjoy rural scenery." Other reasons were to learn "where food comes from," visit "family or friends," "watch/participate in farm activities," "purchase agricultural products," "pick fruit or produce," or "hunt and fish."[8] Colorado State University's (CSU) Cooperative Extension conducted a similar study in 2006 to explore agritourism specifically in Colorado. Researchers found that on-farm educational and nature experiences were the favorite type of agritourism activity, with food and culinary activities the second most popular.[9] In 2006 more than thirteen million people took part in agritourism activities, and the total economic impact for the state was $2.2 billion.[10] These researchers, however, found that the Colorado Tourism Office (CTO) was not doing as much as might have been done for agritourism: "They do not typically consider agritourism to be a part of tourism, and developing this partnership remains a challenge for Colorado agritourism, but a challenge worth pursuing given that CTO has a lot of marketing resources and expertise to share."[11] Since then CTO has changed its ways.

In 2014 Laura Grey, director of Heritage and Agritourism for the CTO, explained, "Farmers and ranchers have no idea how fascinated urban America is in what they do. Even the most basic things that a farmer can do, like irrigation, is fascinating. People want to come and they want to pay them to know about this." Grey wanted to get the word out: "I think the outside world has no idea how aggie we are. I really don't. We have huge numbers nationally in ag and I don't even think Coloradans are aware of that." Her efforts worked. Colorado ranked fourth in the nation in agritourism revenue in the early 2010s.[12]

According to a study authorized by CTO that looked at travel in Colorado from 1996 to 2012, Mesa County is its own travel district. Mesa County has a 1.6 percent share of the state's total overnight stay earnings, largely because of the agritourism industry, which is mainly a summer and fall activity—seasons that correspond to crop growing and harvesting. As researchers pointed out, however, opportunities exist even in winter for agritourism activities. Colorado economists argued that agritourism activities during winter months could serve as "diversions for those accompanying skiers, but who do not ski, such as wine tastings, sleigh or horseback rides, snowmobile excursions and holiday farm or ranch getaways."[13] In the Grand Valley small business owners recognize that they have two or three seasons to make the most of their attractions and work hard to develop recreation-oriented opportunities that go "hand-in-hand with agritourism."[14]

The Colorado Department of Agriculture and the CSU extension have worked together for several years, and the CTO works with these organizations to promote and help develop agritourism events. They have led initiatives that include having dedicated monies from the statewide unclaimed property fund go toward marketing agritourism, which makes Colorado one of the few states to have specific funding for promoting agritourism.[15] They also worked together to put in place a three-year "Come to Life" action plan for promoting agritourism with the stated goal of rural economic development. The plan defined agritourism as "the practice of engaging in activities, events, and services that have been provided to consumers for recreational, entertainment, or educational purposes at a farm, ranch, or other agricultural, horticultural, or agribusiness operation in order to allow consumers to experience, learn about, and participate in various facets of agricultural industry, culinary pursuits, natural resources, and heritage."[16] The plan's guiding objectives are: 1) putting a spotlight on Colorado agritourism businesses that are visitor ready; 2) stimulating the development of fresh and new high-quality agritourism experiences for travelers; and 3) supporting regional clusters of businesses that are working together to develop and promote agritourism.[17]

Colorado sorts its agritourism activities into three general classifications: on-farm or ranch, food-based, and farm or ranch heritage and history activities.[18] As shown by the surveys mentioned, people are more interested than ever in where their food comes from and in the process of growing food. A writer for the *Daily Sentinel* made the point that people are "no longer content to impersonally pick up a box of peaches or a half-bushel of green beans, [and] conscientious consumers are researching farms, engaging farmers and touring and dining in their orchards. If they can't get the dirt underneath their fingernails themselves, they at least want to see for themselves how it gets there." They can have these experiences in a variety of ways, and Colorado's Grand Valley is one region that offers a little bit of everything in the way of agritourism activities. As Carol Zadrozny of Z's Orchards in Palisade puts it, "Agritourism places have their own niches. . . . For High Country [Orchards], you see high-tech, computer-driven stuff. When you go to Alida's [Fruits], you get to talk to Farmer Bob [Helmer]. If you come to Z's, it's like going back to Grandma and Grandpa's farm."[19]

The "Agri-Tourism" link on the Palisade Chamber of Commerce website touts "apples, apricots, cherries, pears, plums, melons, chili peppers, heirloom tomatoes, herbs and more" grown in the area. One can also read that Palisade is the wine capital of Colorado:

Palisade's agricultural businesses offer a great opportunity to learn firsthand how fruit, wine and farm products are grown from the ground up, then prepared and sent to market. Take your pick of tours: orchards and farms, vineyards and wineries, brewery or distillery. Indoor tours of wineries, distillery and brewery operations capture the craftsmanship of beverage-making. In addition, you can learn about lavender uses, milling alpaca wool, hops processing, packing ripe peaches, conventional and organic orchards, packaged fruit producers, fruit stands, and vineyards brimming with an assortment of wine grapes.[20]

Town planners said, "The overall cultural belief system in Palisade is that Palisade is an ag center and that people value the ag industry," and the scope and the variety of the offerings support that assessment.[21] As such Palisade presents a venue for exploring agritourism

FIG. 19. Palisade Peach Festival, August 2012. Photograph by Jeffrey M. Widener.

landscapes that represent the work being done by committed farmers and supportive townspeople in Colorado's upper Grand Valley.

Three Seasons of Upper Grand Valley Festivals

The upper Valley has a lot to celebrate, and its festivals do a good job of publicizing its agricultural attractions. While the Palisade Peach Festival and Colorado Mountain Winefest are the most well-known festivals that take place in the Grand Valley, the region is now hosting several farm-product festivals during the spring, summer, and fall that are growing in popularity (see table 1). Notably the Palisade Chamber of Commerce made a deliberate effort to "weave agritourism into its festivals.... Each festival schedule lists local orchards and farms open for tours that day." Grand Junction Downtown Development Authority spokeswoman Kathy Dirks noted that many places, including her city, benefit from the festivals, "especially the businesses that actively seek to get people in" during them. Grand Junction Visitor and Convention Bureau spokeswoman Jennifer Grossheim-Harris said they encourage new festivals, and they encourage them to be more than one day so that the hotels will benefit too.[22] These festivals not only significantly help the Palisade and Grand Valley communities financially, they also contribute in an important and entertaining way to educating the general public on the importance of agriculture to this fruitful region.

Table 1. Festivals Held in the Upper Grand Valley

Month	Festival	Date Established
January	—	—
February	—	—
March	—	—
April	Palisade International Honey Bee Festival	2010
April	Barrel Into Spring (Wine Tasting, also held in May)	2012
May	Grand Valley Bank Brews & Cruise Festival	2014
June	Palisade Bluegrass Festival	2008
July	Lavender Festival	2011
August	Palisade Peach Festival	1890
September	Colorado Mountain Winefest	1992
October	Quilt and Fiber Art Festival	2014
October	Palisade Fall Harvest Market	2018
November	Blue Pig Art Gallery's Art & Chocolate Walk	2008
December	Olde Fashioned Christmas	"Always"

In August the most famous and historic festival in the Grand Valley takes place—the Palisade Peach Festival. Grand Junction held its first annual Peach Day festival in 1890.[23] Traditionally the festival took place in September, celebrating the end of the peach harvest, as farmers used to only grow one variety of peach, Elbertas.[24] Since the 1960s the festival has occurred in early to mid-August. Although most growers are in the middle of picking their peach crop, visitors can see the working agricultural landscapes. Renee Herman noted the significance of the Peach Festival to the region: "It's one of our biggest revenues. . . . And that's what keeps Palisade, and, I think, the Junction area going" (see fig. 19).[25]

Peach Fest has the highest attendance of the festivals. Some fourteen thousand people attended the 2013 Peach Festival, but more recent years have seen totals surpassing the fifteen-thousand mark.[26] Events take place over four days and include a peach recipe contest, baseball game, Biggest Beauty Peach Contest, parade, live music, peach-eating contest, games, coloring contest at the "Jake's Jungle" children's area, pancake breakfast, free ice cream social, walking tours, the Palisade Peach Plunge down the Colorado River, two Feast in the Fields dinners, the Bag Jump, the crowning of the Peach Queen and the naming of the Town Grouch, and opportunities to view merchandise from numerous vendors.[27] Because of the good 2014 peach crop, planners hoped to include a drawing for a basket of peaches every half hour during the Saturday festival. The previous year, the drawings had been limited to once per hour. The price of admission to the main event, the Saturday festival, was five dollars.[28]

Palisade also hosts Colorado Mountain Winefest in September during the grape harvest, which, in terms of tourism revenue generated for the Grand Valley, is the biggest festival of the year—with an economic impact of around $750,000 to $1 million.[29] It started in 1992 in Veterans Memorial Park in Palisade with five wineries and an attendance of about five hundred.[30] In 2012 Palisade was ninth on the list of the top U.S. wine destinations on Tripadvisor's "2012 Travelers' Choice Wine Destination List."[31] In 2017 *USA Today* named Colorado Mountain Winefest the best wine festival in the nation.[32] Now the four-day destination event is large enough to take place in Riverbend Park. The festival requires the assistance of about three to four hundred volunteers who cater to the six thousand-plus attendees who represent several countries and nearly every U.S. state. Winefest includes cooking demonstrations, live performances, arts and crafts, locally made ciders, and wines.[33] The fifty-plus Colorado wineries that take part in the festival offer well over four hundred different wines for sampling.

Besides residents working hard just to get the word out, several pieces of important legislation have helped the industry and the festival over the years. In 1990 state politicians enacted the Colorado Wine Industry Development Act, creating "a continuously appropriated funding stream from a penny per liter excise tax on all wine sold in the state, an additional $0.01-$0.05 per liter sliding scale excise tax on wine produced by Colorado wineries, and $10 per ton on grapes and other produce used by Colorado wineries to make wine." In the last few years funds have amounted to more than $600,000 per year. One-third of the money generated each year goes toward research and another third goes toward promoting the industry. Doug Caskey, executive director of the Colorado Wine Industry Development Board (CWIDB), called this legislation "the single event that moved Colorado's wine industry further ahead of the other Four Corner states."[34] Caskey also lauded the work of Ron Binz, a former leader of the CWIDB, and former state senator Ron Teck in helping with appropriate legislation. In the late 1990s lawmakers raised a question about the legality of allowing "consumers to carry wine samples from booth to booth." According to Caskey, Binz "drafted a very strong bill that created the wine festival permit within the Colorado Liquor Code, CRS 12-47-403.5, allowing multiple wineries to share a single permit for festival premises as well as addressing liability issues. This allows them to put on all of the events that we have come to love" (see fig. 20).[35] A few years after that there was a question about whether the Colorado Association for Viticulture and Enology (CAVE), a nonprofit trade association, could legally sell "tickets to an event licensed by commercial, independent wineries." Caskey said that Senator Teck "introduced a bill within the last few weeks of the session that allows a nonprofit organization to get a special events permit and sell tickets for happenings that are co-located with the premises of a wine festival permit. As the bill was introduced at the last possible minute, it may have been one of the fastest passed pieces of legislation on record, all thanks to the strong support of then Sen. Ron Teck."[36]

Other activities associated with Winefest include learning about food and wine pairings firsthand at local restaurants, a comparative wine tasting at Palisade's Wine Country Inn, a chocolate and wine

FIG. 20. Colorado Mountain Winefest, 2012. Photograph by Jeffrey M. Widener.

tasting event also held at the inn, and a day of winery tours. Visitors have opportunities to learn about "Colorado's unique terroir," discover common aromas of wines, learn specifics about "Navigating Colorado Wine Country," and even participate in an "introduction to grape growing."[37] One of the highlights is the grape stomp event, for which Talbott Farms donated six hundred pounds of grapes in 2013.[38] The cost of admission to the main festival in 2014 was forty-five dollars for wine tasters and twenty-five dollars for nondrinkers.[39] Tickets in 2019 ranged between $15 and $250, with one-day admission rounding out to $65.

Colorado Mountain Winefest also features a bicycle event. The Tour de Vineyards began in 1993 with about three hundred bicyclists. In 2013 more than eight hundred riders represented eleven states, with 10 percent more female riders than male. For 2014 the event fee for the twenty-five-mile ride was fifty-five dollars and that included a T-shirt, some peaches, and a brunch after the ride.[40]

The proceeds of this festival support much of the work of CAVE, particularly its annual regional trade conference.[41] Caskey believes "the most successful way to convert to drink Colorado wines is to taste it. The Winefest is the best place to go for it, and it's a great event for the growing industry."[42] Certified sommelier and noted wine writer Ben Weinberg said, "I highly recommend you take this unique opportunity to taste Colorado's wines."[43] City planners Rebecca Levy and Richard Sales call Winefest "a great asset to the community" and believe it is helping the Grand Valley get a "stay crowd." Levy and Sales noted that people often book their rooms for the next year before they leave town.[44]

Traditional and Emerging Agritourism Landscapes

While festivals bring large numbers of visitors to the valley, traditional agritourism landscapes are also very popular attractions for locals and outsiders, including u-picks (one of the oldest types of on-farm agritourism activities), farm tours, roadside produce stands, and farmers markets.[45] Newer agritourism landscapes in the upper Valley consist of the Colorado Fruit and Wine Byway, the Palisade Brewery, Palisade's Peach Street Distillers, a meadery, alpaca farms, lavender farms and shops, and, of course, several wineries.

In the upper Valley a few growers allow visitors to pick their products on their own. Mel Rettig is one. His parents had a u-pick on the farm when they managed it, and Rettig wanted to keep the tradition. Rettig has had his for about a decade, and u-pickers primarily come in to pick his tomatoes and peppers. At the time of our talk, which was before the new liability legislation, Rettig admitted that he was "always worried about the liability." Our talk was also a few days after the arrest of the Jensen brothers from Holly, Colorado, near Rocky Ford on the Front Range, for the 2011 cantaloupe-sourced listeria outbreak. This was one of the worst foodborne illness occurrences in U.S. history, so he was referring to that type of danger too. He told me he hoped his customers will continue to have "common sense" about personal safety and food safety. "The best we can do is do all we can to minimize problems," Rettig maintained.[46]

Bruce Talbott, however, explained that Talbott Farms no longer allows u-pickers in their orchards—participants too often caused damage to the fruit, the trees, and their infrastructure. They squeezed the peaches too hard and bruised them, they snapped branches when trying to reach the higher fruit, and they stepped on the irrigation systems, breaking sprinkler heads and lines. For the Talbotts "it's just not worth it to explore agritourism" in that on-farm sense. The Talbotts do, however, have a store on the east side of their packing shed in which they sell their fresh fruits, apple juice, and ciders.[47]

Just as legislation helped the wine industry, there was a need for additional legislation to help the agritourism industry. Farmers interested in having agritourism activities have had to worry about liability issues. People can get hurt when they come on a property and participate in activities that get their hands dirty. Yet this is one of the points of agritourism—providing hands-on experiences.

Carol Zadrozny of Z's Orchard, for example, was "ready to capitalize on the growing interest in food." Carol added a commercial kitchen so that visitors would be able to not only pick their own food but also cook a meal on site. Carol soon found out her insurance company did not like this idea because of the potential for injury for which she would be liable. At the time Zadrozny maintained that a lawsuit could easily put them out of business.[48] She will always need to have insurance, of course, but she can now feel more comfortable about offering farm-to-table activities and her agri-tours that highlight their operation.

In June 2014 Colorado governor John Hickenlooper signed HB 1280, which reworked previous laws protecting farmers by limiting liability for accidents related to tourism activities to protecting them in "agricultural recreation activities" or agritourism activities.[49] Essentially HB 1280 "enhances civil liability protections for farms, ranches and other rural properties that offer tourist activities as a way to supplement their agricultural income" by giving farmers "additional protections against lawsuits if they post a sign regarding the risks of the activities and get participants in activities like horse riding to sign a statement." The CTO helped warrant the bill, believing that the piece of legislation would further enable a budding industry. Republican Rep. Tim Dore stated that he believes the new bill "will help the agritourism industry grow in Colorado," calling agritourism a "valuable economic driver" in rural areas of the state. "Businesses will be able to have the security they need to expand and the piece [sic] of mind to participate in the agritourism activities," added Dore.[50]

A variety of other activities are available for agritourists who want to experience agritourism and purchase fruits, vegetables, wines, and value-added Grand Valley products. Wineries, with their tasting rooms and product/gift shops, also bring in people for concerts, meetings, weddings, birthday parties, and classes. Many wineries, the meadery, the Palisade Brewery, and the Peach Street Distillers—which offers peach and pear brandy, Jackelope Gin, and Goat Artisan Vodka—are open for business all year.[51] There are about eighteen upper Valley fruit stands noted on the Colorado Fruit and Wine Byway map; however, the list of those who paid to get on that map does not accurately portray the true number of stands that dot the landscape depending on the time of year.[52] Some fruit stands are in historic packing sheds. Others take up a small amount of square footage in larger, modern-day packing sheds as the Talbotts do with their Mountain Gold products. Some operate stands located off their farm property such as Alida's Fruits. This stand uses locally grown fruits to manufacture value-added products such as jams, jellies, syrups, and salsas. These are made in Palisade and sold along with fresh fruit and vegetables at retail outlets in downtown Grand Junction and East Orchard Mesa and through an online store. The business receives customers from all fifty states and many international visitors according to the owner.[53] Residential-type fruit stands vary. Some growers set up shop in garages attached to their homes. One might also see a temporary structure built at the end of a driveway. Signage, brightly painted buildings and decor, and just the knowledge of the presence of mouth-watering fruit and vegetables will snag passersby to fruit stands.

Anita Hix has been in the upper Valley for fifteen years, opening her first fruit stand, Anita's Pantry and Produce, in 1999. Her stand is an old packing shed sitting just a few feet—space enough to get a few moderate-sized vehicles in the parking lot—off F Road on Orchard Mesa. Peach orchards hug her stand, and her storefront offers a beautiful view of Grand Mesa. "People will stop at my place because it looks like a circus," she explained. Anita has made a name for herself over the last fifteen years among both her customers and the local growers from whom she purchases her produce. Anita not only sells produce but also various homemade salsas. Anita's exceptional customer service and business savviness enabled her to open her second stand in 2013 outside of Palisade on U.S. Highway 6, just where it winds its way to meet up with the Interstate 70 eastbound on-ramp. Anita says she "goes the extra mile" for her customers: "Customers can order several boxes of peaches, and I can set them to ripen upon their arrival." She also will store her customers' purchases until they are ready to pick them up—either at the end of their stay in a hotel across town or after they have pedaled the Colorado Fruit and Wine Byway.[54]

There are also three farmers markets held throughout the Grand Valley that locals and visitors can attend. Fruita, a growing community west of Grand Junction, has its town market on Saturdays at the civic center from eight o'clock to noon from late June to mid-September. Grand Junction blocks off Main Street on Thursday nights from five thirty to eight thirty from mid-June to late September. In Palisade parts of Third Street and Main Street are blocked off on Sundays from ten to two o'clock from mid-June to mid-September so pedestrians may stroll through the streets to get fresh produce. All of these farmers markets have music, artwork, clothing, and family-friendly activities, but Palisade's market offers something a bit more special—the opportunity to take a carriage ride through peach and wine country for thirty-five to fifty dollars per person.

The newest and perhaps the most novel agritourism attraction/activity is the Colorado Fruit and Wine Byway. The byway showcases what the upper Valley is all about, and Sandie Cooper and Cassidee Shull of CAVE firmly believe that this will help Mesa Land Trust (MLT) in their Fruitlands Forever endeavor.[55] In May 2014 a group from CTO's Agritourism and Heritage Program took a two-day tour of agritourism attractions in Grand Junction, Fruita, and Palisade as part of their work "to develop a marketing plan and work to promote agritourism throughout the state."[56] One thing they were looking over was the Fruit and Wine Byway in Palisade, the result of

FIG. 21. Fruit and Wine Scenic Byway signs, 2012. Photograph by Jeffrey M. Widener.

what Cooper called a "grassroots community effort."[57] The ribbon-cutting for this project was held on May 11, 2012.

State enologist Steve Menke—trained for everything dealing with wine-related issues in Colorado—was responsible for securing the first funding for the project. He obtained $20,000 in 2010 and $20,000 in 2011, with about half of the money coming from the Colorado Department of Agriculture and the rest coming from CAVE, local governments, and local businesses. At the opening he said, "I think it behooves all of us to think about this as a first step in a permanent kind of agritourism effort." The byway is twenty-seven miles long and has at least ninety signs advertising the route. Cooper stressed the importance of the signs in getting people off Interstate 70 and other highways. She said, "We wanted something that would help do some branding of routes and provide safety measures and ways to help market businesses along those routes."[58] The byway has car, bike, and foot routes and includes access to "wineries, orchards, lavender shops, alpaca farms, and more."[59]

Small Town Development and Community Resources

Agritourism, just like other forms of tourism, benefits from having a variety of available activities, including other attractions nearby, complementary businesses that indirectly support it, and promotion—all of which support communities economically. The CTO plan for action noted all of these as factors for success.[60] Juliann Adams is the executive director of the Palisade Chamber of Commerce. She knows firsthand about the community effort that is an essential part of what is ongoing in the Grand Valley. She sees that Palisade is becoming known for its festivals, peach fest, and wine fest and that the Fruit and Wine Byway gives tourists "greater access to all the good things that grow and are made in Palisade." She summed up the experience: "A lot of people like just getting out and biking through the area, maybe stopping and making it a wine tour in combination with different orchards. Most of our area is flat and not very intense so you can really enjoy yourself, stop in at an alpaca farm, a lavender farm, a winery, an orchard. We've got such diverse agriculture. And at the end of the day, you can relax at the distillery and brewery."[61]

The agritourism survey conducted in 2006 by CSU indicates that "people are attracted to an area by its natural amenities and this, in turn, spills over into participation in agritourism activities in these areas."[62] Colorado is a dream state in terms of natural amenities: the Grand Valley, the Rocky Mountains, the Grand Mesa, the Colorado National Monument, and the Colorado River are all within half-a-day's driving distance. Denver is a four-hour drive away. Weather is a natural amenity, of course, and Grand Junction boasts that it was named one of the eight sunniest cities in the United States by the website TourismReview.[63]

Numerous businesses in the Palisade region not directly associated with the growing, shipping, and processing of agricultural products support agritourism and are supported by agritourism. Even though the Palisade Chamber of Commerce homepage says, "Play and Stay in Palisade ... Life Tastes Good Here ... All Year Long," Palisade is realistically, at this point anyway, a three-season tourist destination.[64] Local business owners like Rondo Buecheler and Julie and Bob Commons agree that the winter months, and even the early spring and late fall, are slow business-wise.[65] Julie Commons commented, "There's room in the inn by the first week of October.... They [Front Range residents] are just too scared to drive over the [Vail] pass." Indeed Julie has always worked a second job to make ends meet since opening the Dreamcatcher Bed and Breakfast.[66]

Rondo explained that he, too, takes on a second and sometimes a third job. When he is not renting and selling bikes and paddleboards, he gives tours down the Colorado River. And in the winter months he gives ski lessons on the slopes at Powder Horn Ski Resort.[67] Businesses like Rapid Creek Cycles and Sports and Dreamcatcher Bed and Breakfast indirectly support agriculture, and such community resources are imperative in maintaining an agritourism industry.

In 2008 Wine Country Inn opened its doors. The inn is situated between vineyards and Interstate 70. The eighty-room hotel has a gourmet restaurant and a smaller pub-style restaurant on its grounds, which may keep some visitors from branching off the premises. After all, Palisade has only a handful of restaurants, and a couple of them are open only on Fridays and Saturdays. One of the only restaurants open seven nights a week is at the Palisade Brewery, so it has its own agritourism flair. Some bed and breakfast owners, such as Julie and Bob Commons, worried that the inn would destroy their businesses. But Julie framed it this way: "People who stay in hotels will always stay in hotels.... Luckily for our small businesses the hotel is always double-booking, and they'll refer their outraged customers to us." Julie also commented that when visitors staying with her in the Sunday-to-Thursday timeframe ask where to eat, she typically points them to Grand Junction.[68]

In 2014 Palisade town leaders said they were going to phase in $1.2 million in improvements to the downtown square area to make it more attractive for retail businesses. The improvements would take place in between the festivals so they would not negatively affect visitors' temperaments. These anticipated additions encouraged some locals to consider investing in downtown store frontage. For instance Cory Johnson talked about opening a sushi restaurant in a former coffee shop. In May 2014 Johnson was waiting for clearance from the Mesa County Health Department.[69]

Indeed visitors expect certain amenities when they travel with leisure in mind. For agritourism and Palisade's economic well-being, more investments like what the town of Palisade proposed are needed. Palisade may be able to round out its calendar with events in other months; it already features Halloween activities and pumpkin patches, an Art and Chocolate Walk of downtown in November, and various Christmas activities. More advertisement on the opportunities for winter activities in the upper Grand Valley would be a step in the right direction.

Advertisement is vital all year long. According to the Longwoods International *Colorado Travel Year 2012 Final Report*, 71 percent of those who planned their leisure trips to Colorado used the internet for trip planning purposes.[70] Online one can find Grand Junction's annual *Daily Sentinel Vacationland* supplement and various CTO website offerings, like the new Colorado Roots guide or app for "local-food eaters, craft-beer lovers, scenic-byway drivers, fresh-fruit pickers, history-museum browsers, tiny-lamb petters, dude-ranch fanciers and everything in between."[71] In summer 2013 *Sunset* magazine featured Palisade in a two-page spread.[72] In June 2014 Mesa County was featured in a thirty-six-page article in *US Airways Magazine*, available online and in print in airline seatbacks, with the expectation that more than six million passengers would fly US Airways that month and perhaps view the article.[73] The CTO action plan is solidly behind promotion, regional roadshows, online resources, peer mentors, matching grants, quality standards, and legislation to bolster agritourism's niche in Colorado's tourism industry.[74]

Most of all, however, businesses recognize the value of working together. Recently Valley businesses joined the Quilt Trail, a tradition beginning in Ohio and led in the United States by residents in two North Carolina counties. The objective is for tourists to visit structures, typically barns, that have painted boards attached to the facade with depictions of quilt designs. Barbara Webster from Quilt Trails of Western North Carolina called the quilt squares "a history repository," noting they "tell the story of the site where they hang, so in a way we are giving a voice to the land and the buildings.... I like to think of the blocks as mirrors of who we are."[75] It is too early to tell how much of an increase there will be in visitors and in revenue in the Grand Valley from its additions to the Quilt Trail, but local businesses such as SunCrest Orchard Alpacas and Fiber Works, Dreamcatcher Bed and Breakfast, Kokopelli Fruit Stand, and several others have indeed created another reason to visit this special agricultural region that encourages visitors to learn about its heritage.

Agritourism as Land-Saving Action

Agritourism is blooming across the United States. In the American West many farmers are seeing this additional activity on their landscapes as a valuable enterprise for preserving the lifeways more attributable to the Old West while adapting to the pressures of the New West to stay relevant. The examples in the Grand Valley could likely be proven elsewhere in the American West where agriculturalists are trying to hold on to their heritage in a sea of development: such as in Utah's Fruit Way; Napa, California (among others); Ashland and Medford, Oregon; and Hatch, New Mexico. With that said, the Grand Valley is still different from these noteworthy communities. The sheer number of diverse agritourism sites and events concentrated in this small valley likely exceed most regions in the American West and, quite possibly, in all of the United States.

Biologist Richard Brewer was talking about land trusts and protecting land when he said, "Education, education, education."[76] That refrain should be echoed for agritourism. Martha Sullins, a CSU Extension specialist in agriculture and business management, said agritourism "is a tremendous opportunity for farmers and ranchers if they can find the right fit. We all eat, and it's a great way to introduce people to other aspects of farming, including ecology and environmental management."[77] Agritourism, in fact, may be one of the most encouraging means in recent years to inform citizens about agricultural heritage, teach them about where their food comes from, and show them why it is important to protect the resources needed for agriculture to be sustainable, especially land and water.

The focus on land and water in the historiography of the American West is paramount. When I began this project I was reading works by historian Donald Worster and geographer James Parsons—two scholars with two opposing ways for reading the landscape in this attractive region. Worster's writings focused on the techno-environments that took shape along irrigation canals, and he left us with an image that there was "nothing harmonious, nothing picturesque about the western world that has developed beside the irrigation ditch," that "there is little peace or tidiness or care, little sense of a rooted community," that "there is not equitable sharing of prosperity," and that "the human presence here often seems very much like the tumbleweeds that have been caught in . . . fences."[78] Parsons, however, wrote that regions in the American West were rich in "promise, for exploration and discovery, for landscape appreciation, and for the study of changing human imprints."[79] There is not one vantage point that is better than the other here, as each contributes in its own ways to our understanding of the shaping of the West. I do hope, though, that this essay captured which view I appreciated more.

And yet as we dig deeper into the works of the historians of the New West, we can discern that what we should be studying, or what we should be exploring, are what Richard White called blurred boundaries. More specifically, in *The Organic Machine* White suggested that we look for and emphasize blurred boundaries and impurities and "find, paradoxically, along those blurred and dirty boundaries ways to better live with our dilemmas."[80] And more recently in *A Ditch in Time* Limerick argued that the population in the West is "dependent on, complicit with, and indebted to the organizations and institutions that disrupted the ecosystems and disturbed the landscapes that, a little late in the game, we came to treasure."[81] As William Cronon reminds us, "Stories about the past are better . . . if they increase our attention to nature and the place of people within it."[82] It is my sincere hope that agritourism in the Grand Valley is not too late in the game to make people aware of the importance of agriculture here—and that it does not go the way of the Silicon Valley that Stegner captured in his *American West as Living Space*.

Farmers in the Grand Valley are undoubtedly trying to better live with their dilemmas. The problems of too much growth on prime agricultural land, the significance of drought and the need to use available water in the best ways possible, and the obligation to have something good to leave our children are not easy themes to demonstrate to individuals who want to develop agricultural land. Agritourism puts the important, and often unnoticed, work of farmers in an attractive package for those who visit. If visitors listen closely enough, they can understand the love farmers have for their land and their life. Visitors can taste, see, hear, touch, and smell their way to a new appreciation for agricultural landscapes. The repackaging of these Old West ways with New West amenities might help people appreciate the places, the work involved, the people who do the work, and the heritage behind it all.

Notes

1. Stegner, *The American West as Living Space*, 75–76.
2. For more on this topic, see Travis, *New Geographies of the American West* and Wyckoff, *How to Read the American West*.
3. "Colorado Agritourism Gets a Helping Hand," *Copper* (blog), June 7, 2014, https://www.coppercoloradocondos.com/copper-mountain-blog/post/colorado-agritourism-gets-a-helping-hand/.
4. "Farming Matters," *Out West* (Colorado Springs), September 5, 1872.
5. Sylvester Baxter, "Vineyards in the Rio Grand [sic]," *Colorado Transcript*, April 1, 1885.
6. Loyd Files Research Library, *All About Grand Junction and the Grand Valley Colorado*, 30.

7. Riebsame, *Atlas of the New West*, 72; Walden et al., "A Three-Year Action Plan," 5.
8. See Wilson, Thilmany, and Sullins, "Agritourism: A Potential Economic Driver."
9. Gascoigne, Sullins, and McFadden, "Agritourism in the West," 19.
10. From 2002 to 2007 the number of farms in Colorado with some kind of agritourism and recreational service went from 867 to 679, but income nearly tripled from $12,042,000 to $32,913,000. From 2007 to 2012 the number of farms with some kind of agritourism and recreational service went to 864, almost back to the 2002 count, but overall revenue decreased by about 15 percent. For more information see United States Department of Agriculture, State Level Data and United States Department of Agriculture, County Level Data.
11. White and Thimany, "Exploring Consumer Preferences," 7–8.
12. Luke Runyon, "Working Out the Kinks to Rebrand Colorado as an Agritourism Destination," Harvest Public Media, June 26, 2014, https://www.kunc.org/post/working-out-kinks-rebrand-colorado-agritourism-destination#stream/0.
13. Thilmany, Sullins, and Ansteth, "Of Wine and Wildlife," 3.
14. Penny Stine, "Agriculture and Tourism Still a Mainstay in Palisade," *Daily Sentinel*, May 13, 2011; Rondo Buecheler (owner, Rapid Creek Cycles and Sports), in discussion with the author, August 2012; Bob and Julie Commons (owners, Dreamcatcher Bed and Breakfast), in discussion with the author, September 2012.
15. Walden et al., "A Three-Year Action Plan," 6–7.
16. Walden et al., "A Three-Year Action Plan," 3.
17. Walden et al., "A Three-Year Action Plan," 4.
18. "What Is Agritourism," Colorado Department of Agriculture, September 1, 2012.
19. "Visitors Inquisitive About How Their Food Is Produced," *Daily Sentinel*, September 2, 2011.
20. "Agri-Tourism," Palisade Chamber of Commerce, access date July 1, 2012, http://palisadecoc.com/co/agri-tourismnew.
21. Rebecca Levy (city planner, Town of Palisade) and Richard Sales (city planner, Town of Palisade), in discussion with the author, August 2012.
22. Emily Shockley, "Summer Festival Season Kicks Off," *Daily Sentinel*, April 16, 2010.
23. Wyckoff, *Creating Colorado*, 230.
24. Priscilla Walker (orchard owner and president, Walker Innovations, Inc.; chair, Palisade Historical Society), in discussion with the author, August 2012.
25. Kattey Ortiz, "Peach Farmers in Palisade Prepare for Their Favorite Time of Year," KREXTV, August 15, 2014, http://www.westernslopenow.com/story/d/story/peach-farmers-in-palisade-prepare-for-their-favori/38910/-HN54pxAbEuxc8xS2czEsA.
26. Ortiz, "Peach Farmers in Palisade," KREXTV, August 15, 2014; "Mark Your Calendars! Next Year's Peach Festival Will Be August 13–16, 2015," Palisade Peach Fest, accessed October 11, 2014, http://palisadepeachfest.com/pf/.
27. "Peach Festival Schedule," Palisade Peach Fest, accessed October 11, 2014, http://palisadepeachfest.com/pf/peach-festival-schedule/.
28. "Palisade Peach Festival," *Vacationland*, May 18, 2014, M43.
29. Caskey, "Colorado Wine," 4.
30. Caitlin Row, "Colorado Mountain Winefest Attracts Record Numbers to Palisade," *Grand Junction Free Press*, September 24, 2013, https://www.postindependent.com/news/local/colorado-mountain-winefest-attracts-record-numbers-to-palisade/; Sandie Coo-

per (executive director, CAVE) and Cassidee Shull (program director, CAVE), in discussion with the author, August 2012.

31. "Colorado's Wine Ranking Nothing to Whine About," *Denver Business Journal*, October 16, 2012, https://www.bizjournals.com/denver/news/2012/10/16/colorados-wine-ranking-nothing-to.html.

32. "Colorado Mountain Winefest Named Best Wine Festival," *USA Today* (10Best), September 1, 2017, https://www.10best.com/awards/travel/best-wine-festival-2017/.

33. Cooper and Shull, discussion, August 2012.

34. Caskey, "Colorado Wine," 4.

35. Ben Weinberg, "Wine, Chocolate and Food in the Vineyards of Western Colorado," *Colorado Statesman*, September 19, 2013.

36. Weinberg, "Wine, Chocolate and Food," *Colorado Statesman*, September 19, 2013.

37. Weinberg, "Wine, Chocolate and Food," *Colorado Statesman*, September 19, 2013; Brittany Markert, "Colorado Mountain Winefest Infused with Tasting Options in Palisade, Colorado," *Grand Junction Free Press*, September 16, 2014, https://www.postindependent.com/entertainment/colorado-mountain-winefest-infused-with-tasting-options-in-palisade-colorado/; "Colorado Mountain Winefest," Wine Colorado, September 1, 2014, http://www.winecolorado.org/events/mountain-winefest/.

38. Row, "Colorado Mountain Winefest," *Grand Junction Free Press*, September 24, 2013.

39. Row, "Colorado Mountain Winefest," *Grand Junction Free Press*, September 24, 2013.

40. Markert, "Colorado Mountain Winefest," *Grand Junction Free Press*, September 16, 2014; Row, "Colorado Mountain Winefest," *Grand Junction Free Press*, September 24, 2013.

41. Row, "Colorado Mountain Winefest," *Grand Junction Free Press*, September 24, 2013.

42. Markert, "Colorado Mountain Winefest," *Grand Junction Free Press*, September 16, 2014.

43. Weinberg, "Wine, Chocolate and Food," *Colorado Statesman*, September 19, 2013.

44. Levy and Sales, discussion, August 2012.

45. Walden et al., "A Three-Year Action Plan," 15.

46. Mel Rettig (owner, Rettig Farms), in discussion with the author, September 2013.

47. Bruce Talbott (orchard and vineyard manager, owner, Talbott Farms), in discussion with the author, September 2012.

48. Runyon, "Working Out the Kinks," Harvest Public Media, June 26, 2014

49. "Colorado Agritourism Gets a Helping Hand," *Copper* (blog), June 7, 2014.

50. Ed Sealover, "Hickenlooper Signs Five Final Business Bills on Last Possible Day," *Denver Business Journal*, June 6, 2014, https://www.bizjournals.com/denver/blog/capitol_business/2014/06/hickenlooper-signs-five-final-business-bills-on.html.

51. "Palisade Must-Dos," *Vacationland*, May 18, 2014, M23.

52. Palisade Chamber of Commerce, "Palisade & East Orchard Mesa Area Map: The Heart of Colorado Fruit & Wine Country."

53. "Colorado, Palisade Fruitlands—FRPP Economic Research," Land Trust Alliance, 2012, http://www.landtrustalliance.org/policy/documents/colorado-frpp-report.

54. Anita Hix (owner, Anita's Pantry), in discussion with the author, September 2013.

55. Cooper and Shull, discussion, August 2012.

56. Amy Hamilton, "Valley's Rural Roots Run Deep," *Daily Sentinel*, May 15, 2014.

57. Penny Stine, "Agriculture and Tourism Still a Mainstay in Palisade," *Daily Sentinel*, May 13, 2011.

58. "Palisade Byway Beckons," *Daily Sentinel*, May 12, 2012.
59. "Agritourism Must-Dos," *Vacationland*, May 18, 2014, M21.
60. Walden et al., "A Three-Year Action Plan," 3–4.
61. Rachel Sauer, "PALISADE: Bask in the Glow of Orchards, Vineyards and Art," *Vacationland*, May 18, 2014, M22.
62. Gascoigne, Sullins, and McFadden, "Agritourism in the West," 16.
63. "Grand Junction Announces Five Ways to Fall in Love with Fall," Visit Grand Junction, October 14, 2014, http://www.visitgrandjunction.com/grand-junction-announces-five-ways-fall-love-fall-0.
64. "Palisade Chamber of Commerce," Palisade Chamber of Commerce, August 1, 2012, http://palisadecoc.com/co/local-attractions.
65. Buecheler, discussion, August 2012; Commons, discussion, September 2012.
66. Commons, discussion, September 2012.
67. Buecheler, discussion, August 2012.
68. Commons, discussion, September 2012.
69. Penny Stine, "New Festivals, New Business Ventures Keep Palisade in a Celebratory Mood," *Daily Sentinel*, May 8, 2014, https://www.gjsentinel.com/lifestyle/agritourism/new-festivals-new-business-ventures-keep-palisade-in-a-celebratory-mood/article_4826a336-eca9-5dea-808a-2993091de6b1.html.
70. Longwoods International, "Colorado Travel Year 2012 Final Report," 175.
71. "Colorado Roots," Colorado, September 1, 2012, http://www.colorado.com/roots.
72. Elisa Bosley, "Why You'll Love Palisade, CO," 23–24.
73. "US Airways Magazine to Feature Mesa County," Mesa County Headlines, March 12, 2014, http://blog.mesacounty.us/2014/03/us-airways-magazine-to-feature-mesa.html.
74. Walden et al., "A Three-Year Action Plan," 22–23.
75. Barbara Webster, "What Is Quilt Trails All About?," Quilt Trails, October 15, 2014, http://quilttrailswnc.org/What-is-Quilt-Trails-All-About.pdf.
76. Brewer, *Conservancy*, 229.
77. Stacy Nick, "Farms, Fans Eat up 'Agritainment,'" *Coloradoan*, August 10, 2014, https://www.coloradoan.com/story/entertainment/music/2014/08/10/farms-fans-eat-agritainment-calmly/13878891/.
78. Worster, *Rivers of Empire*, 6.
79. Parsons, "A Geographer Looks at the San Joaquin Valley," 388.
80. White, *The Organic Machine*, xi.
81. Limerick, *A Ditch in Time*, 4.
82. Cronon, "A Place for Stories," 1375.

Bibliography

Archival Sources

Loyd Files Research Library. Museum of Western Colorado. Grand Junction, Colorado.

Published Works

Bosley, Elisa. "Why You'll Love Palisade, CO." *Sunset* (August 2013): 23–24.

Brewer, Richard. *Conservancy: The Land Trust Movement in America*. Lebanon NH: University Press of New England, 2003.

Caskey, Doug. "Colorado Wine: Rooted in History." *Colorado Business Review* 78, no. 4 (2012): 4–5.

Cronon, William. "A Place for Stories: Nature, History, and Narrative." *Journal of American History* 78, no. 4 (1992): 1347–76.

Gascoigne, William, Martha Sullins, and Dawn Thilmany McFadden. "Agritourism in the West: Exploring the Behavior of Colorado Farm and Ranch Visitors." Western Economics Forum, Lincoln NE, 2008. http://ageconsearch.umn.edu/bitstream/92849/2/0702002.pdf.

Limerick, Patricia. *A Ditch in Time: The City, the West, and Water*. Golden CO: Fulcrum, 2012.

Longwoods International. "Colorado Travel Year 2012 Final Report." Columbus OH, May 2013. gov3415112012internet.pdf (state.co.us).

Palisade Chamber of Commerce. "Palisade & East Orchard Mesa Area Map: The Heart of Colorado Fruit & Wine Country." Palisade CO: Palisade Chamber of Commerce, 2015.

Parsons, James J. "A Geographer Looks at the San Joaquin Valley." *Geographical Review* 76, no. 4 (1986): 371–89.

Riebsame, William E., ed. *Atlas of the New West: Portrait of a Changing Region*. New York: W. W. Norton, 1997.

Stegner, Wallace. *The American West as Living Space*. Ann Arbor: University of Michigan Press, 1987.

Thilmany, Dawn, Martha Sullins, and Alex Ansteth. "Of Wine and Wildlife: Assessing Market Potential for Colorado Agritourism." *Economic Development Report*, Colorado State University Extension, Fort Collins, 2007.

Travis, William. *New Geographies of the American West: Land Use and Changing Patterns of Place*. Washington DC: Island, 2007.

United States Department of Agriculture. Census of Agriculture. Chapter 2: County Level Data, Colorado, vol. 1. "Table 6. Income from Farm-Related Sources: 2012 and 2007," 2012. http://www.agcensus.usda.gov/Publications/2012/Full_Report/Volume_1,_Chapter_2_County_Level/Colorado/st08_2_006_006.pdf.

United States Department of Agriculture. Census of Agriculture. Chapter 2: State Level Data, Colorado, vol. 1. "Table 6: Income from Farm-Related Sources: 2007 and 2002," 2007. http://www.agcensus.usda.gov/Publications/2007/Full_Report/Volume_1,_Chapter_2_US_State_Level/st99_2_006_006.pdf.

Walden, Judy, Amy Webb, Dan Hobbs, and Kelli Harper. *A Three-Year Action Plan for the Promotion of Agritourism in the State of Colorado*. Denver: Colorado Tourism Office, 2013. https://www.colorado.com/sites/default/master/files/hagplanfinal.pdf.

White, Richard. *The Organic Machine: The Remaking of the Columbia River*. New York: Hill and Wang, 1995.

White, Wendy, and Dawn Thilmany. *Exploring Consumer Preferences and Travel Plans for Agritourism in Colorado*. Fort Collins CO: FSMIP Final Report, September 2006–2007. https://web.archive.org/web/20111022193056/http://www.ams.usda.gov/amsv1.0/getfile?dDocName=stelprdc5064320.

Wilson, Joshua, Dawn Thilmany, and Martha Sullins. "Agritourism: A Potential Economic Driver in the Rural West." In *Colorado State University Cooperative Extension Economic*

Development Report EDR 06–01. Fort Collins CO: Colorado State University Cooperative Extension, February 2006. http://citeseerx.ist.psu.edu/viewdoc/download?doi=10.1.1.522.4328&rep=rep1&type=pdf.

Worster, Donald. *Rivers of Empire: Water, Aridity, and the Growth of the American West*. New York: Oxford University Press, 1992.

Wyckoff, William. *Creating Colorado: The Making of a Western American Landscape, 1860–1940*. New Haven: Yale University Press, 1999.

Wyckoff, William. *How to Read the American West: A Field Guide*. Seattle: University of Washington Press, 2014.

PART 4

Migrant Lives and Labor

8

"A Violation of the Most Elementary Human Rights of Children"

The Rise of Migrant Youth Detention and Family Separation in the American West

IVÓN PADILLA-RODRÍGUEZ

In August 1983 Ana Margarita Ramirez arranged for her son, Orlando, to be transported to her in the United States a year after his father was murdered by a right-wing "death squad" in El Salvador. Only four years of age, Ramirez was transported across the U.S.-Mexico border along with a dozen other Salvadoran minors inside of the concealed compartment of a truck belonging to a *coyote* smuggler.[1] Upon arriving in Southern California without authorization, Ramirez was apprehended by the U.S. Border Patrol and incarcerated for fifteen days.[2] After spending two weeks imprisoned—away from his mother—Ramirez was placed in the custody of a foster care program, which the Immigration and Naturalization Service (INS) had contracted with the U.S. Marshals Service, Catholic Community Services, and the Salvation Army beginning in 1979 as a "humane" alternative to child incarceration. Ramirez was not unlike the children placed in foster care after being separated from their parents by Pres. Donald Trump's 2018 "zero-tolerance" policy.[3] He spent a year in a foster home, separated from his undocumented mother, Ana Margarita, until a protracted legal battle secured their reunification.[4]

Four-year-old Orlando Ramirez's "unaccompanied" migration, incarceration, and separation from his mother reveal that child detention and family separation at the U.S.-Mexico border are not phenomena unique to the twenty-first century, nor are they inventions of the Trump administration. Modern child detention and immigrant family separation practices were born in the 1970s American West, when unaccompanied and accompanied youth from Latin

America increasingly migrated to the United States in search of refuge, work, educational opportunity, and family unity. In an effort to stem this growth of unauthorized migration, the INS started removing undocumented children from their parents to incarcerate them separately as "material witnesses" in the prosecution of *coyote* smugglers. Children who migrated unaccompanied, like Orlando Ramirez, were also forced to sustain prolonged family separation, because the INS required undocumented parents who tried securing their children's release from immigration prison to waive their rights to remain silent and not incriminate themselves, risking their and their child's deportation.[5] These policies demonstrated that twenty-first-century youth detention, family separation, and violence against children in immigration custody were continuations of late twentieth-century border enforcement practices and consequences. Liberal and conservative presidential administrations in the early twenty-first century merely reinforced, expanded, and formalized immigration deterrence tactics initiated under the Nixon and Carter administrations, which relied on injuries to child and family welfare.

This essay expands adult-, Caribbean-, and Florida-centric immigrant detention scholarship by unraveling the western origins of the United States' modern child detention and immigrant family separation practices.[6] The migration of asylum-seeking Haitians and Cubans to Florida in the late 1970s and 1980s helped the United States design and institutionalize its mandatory detention and "prevention through deterrence" techniques.[7] But it was the smuggling, detention, and criminalization of Mexican and Central American minors—which historical scholarship on Latin American immigration elides—that enabled the rise of the United States' mass child incarceration practices and the systematic separation of immigrant families on policy grounds.[8] Immigration and prison authorities justified these rights violations by adopting a rhetoric of protection and humanitarianism, rooted in paternalistic ideas about childhood innocence and the "best interests of the child," which required the criminalization of undocumented parents who dared subject their vulnerable children to the perils of unauthorized migration.

The Fatal Consequences of Border Militarization

The 1965 Immigration and Nationality Act's imposition of numerical restrictions on Latin American immigration and the 1964 termination of the guestworker Bracero Program significantly curtailed avenues for lawful entry, generating an increase in undocumented migration to the United States.[9] In the late 1970s if a legal U.S. resident of Mexican descent wanted to reunify with their spouse and child under U.S. immigration law, the wait for formal documentation had grown to seven years.[10] Numerical restrictions in immigration law facilitated the long-term separation of families just as effectively as the millions of deportations conducted in this period.[11] As a consequence thousands of families and children decided to "reunify themselves ... illegally" during and after the 1970s.[12] Meanwhile growing numbers of unaccompanied youth journeyed to the United States without authorization in search of work and educational opportunities due to the absence of legal paths for immigration and rising inequality, unemployment, and violence in Mexico and Central America.[13] Minors, not just adults, migrated for work in agriculture and construction in order to send money back home to their families.[14]

Educators, labor officials, and Border Patrol agents consistently confirmed that children and families migrated to the United States without authorization after 1965. California labor commissioner George Tockstein detailed to journalist Ronald B. Taylor of the *Fresno Bee* what the migration of undocumented and mostly Mexican minors and families looked like in the 1970s: "They go with their families ... calexico-mexicali [sic] ... come through to work daily. And they stream across every morning, from 1 a.m. on ... figure 12- and 15-year-old kids, get a lot of those. They try to smuggle selves on busses [sic], hide down in busses when ... go out with group ... I go through kick them off busses."[15] The California Labor Commission witnessed the migration of lone and accompanied migrant children who snuck across the border on buses in northern Mexico or were transported by *coyotes*, sometimes for work on rural farm fields, specifically. Border Patrol agents also revealed that border-crossers were now "young men, even boys, eager to work."[16]

Estimates of southwestern border apprehensions confirmed the anecdotal information reported by Border Patrol agents for, in 1979, when 340,000 immigrants were arrested at the border, more than 8,000 were children, and 600 of them were held as "material witnesses" to testify in federal court against their *coyote* smugglers.[17] In the 1960s, when the INS claimed to have arrested seven hundred to eight hundred *coyotes* a year, only about 40 percent of migrants used a *coyote* to transport them across the border.[18] By 1975 this percentage had grown to 75 percent of all migrants. In the 1980s the INS incarcerated about five thousand children a year, and an estimated nine hundred minors were forced to testify against their *coyotes* each year, at least until 1986.[19]

When the 1986 Immigration Reform and Control Act provided for the amnesty of millions of undocumented residents and made circular unauthorized migration far more difficult due to the law's budgetary investment in border enforcement, both *coyote* fees and rates of child migration for the purposes of reunification with newly legalized relatives increased. Between 1986 and 1990 INS officials in the Southwest reported that they were "experiencing more families [and youths] than . . . ever . . . before," and that "the movement [was] here on a permanent basis." In the first six months of 1986 the Border Patrol in San Diego—the busiest crossing point for undocumented migrants in that period—apprehended 8,121 undocumented minors, which represented a 74-percent increase from the same period in 1985. In south Texas family groups accounted for nearly 20 percent of all apprehensions at the border. Juvenile apprehensions represented more than 48 percent of the increase in the overall number of migrant arrests in 1986.[20] Between mid-1988 and mid-1989 the Border Patrol in south Texas apprehended two hundred to four hundred children a month, prompting the INS to open three new shelters for children in that period.[21] By the early 1990s the majority of "illegal alien youths" held in detention were Guatemalan and Honduran citizens.[22] This trend of child migration and detention did not abate in the early twenty-first century, since the rates of migration in fiscal years 2004 and 2014 resulted in the apprehensions of tens of thousands of youths and family units.[23] In 2019 the United States incarcerated a record 69,500 children in government facilities, more than any other country in the world.[24]

The growing numbers of late twentieth-century undocumented child arrivals to the United States coincided not only with the advent of legal restrictions on Latin American immigration and preferential treatment for refugees fleeing communism but also the explosion of the *coyotaje* (human smuggling) business and the hardening of the U.S.-Mexico border. In the late 1970s more than 70 percent of migrants, especially undocumented minors, purchased the services of a *coyote* to transport them across the U.S.-Mexico border, which started to become militarized in the 1970s.[25] Leonard Chapman, the INS commissioner appointed by President Nixon, convinced the Pentagon to lend the INS "paraphernalia of war" such as guns, bullet-proof vests, heat sensors, and infrared scopes left over from the Vietnam War to police the surge in migrant adults, family groups, and unaccompanied children. The commissioner who succeeded Chapman and was appointed by President Carter, Leonel Castillo, built upon this arsenal by securing additional tactical gear for Border Patrol agents during his tenure.[26] Herman Baca of the Committee on Chicano Rights charged that border militarization allowed "an armed force of psycho-paths to wage war on innocent children."[27]

The outfitting of Border Patrol agents with weapons used in war and the introduction of technological advances to border enforcement made possible the infliction of fatal violence against Latin American youth. In the summer of 1979 Border Patrol personnel seriously injured a sixteen-year-old Mexican citizen at the border, Martin Zarate, by shooting at him from a helicopter. In April 1985 Edward D. Cole, a Border Patrol agent with a history of violence against migrants, killed a child.[28] Cole shot and killed twelve-year-old Mexican citizen Humberto Carrillo-Estrada.[29] Migrants' rights advocates complained to Congress that unlawful entry or attempted escape from Border Patrol custody should not be "punishable by the death penalty inflicted by the arresting agent."[30]

Border Patrol officers who directed physical and sexual violence at noncitizen youth regularly benefitted from a culture of impunity, which was fully realized in the 2020 *Hernandez v. Mesa* Supreme Court decision, while migrant youth bore the brunt of criminalization and retaliation. When Calexico police arrested Border Patrol agent Robert M. Ferrick for the kidnapping and assault of a fourteen-year-old Mexican boy, the orphaned migrant was held in Imperial County's juvenile detention facility.[31] That this kidnapped minor's complaint against the abuses of an immigration agent resulted in his incarceration was part of a broader pattern of criminalization and retaliation in which the government used the incarceration of noncitizens, and sometimes targeted retaliation, to demoralize and "tamper with witnesses."[32] When border patrolmen were accused of sexually assaulting undocumented minors and women in their custody, they either had their charges dropped by prosecutors or were allowed to resign from their positions.[33] In February 2020 the U.S. Supreme Court sanctioned deadly Border Patrol violence against noncitizen youth when it barred a lawsuit against the patrol officer who killed Sergio Adrián Hernández Güereca at the U.S.-Mexico border.[34]

Other undocumented migrants, including children, died trying to cross the border because its militarization had forced migrants to cross at night through dangerous "hidden" routes that required minors to cross multiple lanes of highway traffic in the dark.[35] Fourteen-year-old Luis Eduardo Hernández was killed when he was run over by a Border Patrol vehicle just minutes after crossing into the United States.[36] Commissioner Castillo announced that in 1978 the bodies of twenty-four undocumented immigrants who drowned trying to enter the United States had been washed ashore on the U.S. side of the Rio Grande. Others died crossing the desert on foot and while trying to escape Border Patrol officers. In 1979 Castillo called for the compilation of national statistics on the migrant death toll because of the frequency of bodies washed ashore or the discovery of unidentified human remains in the desert.[37]

Migrant youth, many of whom sought to flee poverty and violence—and in the case of Central America, child conscription and societal destabilization accelerated by U.S. intervention—did not just have to evade apprehension and violence by armed Border

Patrol agents, however.[38] They also had to avoid immediate confinement in detention centers, jails, and hotels refashioned into makeshift sites of confinement. Restrictive immigration and refugee laws, paired with the hardening of the U.S.-Mexico border and practice of mandatory detention, made *coyotaje* an extremely lucrative business. Commissioner Castillo conceded that the vulnerabilities of undocumented children and families made them especially "exploitable" by *coyotes* and employers.[39] Paul Carrasco, an attorney for the National Center for Immigrants' Rights (now called the National Immigration Law Center), went further than Castillo by noting that children were also particularly vulnerable to abuses by the INS and Border Patrol.[40]

Detention and Separation in the Borderlands

In a bid to try to thwart the post-1965 increase in unauthorized migration across the U.S-Mexico border, the INS started to prosecute *coyotes* in court in the late 1960s and significantly intensified its prosecution efforts a decade later, particularly in California, Arizona, and Texas.[41] This decision did little to hold accountable well-resourced human smugglers who could secure bail within a single day of arrest. Instead, as authorities attempted to gather "material witnesses" against *coyotes*, the decision caused what Juan Manuel Soliz of the Midwest Coalition in Defense of Immigrants called "a violation of the most elementary human rights of children": the mass imprisonment of thousands of minors and the separation of immigrant families.[42]

Immigration authorities resorted to incarcerating women and children based on a false government belief, which still persists today.[43] The misguided assertion was that undocumented immigrants did not show up for scheduled court appearances if released from detention.[44] As a result between 1977 and 1978 undocumented boys held as "material witnesses" collectively spent 4,983 days in government custody, while the girls spent 1,297 days in detention. Although most minors spent an average of 20 days incarcerated, some children could languish in detention for as many as 145 days, as a seventeen-year-old from Jalisco, Mexico, did.[45]

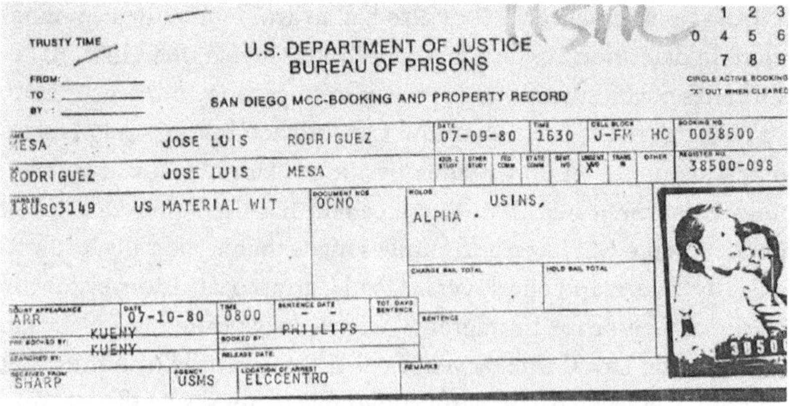
TRUSTY TIME
FROM:
TO :
BY :
U.S. DEPARTMENT OF JUSTICE
BUREAU OF PRISONS
SAN DIEGO MCC-BOOKING AND PROPERTY RECORD
1 2 3
0 4 5 6
7 8 9
CIRCLE ACTIVE BOOKING
"X" OUT WHEN CLEARED
MESA JOSE LUIS RODRIGUEZ 07-09-80 1630 J-FM HC 0038500
RODRIGUEZ JOSE LUIS MESA 38500-098
18USC3149 US MATERIAL WIT OCNO
USINS,
ALPHA
07-10-80 0800
ARR KUENY PHILLIPS
KUENY
SHARP USMS ELCCENTRO

FIG. 22. Photograph of a booking form, documenting the incarceration of a young child and her mother as "material witnesses" at the San Diego MCC. U.S. Department of Justice booking form for "material witnesses," box 25, folder 1, HB.

The detention of migrant minors in the late twentieth century succeeded in criminalizing undocumented youth of all ages and denying them the privilege of childhood innocence. The Marshals Service, which had a contract with the INS to incarcerate migrant youth, conceded that detained undocumented minors were not charged with criminal offenses.[46] Immigration detention was technically considered an administrative process, not a criminal one, as a result of late nineteenth-century Supreme Court cases that ruled that the "order of deportation is not a punishment for a crime."[47] Also detention was "not imprisonment in a legal sense."[48] Prison wardens nevertheless confirmed that children over the age of ten were fingerprinted and photographed for record processing soon after being incarcerated in detention sites like the Metropolitan Correctional Center (MCC) in San Diego and those in El Centro and San Ysidro, California.[49] At MCC and other INS jails in the U.S. Southwest, undocumented youth were provided their first criminal records and incarcerated alongside adults charged with criminal offenses.[50] One Marshals officer admitted that undocumented youth were "generally treated like ordinary offenders" and subjected "to harassment by the general jail population."[51] This physical proximity to adult criminals hardened perceptions of poor, undocumented youth as undoubtedly criminal and blurred the lines between adolescence and adulthood, for the INS did little to differentiate between incarcerated undocumented youth and adult convicts. But this criminalization of minors did not just affect older children. When a detained material witness was pregnant and gave birth at a local San Diego hospital, she was swiftly returned to custody with her infant, who was foot-printed upon being confined.[52]

Late twentieth-century immigration and prison authorities presented journalists with sanitized versions of the incarceration of undocumented minors, just as President Trump did when he assured the public that separated children in immigration custody were "so well taken care of."[53] Immigration authorities in the 1970s and 1980s simultaneously denied that children were being imprisoned at all—just as the Trump administration insisted when it claimed "zero-tolerance" did not intentionally break up families, and that family separation was merely a side effect of the decision to prosecute adults' unlawful entry.[54] The Marshals Service, for example, denied that "youngsters [were] being imprisoned needlessly" while in the same breath maintaining that "no child [was] being held ... unless it [was] for his own interest."[55] Those who openly admitted to children's incarceration justified the imprisonment of minors by claiming their confinement was as "humane as possible."[56] They also asserted that "in no way did these [spaces] resemble a typical jail."[57] Immigration officials in the United States employed paternalistic arguments in which they purported to be "protecting" children and acting in their "best interests" by detaining them to prosecute their smugglers, who were responsible for their unlawful entry—similar to how proponents of "zero-tolerance" weaponized migrant minors' childhood innocence to "protect" them from parents who subjected them to international migration.[58] If the INS did acknowledge the cruelty of child incarceration, they did so to advance another paternalistic argument: that deportation was also in an undocumented minor's best interest because removal from the nation allowed for a child's release from prison.[59]

The realities of immigration detention, brought to light by human rights defenders and migrants on hunger strikes, exposed the unreliability of government narratives about the punitive conditions of immigration detention, which relied on their remote geographies. Minors in detention centers and county jails were deprived of rights to privacy and their bodily autonomy. Even though the Border Patrol admitted that immigrant youth "rarely [carried] a pocketknife [and] almost never a gun,"[60] the INS performed thousands of invasive strip searches a year on boys and girls.[61] They were fed frozen TV dinners, provided limited outdoor recreational activities at best, and received no medical attention or educational opportunities.[62] The remote nature of the United States' constellation of ninety immigration detention centers and county jails where the Marshals Service detained material child witnesses also served to control the mobility of and deliberately disorient children since "they [didn't] even know where they [were] in the U.S.," diminishing their access to legal and social support.[63]

Migrants and their advocates also contradicted the federal government's accounts about how the prosecution of *coyotes* and incarceration of children separated families. Prison wardens reported to journalists that the government "never separated children under 10 years old from their parents."[64] Not only did statements like these indirectly confirm the separation of older children, but the mere design of detention facilities, particularly in Southern California, revealed that incarceration itself involved physical separation, for non-English-speaking children were held separately from their parents in hastily-organized "juvenile units," causing widespread confusion and fear.[65]

Migrants and human rights defenders became further incensed about the removal of young children from their parents for secluded interrogations with immigration officers when the federal government actively suppressed information about these practices. Texas Border Patrol agent Mr. Begley, for example, touted that "if you browbeat them [the children] enough, tell them, 'We're going to leave your mama locked up forever if you don't tell us the truth,' the kid'll tell you everything" about their border crossings and alleged law-breaking activities.[66] Mothers like Para Rosa Rivas also revealed that sometimes migrants were detained as "material witnesses" to testify "against [*coyotes* they] had never seen" and separated from children as young as one year of age.[67] The Marshals Service deliberately withheld reports about the incarceration of material witnesses like Rivas from migrants' rights advocates and sympathetic state welfare personnel, even severing relations with these government offices to keep information about child incarceration and family separation confidential.[68] The Trump administration similarly withheld crucial information from advocates about the separation of migrant families in 2018.[69]

Finally, in an effort to dispel accusations of child imprisonment, the INS and Marshals Service in 1979 partnered with Catholic Community Services and the Salvation Army in San Diego to place incarcerated migrant youth with unrelated foster parents through a pilot program that exacerbated the pathologization of migrant youth.[70] The Marshals Service in August 1980 was in direct contact with officials in Washington DC to expand the program to Texas and Colorado after having "activated" the project in New Mexico and Arizona.[71] Potential foster parents' concerns about housing a migrant Mexican or Central American minor had to be assuaged since the youth were criminalized through their swift imprisonment and in sensationalist media narratives about "hard-core youths" so "disruptive and even violent" that they enticed "newly arrived migrants into petty crime."[72] The foster care program's outreach materials and rhetoric further contributed to this criminalization and the pathologizing of migrant youth by arguing that migrant minors "do not come neatly packaged, well-scrubbed, and with problems that can be solved in thirty minutes or less."[73]

Even though the foster care program was depicted as a "humane" alternative to formal confinement in a detention center or county jail, its federal funding source inside the U.S. Department of Justice and the ways in which it deprived young people of rights crucial to the exercise of childhood laid bare the program's carceral-like nature. Catholic Services representatives assured parents that only "low-risk juveniles" would be eligible for foster care.[74] The juveniles who were deemed "low-risk" were not only the ones who adhered to respectable social norms and behaviors but also were those least likely to abscond.[75] The program made a concerted effort to control migrant children's mobility, for "juveniles deemed likely to run away were not placed in the foster home program."[76] Additionally, similar to detention, noncitizen minors placed in the foster care program were not permitted the opportunity to attend school.[77] Funding from the Law Enforcement Assistance Administration's Office of Juvenile Justice and Delinquency Prevention, which historian Elizabeth Hinton argues "critically shaped the rise of the carceral state," allowed the foster care program to act as a site of carcerality that continued the U.S. immigration regime's deprivation of children's rights to familial integrity, freedom of movement, and education.[78]

While government officials privately acknowledged in manuals for the program that "most foster children are disturbed by separation from their family," the separation of immigrant families through children's release to unrelated foster parents was publicly justified as a humanitarian solution to the plight of undocumented youth in detention.[79] This separation was meant to "protect" children. Advocates ultimately alleged that some of these children were "lost" to the federal bureaucracy and went "missing" inside jails—rhetoric bearing striking resemblance to accusations in 2018 that the government "lost" track of more than a thousand migrant youth in its custody.[80] These actions resulted in permanent family separation due to children's separate incarceration, placement in foster care, and lone deportation.[81]

Although the district director of the INS in 1980 denied "releasing" children to Latin American authorities unless the U.S. government could establish contact with an adult responsible for them, migrants and advocates confirmed that the Border Patrol deported children as young as eight years old to northern Mexico, alone, in the middle of the night.[82] Herman Baca complained to President Carter that when children were no longer needed as material witnesses, they were "tossed" into Mexico "to fend for themselves."[83] A fourteen-year-old boy from Mexico City, for example, was deported from Chicago in 1979 and returned not to the interior of Mexico but to Juarez, on the Mexican border, where he had no relatives and was forced to survive by "garbage-can scrounging, living on rooftops."[84] When Central American teenagers, like Rudy Elmer Barerra of Ilopango, El Salvador, were deported to Mexico alone, they paid Mexican immigration officials bribes and claimed Mexican birthplaces to avoid incarceration in Mexico, then tried to enter the United States again without delay.[85] Deported minors also joined the ranks of informal day laborers in northern Mexico to earn enough money to survive until they could cross the border again.[86] Others made a living working as teenage *coyotes*.[87]

Child deportees incarcerated in overcrowded Tijuana juvenile detention facilities, despite having committed no infraction under Mexican law, were subjected to a double criminalization, beaten by guards, and tortured by Mexican police during interrogations. Here, too, detained children were "wedged between the police department and adult [jails]," which enabled the Mexican government to create proximity between child deportees and notions of criminality.[88] They were mixed in with adult offenders for as long as three months. The head of a Tijuana juvenile detention facility, Daniel Romero Mejia, asserted in 1988 that if migrant youth were not confined in detention, "They might face greater danger on the streets." At the same time, Mejia acknowledged, incarceration made migrant minors vulnerable to "contamination from the criminal element in the jail."[89] Mexican authorities purported to be acting in the best interest of the child while simultaneously cementing the idea that because naïve and immature migrant youth were inherently predisposed to criminality, they were easily corruptible if left unrestrained.

The rise of child detention in the U.S.-Mexico borderlands operated on carceral logics rooted in curtailed mobility, geographic isolation, and punishment, inspiring the earliest demands for the eradication of immigrant enforcement agencies. In 1980 Herman Baca articulated an abolitionist critique of the Border Patrol and INS motivated by violence against and the mass detention of noncitizen infants and children. Baca argued that the "only solution to stopping the abuse of children ... is to abolish the Border Patrol."[90] At a public protest in the summer of 1985, in which most of the marchers were children denouncing Pres. Ronald Reagan and the Border Patrol as "child abusers," Baca asserted that "as long as the Border Patrol exists, you [the children] will never have rights."[91] Baca's child-centered call for the abolition of the

Border Patrol predated contemporary demands for the dismantling of the Immigration and Customs Enforcement agency, or ICE, which gained mainstream popularity in the aftermath of "zero-tolerance."[92]

Even drawn-out legal battles in which incarcerated minors successfully sued the INS in the mid- and late 1980s were not enough to end abuse in child detention into the twenty-first century. When in 1985 an unaccompanied Salvadoran minor named Jenny Lisette Flores filed what would become a class action lawsuit against the INS for its late twentieth-century child detention practices, the federal government and the minor plaintiff's lawyers agreed on what is now known as the 1997 Flores Settlement. In spite of the baseline protections afforded by the Flores Settlement, undocumented youth continued to be incarcerated by the thousands in life-threatening, prison-like spaces that deprived children of their education, health, welfare, and familial and bodily integrity by the Bush, Clinton, Obama, and Trump administrations. In fact it was during the Obama administration that the U.S. government dramatically expanded the United States' family detention infrastructure as an immigration deterrence strategy.[93]

So when the Trump administration held an unprecedented number of undocumented minors in life-threatening "cages" and separated them from their parents to punish and deter unauthorized migration, he was advancing discursive policy tools inherited from late twentieth-century waves of migration to the American West. Leveraging an immigration deterrence infrastructure already in existence, early twenty-first-century policymakers ensnared noncitizen minors into an overlooked arm of the carceral state that had long provided the foundations for permanent immigrant family separation, child detention, and the lone deportation of minors.[94]

Notes

1. Michael Seiler, "After Year Apart, Mother and Her Son, 4, Reunited," *Los Angeles Times*, September 5, 1984.

2. Laurie Becklund, "Suit Claims INS Holds 4-Year-Old 'Hostage,'" *Los Angeles Times*, circa 1983.

3. Ginger Thompson, "What's It Like for an Immigrant Child to Have a Glimpse of the American Dream, Then Have It Taken Away," *ProPublica*, December 28, 2018, https://www.propublica.org/article/trump-administration-zero-tolerance-policy-family-separation-foster-care-immigrant-children.

4. Seiler, "After Year Apart," *Los Angeles Times*, September 5, 1984.

5. Seiler, "After Year Apart," *Los Angeles Times*, September 5, 1984.

6. For historical monographs indicative of the burgeoning scholarship on the modern origins of immigrant incarceration, see Lloyd and Mountz, *Boats, Borders and Bases*; Lindskoog, *Detain and Punish*; and Young, *Forever Prisoners*. While important, these works focus almost overwhelmingly on adults or the asylum-seeking "boat people" from Cuba and Haiti who reached Florida's shores in the 1970s and were mandatorily detained in county jails, detention centers, and military facilities. One notable exception to the mostly Florida- and Caribbean-centric, mid- and late-twentieth-century detention scholarship is Ordaz, *The Shadow of El Centro*.

7. Lloyd and Mountz, *Boats, Borders and Bases*, 54–84; Lindskoog, *Detain and Punish*, 18.

8. For examples of the rich but adult-centric scholarship on late twentieth-century Mexican and Central American immigration, see Goodman, *The Deportation Machine*; Minian, *Undocumented Lives*; and Garcia, *Seeking Refuge*.

9. Ngai, *Impossible Subjects*, 228.

10. Robert Scheer, "Waste, Hope; Illegal Aliens: Endless Cycle of Insecurity," *Los Angeles Times*, November 11, 1979.

11. Some estimates suggest that between 1965 and 1986 the INS carried out around thirteen million deportations, largely through voluntary departures. See Goodman, *The Deportation Machine*, 107–8.

12. Michael Harpold, president of the immigration employees union, quoted in Scheer, "Waste, Hope; Illegal Aliens," *Los Angeles Times*, November 11, 1979. On Central American family reunification, see Patrick McDonnell, "Youths, Families See U.S. as Only Hope, Swell Alien Arrests," *Los Angeles Times*, May 11, 1986.

13. Minian, *Undocumented Lives*, 10. For information about unaccompanied child and family migration after 1985, see McDonnell, "Youths, Families," *Los Angeles Times*, May 11, 1986.

14. Padilla-Rodríguez, "Child Migrants in 20th-Century America," 7. Stories of unaccompanied youth who migrated to work as child laborers can be found in countless newspaper accounts including Ronald B. Taylor, "Hide-and-Seek Plight of 2 Sisters," *Fresno Bee*, circa 1968–1969, Ronald B. Taylor Papers (RBT), box 16, folder 4; John Kendall, "Youths Tell of Privations as Pickers" *Los Angeles Times*, April 10, 1979, Orange County Interfaith Committee to Aid the Farmworkers Records (OCIC), box 1, folder 93.

15. Ronald B. Taylor, interview notes for George Tockstein (investigator, California Labor Commission, San Diego), circa early 1970s, RBT, box 1, folder 1–43.

16. Richard Severo, "The Flight of the Wetbacks: The Hunted Are Also Hunters" *New York Times Magazine*, March 10, 1974, Agricultural Workers History Collection (AWH), box 1, folder 135.

17. "Mexican Children Imprisoned in U.S," *PW*, April 1980, Herman Baca Papers (HB), box 25, folder 1.

18. Ronald B. Taylor, "Valley's Fields Lure Alambristas," *Fresno Bee*, November 3, 1968, RBT, box 16, folder 4.

19. Schrag, *Baby Jails*, 14; John M. Crewdson, "Border Sweeps of Illegal Aliens Leave Scores of Children in Jail," *New York Times*, August 4, 1980. Evidence that youth were held as "material witnesses" at least until 1986 can be found in McDonnell, "Youths, Families," *Los Angeles Times*, May 11, 1986.

20. McDonnell, "Youths, Families," *Los Angeles Times,* May 11, 1986; Marita Hernandez, "Immigrant Teens Find Little Refuge," *Los Angeles Times,* January 25, 1989; Patrick McDonnell, "El Norte Luring More Families: Growing Numbers of Women, Children Risk Perils of Border Crossing for Better Life," *Los Angeles Times,* August 19, 1990.

21. Lisa Belkin, "Lonely Young Aliens Pose Problem for U.S.," *New York Times,* May 25, 1989.

22. Dirk Johnson, "Choice for Young Illegal Aliens: Long Detentions or Deportations," *New York Times,* November 30, 1992.

23. In fiscal year (FY) 2004 the United States apprehended 122,122 minors. See Bhabha and Schmidt, "Seeking Asylum Alone," 16. In FY 2014 the United States apprehended 68,541 unaccompanied youth and 68,445 family units. "Southwest Border Unaccompanied Alien Children FY 2014," U.S. Customs and Border Protection, https://www.cbp.gov/newsroom/stats/southwest-border-unaccompanied-children/fy-2014.

24. Christopher Sherman, Martha Mendoza, and Garance Burke, "U.S. Held a Record of Migrant Children in Custody in 2019," *Associated Press,* November 12, 2019, https://apnews.com/article/us-news-ap-top-news-honduras-trauma-immigration-015702afdb4d4fbf85cf5070cd2c6824.

25. For a history of how the border became militarized in practice after 1978, see Dunn, *The Militarization of the U.S.-Mexico Border.*

26. Edward O'Connor, southwestern regional director of the INS, quoted in Scheer, "Waste, Hope; Illegal Aliens," *Los Angeles Times,* November 11, 1979.

27. Committee on Chicano Rights Press Release, July 3, 1985, HB, box 25, folder 1.

28. Michael D. Lopez, "DA Will Not File Charges in Manacled-Alien Slaying," *San Diego Union,* 1985; John K. Van de Kamp (attorney general of California) to Edwin L. Miller (district attorney, County of San Diego), April 29, 1986, HB, box 25, folder 2.

29. Herman Baca to Mr. Thomas "Tip" O'Neil (speaker of the house), April 26, 1985, HB, box 25, folder 1; Tom Greeley, "Police Probe of Boy's Shooting by Border Patrol for DA," *Los Angeles Times,* April 23, 1985.

30. Legal Aid Society of San Diego, Committee on Chicano Rights, United California Mexican-American Association, "Petition for Congressional Investigation Presented to the United States Senate, United States House of Representatives, United States Department of Justice," July 23, 1979, HB, box 31, folder 1.

31. Marjorie Miller, "Border Agent Arrested on Complaint of Mexican Boy," *Los Angeles Times,* June 4, 1985.

32. When the Federal Bureau of Investigation (FBI) investigated allegations that undocumented and legal U.S. residents of Latin American descent had been beaten by Border Patrol officers, the FBI reported an attempt to harm the witnesses expected to testify. Border patrolmen Steve Iverson, Blake Brown, and Brent King loosened the lug nuts of the tires used by the witnesses in order to cause a car accident. See Ricardo Chavira, "FBI Probes Charge that Aliens Beaten," *San Diego Union,* October 10, 1979.

33. Untitled article, *New York Times,* January 14, 1980, HB, box 25, folder 1.

34. Hernandez et al. v. Mesa, 140 S. Ct. 735 (2020).

35. For an account of two undocumented Mexican teenage workers who had to cross multiple freeway lanes to cross into California, see Kendall, "Youths Tell of Privations as Pickers," *Los Angeles Times,* April 10, 1979, OCIC, box 1, folder 93. For evidence of undocumented children who passed away after being hit by cars while trying to cross the bor-

der unlawfully, see Patrick McDonnell and Lily Eng, "2nd Latino Youth Is Killed on I-5 in Less than a Day," *Los Angeles Times*, August 10, 1990.

36. McDonnell, "El Norte Luring More Families," *Los Angeles Times*, August 19, 1990.

37. Jack Nelson, "Castillo to Study Alien Border Toll," *Los Angeles Times*, March 22, 1979.

38. Garcia, *Seeking Refuge*, 13–30. See also McDonnell, "Youths, Families," *Los Angeles Times*, May 11, 1986.

39. Testimony of Leonel J. Castillo (commissioner of the INS between May 1977 and October 1979), C-24, Oral Hearing on Plaintiffs' Motion for Preliminary Injunction, Testimony Presented by Plaintiffs, February 26, 1980, Mexican American Legal Defense and Educational Fund Records, record group 5, carton 1497, folder "Appendices to the Supreme Court Brief."

40. Bill Ott, "Settlement Disclosed in INS Case," *San Diego Union*, September 1, 1984.

41. Evidence that the INS started to detain "material witnesses" in the late 1960s to prosecute *coyotes* can be found in John V. Tunney (member of Congress) to Raymond F. Farrell (commissioner at the INS), July 25, 1968, RBT, box 7, folder 6; Ronald B. Taylor, "Wetback Investigation" notes, September 1968, RBT, box 16, folder 4. For evidence on the holding of material witnesses in Arizona and Texas, see Patt Morrison, "Border Paradox: Witnesses Jailed, Aliens Held, Smuggler Suspects Get Bail," *Los Angeles Times*, September 4, 1978; Crewdson, "Border Sweeps," *New York Times*, August 4, 1980.

42. Juan Manuel Soliz quoted in "Mexican Children Imprisoned in U.S.," PW, April 1980, HB, box 25, folder 1.

43. Ingrid Ealy and Steven Shafer, "When Trump Says Immigrants Don't Show Up for Court Hearings, He Couldn't Be More Wrong," *Los Angeles Times*, October 29, 2020, https://www.latimes.com/opinion/story/2020-10-29/immigration-donald-trump-joe-biden-presidential-debate.

44. Crewdson, "Border Sweeps," *New York Times*, August 4, 1980.

45. Bill Ott, "Alien Youngsters Who Witnessed Smuggling Wait at MCC," *San Diego Union*, August 20, 1978.

46. Morrison, "Border Paradox," *Los Angeles Times*, September 4, 1978.

47. Fong Yue Ting v. United States, 149 U.S. 698 (1893).

48. Wong Wing v. United States, 163 U.S. 228 (1896).

49. "Federal Official Denies Charge of Imprisoning Alien Children," *San Diego Union*, March 1, 1980.

50. Schrag, *Baby Jails*, 13.

51. Crewdson, "Border Sweeps," *New York Times*, August 4, 1980.

52. Crewdson, "Border Sweeps," *New York Times*, August 4, 1980; Committee on Chicano Rights, Press Release, February 29, 1980, and Rogelio Laventant Siguentes, "Encarcelan Niños Como Testigos en Casos de Detención de 'Polleros,'" *El Mexicano*, March 1, 1980, HB, box 25, folder 1.

53. Kathryn Watson, "Trump Says Children Separated from Their Parents Were 'So Well Taken Care of,'" CBS News, October 23, 2020, https://www.cbsnews.com/news/child-separation-trump-says-taken-care-of/.

54. Christina Wilkie, "White House Denies Separating Families Is 'Policy,' but Insists It Is Needed 'to Protect Children,'" CNBC, June 18, 2018, https://www.cnbc.com/2018/06/18/white-house-denies-separating-families-is-policy.html.

55. "Federal Official Denies Charge of Imprisoning Alien Children," *San Diego Union*, March 1, 1980.

56. Ott, "Alien Youngsters," *San Diego Union*, August 20, 1978.

57. Annie Gutiérrez (regional INS director) quoted in "El Servicio de Inmigración de EU desmiente que haya niños mexicanos detenidos," *Uno + Uno*, November 30, 1980, HB, box 25, folder 1.

58. Wilkie, "White House Denies Separating Families," CNBC, June 18, 2018. See also Philip Bump, "A Frustrated Trump Blames Migrants for Having Their Children Taken from Them," *Washington Post*, July 10, 2018, https://www.washingtonpost.com/news/politics/wp/2018/07/10/a-frustrated-trump-blames-migrants-for-having-their-children-taken-from-them/.

59. Vicki Torres, "Juveniles Return to Mexico with Smiles," *San Diego Tribune*, February 28, 1984.

60. Ronald B. Taylor, "Illegal Aliens: A Growing Labor Force," *Fresno Bee*, September 9, 1973, RBT, box 16, folder 7. See also Dan Wiekel, "The OC Man at the Helm of INS Office: Reagan Loyalist Believes in Need to Stem the 'Silent Invasion' of Illegal Immigrants," *Register*, December 2, 1985, OCIC, box 1, folder 97.

61. Schrag, *Baby Jails*, 14.

62. Michael D. Lopez, "MCC Inmates' Hunger Strike Has Little Bite," *San Diego Union*, October 2, 1979; Schrag, *Baby Jails*, 13; Juvenile Justice Legal Advocacy to Rebecca Mendoza, memo, April 1979, California Rural Legal Assistance Records, box 231, folder 8.

63. Crewdson, "Border Sweeps," *New York Times*, August 4, 1980.

64. Lopez, "MCC Inmates'," *San Diego Union*, October 2, 1979.

65. Ken Mimms, "Inmates Plan Hunger-Work Strike Starting Monday at Prison Here: 28 Grievances Listed," *San Diego Union*, September 27, 1979.

66. Untitled article, *New York Times*, January 14, 1980, HB, box 25, folder 1.

67. "Mexican Children Imprisoned in U.S.," *PW*, April 1980, and "Illegal Aliens Said Separated from Children," *San Diego Union*, February 29, 1980, HB, box 25, folder 1.

68. For a string of communication on the matter, see James R. Laffoon (U.S. Marshal) to Señor Estaban Morales L. (Consul General of Mexico), August 21, 1980; Laffoon to Mario G. Obledo (secretary of State of California Health and Welfare Agency), August 21, 1980; and Obledo to Laffoon, U.S. Department of Justice, September 11, 1980, HB, box 25, folder 1.

69. Jasmine Aguilera, "Judge Requires the Government to Explain Why Undisclosed Data on Missing Separated Parents Was Not Provided Sooner," *Time*, December 3, 2020, https://time.com/5917728/separated-families-border-data-government/.

70. Mitch Himaka, "Alien Juveniles Get Foster Homes," *San Diego Union*, November 30, 1979.

71. Laffoon to Morales L., August 21, 1980, HB, box 25, folder 1.

72. Sebastian Rotella, "Children of the Border: Caught in the Makeshift Life," *Los Angeles Times*, April 3, 1993.

73. Statement on the Catholic Community Services and U.S. Marshals' Pilot Foster Care Program, undated, HB, box 25, folder 1.

74. Pat Calloway, "Church Group Seeking Foster Home for Aliens," July 14, 1979, HB, box 25, folder 1.

75. Laffoon to Morales L., August 21, 1980, HB, box 25, folder 1.

76. Crewdson, "Border Sweeps," *New York Times*, August 4, 1980.

77. Catholic Community Services and U.S. Marshals' Pilot Foster Care Program, HB, box 25, folder 1.

78. Hinton, *From the War on Poverty to the War on Crime*, 223.

79. Catholic Community Services and U.S. Marshals' Pilot Foster Care Program, HB, box 25, folder 1.

80. Ron Nixon, "U.S. Loses Track of Another 1,500 Migrant Children," *New York Times*, September 18, 2018, https://www.nytimes.com/2018/09/18/us/politics/us-migrant-children-whereabouts-.html.

81. "Mexican Children Imprisoned in U.S.," *PW*, April 1980, HB, box 25, folder 1; Torres, "Juveniles Return to Mexico," *San Diego Tribune*, February 28, 1984. See also Committee on Chicano Rights, Press Release, July 3, 1985, HB, box 25, folder 1.

82. Committee on Chicano Rights, Press Release, July 3, 1985, HB, box 25, folder 1; Calloway, "Church Group," July 14, 1979, HB, box 25, folder 1; "Federal Official Denies Charge of Imprisoning Alien Children," *San Diego Union*, March 1, 1980.

83. Baca to President Carter, February 28, 1980, HB, box 25, folder 1.

84. Crewdson, "Border Sweeps," *New York Times*, August 4, 1980.

85. McDonnell, "Youths, Families," *Los Angeles Times*, May 11, 1986.

86. Patrick McDonnell, "Migrant Youths Face Trip to Crowded Tijuana Jail: Tales of Beatings, Torture, Fights Greet Minors Returned by Border Patrol," *Los Angeles Times*, April 10, 1988.

87. Beginning in 1980 the U.S. Department of Justice started charging teenagers who guided migrants across the U.S.-Mexico border with felonies. See John Crewdson, " Teenagers Join in the Business of Smuggling Aliens," *New York Times*, 1980, HB, box 25, folder 1; Sebastian Rotella, "Children of the Border: Caught in the Makeshift Life," *Los Angeles Times*, April 3, 1993.

88. McDonnell, "Migrant Youths Face Trip," *Los Angeles Times*, April 10, 1988.

89. McDonnell, "Migrant Youths Face Trip," *Los Angeles Times*, April 10, 1988.

90. Herman Baca, "From the Desk of" handwritten notes, circa 1980, HB, box 25, folder 1.

91. David Jefferson, "U.S. Agents Targeted by Protesters: Chicanos Critical of Border Patrol," *San Diego Tribune*, July 4, 1985.

92. Matt Loffman, "What's Driving the Movement to Abolish ICE?," *PBS*, July 6, 2018, https://www.pbs.org/newshour/politics/whats-driving-the-movement-to-abolish-ice.

93. Schrag, *Baby Jails*, 8–9, 61–139, and 213–69.

94. Jacob Soboroff and Julia Ainsley, "Lawyers Can't Find the Parents of 666 Migrant Kids," *NBC News*, November 9, 2020; Sherman, Mendoza, and Burke, "U.S. Held a Record," *Associated Press*, November 12, 2019; Caitlin Dickerson, "U.S. Expels Migrant Children from Other Countries to Mexico," *New York Times*, October 30, 2020, https://www.nytimes.com/2020/10/30/us/migrant-children-expulsions-mexico.html.

Bibliography

Archival Sources

California Rural Legal Assistance Records (CRLA). Stanford University, Green Library.
Mexican American Legal Defense and Educational Fund Records (MALDEF). Stanford University, Green Library.

Herman Baca Papers (HB). University of California, San Diego, University Library.
Agricultural Workers History Collection (AWH). Archives of Labor and Urban Affairs. Wayne State University, Reuther Library.
Orange County Interfaith Committee to Aid the Farmworkers Records (OCIC). Archives of Labor and Urban Affairs. Wayne State University, Reuther Library.
Ronald B. Taylor Papers (RBT). Archives of Labor and Urban Affairs. Wayne State University, Reuther Library.

Published Works

Bhabha, Jacqueline, and Susan Schmidt. "Seeking Asylum Alone: Unaccompanied and Separated Children and Refugee Protection in the U.S." The Harvard University Committee on Human Rights Studies, Harvard Kennedy School, 2006. https://idcoalition.org/wp-content/uploads/2008/12/seeking-asylum-alone-us.pdf.

Dunn, Timothy. *The Militarization of the U.S.-Mexico Border, 1978–1992: Low Intensity Conflict Doctrine Comes Home.* Austin: Center for Mexican-American Studies, University of Texas, Austin, 1996.

García, María Cristina. *Seeking Refuge: Central American Migration to Mexico, the United States, and Canada.* Berkeley: University of California Press, 2006.

Goodman, Adam. *The Deportation Machine: America's Long History of Expelling Immigrants.* Princeton: Princeton University Press, 2020.

Hinton, Elizabeth. *From the War on Poverty to the War on Crime: The Making of Mass Incarceration in America.* Cambridge: Harvard University Press, 2016.

Lindskoog, Carl. *Detain and Punish: Haitian Refugees and the Rise of the World's Largest Immigration Detention System.* Gainesville: University Press of Florida, 2018.

Lloyd, Jenna M., and Alison Mountz. *Boats, Borders and Bases: Race, the Cold War, and the Rise of Migration Detention in the United States.* Berkeley: University of California Press, 2018.

Minian, Ana Raquel. *Undocumented Lives: The Untold Story of Mexican Migration.* Cambridge: Harvard University Press, 2018.

Ngai, Mae. *Impossible Subjects: Illegal Aliens and the Making of Modern America.* Princeton: Princeton University Press, 2004.

Ordaz, Jessica. *The Shadow of El Centro: A History of Migrant Incarceration and Solidarity.* Chapel Hill: University of North Carolina Press, 2021.

Padilla-Rodríguez, Ivón. "Child Migrants in 20th-Century America." In *Oxford Research Encyclopedia of American History*, edited by Jon Butler, 1–12. Oxford: Oxford University Press, 2020.

Schrag, Philip G. *Baby Jails: The Fight to End the Incarceration of Refugee Children in America.* Berkeley: University of California Press, 2020.

Young, Elliott. *Forever Prisoners: How the United States Made the World's Largest Immigrant Detention System.* Oxford: Oxford University Press, 2020.

9

Toxins in the Field

The CRLA, Farmworker Families, and Environmental Justice in Contemporary California

TAYLOR COZZENS

In August 2018 a San Francisco jury ordered the giant agrochemical company Monsanto to pay $289 million to California groundskeeper Dewayne Johnson because his diagnosis of non-Hodgkin's lymphoma was "at least partly due to using glyphosate, the primary ingredient in [the herbicide] Roundup."[1] Though a judge later reduced the reparations to $78 million, the jury's acceptance of partial causation set a significant precedent. In March 2019 a federal jury ordered Monsanto to pay $80 million to California resident Edwin Hardeman, who likewise claimed that using Roundup had led to his non-Hodgkin's lymphoma.[2] Furthermore, in May 2019 a California jury ordered the company Bayer, which had recently acquired Monsanto, to pay a record $2 billion to Alva and Alberta Pilliod, who suffered the same type of cancer and also blamed Roundup.[3] As in Johnson's case, a judge eventually reduced the amount, but Bayer was hardly off the hook.[4] In the following months the docket of lawsuits against the company grew exponentially, and in June 2020 Bayer agreed to pay more than $10 billion to settle thousands of cases. As one journalist noted, the payoff was "among the largest settlements ever in U.S. civil litigation."[5]

Throughout the Roundup debates the U.S. Environmental Protection Agency (EPA) has maintained that, if used according to manufacturer's instructions, the herbicide presents no significant health risks, and the controversial ingredient glyphosate is not a carcinogen. Nevertheless, the juries' consistent ruling against Roundup, even when the plaintiffs could only establish partial causation of their illnesses, indicates that many citizens and policy makers may take a harder line against pesticides in the twenty-first century. Indeed, more and more voices, like the nonprofit Environmental Working Group, may call for "a fundamentally new paradigm for pesticides."[6] Near the end of the twentieth century scholar Christopher Bosso observed that the entrenched "pesticides paradigm" in the United States embraced agrochemicals as necessary, safe, and effective.[7] The Roundup verdicts challenge such assumptions more boldly than ever.

If the twenty-first century is to usher in a new pesticides paradigm, however, the public and legal debate must also address the incalculable number of individuals in California who spend their days in fields bathed with agrochemicals and whose communities often receive disproportionate drift from pesticides and waste facilities, namely Latino farmworkers. In the three initial Roundup trials, Hardeman and the Pilliods (who are white) simply used Roundup in their yards; Johnson (who is African American) used the herbicide as part of his groundskeeping job. California field workers await the same level of attention that these individuals received. Perhaps it bears repeating that thanks to these workers, California provides half the nation's produce and generates more than $38 billion in annual sales of fruits, vegetables, and nuts.[8]

At the beginning of this century historian Patricia Limerick emphasized the need for scholars of the American West to see the region as a place of convergence of diverse peoples. She also argued for the relevance of history in understanding current dilemmas.[9] In the spirit of Limerick's approach, a look at California farmworkers' recent experiences with environmental hazards, including agrochemicals and contamination from waste facilities, helps put the Roundup cases into perspective. On one hand it reveals significant incremental victories in the ongoing fight for environmental justice. On the other hand it reveals considerable continuity in a pesticides paradigm that accepts Latino communities' exposure to agrochemicals and other hazards as normal.

To understand farmworkers' stake in pesticide debates, the history of two organizations is fundamental: the United Farm Workers Union (UFW) and the California Rural Legal Assistance (CRLA). Beginning in the 1960s both advocates employed a variety of strategies to protect workers from pesticide exposure. In the 1990s, however, UFW influence waned, whereas the CRLA found new avenues of protest in the nationwide environmental justice movement, which addressed minority communities' disproportionate exposure to environmental hazards.[10] The CRLA helped bring this movement to California farmworkers, using its logic to protest both farmworkers' proximity to waste facilities and their exposure to pesticides. Environmental justice litigation on behalf of farmworker families—though not as successful as the recent Roundup cases—started the century off with bold arguments that deserve the same level of attention as the Roundup debates.

Since the 1800s California's vast crops and orchards have depended on cheap manual labor, often from racial minority groups. It has been just as crucial for growers to fight environmental challenges (including pests) as find field workers. As historian Richard Street writes, in the nineteenth century California growers organized Native American and Chinese laborers "into huge bug-killing crews. Armed with little more than paddles, branches, burlap bags, sulfured rags, smoky torches, and carts full of flaming dung," these workers would "burn, scare, smoke, smash, or otherwise drive away insect infestations." On the eve of the twentieth century growers began experimenting with homemade pesticides, such as sulfur dust, shark oil, and kerosene. By 1912 citrus growers had discovered lead arsenate, and they began requiring workers to spray pesticides from pressure-filled hoses and to fumigate orchards by covering trees with tents and pumping poisonous gases underneath each tent's side.[11]

During World War II scientists developed chemical compounds such as DDT and organophosphates to help control mosquito-borne illness.[12] Following the war as California agribusiness expanded, growers began spraying such chemicals on their crops.[13] As historian Linda Nash points out, in the transition to larger, monoculture farms, the California Department of Agriculture promoted a "modern" agricultural system, based not only on "mechanization, irrigation technology, advances in plant hybridization, and the recruitment of a vast labor supply ... but also on massive amounts of the new agricultural chemicals. By 1955, 7.1 million acres, or two-thirds of California's cropland, was being treated with chemicals. By the mid-1960s more than sixteen thousand pesticides had been registered in California, and farmers increasingly relied on multiple applications of multiple chemicals."[14]

During this same period of post-war growth, Mexican immigrants and Mexican Americans entered the industry in unprecedented numbers to satisfy the need for cheap, seasonal labor.[15] In many cases the entire family worked in the fields.[16] The growth of this seasonal workforce, alongside the increased reliance on pesticides, meant that more and more Latino farmworkers would suffer harmful exposure to agrochemicals. In many crops, as Nash's research indicates, contact was inevitable. When picking fruit, for example, workers had to reach through foliage that was usually covered with pesticide. In the process they not only absorbed the chemicals through their hands and arms but also breathed in dusts that became airborne as the foliage was shaken. Furthermore, neither growers nor workers could control environmental factors such as heat and wind, which, on any given day, could cause pesticides to vaporize or drift.[17] In such scenarios workers in the fields often unwittingly found themselves in the chemicals' path.

Since contact with chemicals was inevitable and accidents were probable, workers needed equipment and labor techniques that would protect them from harmful exposure and prevent accidents. They rarely received them. In fact, many practices flew in the face of caution. Aerial spraying, which many growers adopted for its efficiency, put farmworkers at tremendous risk. Moreover, lack of communication was common. Former field worker Jesús Lopez explained that, in his experience, information about pesticide application—which chemicals, which field, what time, etcetera—went from the sprayer to the grower to the labor contractor to the foreman to the crew.[18] With language barriers and pressure to produce quickly, growers often neglected to warn workers about possible dangers.

Neglect of this kind likely caused a mass poisoning in 1949, one of the first of such tragedies ever reported, when more than a dozen farmworkers in a Sacramento Valley pear field began sweating uncontrollably, vomiting, and convulsing. Studies later indicated that they had absorbed residues of parathion, which had been applied twelve days earlier. Parathion was one of the new organophosphates and was extremely toxic.[19] Nevertheless, growers continued using such chemicals with little overall concern about workers' contact with them. While not all risks were initially understood, the agrochemicals were obviously dangerous. Yet by and large farmworkers' migratory status and cultural differences relegated them to merely another production input. When workers moved on, they took their injuries with them.

From the 1960s onward two organizations that sought to bring dignity and justice to the fields were the UFW and CRLA.[20] In scholarship and popular memory, individuals rightly give the UFW and its leaders, particularly Cesar Chavez, credit for the fasts, strikes, boycotts, and marches that awoke the nation to farmworkers' plight and, for a time, won better contracts from some growers.[21] Yet they usually overlook the equally significant, and in some ways more lasting, legal work of the CRLA on behalf of farmworker communities. Indeed, in the twenty-first century scholars are just beginning to correct the twentieth-century misconception that the farmworker movement of the 1960s and 1970s was about Chavez, Chavez, and Chavez.[22]

Founded in 1966 during Pres. Lyndon Johnson's War on Poverty and funded through the federal government's Office of Economic Opportunity, the CRLA was a private, nonprofit agency of lawyers and Spanish-speaking community workers. In ten (and later seventeen) field offices throughout the state, these employees provided free legal services to farmworkers.[23] In so doing they tackled a variety of social problems and abusive labor practices, often focusing on farmworker families, especially children.[24]

Like the UFW, the CRLA identified exposure to pesticides as one of the greatest injustices that farmworkers lived with, and it employed a variety of strategies to help reduce this exposure. One of the agency's first strategies on this front involved appealing to consumers. In the fight against DDT, the CRLA publicized scientific studies indicating that residues on fruits and vegetables accumulate in mothers' milk and then pass directly to nursing babies.[25] The study led to a general outcry by nursing mothers and confirmed the warnings of Rachel Carson's 1962 *Silent Spring*. Though effective, such appeal to consumers was only a starting point. Using Upton Sinclair's *The Jungle*, historian Matt García argues that pesticide protest focused exclusively on consumers can, at best, result in partial victory.[26] The real battle involves changing the attitude of growers, the government, and society about the importance of farmworkers' health. With this ultimate goal, CRLA lawyers also fought specific practices and specific pesticides. In 1969, for instance, they won a temporary restraining order on aerial spraying when workers were present.[27] That same year the agency filed a case against DDT on behalf of six farmworkers, five of whom were nursing mothers. This case contributed to the federal government's ban on the insecticide in 1972.[28] Unfortunately chemical manufacturers replaced DDT with other pesticides that were also harmful.

By the 1970s a new form of protest involved filing complaints with the EPA. In 1978 the CRLA filed such a complaint on behalf of three workers who were sprayed with pesticides from the air while pruning trees in a Sutter County orchard and subsequently suffered damage to their nervous systems.[29] Cases such as this contributed to growing national awareness of the danger of pesticides. In 1980 the state of California began requiring chemical manufacturers to publish information on their product labels that indicated health risks.[30]

As another strategy in the early 1980s the CRLA educated workers about the dangers of pesticides. In one didactic booklet *¡La Amenaza de los Pesticidas!* (the pesticide threat), CRLA authors used a comic-strip narrative in Spanish to warn workers about the consequences of exposure. In the narrative a kind doctor explains to the Cuerda family that if pesticides are strong enough to kill insects and rodents, they are certainly strong enough to harm humans, especially children.[31] They affect eyes, skin, lungs, and the nervous system. Other effects of exposure appear later, such as cancer, blindness, damage to internal organs, and birth defects. Since growers cannot be counted on to protect their employees, the booklet suggests, workers must protect each other.[32]

The CRLA also used litigation to promote research on the effects of pesticide exposure, especially for pregnant women and fetuses. In

1984 the agency prepared a report on the "reproductive hazards of pesticide exposure" and challenged the "evolving governmental policy which would ban the worker, not the hazard." Aside from challenging the discriminatory idea of banning pregnant women from fieldwork, the CRLA argued that 60 to 70 percent of pesticides in use had not been tested for their effects on fetuses, and it criticized the "glacial pace" of the EPA in carrying out the tests. To emphasize the need for such research, CRLA lawyers pointed out that growers had used the herbicide TOK—whose active ingredient was the carcinogen-bearing nitrofem—for two decades before its potential to cause birth defects became known. The CRLA helped remove it from the market.[33] Yet TOK was not an isolated case. This same year research also demonstrated that the insecticide Metasystox-R was associated with birth defects.[34]

Not only had the EPA failed to test pesticides before their release into the market, but in the mid-1980s California officials found that its test results of ninety-six pesticides were invalid. The CRLA participated in a lawsuit to force officials to retest.[35] Yet even with the health of babies at stake, farmworkers and their allies faced strong opposition from California's pro-industry politicians, who complained that manufacturers already experienced delays in registering their products for use.[36] Clare Berryhill, director of the Food and Agriculture Department, stated that he did not "want to put our growers at a competitive disadvantage." In contrast other officials called for greater controls on pesticides for the sake of public health. "This shouldn't be looked at as an ag issue," said assemblyman Bruce Bronzan, "it's a human issue."[37]

Indeed it was. By the mid-1980s California growers used approximately 11 pounds of pesticide per acre as opposed to the national average of 2.3 pounds per acre.[38] This kind of copious use—combined with the practice of spraying first and researching later (or not at all)—had led to one of the most tragic outcomes of all: "cancer clusters" in places like McFarland, Fairchild, Rosamond, and Earlimart.[39] In these towns an unusually high number of babies and children suffered cancer or birth defects. In many cases the mothers had worked in the fields while pregnant.[40]

FIG. 23. With the booklet *La amenaza de los pesticidas!* (The pesticide threat), CRLA attorneys and community workers sought to educate farmworkers about the dangers of pesticide exposure. One underlying message of these booklets was that since neither growers nor government officials were taking all the necessary steps to protect field workers from agrochemicals, workers had to protect themselves. CRLA Records, MO 750, carton 270, folder 7, Department of Special Collections and University Archives, Stanford University Libraries, Stanford, California.

In 1991 the *Sacramento Bee* released a special issue titled "Fields of Pain," which highlighted the situation of farmworker families. "My co-workers have their fingers all rotten because of the pesticides and the pulling of roots by hand," reported Teresa Sandoval. Similarly Leticia Maravilla shared her story of pesticide poisoning. In 1990 as she worked in lettuce fields in Fresno County, Maravilla sat on the ground to have lunch and, in so doing, absorbed a liquid pesticide. "I began to feel terrible," she recalled. "My skin began to swell up and I began to break into a rash. I tried to keep working but I couldn't. I felt a sense of desperation. My skin was on fire." She continued, "My eyes had swollen shut. And when I went to the clinic my body had welts all over. I felt so weak. I always felt like vomiting."[41] Other articles focused on children, including the problems of hunger, poverty, lack of education, and pesticide exposure. The issue underscored the fact that, looking ahead to the twenty-first century, much work remained in the fight to improve farmworker conditions. By this time the membership and influence of the UFW was declining.[42] The CRLA, by contrast, had grown in personnel and experience.

While CRLA litigation had succeeded in outlawing hundreds of pesticides and in regulating spraying practices, the problem of harmful exposure persisted because, as Julie Sze argues, "Environmental abuse of the most vulnerable populations" had become "normalized."[43] Perhaps such normalization explains why four users of a household herbicide like Roundup can win hundreds of millions in reparations, while the thousands of Latino workers exposed regularly to industrial agrochemicals receive no such attention. To summarize the ideas of sociologist Jill Harrison, California agriculture had come to rest squarely on "social exploitation" of Latino workers, who appeared and disappeared when needed, and on "environmental exploitation" from chemicals that contaminated air and water and forced agricultural ecosystems to produce quickly. These two forms of exploitation reinforced each other: the cheap, seasonal farmworkers suffered disproportionate pesticide exposure and illness, and their low-income, migratory status made them disproportionately unable to challenge pesticide practices.[44] To address such structural problems, Sze argues that activists must expose them "in ways that trigger attention from the state."[45] In the 1990s the environmental justice movement provided such an opportunity for CRLA attorneys and the farmworkers they served.

Environmental justice became a national movement, at least in name, in 1982 Warren County, North Carolina, when residents and activists lay down in the road to prevent garbage trucks from entering the state's first toxic waste landfill. They protested because 75 percent of the residents who would have to live next to the landfill were African American.[46] This event publicized the fact that across the nation waste sites were disproportionately located in minority communities. In 1987 the United Church of Christ used census data to examine the demographics of waste sites in twenty-five states and fifty metropolitan areas. It concluded that three in five Black people and Hispanics lived in neighborhoods with abandoned toxic waste sites. Furthermore, "Communities with commercial hazardous waste facilities had twice the number of minority residents as did areas without these plants."[47]

In light of such realities African American leaders and activists in 1991 held the first People of Color Environmental Leadership Summit in Washington DC, at which they presented "17 Principles of Environmental Justice." Principle 1 affirmed the "sacredness of Mother Earth." Principle 2 stated, "Environmental justice demands that public policy be based on mutual respect and justice for all peoples, free from any form of discrimination or bias."[48] Essentially the movement tackled both social and environmental exploitation, and its focal point was the intersection of the two. In 1994 Pres. Bill Clinton supported the movement by signing Executive Order 12898, which required federal agencies to "make achieving environmental justice part of [their] mission[s] by identifying and addressing... disproportionately high and adverse human health or environmental effects of its programs, policies, and activities on minority populations."[49]

As the work of Ellen Spears illustrates, environmental justice activists tapped into the networks of organizers and political power that civil rights activists had developed in previous decades.[50] In this way the movement stemmed more directly from civil rights activism than from traditional environmentalism. Indeed, as CRLA lawyer Luke Cole explained, environmental organizations had historically prioritized flora and fauna. In 1971, for example, the Sierra Club asked its national membership, "Should the Club concern itself with the conservation problems of such special groups as the urban poor and ethnic minorities?" In response, "58 percent of all members either strongly or somewhat opposed" the idea.[51] By contrast the environmental justice movement prioritized the urban poor. As one journalist observed, local activists who challenged discriminatory contamination often "had little interest in saving Barton Springs, the golden-cheeked warbler or the blue whale," but they did care about their communities.[52] In the twenty-first century scholars have pushed back against this dichotomy and highlighted overlap between the environmental and environmental justice movements.[53] Nevertheless, in the CRLA's fight against pesticide practices, it was clearly the environmental justice movement that offered new strategies. For farmworkers the most significant twenty-first-century shift involved the expansion of the environmental justice movement from urban to rural spaces. Scholarship in many ways now reflects this expansion.[54]

In California Luke Cole was instrumental in bringing the movement to farmworkers. Just days after graduating from Harvard Law School in the early 1990s, Cole joined the CRLA and began helping farmworkers in Kettleman City challenge the construction of a toxic waste incinerator at a large landfill in their community.[55] The case, *El Pueblo Para el Aire y Agua Limpio v. County of Kings*, revealed one of the fundamental challenges of environmental justice litigation, namely proving discriminatory intent. As a journalist pointed out, minorities and their advocates charged that the siting of waste facilities in their communities constituted discrimination, but many officials, including the EPA, claimed that it was "poverty, low property values, and lack of political power—not overt racism—that attracted polluters." After all there was also "strong evidence that whites, too, [were] widely victimized" in the siting of "landfills, incinerators, petrochemical plants and sewage treatment facilities."[56]

In California, however, all three of the toxic waste dumps—Kettleman City, Buttonwillow, and Westmorland—were located in minority communities, and such siting did not appear to be happenstance. In 1984 the government had commissioned a study to learn which groups were least likely to resist the construction of waste facilities. The results identified people who were poor, rural, Catholic, of limited education, and involved in resource extraction jobs. In California, farmworkers matched that description perfectly.[57] When county officials denied charges of discrimination and approved the construction of the incinerator, the CRLA appealed with the argument that the landfill owner, Chemical Waste Management, discriminated by only translating five of the nearly one-thousand-page Environmental Impact Report into Spanish for local residents.[58] A judge upheld this latter charge, agreeing that "failure to translate materials had unlawfully precluded residents from meaningful involvement." Eventually the company canceled its plan to build the incinerator.[59]

In the wake of this victory, Cole and other CRLA lawyers began considering how environmental justice also included protection from pesticide exposure, a problem largely unique to farmworker families. While scholars marked Warren County as the beginning of the movement, Cole argued that lawsuits to protect farmworkers from pesticides, such as the 1969 case against DDT, could also be considered the beginning.[60] In other words pesticide exposure clearly fell within the purview of the environmental justice movement.[61] One new option that Cole considered was using Title VI of the Civil Rights Act to file administrative complaints with the EPA. In his words Title VI, which "prohibits discrimination on the basis of race, color or national origin," is "a potentially powerful tool for community groups engaged in local environmental justice struggles because, under EPA regulations, it bars disproportionate impact in the administration of environmental programs." Moreover, Cole argued, administrative complaints could work more effectively than traditional litigation because the EPA handled them directly, and they did not involve expensive court proceedings.[62]

Significantly Title VI moved beyond intentional discrimination. As the U.S. Department of Justice explains, "Title VI itself prohibits intentional discrimination. However, most funding agencies have regulations implementing Title VI that prohibit recipient practices that have the *effect* of discrimination."⁶³ Throughout the 1990s CRLA lawyers followed Title VI complaints around the nation.⁶⁴ In 1999 they were ready to test the strategy on pesticides. Not surprisingly they prepared a case that focused on children. With the help of community workers CRLA lawyers contacted parents in the counties of Monterey, Ventura, and Santa Cruz and selected six schools that were surrounded by produce fields.⁶⁵ Then, working with the Center on Race, Poverty, and the Environment, CRLA lawyers prepared a Title VI complaint on behalf of children who attended these schools, including Thalia, who attended Ohlone Elementary School in Pajaro, and David, who attended Rio Mesa High School in Oxnard. The complaint was titled *Angelita C. et al. v. California Department of Pesticide Regulation* for Thalia's mother, Angelita.

In this complaint the CRLA charged that given the location of public schools, farmworker children faced a "disparate impact" of pesticide use.⁶⁶ Specifically the schools in question were surrounded by strawberry fields that were treated with a toxic fumigant called methyl bromide. Growers usually pump fumigants of this kind into the ground to prepare the soil for planting. As Harrison notes, the chemicals are designed to vaporize and then "permeate and sterilize the soil structure."⁶⁷ Put differently, they kill virtually everything and are extremely dangerous. As the EPA later indicated, methyl bromide is an effective acaricide (for ticks and mites), fungicide, herbicide, insecticide, nematicide (for nematode worms), vertebrate control agent, and antimicrobial substance.⁶⁸ The gas is so toxic that growers are required to stretch thick plastic tarps over each strawberry row; the strawberry stem grows through a tiny hole in the plastic.⁶⁹

Despite such precautionary measures, fumigant vapors can drift.⁷⁰ In a 2012 case of mass poisoning, lettuce workers in Salinas smelled an acid odor that reminded them of paint, cilantro, and diesel fuel. They then began to suffer eye irritation, nausea, headaches, dizziness, and shortness of breath. In total forty-three people fell ill. Investigation revealed that on the previous day, to prepare a nearby field for strawberries, growers had fumigated the soil with a mixture of chemicals, including 1,3-dichloropropene (brand name Telone) and chloropicrin. In the morning sun on the day of the poisoning, the

FIG. 24. On the threshold of the twenty-first century, the Angelita C. case presented a bold argument about environmental justice in rural California, namely that agrochemicals not only threatened farmworkers but also children whose schools were surrounded by produce fields. This image captures the proximity of Rio Mesa High School in Oxnard, California, to the surrounding strawberry fields.
Courtesy Todd Bigelow Photography.

fumigant mixture had re-vaporized and traveled nearly half a mile through the air to the lettuce field. Because the growers had not violated any regulations, the Monterey County Agricultural Commissioner issued no fines. As this case indicates, fumigants are designed to vaporize and permeate the soil, but on hot, breezy days, nobody can make the vapors stay in the soil. When the toxins drift, authorities commonly treat any damage as an uncontrollable accident. As CRLA lawyer Pearl Kan noted after the incident, California law regarding fumigant drift simply "doesn't protect farmworkers or community members from exposure."[71]

In 1999, with the health of their children in mind, farmworkers proposed a real solution: simply stop using the dangerous pesticides. In the Title VI complaint the CRLA called for a complete ban on methyl bromide and the use of less toxic alternatives in its place, as well as a ban on all toxic pesticides within five miles of schools.[72] In making their argument CRLA lawyers first pointed out that pesticides like methyl bromide could easily drift onto school property. Second, they established that most of the students who attended schools in these high-risk areas were minorities. As attorney Michael Meuter noted, of "twenty-one public schools within 1.5 miles of the state's most heavily fumigated areas, eighty-two percent of [the] students were non-white," and most were Latino.[73] Thus fumigation practices had a discriminatory impact. In the words of the complainants, "Imagine [these] children running track, practicing football, playing at recess, or just studying in an area where long-term and short-term pesticide exposures threaten their health and well-being."[74]

In many ways this Title VI complaint broadened the debate over pesticides. It was not a reaction to a specific poisoning incident nor did it involve workers, though the parents of the schoolchildren were farmworkers.[75] Rather it preemptively addressed schoolchildren's proximity to pesticides, and it challenged the accepted idea that fumigants like methyl bromide were agricultural necessities. On the threshold of the twenty-first century, it was an ambitious test case for farmworker justice and pesticide control. It also symbolized parents' efforts to free their children from some of the injustices that they faced in the fields.

The CRLA's 1980's critique of the EPA's "glacial pace" in carrying out investigations proved worthy of repetition in 1999. The federal agency took two years to accept the complaint for investigation, and it was not until 2011 that it released its preliminary ruling. Such delay made a joke of its 180-day deadline for issuing preliminary findings.[76] Indeed, from experiences such as this, Luke Cole concluded that complaints at the EPA just "sat on a shelf."[77] The fact that the subjects of the case were children made the delay all the more significant. By the time the EPA responded, children like Thalia and David were grown. They had not seen justice served.

In 2009, however, the EPA received a censure from the U.S. Court of Appeals when, in relation to a different case, the court noted a "consistent pattern of delay." Following the reprimand EPA administrator Lisa P. Jackson announced that "environmental justice . . . is an area that calls for innovation and bold thinking. . . . The protection of vulnerable subpopulations is a top priority, especially with regard to children."[78] Two years later the EPA declared that, in relation to the 1999 complaint, it had found a *prima facie* violation of Title VI. In a letter from the EPA's Office of Civil Rights to the California Department of Pesticide Regulation (CDPR), EPA officials explained the results of their investigation of daily methyl bromide concentrations and exposure scenarios. Specifically, they found "exceedances, to a limited extent, for short term exposures"; "exceedances, to a wider extent, for chronic exposure"; and "an adverse disparate impact upon Latino schoolchildren with respect to the application of methyl bromide between 1995 and 2001."[79] In other words current fumigation practices did appear to violate schoolchildren's civil rights. The EPA then directed the CDPR to address the situation.

Though these findings were promising, the case fell short of a victory because the CDPR engaged in private negotiations with the EPA and came to an agreement. Completely excluding the CRLA and the complainants, the resulting consent decree required nothing more than greater monitoring of "methyl bromide air concentrations by adding a monitor at or near one of the schools named in the original complaint" and "community outreach and education efforts to schools that are in high methyl bromide usage areas."[80] Essentially the EPA told the CDPR, "Just try to help people stay out of the way." Neither organization cared enough to require more than one token air monitor, which left the other high-risk areas virtually unchanged. In the wake of this resolution, the CRLA appealed the EPA's decision to reach an agreement behind the backs of the complainants. The appeal was denied and the case closed.

In a press release the EPA spoke of the decision as an environmental justice victory. "EPA is committed to ensuring that all Americans receive equal environmental and health protections," said Rafael DeLeon, director of the Office of Civil Rights. "Environmental protection is public health protection, and everyone, especially children, deserve the opportunity to live, play, and learn in healthy communities."[81] By contrast, Latino parents and CRLA lawyers felt that the "wimpy" new requirements failed to restrict the real problem of methyl bromide use.[82] Indeed the fact that the EPA and the CDPR did not include the complainants in the agreement—though such exclusivity was within their prerogative—indicated only the most limited interest in making changes. Adding insult to injury was the EPA's eleven-year delay. The *prima facie* finding of a Title VI violation was significant because it was the first of its kind; nevertheless, the result was frustratingly devoid of real action. In the words of one journalist, "The case is both EPA's biggest success and one of its most notorious failures."[83]

While *Angelita C.* fell short of a full victory, the Title VI complaint posited ideas that deserve public debate. Chief among them is the argument that the civil rights of farmworker children—indeed, of all children—should protect them from exposure to agrochemicals; therefore, certain pesticides should not be used near schools. More broadly the case questioned the need for dangerous agrochemicals at all and emphasized the need to find alternatives. These arguments should inform ongoing debates.

Equally relevant in the twenty-first century are farmworkers' arguments regarding additional environmental hazards. In Kettleman City, for instance, exposure to chemicals is not limited to pesticides; rather a second hazard is air and water contamination from Waste Management's Kettleman Hills landfill. Using the reasoning of the environmental justice movement, Kettleman City residents began the twenty-first century charging that the expansion of this landfill constituted a violation of their civil rights. Although, as with *Angelita C.*, their initial protest did not lead to many concrete changes, their experience will serve as a touchstone in twenty-first-century debates regarding environmental justice.

Kettleman City is located in Kings County, California, and has approximately 1,500 residents: 93 percent are Latino, around 62 percent are foreign-born and monolingual Spanish speakers, and many are employed as farmworkers.[84] Although these residents and the CRLA halted Waste Management's construction of an incinerator in the early 1990s, their battle for environmental justice never ended. After all they still lived next to the largest hazardous-waste facility west of the Mississippi—a facility that, since its creation in 1979, had a record of environmental violations, including mismanagement of toxic substances like polychlorinated biphenyls (PCBs).[85] Moreover, as the work of anthropologist Yalda Asmatey demonstrates, the facility constantly received new contracts and constantly sought to expand. In 1997, for example, CRLA lawyers again helped residents oppose the landfill's expansion. This time, however, they had less success. The company won the right to expand, quid pro quo a yearly donation of $70,000 to the Latino community, in addition to twenty-five cents for every ton of waste and one dollar for every ton of PCB waste.[86] Though the neglected community needed the funds, the victory for Waste Management was an ominous harbinger for the twenty-first century.

Indeed expansion efforts never ceased. In order to expand the company must receive permits from Kings County and from the California Department of Toxic Substance Control (DTSC), a branch of the state EPA (Cal EPA). As part of the permit approval process, officials often hold open meetings at which different parties, including Latino residents, can share their opinions. Some of most important debates over expansion took place at the beginning of the twenty-first century. In 2005 Waste Management requested a thirty-two-year renewal of its permit from Kings County officials, as well as permission to add 221.5 acres to their existing property. This expanded landfill, as community members pointed out, "would accept approximately 2,900 tons of hazardous waste daily, including . . . materials containing PCBs, cyanides, asbestos, solvents, corrosives, lead, metals, and halogenated organics."[87] In 2008 Waste Management requested an additional permit for expansion.[88]

In these cases and others, numerous community groups, including a youth organization named Kids Protecting Our Planet, argued that such expansion would violate their civil rights. In 2008 opposition became even more impassioned when investigation revealed a tragedy: of the twenty babies born in Kettleman City during the past fourteen months, five had been born with cleft palates, and three of those babies had passed away. During the next two years six more babies were born with similar defects. Studies also revealed that nearly one-fourth of all the town's children suffered from asthma.[89] The most obvious cause of the crisis was contamination from the nearby landfill. Of specific concern were the PCBs, which scientific study had linked to cleft palates in the 1980s.[90] Congress had banned these toxins in 1976, and the Kettleman Hills landfill remained the only facility in California authorized to receive PCB waste.[91]

Despite the birth defects Waste Management lobbied successfully for expansion. At a crucial public hearing in October 2009, Kettleman City parents hoped their personal experience would convince the Kings County Planning Commission that babies' lives were at stake. Waste Management, however, bused in scores of employees and their family members. With their green company T-shirts and hats, this sea of supporters filled the auditorium and vastly outnumbered Latino attendees. As another obstacle Waste Management had provided for consecutive interpreters to help monolingual Spanish speakers, but county officials applied a strict five-minute limit to each participant's comments. This meant that those who needed consecutive interpretation could only speak for two-and-a-half minutes.[92] Outnumbered and cut short, Latino residents were unable to change officials' opinion.

In December 2009 Waste Management received approval to expand, which sparked additional protest from the community. As debate continued, company officials described their facility as a "critical resource for the state of California." After all, they said, "It is because of the Kettleman Hills landfill that sites like PacBell (now AT&T) Park in San Francisco can be built, all of the lead paint from Golden Gate Bridge could be cleaned up and the Archie Crippen Tire Fire site in Fresno could be cleaned up." Latino residents, on the other hand, pointed to the contamination and birth defects. Maria, who had lost a baby, declared, "It is [not] a coincidence that my daughter was born unhealthy, that other babies were born unhealthy, that infants have died, and that more are being born with defects." Similarly, Magdalena Romera, whose baby passed away in 2007, told a reporter, "My daughter America was the first of the babies born with a cleft and other problems. . . . She was four-and-a half months old when she died. At first, I thought it was an act of God. Then I started hearing about the others."[93] To explain the problems, farmworker Adrian Alatorre said simply, "It's the toxic waste. It's got to affect you." Alatorre's son Emmanuel was born with a cleft lip and underdeveloped brain.[94]

To many farmworker families who resided in Kettleman City, contamination from the landfill was not a separate problem from pesticide exposure. Rather, each problem was a manifestation of the same injustice. Many residents spoke of the problems in the same breath. Romera stated, "I may not know much, but I do know one thing.... Living next to the largest toxic landfill is no good. I know that can't be good and I know it's not good to work in the fields, to be exposed to those chemicals they put on the fruit and vegetables." She added, "I see the water coming from the tap. It's disgusting." Other residents compared the two environmental hazards, concluding that the waste company's expansion constituted the greater injustice. While some farmworkers accepted pesticide risks as part of their job, they did not accept the landfill in their backyard and the harm it had caused. "We don't blame the farmers," said one worker, "because we depend on the fields as much as the fields depend on us." Another resident declared that while "pesticides should be banned," she and other activists had "turned [their] attention to Chem Waste" as the greatest threat to their health.[95]

While county officials approved the landfill's expansion, they also, under pressure from the community, requested a state investigation into the birth defects. Initially the California Department of Public Health denied the request, asserting that an investigation would not be fruitful.[96] Immediately thereafter, however, Gov. Arnold Schwarzenegger directed Cal EPA and the Department of Public Health to investigate. To do so Cal EPA created a list of chemicals and pesticides known to cause birth defects and searched for such substances in Kettleman City. As a report later indicated, the study "did not find any source of exposure that could likely be associated with birth defects." Similarly the Department of Public Health looked for "genetic, medical or pregnancy-related risk factors," lifestyle risk factors, and occupational exposure that could be related to the birth defects. Again the results "did not find a specific cause of environmental exposure that would explain the increase in the number of children born with birth defects in Kettleman City." Given the results of the study the DTSC declared, "[Our department] does not agree that approval of [Waste Management's] permit modification violates Title VI."[97]

In addition to the work of state agencies, U.S. EPA officials inspected the landfill in 2010, and in 2011 they collected samples of agricultural pesticides from Kettleman City homes to determine community members' level of exposure at home. The results, they said, indicated that people were exposed in their homes but "at levels that are too low to present a significant health risk."[98] In all studies and at all levels officials concluded that neither pollution nor pesticides had directly caused the birth defects and sicknesses of Kettleman City babies, and the case was closed. Unlike the Roundup cases, which occurred just a few years later, partial connections between the toxins and the diseases were not considered.

The California DTSC did acknowledge, however, "the multiple environmental pollution burdens born by the Kettleman City community, and the presence of poverty, language barriers and other factors which tend to make people vulnerable to the impacts of pollution."[99] As with *Angelita C.*, state officials recognized environmental injustice with unprecedented honesty, but they stopped short of real action. All Kettleman City residents received was a promise that, beginning in 2018, the DTSC would require all dump trucks that entered the landfill each day to have post-2007 engines, which would reduce air emissions. DTSC also pledged to help bring clean drinking water to Kettleman City residents.[100] These measures were something, but the landfill still expanded.

While neither *Angelita C.* nor the Kettleman City cases achieved the changes that farmworkers hoped for, they presented bold, convincing arguments that should inform twenty-first-century debate regarding exposure to environmental hazards. Moreover, in this century these cases represent the beginning of the battle rather than the end. In the last few years the CRLA has helped farmworker families win several incremental victories in the fight for environmental justice. In 2017 CRLA lawyers successfully established a "medical-legal partnership," which allows the attorneys to work directly with doctors who treat injured farmworkers. Among other advantages, this partnership permits attorneys to make use of medical reports that deal with pesticide exposure. Additionally, the CRLA in recent years has successfully included pregnant farmworkers in the State Disability Insurance Program.[101] Disability payments remove the economic pressure for pregnant women to work in the fields, thus significantly reducing the risk of pesticide poisoning to fetuses. As a final success in 2018, partially because of *Angelita C.*, the CDPR released new regulations regarding pesticide use near schools. These regulations required a quarter-mile safe zone around all schools during school hours as well as notifications sent from growers to schools when pesticides are applied.[102] Although the dangerous pesticides remain, the regulations will help.

The CRLA has also continued to work with Kettleman City. In 2014 Waste Management requested another permit to expand, which DTSC immediately approved. Again community members objected on the grounds that the expansion would violate their civil rights by exposing them disproportionately to contamination. Representing the community the CRLA filed a Petition for Review of the permit decision. When the DTSC denied the petition, the CRLA moved to the U.S. EPA, which accepted the complaint for review. In 2016 the EPA held six mediation sessions between state officials and community members.[103] With the town's medical history and the state's empty investigations on everyone's mind, the meetings led to a favorable settlement. CRLA lawyer Mariah Thompson recalled that, ideally, officials would close the landfill, but the settlement was perhaps the next best option because it began to address the need for systematic change.[104] Specifically DTSC committed to monitor Waste Management's compliance with regulations more closely and to consider such compliance before granting permit approvals—something it had not previously done.[105] Moreover, Cal EPA and DTSC agreed to provide "immediate support to the residents of Kettleman City," including "public health programs, asthma intervention activities, clean water and air monitoring, and a commitment to providing information in Spanish." The settlement also enlisted the aid of researchers from the University of California.[106]

Notably the language-access plan applies to waste facility discussions across the state, not just Kettleman City. The settlement, in other words, set a new standard for state authorities, which will require them to pay more attention to the voices of Spanish speakers in all debates over environmental justice. As CRLA lawyer Ilene Jacobs declared, the agreement confirmed "the importance of meaningful public participation, language access and protection of civil rights, regardless of race or national origin." Public participation and language access are crucial, she reiterated, because "the impact of [environmental] decisions falls so disproportionately on lower income residents in racially and ethnically concentrated areas who have few choices about where to live or work."[107] While this reality may persist in the twenty-first century, the experiences of Latino farmworkers and the CRLA can help communities move continually closer to achieving environmental justice.

Notes

1. Mike James and Jorge L. Ortiz, "Jury Ordered to Pay $289 Million to Cancer Patient in Roundup Lawsuit," *USA Today*, August 10, 2018, https://www.usatoday.com/story/news/2018/08/10/jury-orders-monsanto-pay-289-million-cancer-patient-roundup-lawsuit/962297002/; see also Emily Sullivan, "Groundskeeper Accepts Reduced $78 Million Award in Monsanto Cancer Suit," *NPR*, November 1, 2018, https://www.npr.org/2018/11/01/662812333/groundskeeper-accepts-reduced-78-million-in-monsanto-cancer-suit.

2. Julia Jacobs, "Monsanto Order to Pay $80 Million in Roundup Cancer Case," *New York Times*, March 27, 2019, https://www.nytimes.com/2019/03/27/us/monstanto-roundup-california-verdict.html.

3. Rachel Siegel, "Roundup Is Embroiled in Cancer Cases. Now Its Maker Is Putting $5.6 Billion toward a New Kind of Weedkiller," *Washington Post*, June 14, 2019, https://www.washingtonpost.com/business/2019/06/14/roundup-is-embroiled-cancer-cases-now-its-maker-is-putting-billion-toward-new-kind-weed-killer/; Tina Bellon, "California Jury Hits Bayer with $2 Billion Award in Roundup Cancer Trial," *Reuters*, May 13, 2019, https://www.reuters.com/article/us-bayer-glyphosate-lawsuit/california-jury-hits-bayer-with-2-billion-award-in-roundup-cancer-trial-idUSKCN1SJ29F.

4. Tina Bellon, "Bayer Asks California Court to Reverse $86 Million Roundup Cancer Verdict," *Reuters*, February 10, 2020, https://www.reuters.com/article/us-bayer-glyphosate-lawsuit/bayer-asks-california-court-to-reverse-86-million-roundup-cancer-verdict-idUSKBN2041QY.

5. Patricia Cohen, "Roundup Maker to Pay $10 Billion to Settle Cancer Suits," *New York Times*, June 24, 2020, https://www.nytimes.com/2020/06/24/business/roundup-settlement-lawsuits.html#:~:text=Bayer%20still%20faces%20at%20least,agreed%20to%20join%20the%20settlement.

6. Siegel, "Roundup Is Embroiled," *Washington Post*, June 14, 2019.

7. Bosso, *Pesticides and Politics*, 28, 32–33, 237.

8. Harrison, *Pesticide Drift*, 25.

9. Limerick, *Something in the Soil*, 13–27.

10. The EPA defines environmental justice as "the fair treatment and meaningful involvement of all people regardless of race, color, national origin, or income, with respect to the development, implementation, and enforcement of environmental laws, regulations, and policies. This goal will be achieved when everyone enjoys: the same degree of protection from environmental and health hazards and equal access to the decision-making process to have a healthy environment in which to live, learn, and work." See "Environmental Justice," U.S. EPA, https://www.epa.gov/environmentaljustice.

11. Street, *Beasts of the Field*, 155, 334–35, 512–14.

12. See Kinkela, *DDT and the American Century*.

13. "*California Agriculture* Time Line," 22; Bosso, *Pesticides and Politics*, 28–31.

14. Nash, *Inescapable Ecologies*, 130–33.

15. Joon Kim argues that Mexicans gradually replaced other groups, like the Chinese, because the California Farm Bureau Federation and the American Farm Bureau Federation recognized that Mexican laborers were easier to deport once harvest season ended. See Kim, "California's Agribusiness."

16. An important exception to family labor was the Bracero Program (1942–1964), an agreement between the U.S. and Mexican governments through which Mexican men immigrated as temporary field laborers. See Cohen, *Braceros*.

17. Nash, *Inescapable Ecologies*, 141–48.

18. Jesús Lopez (CRLA community worker), in discussion with the author, March 18, 2019. Lopez worked in the fields from 1971 to 1989.

19. Nash, *Inescapable Ecologies*, 128.

20. These were by no means the first farmworker advocates in California. During the previous two decades, for example, Ernesto Galarza and the National Farm Labor Union fought for better treatment of workers. In their case, however, growers and government leaders repeatedly used braceros, temporary guest laborers from Mexico, to break their strikes. See Galarza, *Spiders in the House*; see also, Valdés, *Organized Agriculture*.

21. Historians who have studied Chavez and the UFW include Jacques Levy, Richard Jensen, John Hammerback, Miriam Pawal, Frank Bardacke, Matt García, and Randy Shaw. Shaw goes so far as to argue that the legacy of the UFW set the course for virtually all social justice projects that followed. This argument, and much of the scholarship, overlooks the CRLA. Shaw, *Beyond the Fields*, preface and introduction. To see one journalist's appraisal of Chavez's authentic leadership, see Frank del Olmo, "Cesar Chavez Suffers for and Revives the Cause of Farm Workers' Contracts," *Los Angeles Times*, August 26, 1988.

22. While Chavez and the UFW still dominate the historiography, Lori Flores's 2016 *Grounds for Dreaming* provides an excellent example of how historians can examine both organizations alongside each other, thereby pulling the CRLA out of Chavez's shadow and giving its members credit for their tremendous contributions to the farmworker movement.

23. See "A CRLA Casebook: Selected Clippings and Summaries of 1968 Cases," CRLA Records, box 28, folder 1, (M0750).

24. For example, CRLA lawsuits prevented welfare officials from obligating children to work in the fields, provided free milk for low-income schoolchildren, and halted the state's practice of placing farmworker children in classes for the "mentally retarded" because they did not speak English. See Gene Blake, "Children on Welfare Forced to Pick Grapes, Suit Charges," *Los Angeles Times*, June 27, 1968, CRLA Records, box 28, folder 1; "Suit Settled:

More Free Milk for State's Kids," *San Francisco Chronicle*, March 17, 1970, CRLA Records, box 65, folder 3; Mary Ellen Leary, "Children Who Are Tested in an Alien Language: Mentally Retarded?," *New Republic*, May 30, 1970, CRLA Records, box 65, folder 6.

25. "CRLA Press Release: July 27, 1969," CRLA Records, box 65, folder 1.

26. García, *From the Jaws of Victory*, 2.

27. "Court Order Halts Aerial Crop Sprays," *Santa Barbara News*, August 5, 1969, CRLA Records, box 65, folder 6.

28. Cole and Foster, *From the Ground Up*, 221, footnote 32; Sze, "Denormalizing," 111.

29. See "Before the United States Environmental Protection Agency: Administrative Petition," CRLA Records, box 286, folder 9.

30. See Larry Parsons, "Insecticide Linked to Birth Defects," *Salinas Californian*, March 16, 1984, CRLA Records, box 167, folder 4.

31. The family's name is probably not by chance. In conversational Spanish, *cuerda* can mean rational or intelligent.

32. ¡*La Amenaza de los Pesticidas!*, CRLA Records, box 270, folder 7.

33. *Report V: Pesticides*, CRLA Records, box 271, folder 1.

34. Parsons, "Insecticide Linked," *Salinas Californian*, March 16, 1984.

35. "State Retests 96 Pesticides that EPA Had OK'd on Basis of Invalid Data," *Mercury News* (Santa Clara County), March 11, 1984, CRLA Records, box 167, folder 4.

36. See "Attack on Pesticide Controls," *Sacramento Bee*, July 24, 1982, CRLA Records, box 27, folder 1.

37. Rick Rodriguez, "Pesticides: A Growing Public Awareness," *Fresno Bee*, March 29, 1984; *Sacramento Bee*, April 29, 1984, CRLA Records, box 167, folder 4.

38. See *Report V: Pesticides*, CRLA Records.

39. Nash, *Inescapable Ecologies*, 185–95.

40. Perhaps the most publicized case from the 1980s is that of Felipe Franco, son of farmworkers in McFarland, who was born without arms or legs. During her first trimester, Felipe's mother, Ramona, worked as a grape picker in fields that had been sprayed with various pesticides. The growers told her the chemicals were harmless, just "medicine" for the plants. See Hoffman, "UFW Fights Harvest of Poison"; Street, *Everyone Had Cameras*, 523–27; Ferriss and Sandoval, *Fight in the Fields*, 235–39.

41. "Special Edition: Fields of Pain," *Sacramento Bee*, December 8–11, 1991, CRLA Records, box 271, folder 2.

42. See Hammerback and Jenson, *Rhetorical Career of César Chávez*, 156–57.

43. Sze, "Denormalizing," 108.

44. Harrison, *Pesticide Drift*, 26–30.

45. Sze, "Denormalizing," 109.

46. Wells, *Environmental Justice*, 3–7.

47. Michael Satchell, "A Whiff of Discrimination? 'Racism' Is the New Ecological Buzzword. But That Is a Mistake," *U.S. News and World Report*, May 4, 1992, CRLA Records, box 270, folder 2.

48. "Principles of Environmental Justice," adopted October 27, 1991, CRLA Records, box 270, folder 2.

49. "Presidential Documents: Executive Order 12898 of February 11, 1994," National Archives, February 16, 1994.

50. See Ellen Griffith Spears, *Baptized in PCBs*, 118.

51. Cole, "Empowerment as the Key," 620, footnote 1.

52. Mike Ward, "'Greening' Closes Gap in Austin: Environment Fuses East, West," *Austin American-Statesman*, March 8, 1992, CRLA Records, box 270, folder 2.

53. Martin Melosi argues that while the environmental justice movement's focus on cities and people did differ from environmentalism's focus on national parks and nature, the environmentalism of the Progressive Era and of the 1960s and 1970s also included care for the urban poor. Furthermore, while he acknowledges that many urban residents became activists only when contamination threatened their communities, he challenges the stereotypes that "minorities have little . . . concern for the full range of environmental issues" and that traditional environmentalism was "a white thing." Notwithstanding these arguments, Melosi still sees a strong connection between the environmental justice and Civil Rights movements. Melosi, "Environmental Justice," 46–48.

54. For example, in her 2017 presidential address to the American Society for Environmental History, Kathleen Brosnan emphasizes the need to study rural workers and their relationship with the environment. She also invites scholars to move beyond questions of injustice. Brosnan, "The Lifting Fog," 10.

55. Marcia Coyle, "Lawyers Try to Devise New Strategy," *National Law Journal*, September 21, 1992, CRLA Records, box 270, folder 2.

56. Satchell, "Whiff of Discrimination?," *U.S. News and World Report*, May 4, 1992.

57. See Cerrell Associates, "Political Difficulties."

58. See Cole and Foster, *From the Ground Up*, preface.

59. See Report, "El Pueblo Para El Aire y Agua Limpio."

60. Cole, "Environmental Justice Litigation," 527.

61. In his recent work, Josiah Rector makes a related argument, pointing out that union protest of environmental hazards throughout the mid-twentieth century can also be considered the beginning of environmental justice. In his view, important union activity includes the UFW's fight against pesticides and the United Automobile Workers (UAW's) fight to end African Americans' disproportionate exposure to dusts, fumes, oils, and other hazards in auto plants. See Rector, "Environmental Justice at Work."

62. Luke W. Cole, "Civil Rights, Environmental Justice, and the EPA: A Brief History of Administrative Complaints under Title VI," CRLA Records, box 270, folder 4.

63. "Title VI of the Civil Rights Act of 1964," The United States Department of Justice, https://www.justice.gov/crt/fcs/TitleVI, emphasis added.

64. Cole, "Civil Rights, Environmental Justice, and the EPA," CRLA Records.

65. See Talia Buford, "In California, an Unsatisfying Settlement on Pesticide-Spraying," Center for Public Integrity, August 11, 2015, https://publicintegrity.org/environment/in-california-an-unsatisfying-settlement-on-pesticide-spraying/.

66. The Center on Race, Poverty, & the Environment, "A Right without a Remedy," 5.

67. Harrison, *Pesticide Drift*, 31.

68. U.S. EPA, "Title VI Complaint 16R-99-R9: Fact Sheet."

69. Lopez, discussion; U.S. EPA, "Title VI Complaint 16R-99-R9: Fact Sheet."

70. Harrison, *Pesticide Drift*, 31.

71. See Lily Dayton, "Dangerous Drift," California Health Report, September 2, 2015, http://www.calhealthreport.org/2015/09/02/dangerous-drift.

72. The Center on Race, Poverty, & the Environment, "A Right without a Remedy," 5.

73. Sara Rubin, "Latino Families Sue EPA, Seeking Environmental Justice for Exposure to Pesticides," *Monterey County Weekly*, September 19, 2013.

74. The Center on Race, Poverty, & the Environment, "A Right without a Remedy," 1.

75. The Center on Race, Poverty, & the Environment, "A Right without a Remedy," 4.

76. The Center on Race, Poverty, & the Environment, "A Right without a Remedy," 6. See also, U.S. EPA, "Title VI Complaint 16R-99-R9: Fact Sheet."

77. Michael Meuter (CRLA attorney), in discussion with the author, March 18, 2019.

78. The Center on Race, Poverty, & the Environment, "A Right without a Remedy," 7.

79. U.S. EPA, Letter from OCR Director Rafael DeLeon to CDPR Director Christopher Reardon.

80. U.S. EPA, "Title VI Complaint 16R-99-R9: Fact Sheet."

81. Buford, "In California, An Unsatisfying Settlement," Center for Public Integrity, August 11, 2015.

82. Meuter, discussion.

83. Buford, "In California, An Unsatisfying Settlement," Center for Public Integrity, August 11, 2015.

84. Report, "El Pueblo Para El Aire y Agua Limpio."

85. Report, "El Pueblo Para El Aire y Agua Limpio"; Yalda Asmatey, "Corporation," 7, 19.

86. Asmatey, "Corporation," 95.

87. Report, "El Pueblo Para El Aire y Agua Limpio."

88. See Asmatey, "Corporation," 95–97; Report, "El Pueblo Para El Aire y Agua Limpio"; "Settlement Agreement," Greenaction for Health and Environmental Justice and El Pueblo Para el Aire y Agua Limpia (Complainants) and the Cal EPA and DTSC. http://www.crla.org/crla-wins-precedents-setting-environmental-justice-.

89. See Asmatey, "Corporation," 53, 100–101, 110; Sze, "Denormalizing," 109.

90. See Watanabe and Sugahara, "Experimental Formation," 49–53.

91. Asmatey, "Corporation," 95.

92. Asmatey, "Corporation," 101–2.

93. Asmatey, "Corporation," 104, 112–13. It is a tragic irony that Romera named her baby America when, in the United States of America, she had been unjustly exposed to chemicals that took the life of her infant daughter.

94. Jesse McKinley, "In a California Town, Birth Defects, Deaths, and Questions," *New York Times*, February 6, 2010, https://www.nytimes.com/2010/02/07/us/07kettleman.html.

95. Asmatey, "Corporation," 107–9.

96. Asmatey, "Corporation," 105.

97. California Department of Toxic Substance Control, Part III, 8–9.

98. California Department of Toxic Substance Control, Part III, 89; see also, McKinley, "In a California Town," *New York Times*, February 6, 2010.

99. California Department of Toxic Substance Control, Part III, 89.

100. California Department of Toxic Substance Control, Part III, 89, 91, 99.

101. Aaron Voit (CRLA attorney), in discussion with the author, February 14, 2019.

102. "California Code of Regulations, Division 6, Article 5: Pesticide Use Near Schoolsites," California Department of Pesticide Regulation, https://www.cdpr.ca.gov/docs/legbills/calcode/030205.htm.

103. "Settlement Agreement," 1–3.

104. Mariah Thompson and Marison Aguilar (CRLA attorneys), in discussion with the author, March 4, 2019.

105. "Settlement Agreement," 4.

106. "CRLA Wins Precedent Setting Environmental Justice Victory," CRLA Press Release, August 16, 2016, http://www.crla.org/crla-wins-precedents-setting-environmental-justice-victory.

107. "CRLA Wins," CRLA Press Release, August 16, 2016.

Bibliography

Archival Sources

California Department of Toxic Substance Control. "Part III: DTSC Response to Comments on Chemical Waste Management Request for Class 3 Permit Modification Expansion of Hazardous Waste Landfill." May 2014. In author's possession.

CRLA Records (M0750). Department of Special Collections and University Archives. Stanford University Libraries.

El Pueblo Para El Aire y Agua Limpio; Kids Protecting Our Planet, Complainants v. Board of Supervisors of Kings County, Respondents. 2010. https://www.epa.gov/sites/production/files/2014-06/documents/16r-10-r9_complaint_redacted.pdf.

U.S. Environmental Protection Agency. "Title VI Complaint 16R-99-R9: Fact Sheet." https://19january2017snapshot.epa.gov/sites/production/files/2016-04/documents/title6-c-factsheet.pdf.

U.S. Environmental Protection Agency. "Title VI Complaint 16R-99-R9." Letter from Rafael DeLeon to Christopher Reardon, April 22, 2011. https://www.epa.gov/sites/production/files/2016-04/documents/title6-c42211-preliminary-finding.pdf.

Published Sources

Asmatey, Yalda. "Corporation, People, and Government: A Look at the Rise of the Waste Management Corporation from Rural California to the Rest of the World." PhD diss., University of California, Berkeley, 2013.

Bosso, Christopher. *Pesticides and Politics: The Life Cycle of a Public Issue*. Pittsburgh: University of Pittsburgh, 1987.

Brosnan, Kathleen A. "The Lifting Fog: Race, Work, and the Environment." *Environmental History* 24 (2019): 9–24.

"California Agriculture Time Line." *California Agriculture* 50, no. 6 (November 1996): 22–31.

The Center on Race, Poverty, & the Environment. *A Right without a Remedy: How the EPA Failed to Protect the Civil Rights of Latino Schoolchildren*. Emeryville CA: CRPE Publications, 2016.

Cerrell Associates, Inc. *"Political Difficulties Facing Waste-to-Energy Conversion Plant Siting."* Report, California Waste Management Board, 1984. https://www.ejnet.org/ej/cerrell.pdf.

Cohen, Deborah. *Braceros: Migrant Citizens and Transnational Subjects in Postwar United States and Mexico*. Chapel Hill: University of North Carolina, 2011.

Cole, Luke W. "Empowerment as the Key to Environmental Protection: The Need for Environmental Poverty Law." *Ecological Law Quarterly* 19, no. 4 (1992): 619–83.

Cole, Luke W. "Environmental Justice Litigation: Another Stone in David's Sling." *Fordham Urban Law Journal* 21, no. 3 (1994): 523–45.

Cole, Luke W., and Sheila R. Foster. *From the Ground Up: Environmental Racism and the Rise of the Environmental Justice Movement*. New York: New York University, 2001.

Ferriss, Susan, and Ricardo Sandoval. *The Fight in the Fields: Cesar Chavez and the Farmworkers Movement*. New York: Harcourt Brace, 1997.

Flores, Lori. *Grounds for Dreaming: Mexican Americans, Mexican Immigrants, and the California Farmworker Movement*. New Haven: Yale University, 2016.

Galarza, Ernesto. *Spiders in the House and Workers in the Field*. Notre Dame: University of Notre Dame, 1970.

García, Matt. *From the Jaws of Victory: The Triumph and Tragedy of Cesar Chavez and the Farm Worker Movement*. Berkeley: University of California, 2012.

Hammerback, John C., and Richard J. Jenson. *The Rhetorical Career of César Chávez*. College Station: Texas A&M University, 1998.

Harrison, Jill Lindsey. *Pesticide Drift and the Pursuit of Environmental Justice*. Cambridge: MIT, 2011.

Hoffman, Pat. "UFW Fights Harvest of Poison." *Witness* (July/August 1988). https://libraries.ucsd.edu/farmworkermovement/essays/.

Kim, Joon. "California's Agribusiness and the Farm Labor Question: The Transition from Asian to Mexican Labor, 1919–1939." *Aztlan* 37, no. 2 (2012): 47–72.

Kinkela, David. *DDT and the American Century: Global Health, Environmental Politics, and the Pesticide that Changed the World*. Chapel Hill: University of North Carolina, 2011.

Limerick, Patricia. *Something in the Soil: Legacies and Reckonings in the New West*. New York: W. W. Norton, 2000.

Melosi, Martin V. "Environmental Justice, Political Agenda Setting, and the Myths of History." *Journal of Policy History* 12, no. 1 (2000): 43–71.

Nash, Linda. *Inescapable Ecologies: A History of Environment, Disease, and Knowledge*. Berkeley: University of California, 2006.

Pawal, Miriam. *The Union and Their Dreams: Power, Hope, and Struggle in Cesar Chavez's Farm Worker Movement*. New York: Bloomsbury, 2009.

"Presidential Documents: Executive Order 12898 of February 11, 1994." National Archives, Washington DC, February 16, 1994. https://www.archives.gov/files/federal-register/executive-orders/pdf/12898.pdf.

Rector, Josiah. "Environmental Justice at Work: The UAW, the War on Cancer, and the Right to Equal Protection from Toxic Hazards in Postwar America." *Journal of American History* 101, no. 2 (2014): 480–502.

Shaw, Randy. *Beyond the Fields: Cesar Chavez, the UFW, and the Struggle for Justice in the 21st Century*. Berkeley: University of California, 2008.

Spears, Ellen Griffith. *Baptized in PCBs: Race, Pollution, and Justice in an All-American Town*. Chapel Hill: University of North Carolina, 2014.

Street, Richard Steven. *Beasts of the Field: A Narrative History of California Farmworkers, 1769–1913*. Stanford: Stanford University, 2004.

Street, Richard Steven. *Everyone Had Cameras: Photography and Farmworkers in California, 1850–2000*. Minneapolis: University of Minnesota, 2008.

Sze, Julie. "Denormalizing Embodied Toxicity: The Case of Kettleman City." In *Racial Ecologies*, edited by Leilani Nshime and Kim D. Hester Williams, 107–22. Seattle: University of Washington, 2018.

Valdés, Dionicio Nodín. *Organized Agriculture and the Labor Movement Before the UFW: Puerto Rico, Hawaii, California*. Austin: University of Teas, 2014.

Watanabe, Masao, and Toshio Sugahara. "Experimental Formation of Cleft Palate in Mice with Polychlorinated Biphenyls (PCB)." *Toxicology* 19 (1981): 49–53.

Wells, Christopher W. *Environmental Justice in Postwar America: A Documentary Reader*. Seattle: University of Washington, 2018.

10

NAFTA's Legacy in the High Country

Mexican Migration to Colorado's Western Slope

ERNESTO SAGÁS

Colorado experienced major changes in the last decades of the twentieth century. The economic boom years of the 1990s, the aging of the baby boomers, and the attractive amenity lifestyle of Front Range metro areas fueled rapid demographic shifts. Thousands of transplants from other states moved in during the 1990s and 2000s. New companies set up shop in Colorado, while existing ones relocated there to attract new talent. Traditional Old West economies of agricultural production, ranching, mining, and oil and gas extraction have had to make room for a New West of high-tech industries (including defense), tourism, and real estate. As thousands moved into the state, international migrants followed suit, also attracted by new job opportunities.

Starting in the 1990s the arrival of thousands of Mexican immigrants after the implementation of the North American Free Trade Agreement (NAFTA) added a new layer and bolstered the long-standing presence of Latinos in Colorado.[1] NAFTA's economic shock waves penetrated deeply into Mexico's rural areas, where agricultural imports from the United States forced traditional small-scale farmers to seek opportunity elsewhere. Thousands of Mexicans eventually migrated to Mexico City and other large cities, to the *maquiladora* towns of the northern border, and to the United States.[2] In Colorado many of these new immigrants ended up in large metropolitan areas, such as Denver, Aurora, and Colorado Springs—traditional destinations for previous waves of immigrants from Mexico. However, the NAFTA migrants also found jobs and settled in parts of the state

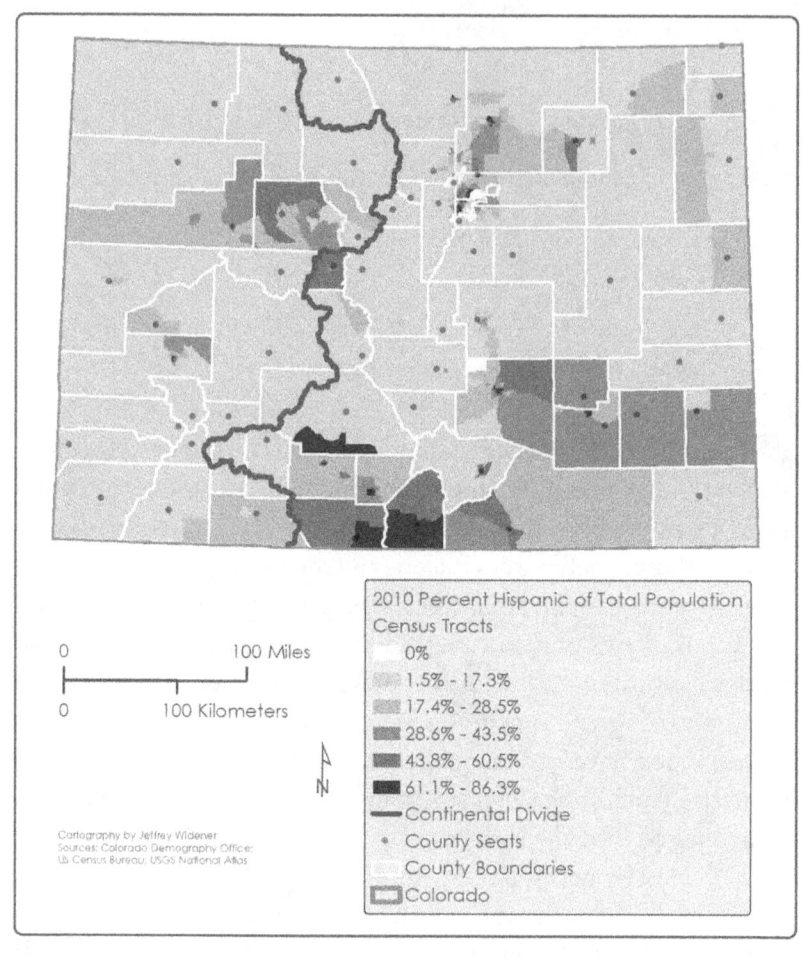

FIG. 25. Map of Colorado's Western Slope with Hispanic percentage of total population, 2010. Map by Jeffrey M. Widener.

hitherto devoid of a sizable Mexican population, such as the Western Slope—a trend that quickly reshaped the region's demographics.

The Western Slope occupies the western third of the rectangular-shaped state, encompassing most of the counties west of the Rocky Mountains and Continental Divide (see fig. 25). The area is sparsely populated. Decades ago its economy relied upon oil and gas extraction, ranching, and agriculture, but the economic boom of the 1990s fueled the expansion of the resort industry in ski towns along the I-70 highway corridor and other parts of the region. Moreover, an aging baby boomer generation and rapid statewide population increase led to the growth of regional trade and service hubs such as Grand Junction and Durango.[3] This rapid economic expansion and diversification created thousands of jobs in ranching and agriculture but mostly in the construction and service sectors, where Mexican workers met the demand for cheap, low-skill labor. The NAFTA immigrant cohort initially came for the jobs, but a generation later it represents an integral part of the region's population. Thousands of Mexican immigrants (and their descendants) now live and work throughout the Western Slope, where they make up a large segment of the population. Equally important, this new labor force occupies a vital space in an affluent economy that relies upon cheap labor.

It is essential to understand the role that (mostly) Mexican immigrants have played in the Western Slope's booming economy during the rapid demographic changes since the mid-1990s. Recent Mexican migration to Colorado is not a "new" historical development but rather the latest iteration of a long-term trend with local, regional, and global repercussions. On the other hand this new Mexican migratory cohort has such unique characteristics (e.g., different places of origin, new settlement patterns, and modes of insertion into a New West economy) that it can be argued that its migration represents a "new" development in the New West. This story is revealed by dozens of interviews with immigrants, community leaders, and staff from local agencies as well as research carried out in libraries throughout the state.[4] As such this chapter offers the first comprehensive scholarly examination of Mexican migration to Colorado's

Western Slope, its economic contributions, and the challenges that such swift demographic changes brought about to the region—and to the American West.

Latino History in the Western Slope

Colorado's Latinx history is often seen by non-Latinx Coloradoans as consisting of two distinct periods: old Hispano families that predate the Mexican-American War and 1848 purchase and annexation of the territory, and the late twentieth-century influx of (mostly) Mexican immigrants.[5] The historical reality is more complex. This popular binary narrative gives little regard to the continuous presence of Latinos in the state. Latinos are imagined as both ancient relics of a distant past (like Native Americans) and as "new" (in the form of Mexican immigrants). They are rarely seen as part of Colorado's (or the West's) continual mainstream.[6] The mainstream narrative is still one of white trappers, miners, and pioneer families that settled an "emptied" territory.[7] Popular imagination erases the continuous presence of Latinos and does not reintroduce their presence until well into the twentieth century—and then mostly as immigrants. This narrative has acute impacts for the Western Slope, where the Latino population is predominately from the "new" immigration wave.[8]

Ironically it was not until the end of the Mexican-American War in 1848 and the arrival of Anglo settlers that Latinos became a permanent fixture on the Western Slope.[9] Indigenous resistance had thwarted previous Spanish and Mexican attempts to establish permanent settlements in what is now Colorado (e.g., in the San Luis Valley). The founding of U.S. army outposts throughout the territory, significant Indian defeats at the hands of the U.S. military, and confinement of Utes, Navajos, and other Indigenous peoples onto reservations opened up the Western Slope to American settlements.[10] Most of the settlers were Anglos, though some Hispanos from the San Luis Valley and northern New Mexico also came to southwestern Colorado. Like Anglos, Hispanos came attracted by the opportunity to work in the expanding industries of the region (mining, railroads, and cattle and sheep ranching) and settled in the new towns of Durango, Mancos, and Cortez.[11]

Other parts of the Western Slope, such as the Grand Valley, were settled later. The construction of irrigation canals in the late nineteenth century boosted commercial agriculture, especially in grapes, peaches, apricots, and, later, sugar beets. When the first sugar beet factory in the state opened in Grand Junction in 1899, it attracted dozens of Hispano families to the area.[12] Displacement by Anglo settlement, legal dispossession of lands, and the demand for cheap labor as American capitalism expanded in the late nineteenth century had led Hispanos to migrate out of the San Luis Valley and elsewhere, but they mostly settled along the Front Range. Some opted to work in the Grand Valley's fruit orchards, railroad industry, and as stoop laborers in the growing sugar beet industry.[13] Need for their labor grew as sugar beet demand and prices increased during World War I, and the construction of the Grand Valley Diversion Dam in 1916 and the Government Highline Canal in 1917 opened up thousands of additional acres for sugar beet cultivation.[14] The labor shortage pulled many from Mexico as violent revolution and destruction of agricultural lands there pushed them north.

The Lucero and Bernal families provide an example of how these labor markets led to the blending of existing Hispanos and new Mexican immigrants. The Luceros came to the Grand Valley to do stoop labor after their Eastern Plains family farm in Hoehne, Colorado, failed in 1925. In 1927 Plácida Lucero married José Celso Bernal, whose family had come to the Grand Valley from Ocate, New Mexico. They were like many Mexican immigrants and refugees who arrived in the Grand Valley to work as *betabeleros* (i.e., stoop laborers) for the Holly Sugar Company. Many were seasonal workers, who would return to Mexico at the end of their contracts, but Holly built quarters near its Grand Junction factory to house workers and foster a steadier work force. This area became a Latinx neighborhood known as Las Colonias, shared by Hispano and Mexican immigrant families.[15] As for the Luceros and Bernals, they eventually rented a farm west of Grand Junction in Loma, Colorado, growing sugar beets and selling them to the Holly Sugar Company.[16]

After the Great Depression crippled the region's economy, the economic boom of World War II and attendant Bracero Program brought more Mexican workers to the Grand Valley.[17] These braceros and their descendants intermarried with the Hispano families already living in the Grand Valley, giving rise to a multigenerational, diverse Latinx community that persists to the present. Their second- and third-generation children moved out of the fields and into urban, middle-class occupations thanks to public education and their command of the English language. As a result, Grand Junction, the commercial hub of the Western Slope, has a Latinx core, and for decades cities and small towns throughout the Western Slope have had significant Latinx populations.

The end of the Bracero Program in 1964 did not stop the arrival of Mexican immigrants into the United States. Instead unauthorized workers filled the need for cheap agricultural labor in the country. The Bracero Program left a major legacy in the United States: the children of the braceros grew up to become the activists of the Chicano Movement in the 1960s and 1970s. Although El Movimiento (as the Chicano Movement was known by its members) had deep roots in Colorado, it mostly bypassed the Western Slope.[18] Some of the second- and third-generation Mexican Americans in the region started identifying as Chicanos in the 1960s and 1970s, but several factors undermined the movement in Colorado's Western Slope. First, the area did not have the sheer numbers—and geographical concentration—of Mexican Americans that parts of the Front Range (such as Denver, Colorado Springs, and Pueblo) had. With the exception of Las Colonias in Grand Junction, most Latinos were dispersed throughout the Western Slope, and their numbers were small in comparison to Front Range metro areas. Second, unlike places like the San Luis Valley, Latinos in the Western Slope were disenfranchised racial minorities who had learned to survive in a white world by keeping their heads low, trying to assimilate, and not challenging the system.[19]

Fearing discrimination, many Mexican parents encouraged their children to assimilate into the Anglo world. Thus, comparatively few Latinos from the Western Slope joined the Chicano Movement. Third, the Western Slope was—and to a certain extent still is—a geographically and socially isolated region; conservative in its cultural and political outlook, it is worlds apart from the hustle and bustle of the Front Range. Thus, Western Slope Latinos did not have the same exposure to the Chicano Movement as their counterparts on the Front Range did, and their conservative milieu and perennial minority status meant that few of them were inclined to join it. Most retained a Mexican American or Hispano identity over a Chicano one. Fourth, the rural Western Slope lacked the institutions of higher education that became incubators of the Chicano Movement elsewhere (such as the University of Colorado, Boulder). Grand Junction had Mesa College, but very few Latinos attended it. According to José Chavez, a Chicano activist from Grand Junction who attended Mesa College in the mid-1970s, there were only about twenty Latinx students on campus at the time. They founded a chapter of United Mexican American Students (UMAS, which he presided over from 1975 to 1976), but because of their small numbers they usually ended up going to the San Luis Valley or the Front Range to meet and march with fellow Chicanx activists there. His political activism with UMAS felt threatening and unpatriotic to conservative Anglos, and Chavez received death threats in the mail.[20]

The Coming of NAFTA

Even after the decline of the sugar beet industry in the 1970s, the Western Slope remained a destination for Mexican immigrants, who sought work in the region's orchards, farms, and ranches as well as in a budding service industry in Grand Junction and other towns.[21] The region's economy—also based upon extractive industries such as uranium, coal, and oil—went through boom-and-bust cycles in the 1980s and 1990s, placing the region's inhabitants on an economic rollercoaster ride of unemployment and underemployment. This caused much distress in small towns that found themselves without consistent tax revenues to provide basic services.

These economic challenges coexisted with new growing real estate and recreation economies. Western Slope cities like Durango, Grand Junction, Montrose, Glenwood Springs, Pagosa Springs, Vail, Aspen, and Telluride grew in the late twentieth century. Weather, lifestyle, and jobs in the new technology and service industries attracted new populations. The economic and demographic changes were more drastic along the Front Range but equally noticeable in the small cities and towns of the Western Slope. The other newcomers to the region were retirees, most of them baby boomers seeking an amenity lifestyle, sparking a real estate and construction boom in the aforementioned towns.[22] Finally, these newcomers were joined by hundreds of thousands of tourists, as the recreation industry took off and became one of the pillars of Colorado's economy. The economic and demographic growth created thousands of new jobs, some in industries that needed cheap labor such as retail and hospitality. As ski resorts, hotels, and restaurants thrived in the new economy, thousands of servers, dishwashers, maids, clerks, and other entry-level positions needed to be staffed. The attendant construction boom also created demand for cheap labor. Mexican immigrants filled that void—as they have done so many times before in our nation's history.

As it had generations prior, the pull of labor demand was matched by the push of economic hardship in Mexico during the 1980s and 1990s.[23] Economic crises forced Mexico to cut back on social spending, restructure its economy, and accept conditions imposed by the International Monetary Fund in order to secure new loans. A new slate of technocratic presidents in Mexico embraced globalization, opening up the country's economy. This culminated in the signing of NAFTA with Canada and the United States in 1992, with implementation starting January 1, 1994. More American companies began investing in Mexico.[24] But NAFTA also had significant deleterious effects on Mexico's countryside. U.S. agricultural imports soon flooded Mexico's consumer market, making it impossible for family farms to turn a profit. Mexican farmers began abandoning the countryside by the thousands, seeking jobs in Mexico's industrial cities (e.g., Mexico City and Monterrey), the rapidly growing *maquiladora* border towns (e.g., Tijuana and Ciudad Juárez), and *el Norte* (i.e., the United States).

The ripple effects of NAFTA not only sparked a new wave of Mexican immigration to the United States, but it also altered the nature of the flow.[25] Whereas the majority of previous Mexican immigrants to the United States came from northern states such as Sonora and

Chihuahua, central and southern states such as Jalisco, Guanajuato, Guerrero, and Michoacán produced the bulk of emigrants by the 1990s. Most were young men. They completed migratory circuits, located seasonal or temporary employment, sent remittances home to their families, eventually returned to Mexico, and often repeated the process year by year.

The first decades of the twenty-first century have complicated these labor migration patterns. Increased border barrier infrastructure and enforcement post-9/11 have disrupted circular migration routes and make transnational passage more difficult. Simultaneously, Mexican drug cartel violence, extortion rackets, and human smuggling have made border crossing more dangerous. Hundreds died in the desert or at the hands of smugglers and the drug cartels, who frequently rob, beat, and rape those attempting to cross.[26] While these factors make immigrants' journey to the United States more difficult, dangerous, and expensive, the potential for significantly higher wages continues to pull thousands of Mexicans north. New patterns have emerged in response—less cyclical migration of young men and more family migration—viewing the path to the United States as a one-way road.

New Mexican Migrants in the Western Slope

The 1990s witnessed an unprecedented surge of Mexican immigration to the Western Slope in response to NAFTA and other factors. Traditional migrant flows from northern Mexican states were joined by central and southern Mexicans as well as Central Americans from El Salvador, Guatemala, and elsewhere. Initially, many were young men from rural backgrounds and with little education beyond elementary school. More full-family immigration followed post-9/11, as previously discussed. While men tended to concentrate in construction, landscaping, and agriculture, women found jobs in hotels, restaurants, and domestic service.[27] From the 1990 to 2000 census, the Western Slope's Latino population grew by 100 percent, and their overall representation in the region grew from 8.06 percent to 11.49 percent of the population.[28]

Parsing Latino demographic data from the U.S. census for the

Western Slope is challenging. The United States Census Bureau does not ask questions about immigration, so it is impossible to determine immigration numbers to Colorado. The long census form (sent to one in six households) asks the respondent's country of birth, but many immigrants do not answer this question. Moreover, the data is not available at the county level and thus is impossible to determine for the Western Slope region. Both the short and long census forms include a question about Latino/Hispanic origin that asks if the respondent is Mexican/Mexican American/Chicano, but this question concerns ancestry, not necessarily national origin, and it is meant to be answered by all Latinos. Regardless of ancestry or national origin, some Latinos answer the less specific "Other Latino." There were 757,181 individuals in Colorado who indicated Mexican ancestry in the 2010 census, which is about 73 percent of all Latinos in the state. Assuming a similar percentage for the Western Slope, that is about sixty-four thousand individuals of Mexican ancestry living in the region—though it is impossible to tell which identify as Hispanos, Mexican immigrants, Mexican Americans, Chicanos, etcetera.[29] Thus, demographic growth analysis relies upon data for Colorado Latinos as a whole, assuming trends for the region's Latinx population are reflective of the region's Mexican immigrant population (see table 2).[30]

Table 2. Latinx Population of Colorado's Western Slope, 1990–2017

	1990	2000	2010	2017 (est.)
Total number	26,433	52,781	88,050	101,015
Percent of population	8.06	11.49	15.93	17.55

Sources: Colorado Department of Local Affairs, State Demography Office, "Race and Hispanic Origin"; U.S. Census Bureau figures, 1990, 2000, and 2010.

The fastest growth—a doubling of the Latinx population—took place in the 1990s, concurrent with the state's economic boom and NAFTA's implementation. By 2010 Latinos had become 15.93 percent of the Western Slope's population—a 66.82 percent increase—and by 2017 the State Demography Office estimated that the region's Latinx population had increased to 17.55 percent of the whole.[31] These figures are dwarfed by the hundreds of thousands of Latinos who

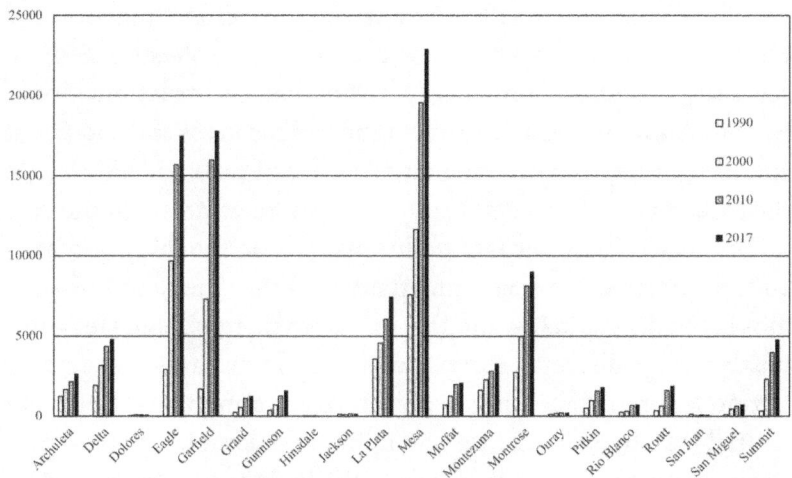

FIG. 26. Latinx population of western Colorado, by county, 1990–2017. State of Colorado, Department of Local Affairs, State Demography Office, https://demography.dola.colorado.gov/population/data/race-estimate/#county-race-by-age-estimates; U.S. Census Bureau, "Annual Estimates of the Resident Population by Sex, Race, and Hispanic Origin for the United States, States, and Counties: April 1, 2010 to July 1, 2013."

live in Colorado's Front Range, but the demographic trends reflect a rapidly growing population in a region of the state with historically below-average numbers for Latinos. It seems like the Western Slope's Latinx population is getting close to matching the state's average of 22 percent Latinos, and it could even surpass it in the near future.

Where these Latinos choose to live is equally important. The Western Slope is not only a sparsely inhabited region of the state but also an unevenly inhabited one. The rugged topography of the region, broken up by mountains, mesas, and canyons, concentrates most of the population in valleys, lowlands, and highway corridors. Some counties—like Hinsdale or San Juan—have fewer than a thousand inhabitants, whereas Grand Junction's Mesa County has more than 150,000.[32] Latinx populations follow these general patterns (see fig. 26). Moreover, ski resort towns like Aspen, Vail, and Telluride are well-known for having a small year-round population and hundreds of part-time "residents," who own a second home they occupy only seasonally. High costs of living in ski resort towns mean that some of the "locals" cannot afford to live there and are forced to commute from places where rents are cheaper.

Mesa County and La Plata County, home to Grand Junction and Durango respectively (the largest towns on the Western Slope), saw a large influx of Latinos as a result of their construction booms. Both towns went through a growth spurt in the 1990s and 2000s that spilled over into neighboring areas, such as Fruita and Clifton (in the case of Grand Junction) and unincorporated areas (in the case of Durango). In both cases traditional jobs in ranching and agriculture attracted Mexican immigrants, but the cities also provided jobs in retail, hospitality, and tourism. Both metropolitan areas now bustle with malls, retail stores, hotels, and restaurants that employ Latino laborers, including many Mexican immigrants. Entrepreneurial members of the Mexican immigrant community have now started small businesses that cater to the Latinx community, such as Mexican restaurants, taquerías, small grocery shops, clothing stores, butcher shops, bakeries, and centers to send remittances back home. Some of these stores are veritable multipurpose businesses where people can shop, eat, and send money home to Mexico.

The growth of existing metropolitan centers like Grand Junction and Durango (and their Latinx populations) is unsurprising. The growth of Latinx communities within driving distance of resort towns such as Vail, Aspen, and Telluride has been more unexpected. This is evident in Eagle, Garfield, and Summit Counties (see fig. 26). All three are on the I-70 corridor, just west of the Continental Divide. Eagle County is home to Vail, an affluent, world-class ski resort destination, and nearby ski areas lie near I-70, including Breckenridge in Summit County. The region is also dotted with small towns like Frisco and Silverthorne that host associated retail, dining, and lodging options. This recreation-based economy relies on the hard work of Latinos (mainly Mexican immigrants), who clean, cook, and serve the thousands of tourists that flock to the slopes every winter.

Low-wage Latinx workers employ multiple strategies to survive in the high-cost ski country. Many cannot afford to live where they work. Costs of living are driven to astronomical levels by real estate markets catering to luxury homes and condos. Instead workers can only afford rent or real estate farther down I-70, away from the resort towns, in mobile home parks or substandard housing. In those locations many live with extended family members and pool resources to make conditions tenable. Though requiring a commute, some strategize by working multiple jobs. For example Rocío Guzmán, a middle-aged immigrant from central Mexico, works back-to-back eight-hour shifts in two fast-food establishments in Vail in order to justify her long commute from Gypsum, a small mining community about forty miles away. Luckily for her there is bus service to Vail from Gypsum, and her two jobs are in the same strip mall, so she just changes clothes and walks next door to start her second shift.[33] Others are not so lucky. Many Latinos in the region endure long, treacherous commutes in winter to and from work.

Similar stories can be found in tiny Pitkin County, which boasts the most expensive real estate market in Colorado. Home to Aspen, another world-class ski resort, and Glenwood Springs, a tourist destination with hot springs right on I-70, the median home value in Pitkin County is $662,964, and a third of its homes value at more than a million dollars.[34] As a winter playground where millionaires arrive by private jets for ski vacations, even middle-income teachers, police officers, and city workers cannot afford to live in and around Aspen. For low-wage Mexican immigrant workers the situation is all the worse, and most reside down the I-70 corridor, commuting from mining towns like Silt, Rifle, and Parachute. Aspen's spectacular growth was made possible and is only sustained by the labor of Mexican immigrants, who drive long distances to work lengthy shifts in Colorado's most expensive place. The luxury living and environmental privilege of Aspen's residents and tourists stand in sharp contrast to the dilapidated housing that Mexican immigrant workers rent miles away in run-down boom-and-bust mining towns.[35]

New West economies based on immigrant labor are also evident in Telluride, a major luxury ski resort destination second only to Aspen. The old mining town is set in a stunning Rocky Mountain valley, and its growth has spilled over into a new development next door in Mountain Village, connected to Telluride by a gondola. Despite efforts by the city of Telluride to provide affordable housing to middle-income workers, most cannot afford to live there.[36] This was a vexing problem when the town went through its construction boom in the 1990s and early 2000s. It needed hundreds of construction and service workers, but there was no affordable housing for them. Immigrants filled this void. According to Ricardo Pérez, executive director of the Hispanic Affairs Project, more than a thousand Latinx immigrant workers commuted more than an hour daily from Montrose and Olathe to Telluride. These immigrants came mostly from northern and central Mexico, though there were also some Central Americans. Initially they were attracted to familiar agricultural jobs in the Montrose area, but they soon moved into better-paying construction and service jobs in Telluride.[37] Entrepreneurial immigrants purchased vans and earned a living making several round trips a day from the Montrose/Olathe area to Telluride, ferrying hundreds of immigrant workers to support Telluride's booming economy.[38] Naturally Montrose County's Latinx population grew in the 1990s and 2000s, but no such increase is evident in San Miguel County (Telluride) where most immigrant workers could not afford to live (see fig. 26).

A similar phenomenon—albeit on a much smaller scale—can be seen in Gunnison, where male Mexican immigrants came for sheepherding jobs in the 1980s. By the 1990s they had brought their families with them and created a community that now works primarily in the service and hospitality industry. Gunnison is a short thirty-minute drive from Crested Butte, where the former Club Med was one of the first ski resorts to hire Mexican immigrants in the 1990s. Nowadays dozens of them commute to work in Crested Butte's ski resorts, mansions, and ritzy vacation condos. While many hail from Tabasco or Chihuahua, more than half of Gunnison's Mexican immigrant community are Cora peoples, an Indigenous group from the mountainous region of the state of Nayarit (in central Mexico).[39] The Coras are a very tightly knit community, and some are not fluent in Spanish, creating linguistic and ethnic divisions between them and other Spanish-speaking Mexican immigrants, who often view the Cora as backward Indians.[40]

A Changing Ethnic Landscape

Compared to the enormous post-NAFTA migration of Mexicans to Colorado's Front Range, the small numbers of Mexican immigrants in the Western Slope may seem relatively irrelevant. However raw

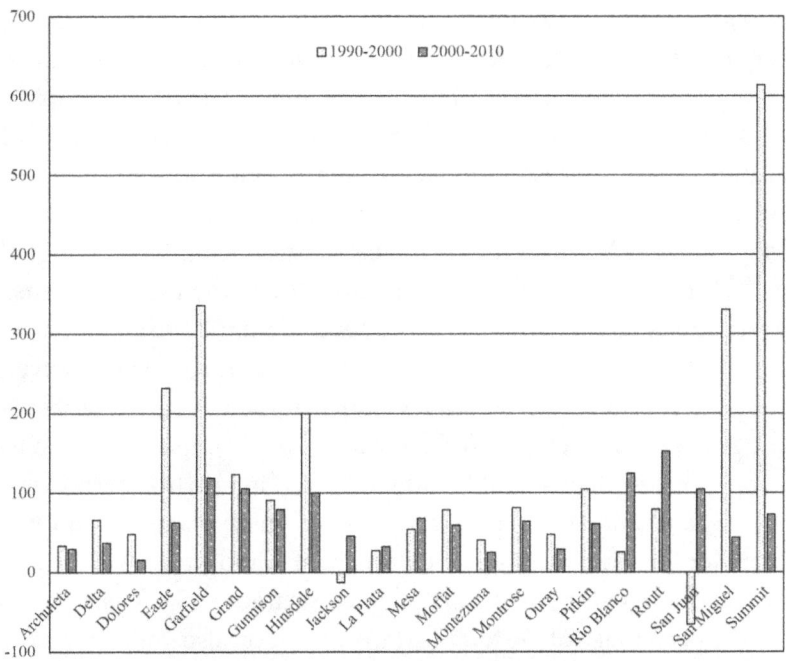

FIG. 27. Percent rate of change of Latinx population in western Colorado, 1990–2000 and 2000–2010. State of Colorado, Department of Local Affairs, State Demography Office, https://demography.dola.colorado.gov/population/data/race-estimate/#county-race-by-age-estimates; U.S. Census Bureau, "Annual Estimates of the Resident Population by Sex, Race, and Hispanic Origin for the United States, States, and Counties: April 1, 2010 to July 1, 2013."

numbers do not tell the whole story, particularly in a region characterized by few cities, a scattering of small towns, and vast rural areas that only holds about 10 percent of Colorado's population. A closer look at how quickly these population changes took place and the current standing of the Latinx immigrant population in the Western Slope helps reveal the powerful impact of recent Mexican immigration on this region of Colorado. Due to its generally sparse population, Mexican migrants have profoundly transformed the Western Slope's ethnic landscape.[41] The percent changes of Latinx populations in western Colorado counties are uneven and reveal important patterns (see fig. 27).

It is unsurprising that the greatest changes (by far) took place in rural areas hitherto devoid of Latinx communities that saw a sudden influx of Mexican immigrants in the 1990s as NAFTA was being implemented. Eagle, Garfield, and Summit Counties experienced triple-digit growth rates as Mexican immigrants flocked to construction, service, and hospitality jobs in the 1-70 ski resort towns of Aspen and Vail. These were counties in which few, if any, Latinos resided before 1990, unlike places like Grand Junction, which had a long-standing Mexican American/Chicanx community. San Miguel and Hinsdale Counties are statistical outliers: the former because few Latinos could afford to live in Telluride until affordable housing was built in the 1990s, the latter because only four Latinos lived in sparsely populated Hinsdale County in 1990. Also noticeable is the greater rate of change from 2000 to 2010 (compared to 1990 to 2000) for Rio Blanco and Routt Counties (in northwestern Colorado), as immigrants began "discovering" these places and moved there for jobs in ranching, agriculture, and mining as well as the service economy in the ski resort town of Steamboat Springs.

The percentage of the total Latino population also grew from 1990 to 2010 in geographically distinct ways (see fig. 28). Again the biggest Latinx populations (percentagewise) are found in the rapidly growing immigrant bedroom communities of Eagle and Garfield Counties, where small mining towns became affordable destinations for Mexican immigrants working in Aspen and Vail. Garfield County's low-cost rural communities like Parachute, Rifle, and Silt saw its Latinx population grow from 5 percent of the population in 1990 to 28 percent in 2010. In neighboring Eagle County close to a third of the population is now Latinx. Similarly 20 percent of Montrose County's population is now made up of Latinos—a direct result of Telluride's economic boom. Even Archuleta County, home to vacation resorts in Pagosa Springs and the gateway community to Wolf Creek ski area, is now 18 percent Latinx, compared to just 2 percent back in 1990. With the exception of tiny San Juan County, Latinx population statistics increased in all Western Slope counties numerically and by percentage. These increases are the direct result of Mexican immigration flows in the 1990s and 2000s, fueled by the push of NAFTA's deleterious impact on rural Mexico and the pull of Colorado's booming economy. The 2008 recession brought

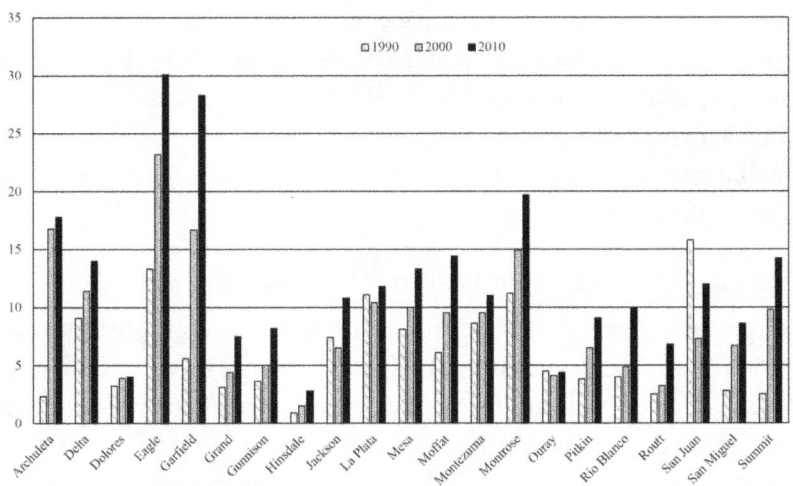

FIG. 28. Latinos as a percentage of the population in western Colorado, by county, 1990–2010. State of Colorado, Department of Local Affairs, State Demography Office, https://demography.dola.colorado.gov/population/data/race-estimate/#county-race-by-age-estimates; U.S. Census Bureau, "Annual Estimates of the Resident Population by Sex, Race, and Hispanic Origin for the United States, States, and Counties: April 1, 2010 to July 1, 2013."

this sustained labor migration to a screeching halt. The recession not only slowed down Mexican migration across the nation but increased out-migration to Mexico and seems to have provoked a net reverse flow.[42] The 2008 recession hit the immigrant community hard. Stalled construction projects and decreased tourism eliminated jobs in construction and service industries.[43] Faced with few decent job prospects and having to support families in two countries, some immigrants returned home. Entire families were (again) uprooted by the economic crisis, tearing apart the social fabric of immigrant communities and displacing people who were yet in the process of establishing secure lives in the United States.[44] Nonimmigrant populations were also hurt by the recession, and anti-immigrant feelings emerged. Repeating historic cycles, immigrants were accused of stealing jobs, depressing wages, and draining social services. This deepened already extant linguistic and cultural gaps between "Americans" and Mexican immigrants.[45] In Durango the influx of affluent, white Texans concurrently turned the former liberal college town into an increasingly conservative enclave less welcoming to Latinx immigrants.[46] Across the Western Slope the worlds of these disparate populations overlapped less and less. In spite of these hardships Mexican immigrants to the Western Slope have managed to create stable communities with deep roots now extending into a second (and a third) generation.

Creating Immigrant Communities

In popular discourses Mexican immigrants are often portrayed as sojourners who come to the United States just to work and send money home, without developing meaningful attachments to the places where they reside. This stereotype is fueled by the huge cultural gap between Anglos and Mexicans and by the extended family connections in Mexico that most first-generation immigrants maintain. But this stereotype, like most, is overblown. Mexican immigrants to the Western Slope (and their children) reside in thriving ethnic communities, and the second generation is now moving into the U.S. middle class. Across the Western Slope new Mexican shops, restaurants, businesses, community organizations (like Hispanic Affairs Project, Compañeros, and Child & Migrant Services), a Western Colorado Latino Chamber of Commerce (based in Grand Junction), and even a monthly Spanish-language newspaper (*La Voz del Pueblo*, or the people's voice) all cater to immigrant communities.[47]

In the twenty-first century the second generation is moving into the U.S. middle class. Benefiting from U.S. education and English fluency, many young women have found employment in pink-collar occupations, and many young men are keen to join the U.S. military—a ticket to seeing the world beyond the Western Slope while also providing gainful employment. Intermarriages with the nonimmigrant and older Hispano/Chicanx populations are slowly taking place too. The second-generation children of Mexican immigrants are behaving just as scores of previous immigrants before them did: they are being assimilated and acculturated by schools and other socializing agents, while still retaining traces of their parents' culture (such as bilingualism). While racial prejudice and daily microaggressions against "Mexicans" are still commonplace, the second-generation

Mexican Americans of the Western Slope are deeply immersed in American society and worlds away from their parents' lived experiences as immigrants. Casual observers may not notice this as it is obscured by a process known as "replenished ethnicity"—ongoing new immigration gives the appearance of a wholly "Mexican" community that does not intend to become Americanized.[48] The trope of the "unassimilable Mexican" runs deep throughout the West and delegitimizes Latinos by alleging that they—because of their cultural ancestry—cannot become full-fledged Americans. The struggle for legitimacy in American society is one that Hispanos faced in the past and that Mexicans and other Latinos still face to this day.[49]

Meanwhile the progress of the old Hispano/Chicanx families in the region continues. Most form part of a solid middle class of businesspeople and professionals. In 2000 one of them, Cindy Enos-Martinez (third-generation Latina), became the mayor of Grand Junction—the largest city in the Western Slope. Many Hispanos have assimilated and trend politically conservative. Others retain their Latinx identity and see in the plight of recent Mexican immigrants the story of their own families, thus supporting efforts for comprehensive migratory reform, to provide the undocumented with driver's licenses, and for Congress to pass the Development, Relief, and Education for Alien Minors (or, DREAM) Act.[50]

Finally, Mexican immigrants also contribute to their communities and a robust economy in Colorado in roles beyond construction and domestic labor. They increasingly operate as small-business owners and white-collar professionals. Moreover throughout the American West Latinx immigrants have infused rural counties with new blood, while white populations age and their younger generations leave for education and employment in larger cities.[51] In rural Colorado most ranchers and farmers are older, white men, but their workforce is Latinx.[52] As the children of white farmers and ranchers leave the land, Latinx immigrants from rural backgrounds have picked up the mantle—Anglos and Mexicans united by their love for the land. John Harold, the king of Olathe's Sweet Corn, has employed thousands of Mexican immigrant workers over the course of more than two decades, some of whom now return with their grown children to harvest corn in his fields. John defends his immigrant labor force. Currently one of his children even grows sweet corn in Mexico thanks to the connections that the family developed over the years with their Mexican workers.[53]

In the immediate post-NAFTA period immigrants from Mexico have become the latest cohort in Colorado's lengthy Latinx history. They are major contributors to the state's economy and have built resilient communities in the face of adversity, and the second generation has moved into the ranks of the U.S. middle class. When NAFTA was signed in 1992, few thought that Colorado's Western Slope would be so radically transformed in just two decades. In hindsight their arrival is not a new story but a new chapter in the history of Latinos in Colorado.

Migration in the Twenty-First-Century West

Although this work has limited itself to examining the experience of Latinos in Colorado's Western Slope, it also sheds light on certain themes germane to the (re)definition of the twenty-first-century American West. Latinos (including Mexican migrants) are an intrinsic part of the West, and their impact must be recognized as omnipresent in historical and contemporary narratives. Three key ideas can inform ongoing discussions of Latinos in western histories, imaginations, and identities.

First, Latinos/Hispanics are not foreign; they are part of the West. In spite of nativist political discourses that sought—and still seek—to portray Latinos as perpetually "foreign," the latter have always been part of the American West. From the Hispano populations that settled parts of the West long before it became part of the United States, to the waves of Mexican, Central American, and other Latinx immigrants who have arrived in the last few decades, their presence long-defined the region. Ironically much of this "othering" has been carried out by Anglo groups with shallower roots in the region themselves. Racializing Indigenous and Hispano populations served to justify American expansion and land acquisition as well as a pliant cheap labor pool. Presently Anglo transplants view Colorado's Latinos as "foreign," surprised by the presence of "Mexicans" in "their" state—regardless of whether these Latinos are old stock Hispanos or recently arrived immigrants from Latin America. The Western Slope, with a growing population of Anglo transplants and retirees, is a good case study of this pernicious trend. Throughout the American West whiteness still amounts to unquestionable nativity, whereas communities of color have never been able to totally shed their foreignness.[54]

Second, Western labor is "Mexican" labor. Mexicans may not have been a good fit for Anglo standards of whiteness but have always had a place in western industries as cheap laborers. The West is a "Third World" region of the U.S. First World, which has many elements in common with other frontier territories: dependence on government, extractive industries, and tourism; geographically distant from the centers of power, decision-making, and capital; conquered and exploited from elsewhere; and vast, rural, and underpopulated. In the West the "Mexican" label became a placeholder for Hispanos, Chicanos, Mexican Americans, and other Latinos, who toil in economic sectors where labor is racialized, low wages and harsh working conditions are the norm, and Anglos rarely work alongside Mexicans. Since 1848 "Mexicans" have been the preferred cheap labor force in Western farms, ranches, mines, and other industries (e.g., the railroad industry). As the Old West transitions to—and coexists with—the New West, "Mexicans" continue to be the main cheap labor force of the twenty-first-century American West. In a sense Mexican migrants travel from the Global South to a peripheral region of the Global North. Construction sites, retail businesses, and the hospitality and amenity industries of Colorado's Western Slope rely on "Mexican" labor to turn a profit while keeping labor costs down (as is the case throughout the West). The background of the workers has changed since the last two centuries, with more immigrants from central and southern Mexico, Central America, and some South American countries (e.g., Bolivia, Peru, and Chile), but their racialization in western industries continues unabated. Throughout the Western Slope Peruvian sheepherders, Cora housekeepers, and Guatemalan mushroom farmworkers perform "Mexican" labor: racialized, low-paying, menial jobs that Anglos would not do. In American society arduous labor often goes beyond a low wage and a job description—it involves race, too. Hired en masse during boom years but compelled to leave during bust periods, "Mexican" labor maintains a long-standing, continuous presence in the American West unlike other regions of the United States.

A case may be made that the September 11, 2001, attacks and the subsequent militarization of the U.S.-Mexico border, tougher immigration policies, and the immigrant humanitarian crisis may present a discontinuity between the twentieth-century and the twenty-first-century American West. While the increased danger and difficulty of crossing the U.S.-Mexico border has certainly altered the nature of Mexican migration to the United States in the first twenty years of this century, "Mexican" workers remain the backbone of many Western industries. George W. Bush's new border wall, Barack Obama's mass deportations, and Donald Trump's draconian refugee policies may have slowed down immigration from the Global South, but racialized "Mexican" labor is still as much a part of the landscape of Colorado's Western Slope and the rural American West as the iconic cattle ranches, oil rigs, and plains, mesas, and mountains that passersby see from their car windows.

Third, we can ask how Latinos get to (re)define "the West." Our (American) West is a geographical figment of the nation's imagination based on the westward expansion of the United States. We have a West just because we look at it from the East. For Asian migrants, it was their East, while for Indigenous peoples, it is home. For Latinos the American West has been their North (*el Norte*), a designation that overlaps with distinctions between the Global North (which includes the American West) and the Global South (which includes Latin America). Therefore for Latinos el Norte is more than a geographical label; it is a socioeconomic realm with sharp economic distinctions but blurred cultural ones. El Norte can be an extension of home but also a foreign land. The borderlands—a cultural zone that extends far away from the international border into the western United States and northern Mexico—blend the Global South into the Global North as much as they blend Mexico into the United

States. Here history moves in a northerly fashion, north from Mexico (and before that, New Spain). Yet the borderlands are also a region on their own, distinct from points farther north and south. It is a Chicanx homeland that also partakes in the West's ethnic diversity. When Mexicans migrate to Colorado's Western Slope, they encounter an unfamiliar land with familiar faces—a region foreign in a domestic sense. Therefore for Latinx peoples the American West revolves on a north-south axis as visualized from the Global South. From this perspective Anglos are not native to the area but newcomers, and Latinos have always been part of the history of el Norte.

Latinos (i.e., Hispanos, Chicanos, Mexicans, and others) represent an element of continuity in the American West. They were here before the arrival of the United States to its "West," and they remain an intrinsic part of the American West (their Norte) to this day. Moreover Latinos have shaped the West into a homeland, an element that they hold in common with Indigenous peoples, Mormons, and other communities (re)created in the American West. Yet in spite of historical continuities twenty-first-century Latinx migration brings an element of diversity, disruption, and discontinuity to the West. Latinos are as much a part of the New West as they were of the Old West. As this case study points out, Latinx immigrants are not only adding a new layer to the long-standing presence of Latinos in Colorado, but they are also establishing a new presence—and creating new communities—in places from which they had been absent. For Latinos the American West is still a frontier; a new frontier that may involve vast distances, economic uncertainty, and personal peril. But as in the frontier past, global forces still set people in motion. They, in turn, (re)shape the character of the American West into the early twenty-first century. Latinos are major agents of continuity and change in this ongoing western (hi)story.

Notes

1. The stated goal of NAFTA was to lower—and in some cases, eliminate—trade barriers between the United States, Canada, and Mexico, thus increasing trade and creating a large trading bloc that would rival the European Union. See Boskin, NAFTA at 20.

2. *Maquiladoras* are factories established by foreign companies throughout the Global South (in this case, Mexico). They take advantage of cheap labor and low tariffs to assem-

ble or manufacture products that are exported to the Global North. Massey, Durand, and Malone, *Beyond Smoke and Mirrors*, 73–81.

3. Both cities have airports, large malls, and dozens of stores, restaurants, and offices that cater to local and regional growing populations. Ricardo Pérez (executive director of the Hispanic Affairs Project), in discussion with the author, June 4, 2014.

4. This research was made possible by grants from the Charles Redd Center for Western Studies at Brigham Young University and the College of Liberal Arts at Colorado State University.

5. *Hispanos* (from *hispanoamericano*) is the name used to refer to the former Spanish/Mexican settlers of northern New Mexico and southern Colorado and their descendants. Facing widespread discrimination from U.S. authorities, many of them resorted to highlighting their Spanish (i.e., white European) cultural roots—and downplaying their Mexican/Indigenous ancestry—through the use of terms such as "Spanish American" (or simply "Spanish") at a time when only whites could hold U.S. citizenship. The term also serves to differentiate these old-stock families from more recent immigrants from Mexico. Nostrand, *The Hispano Homeland*, 3–25. *Latinx* is a gender-neutral term used nowadays to refer to Latinas/os in general.

6. Limerick, *The Legacy of Conquest*, 255.

7. The state of Colorado issues a "Pioneer" special license plate for those who want to display their pioneer heritage. No similar license plates exist for Native Americans or Latinos. See https://colorado.gov/pacific/dmv/group-special-license-plates.

8. Lopez Tushar, *The People of El Valle*, 48–49.

9. *Anglo* is a term widely used throughout the American West to refer to non-Hispanic whites of European ancestry (i.e., Anglo Americans). In Colorado it referred mostly to Americans (and recent European immigrants) settling into the territory from the East. Besides being an ethnic label, it also implies an outsider, non-native status (unlike Native Americans and Hispanos). Nostrand, *The Hispano Homeland*, 99.

10. Abbott, Leonard, and Noel, *Colorado*, 116–17.

11. Such was the case of the Archibeque family (sheepherders of Navajo, Ute, Pueblo, and French/Basque ancestry), who in the 1870s migrated north from Bloomfield, New Mexico, to southwestern Colorado, eventually settling in Mancos and Cortez. Larry Archibeque (retired teacher and school principal), in discussion with the author, June 1, 2015.

12. Carr and Kempa, *The History of Las Colonias Park*, 24.

13. Abbott, Leonard, and Noel, *Colorado*, 354–55.

14. Carr and Kempa, *The History of Las Colonias Park*, 27.

15. Carr and Kempa, *The History of Las Colonias Park*, 38–39. Latinx residents nicknamed their neighborhood "La Gara" (i.e., the rag) after the bandana used by *betabeleros* to protect themselves from the sun while working in the fields. José Chavez (Chicano activist), in discussion with the author, June 16, 2014.

16. One of their children, Santiago Bernal, would eventually own a farm in Loma (which the family purchased from Jesús Maldonado, a Hispano from the San Luis Valley). The Bernals and the Luceros were part of about twenty Hispano land-owning families in the area; all of which are now gone save for the Bernals. Santiago Jorge Bernal (farmer), in discussion with the author, June 11, 2014.

17. The Bracero Program was an international agreement between the governments of Mexico and the United States that legally imported hundreds of thousands of rural Mexi-

can workers into the American West. The Spanish word *bracero* means "field hand" (i.e., a manual laborer). Millions of Mexican braceros came into the United States between 1942 and 1964, when the program ended. Mize and Swords, *Consuming Mexican Labor*, 1–4.

18. Vigil, *The Crusade for Justice*, 18.

19. Most of the sources recount Latinos being forced to speak only English in school and punished by their teachers if they used their maternal Spanish tongue—even outside of class.

20. José Chavez's mother was a Hispana, who came to the Grand Valley from Del Norte, Colorado, whereas his father was a Mexican immigrant of Tarahumara Indigenous ancestry. He grew up in Las Colonias and was bullied in school by both teachers and Anglo classmates for being "Mexican." He identified as Mexican as a child, then as a *cholo* (i.e., an Americanized Mexican American), and finally as a Chicano once he entered college. Chavez, discussion.

21. William Nye Curry, "The Death of a Colo. Sugar Beet Crop," *Washington Post*, April 4, 1977.

22. It also conjured up renewed fears about the "Californication" of Colorado. Michelle P. Fulcher, "A Menace, a Scapegoat, an Emblem: What 'California' Really Means to Colorado," Colorado Public Radio, August 27, 2018, https://www.cpr.org/news/story/a-menace-a-scapegoat-an-emblem-what-california-really-means-to-colorado.

23. The country had borrowed heavily in order to fund ambitious infrastructural development projects and import substitution industrialization programs in the 1960s and 1970s. When oil prices plummeted in the early 1980s, Mexico found itself unable to pay its external debt. In 1982 Mexico's finance minister announced that it could no longer service its debt, triggering a regional financial crisis known as "the lost decade" in Latin America. See Bulmer-Thomas, *The Economic History of Latin America since Independence*; Massey, Durand, and Malone, *Beyond Smoke and Mirrors*, 75–77.

24. In particular dozens of assembly plants known as *maquiladoras* opened up in Mexico's interior and along the border, taking advantage of Mexico's low taxes and cheap wages.

25. For a good overview of Mexican migration to the United States (and the literature), see Jiménez, *Replenished Ethnicity*.

26. See the Migration Data Portal for data on migrant deaths and disappearances at https://migrationdataportal.org/themes/migrant-deaths-and-disappearances.

27. Though the male-dominated industries paid better, women had the most stable jobs among immigrants, particularly as construction work dried up after the 2008 recession. Karla Gonzales García (immigrant rights advocate), in discussion with the author, June 5, 2014.

28. The 1990 census enumerated 23,433 Latinos, and the 2000 census enumerated 52,781. It must be kept in mind that it is particularly difficult to count poor, immigrant populations—particularly unauthorized immigrants—so these numbers very likely represent an undercount of the state's Latinx immigrant population. "Race and Hispanic Origin," Colorado Department of Local Affairs, State Demography Office, https://demography.dola.colorado.gov/population/race-hispanic-origin/#race-and-hispanic-origin.

29. Most other Latinx populations (e.g., Puerto Ricans) are concentrated in the metro areas of the Front Range, so the percentage of Latinos of Mexican ancestry in the Western Slope is probably slightly higher.

30. Given the well-documented anecdotical evidence of Mexican migration to the state and the Western Slope, it is safe to assume that the "Latino/Hispanic" census category is a good proxy for Mexican immigrants.

31. "Race and Hispanic Origin," Colorado Department of Local Affairs, State Demography Office.

32. "County Data Lookup," Colorado Department of Local Affairs, State Demography Office, https://demography.dola.colorado.gov/population/data/profile-county/.

33. Rocío Guzmán (pseudonym), in discussion with the author, August 2, 2013.

34. Samuel Stebbins, "What Counties in Each State Have the Most Expensive Housing Market? Check This List," *USA Today*, April 5, 2019, https://www.usatoday.com/story/money/2019/04/05/the-county-with-the-most-expensive-housing-market-in-every-state/39270013/.

35. Park and Pellow, *The Slums of Aspen*, 2.

36. This is the case with other resort towns throughout the West. Some young teachers resort to sharing apartments with roommates, trying to get a rent-subsided apartment in Mountain Village (there is a long waiting list), or living farther away in towns such as Norwood or Naturita. Most new teachers leave after a few years because they cannot afford to live and raise a family in Telluride. Jenna Hagen (teacher), in discussion with the author, June 13, 2014.

37. Pérez, discussion.

38. A few lucky immigrants have been able to get rent-subsidized apartments in Telluride after the city built Shandoka Apartments. Currently there is a waiting list of more than 130 individuals to get into one of these coveted apartments. María Perla (housecleaner), in discussion with the author, June 13, 2014.

39. Some Coras came to the Montrose area before moving to Gunnison. Paula and her husband, for example, came from Tepic (Nayarit) in 2000 and worked in ranches and farms in Olathe. They moved to Gunnison in 2010, where she now works in a hotel. Paula (last name withheld), in discussion with the author, June 29, 2014.

40. Marketa Zubkova (immigrant rights advocate), in discussion with the author, June 29, 2014.

41. They—and other Latinos—are transforming the American West as well. Wyckoff, *How to Read the American West*, 178.

42. Gonzalez-Barrera, *More Mexicans Leaving than Coming*, 5–7.

43. Many immigrant men found themselves without jobs after the halt in construction, and women became the main breadwinners at home, leading to increased levels of alcohol abuse, marital conflicts, and domestic violence among immigrant families. Gonzales García, discussion.

44. Pérez, discussion.

45. "Anglos see Latinos as a mystery." Tom Acker (college professor), in discussion with the author, June 10, 2014.

46. Danny Quinlan (immigrant rights advocate), in discussion with the author, June 5, 2015.

47. Martín Valdez (newspaper publisher), in discussion with the author, June 15, 2014.

48. Jiménez, *Replenished Ethnicity*, 21–22.

49. Huntington, *Who Are We?*, 230–47.

50. Nicole Bernal Ruiz (immigrant rights advocate), in discussion with the author, June 9, 2014.

51. The trends observed in Colorado's Western Slope are also taking place elsewhere in the American West, particularly in rural communities where the increase in Latinx populations is staving off demographic and economic decline. See Pohl, *Minority Populations and The Growth of Hispanic Populations*.

52. In 2012 the average farmer in Colorado was fifty-nine. Sophie Quinton, "As Farmers Retire, Their Families Face Difficult Choices," *Stateline* (blog), March 27, 2019, https://www.pewtrusts.org/en/research-and-analysis/blogs/stateline/2019/03/27/as-farmers-retire-their-families-face-difficult-choices.

53. Carole Ann McKelvey, "Tuxedo's Owner One of Festival Founders," *Montrose Daily Press*, August 6, 2016. In a surprising turn of events, Mexican corn, once devastated by NAFTA's subsided imports, is making a comeback thanks to the migration of Mexican workers to U.S. farms.

54. See Pierce, *Making the White Man's West*.

Bibliography

Abbott, Carl, Stephen J. Leonard, and Thomas J. Noel. *Colorado: A History of the Centennial State*. Boulder: University Press of Colorado, 2005.

Boskin, Michael J., ed. *NAFTA at 20: The North American Free Trade Agreement's Achievements and Challenges*. Stanford CA: Hoover Institution Press, 2014.

Bulmer-Thomas, Victor. *The Economic History of Latin America Since Independence*. 2nd ed. Cambridge: Cambridge University Press, 2003.

Carr, Jonathan, and Claire Kempa. *The History of the Las Colonias Park: Historic Crossroads along the Riverfront of Grand Junction, Colorado*. Grand Junction CO: City of Grand Junction Parks and Recreation Department, 2015.

Gonzalez-Barrera, Ana. *More Mexicans Leaving than Coming to the U.S.* Washington DC: Pew Research Center, 2015.

Huntington, Samuel P. *Who Are We? The Challenges to America's National Identity*. New York: Simon & Schuster, 2004.

Jiménez, Tomás R. *Replenished Ethnicity: Mexican Americans, Immigration, and Identity*. Berkeley: University of California Press, 2009.

Limerick, Patricia Nelson. *The Legacy of Conquest: The Unbroken Past of the American West*. New York: W. W. Norton, 1987.

Lopez Tushar, Olibama. *The People of El Valle: A History of the Spanish Settlers in the San Luis Valley*. Pueblo CO: El Escritorio, 2007.

Massey, Douglas S., Jorge Durand, and Nolan J. Malone. *Beyond Smoke and Mirrors: Mexican Immigration in an Era of Economic Integration*. New York: Russell Sage Foundation, 2002.

Mize, Ronald L., and Alicia C. S. Swords. *Consuming Mexican Labor: From the Bracero Program to NAFTA*. Toronto: University of Toronto Press, 2011.

Nostrand, Richard L. *The Hispano Homeland*. Norman: University of Oklahoma Press, 1992.

Park, Lisa Sun-Hee, and David N. Pellow. *The Slums of Aspen: Immigrants vs. the Environment in America's Eden*. New York: New York University Press, 2011.

Pierce, Jason E. *Making the White Man's West: Whiteness and the Creation of the American West*. Boulder: University Press of Colorado, 2016.

Pohl, Kelly. *The Growth of Hispanic Populations across the West*. Bozeman MT: Headwaters Economics, 2017.

Pohl, Kelly. *Minority Populations Driving County Growth in the Rural West*. Bozeman MT: Headwaters Economics, 2017.

Vigil, Ernesto B. *The Crusade for Justice: Chicano Militancy and the Government's War on Dissent*. Madison: University of Wisconsin Press, 1999.

Wyckoff, William. *How to Read the American West: A Field Guide*. Seattle: University of Washington Press, 2014.

PART 5

Unresolved Politics and Law

11

"I Oppose the ERA, but I Do Approve of Equal Rights for Women"

Gender and Politics in the Aftermath of the Equal Rights Amendment Campaign in the U.S. West

CHELSEA BALL

Section 1. Equality of rights under the law shall not be denied or abridged by the United States or by any state on account of sex.

Section 2. The Congress shall have the power to enforce, by appropriate legislation, the provisions of this article.

Section 3. This amendment shall take effect two years after the date of ratification.

– Full text of the Equal Rights Amendment[1]

On March 20, 2017, a curious thing happened in the Nevada State Capitol. Thirty-five years after its lapsed ratification deadline, Nevada legislators voted to approve the Equal Rights Amendment (ERA).[2] This was not an isolated incident. Eight other state legislatures, including those in Utah, Arizona, and Illinois, also had members working to bring the amendment back up for a vote.[3] In Oklahoma the majority-female Norman City Council, with the help of house minority leader Emily Virgin as well as its female mayor, unanimously approved a resolution urging their state to revive the ERA.[4] The Greater Oklahoma City area chapter of the Coalition of Labor Union Women (CLUW) separately urged their state legislators to consider revisiting the ERA. At their 2018 national convention in Arizona, CLUW also made the amendment a priority issue in all remaining unratified states.[5] Then in May 2018 Illinois, another previously unratified and former battleground state, successfully approved the amendment, technically bringing the ERA's approval count to thirty-seven states, just one short of the necessary three-fourths majority for constitutional ratification.

None of these states were strangers to the ERA debate. In fact they each held a long, painful history with the amendment, one that divided parties, political allies, church congregations, and neighborhoods.[6] In all, the initial ratification failure of the amendment set state-based women's organizations back decades behind other regions as well as damaged the public's perception of feminism.[7] In the 1970s and 1980s Arizona, Nevada, Oklahoma, and Utah in particular were targeted by pro- and anti-ERA political campaigns; those campaigns affected not just the amendment's future but also shaped the evolving Democratic and Republican Party platforms. While progressives campaigned for the ERA's passage in the region where suffrage had thrived fifty years earlier, a new politically active sect of the Republican Party also mounted an impressive media-heavy campaign against the amendment: conservative women. The ERA initially represented a mainstream issue for all men and women to support, but its perception quickly evolved to something more radical. By the end of the ratification period in the early 1980s, the amendment was—for many—no longer about constitutional equality based on sex. For pro-ERA women the amendment became the ultimate symbol of liberal feminism, a way to force states and the federal government to address sexist legislation. With the rise of the New Right the ERA became another example of the new liberal agenda, another move away from "traditional" Christian moral and gender values, and another incursion into family life, reinforced by increased federal oversight.[8] To both progressives and conservatives the ERA came to represent an unfinished form of mainstream feminism.

With such a contentious history with the amendment, why then has the ERA suddenly risen from the dead in the West? To understand this phenomenon, we must look more closely at the backlash against feminism and the women's movement in the 1980s and 1990s, especially in the American West. Americans and westerners in particular were not opposed to expanding women's rights and revising sexist legislation in their states, but many *were* opposed, by

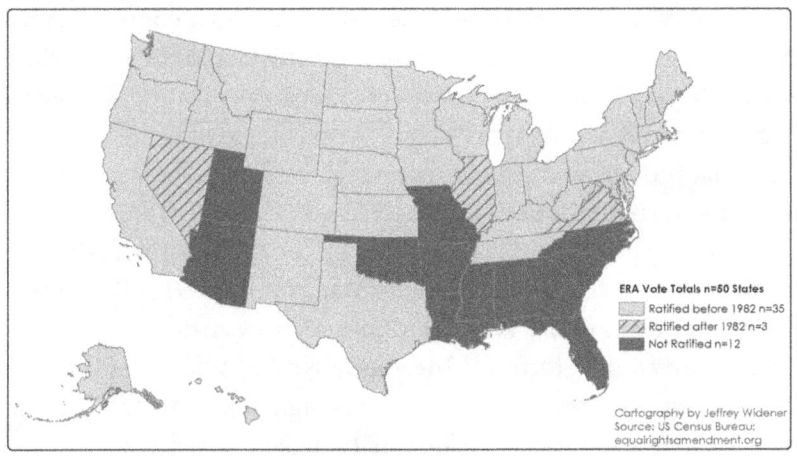

FIG. 29. ERA vote totals by state. Map by Jeffrey M. Widener.

1982, to the "E.R.A." By this time the conservative opposition had successfully packaged the numerous insecurities many westerners had—namely the increasing urban population, a rise in minority populations, the civil rights movement, abortion legalization in *Roe v. Wade* (1973), the women's movement, and increased federal power and subsidies—into a single political problem: liberalism. And while there was not much to be done about many of these insecurities by the 1980s, stopping what conservatives viewed as feminism through the defeat of the ERA became an achievable and highly visible goal. The campaign against the ERA in the West was not about preventing constitutional equality but about stopping feminism and all that it represented. This New Right campaign was successful, as the ERA died in the West, taking numerous liberal women's organizations in the region with it.

Progressive women themselves viewed the ERA as a symbol of feminism as well, thirty-five years ago and still today. While many scholars continue to debate the legality of reviving a constitutional amendment after 1982—its congressionally given deadline—the consensus remains that states like Nevada and Illinois are performing symbolic gestures when they pass the ERA now. The ERA could not become part of the U.S. Constitution without further congressional legislation. So why are state legislators spending their time and political clout on a symbolic issue? It seems that the ERA continues, into the twenty-first century, to represent feminism and the unfinished women's movement in the West, one that is only just now recovering from the backlash of the past. It is no coincidence that Nevada, Arizona, and Oklahoma have recently elected the largest number of female state representatives in their states' histories as well as some of the most unconventional. Since the Donald Trump presidency in 2016 and the rise of the Women's March and the #MeToo movement, feminism in the West continues to grow, inside and outside formal government forums.[9] The ERA, a symbol of feminism's unfinished business, now seems an obvious legislative choice for these new western representatives hoping to make a statement.

Numerous state legislatures initially supported the ERA when Congress approved the amendment in 1972. Both the Democratic and Republican Parties included the amendment in their national platforms. Thirty states ratified the ERA by 1973; it only needed thirty-eight total. Indeed in the first years after Congress sent the ERA to the states for approval the amendment faced little visible or organized opposition. At the state level, Republicans and Democrats, self-proclaimed feminists, and even the prominent Relief Society (the women's charity organization within the Church of Jesus Christ of Latter-day Saints [LDS]) initially supported and voted in favor of the amendment. The Oklahoma Senate was one of the first state legislative bodies to approve of the amendment, giving the ERA a voice vote of "yea" the very same day Congress passed it.[10] State legislatures in California, Idaho, Oregon, New Mexico, Wyoming, and Washington all ratified the amendment by 1973 along with most of the East Coast.[11] Yet as early as 1974 opposition mounted in the form of conservative women's organizations that offered themselves as the "alternative" to women "libbers."[12] Phyllis Schlafly's Eagle Forum and STOP ERA are just a few examples of conservative and religious-based opposition organizations that quickly changed the perception of the amendment from a mainstream extension of the rights revolution to a radical intrusion into American private life. The LDS president Spencer W. Kimball initially called the ERA's motives "praiseworthy," but just two years later in 1976, with the rise of religious opposition, he held a different opinion: "A blanket attempt to help women might bring far more restraints and repressions.... We fear it will even stifle many God-given feminine instincts."[13] This equation between the ERA and ungodly gender norms was a successful tactic. Over the next decade more and more people began to associate the amendment with feminism rather than equality.

The opposition to the ERA also capitalized on the unease brought about by rapid urbanization and an increase in minority populations as well as their demands for recognition and representation in the West. While some western politicians joked that their region did not need a civil rights movement due to the relatively low numbers of African Americans, this was not the case.[14] While the Great Migration brought thousands of African Americans out of the South in the first half of the twentieth century, the expansion of the military industrial complex during and after World War II continued to draw young Black and white Americans to the West. By the 1960s western civil rights activists examined race-based as well as gender- and class-based issues. It is no coincidence that Hannah Atkins, the first African American woman elected in Oklahoma, was also the first member of the Oklahoma House to sponsor and present the ERA.[15] She championed the ERA in her state, viewing it as an extension of the civil rights movement.

When the ERA came up for debate in 1972 Nevadans had already spent a decade uncovering and facing a range of difficult civil rights issues. Long known as the "Mississippi of the West" for its stubborn hold on segregation and racialized labor, Nevada and more specifically Las Vegas had for decades thrived on the underpaid and behind-the-scenes labor of African Americans and Latino/a peoples desperate to escape the South. Postwar suburbanization widened racial dividing lines within the state, making the integration of schools and neighborhoods bitter and slow. Additionally, Nevada's legislators refused federal funds for welfare, minimizing benefits to the state's most vulnerable citizens: women and children of color. State officials took extreme measures to police welfare recipients, including random "welfare checks" when officials looked for potential violations (mostly unclaimed, live-in boyfriends). In response

Black women began to organize. A growing Nevada National Association for the Advancement of Colored People chapter, a vibrant welfare rights organization, and a Supreme Court reprimand, however, did not deter leaders in Carson City. The welfare department continued to raid Black women's homes and cut their already illegally low benefits. The mothers responded by organizing a massive 1,500-person march down Las Vegas Boulevard toward Caesars Palace.[16] This successful campaign proved to Nevadans that Black women could drive social issues in the West and create real change.

Anti-ERA leader Phyllis Schlafly successfully connected the ERA to these racially charged fears. Early on she harnessed the disdain many white westerners felt for the civil rights movement and federal intervention into what they viewed as state issues. In 1973 Schlafly wrote in a white nationalist journal the *Thunderbolt* that in states that had passed the ERA, white women were being put in cells with Black men where the women were then raped. To make these conservatives' imagined dangers real, Schlafly played on age-old anxieties of white masculinity by claiming that it was "a negro judge" that oversaw this ruling.[17] At the 1977 National Women's Conference Schlafly's forces opposed almost every measure the delegates debated, stating that the only women being represented inside were "lesbians and libbers."[18] Their protest conference across town called for "the defeat of the ERA and a return to God, family, and country." One reporter described the scene as militant, stating, "They thunderously shouted 'Yes!' to resolutions calling for a constitutional amendment against abortion, defeat of the ERA, a ban on federally funded child care centers, and laws which would allow homosexuals to teach in schools." The protest conference attendees also compared the government childcare centers to Hitler youth camps.[19] Reporters photographed Ku Klux Klan members protesting the women's conference as well, holding signs that read, "Get out of town: N—s, D—s, and K—s."[20] Clearly the fight against feminism, which was now fully aimed at the ERA, also hoped to undermine racial equality as well.

Yet even after the opposition to the ERA had successfully remade the image of the amendment, private citizens and legislators alike in the West continued to work toward stronger equality for women under the law outside the push for ratification. Through either impatience with the amendment or as a compromise with feminists, legislators in the unratified western states amended some sexist state statutes and passed new legislation to strengthen women's rights in the areas of labor and marriage law. They viewed this as a successful alternative for conservative representatives or those wanting to avoid the controversy surrounding the ERA. The majority of these measures held bipartisan support, but many still did not pass. Just a month after the Arizona legislature voted down the ERA in 1975 (and for the last time), the state senate passed Concurrent Resolution 1003, which added "an equal rights provision to the Arizona constitution."[21] The legislature added equal pay measures to its state statutes as well.[22] The ERA also held its final defeat in 1975 in Utah. Eight years later, after the ERA's deadline had passed, the Utah legislature successfully passed legislation that removed gender-based or sexist language in the Utah State Statutes. Conservatives were appropriating equality now that they had successfully developed a "movement against feminists and the ERA."[23]

In other unratified states ERA activists themselves led the drive to deal with gender-based discrimination within their own state laws and constitutions. A few months after the Oklahoma House voted the amendment down in 1973, ERA activist Hannah Atkins put her past experience as a law librarian to use, compiling a comprehensive list of every mention of sex on the state books. After finding almost thirty sexist statutes, Atkins began to focus on the laws that disturbed her most, including the legal sex discrimination of state and public-school employees.[24] The first bill Atkins proposed and passed was one that forbade sex discrimination in state agencies, most notably in the employment of Oklahoma House pages. A similar bill allowing women to serve as pages also passed in Arizona.[25] Atkins succeeded in the passage of thirteen bills addressing sex discrimination in Oklahoma while still actively campaigning for the ERA in the house.[26]

The other remaining unratified states in the West worked toward similar goals as well, either because activists themselves pushed the issue or because legislators hoped by reforming state-based laws the ERA would become unnecessary and essentially go away. In either case legislators and private citizens alike were not generally opposed to basic equality measures for women in their states. Yet the disdain remained against the ERA as a principal matter. Oklahoma ERA activist Penny Williams stated, "That was something that we were trying to do, was to show that the Equal Rights Amendment was just this mainstream American 'blah, blah, blah' to make it so boring. I remember one of the things I did was never call it the ERA, always call it the Equal Rights Amendment."[27] While pro-ERA activists were not successful in promoting the amendment as mainstream and "boring," they did force state legislatures to evaluate and change numerous sexist laws. By 1977 using the term "ERA" instead of the "Equal Rights Amendment" made a difference, as ERA was now securely linked with feminism and liberalism. This backlash against feminism remained in the West even after the ERA's defeat in June 1982 when the ratification deadline expired.

The 1980s was a particularly difficult time for women across the country. With an increase in sexual violence, decline in child support payments, and attacks on reproductive rights, places like Arizona, Nevada, Oklahoma, and Utah, where the ERA remained unratified and the debate over gender and politics raged on, the pushback against liberal feminism was even harsher.[28] Pres. Ronald Reagan's economic policy and the federal cuts that ensued deeply affected women, as one-third of these cuts came from "programs primarily serving women."[29] As early as 1978 the Governor's Commission on the Status of Women in the state of Utah was defunded. California's commission lost its funding as well due to its support of political measures like the ERA. In the West moderate and even conservative women's organizations came under attack because of the successful demonization of the amendment. Utah did not reestablish its women's commission until 1990, renaming it the Governor's Commission for Women and Families.[30] In Nevada a Governor's Commission on the Status of Women was not established until 1994, and even then it was not fully "activated" or given any real authority or funding until 2016.[31] Other moderate women's organizations lost membership as well, including local chapters of the Women's Political Caucus, League of Women Voters, and Equal Rights Coalition. Carol S. Palmer writes, "Forty years after they led the fight for the ERA, the Arizona chapters of organizations such as the League of Women Voters and the American Association of University Women struggled to find women willing to assume leadership positions."[32]

Women in elected positions decreased in these states despite increasing in other regions.[33] The first Nevada woman elected to U.S. Congress occurred in 1982, a hurdle passed by almost every other state decades earlier. And it was not until 1990 that women really began to make their mark in state politics again, with the *Las Vegas Times* celebrating the highest number of state representative seats filled by women in the state to date: 27 percent.[34] Female representation in Arizona slowed as well in the years after the ERA failed. Because ERA activists there began organizing much earlier than other western states, many of their leaders, like Shirley Odegaard of the Arizona Coalition for ERA, were simply worn out after years of campaigning to a relatively unwavering legislature.[35] Yet the lack of substantial female representation in Phoenix and Carson City in the years immediately following 1982 does not necessarily mean former ERA activists were no longer involved in social change. Many transitioned their activism back into other social justice movements.

After the ERA campaign failed many activists refocused their energies into programs that would directly benefit women in their own communities, shrinking, for a time, from the formal political scene. Historian Joanne L. Goodwin writes that women in Nevada, especially Las Vegas, were involved in "labor organizations, civil rights, women's rights, combating violence against women and children, and antipoverty."[36] Pointing to Florence Shilling McClure, a working-class woman who founded Community Action Against Rape, as an example, Goodwin states that women during this period in Las Vegas "did not set out to be agents of change, but saw a problem that needed a solution and worked to make it happen."[37] In Arizona former ERA activist Allison Hughes took a similar path, focusing her time on grant writing in order to raise funds for domestic violence and rape crisis centers. Carol Papalas, another pro-ERA activist, founded Arizona's Center Against Sexual Assault.[38] Oklahoman ERA activist Pat Reaves used her master's degree in counseling and psychology to help found and direct one of the first battered women's shelters in her home state in the early 1980s.[39] Women's organizations in Utah evolved into similar centers aiding women in crisis.

Despite western women's continued support of social issues in the wake of the ERA's rejection, the clearest indicator of the public backlash against feminism is the decline of women in state and local politics. Historian Martha Sontag Bradley observed that many Utahan women "who toiled for the ERA have become complacent or discouraged—even fearful, based on past experience—to reexamine why women have not fully arrived."[40] While serving in political office is certainly not the only avenue for feminists or women in general to create change, it remains one of the most important and impactful ways of doing so. Political scientists Anne Marie Cammisa and Beth Reingold write, "Female legislators statistically are more likely to vote in favor of women's 'issues' like reproductive rights or the ERA, but they are also almost always the ones to 'initiate' legislation for women."[41] Nevada representative and future lieutenant governor Sue Wagner spoke about this issue in her own state when recalling her time as one of the only women in the Nevada State Capitol:

Women needed to be there, or these issues that we cared about would never be dealt with by men, because they would not be on their radar screens. Yes, the Equal Rights Amendment would have come up, because it was a constitutional amendment. They had to deal with it. But would they have heard another side? Would they have dealt with domestic violence? Would they have dealt with all the sex discrimination that was pervasive throughout our Nevada Revised Statutes? Probably not—because they were all led by women.[42]

Women hold different perspectives than men and can provide valuable insights to issues and legislation. Conservative and progressive female representatives are statistically drawn to issues surrounding women and the family. This phenomenon is not only beneficial to women either. Cammisa and Reingold also note that women "have brought a more constituent-oriented, consensual state legislature, a style that men legislators may now be adopting."[43] Women's presence in state and local politics affects not just women or their own constituents; they influence how their fellow representatives think about and present their own issues as well as how they interact with and understand women as colleagues and as people. While on the surface a decrease in female legislators or representation through women's commissions in western states may seem small, this lack of perspective and representation only added to these states' already precarious position of lagging behind in the safety, happiness, and equality of their female citizens. This backlash against perceived liberal feminism, in part due to the ERA campaign, continued on into the 1990s and beyond. While some dubbed 1992 as the new "year of the woman" because of the notable increase of women in politics, that increase still only brought the number of female representatives across the country to 20 percent.[44] Arizona, Nevada, Oklahoma, and Utah did not see a viable, statewide feminist movement or substantial female visibility in local and state politics until the last few years.

While other nations boast female presidents, gender-balanced legislatures, and strict equal pay laws, the United States still struggles to obtain a gender balance at the local levels of politics. State legislatures remain highly male-dominated. Women elected to state office are still mostly white and upper or middle class. As of 2004 only 18 percent of all female state legislators were from a minority population, meaning only 4 percent of all state representatives, male and female, were minority women.[45] The media named 2018 the next "year of the woman" for numerous reasons, including the visibility of a mainstream feminist movement through the Women's March and the #MeToo movement as well as the one-hundredth anniversary of the Nineteenth Amendment in 2020. Less heralded but as important was the increase in female representatives in elected office. Women now made up 28 percent of state and federal representatives in the United States, many of whom identified as feminists.[46] The states that led the way in elected female representatives were the old ERA battlegrounds: places like Nevada, Oklahoma, Arizona, and other western states. Feminism was finally recovering from its post-ERA backlash.

In 2018, for the first time in the nation's history, a state legislature held a majority of women lawmakers. Nevada's legislature was 50.8 percent women. Colorado also came close to breaking this record that same year, with women holding a majority of its seats in the Colorado House of Representatives. One female representative from Nevada commented, "It's been a long, hard fight," noting the decades it had been since feminists felt they held real power in the Colorado State Capitol.[47] That same year Oklahoma also boasted a record-breaking year for female state representatives when the percentage increased from 14 percent to 21 percent, the highest in the state's history.[48] Candidates who won in this cycle were not only feminists but queer feminists and feminists of color, groups long denied access to elected office. In 2018 many were now representing their states at the local and national levels. Kyrsten Sinema became the first female and openly bisexual U.S. senator from Arizona when she won her campaign in 2018. Sharice Davids became the first Native American women in Congress and the first openly queer representative from Kansas. Two other queer female representatives in the West—Annie Craig of Michigan and Katie Hill of California—became the "firsts" in their states as well and unseated anti-LGBTQ candidates in the process. The U.S. Congress also received its first female Muslim American representatives: Rashida Tlaib of Michigan and Ilhan Omar of Minnesota.[49] This increase in female representation in the West continued in 2019 and 2020: Deb Haaland (Laguna Pueblo) not only became one of the first Native American women elected to office but Pres. Joe Biden's pick to head the Department of the Interior, a position no woman or American Indian has ever been appointed to.[50]

Not coincidentally, one of these queer, female, western representatives led the newly revived ERA campaign in Nevada. Pat Spearman is about as unconventional as they come as far as state representatives. She is a Black woman, a lesbian, a retired army lieutenant colonel, and an ordained minister. She was also transparent when it came to her motivation to pass the ERA in her state forty years after its failure: "I've had to fight for everything that I have. All the titles, none of that was given to me." When asked why the ERA remains important to women in her home state, Spearman explained, "It's time to do away with the patriarchy that holds people down."[51] Here Spearman articulates what activists on both sides of the ERA issue have understood and accepted for many years: the ERA represents an unfinished feminist movement. When asked why her CLUW chapter in Oklahoma brought the ERA back to their legislators in 2018, treasurer Debra Donwerth was clear: "We hoped for more union participation from women. Not all women are lucky enough to be protected by a union. Sometimes equal pay for equal work cannot be achieved in male-dominated careers. The ERA is still needed."[52] For places like Arizona, Nevada, Oklahoma, and Utah, feminists are rebuilding their power in mainstream politics for the first time since the late 1970s. These women have made the ERA an important part of that resurgence.

The ERA faces real hurdles, not only because the deadline has long past, but because its opponents still hold on to their contention that the amendment would radically remake American gender roles. Supporters and opponents of the amendment continue to battle tooth and nail over the issue in their state, with many against the ERA using the same assumptions and "radical" implications the amendment could have on American public and private life. A *New York Times* article argued, "The legislative losers in Nevada tended to be Republican men complaining rather antiquely that the E.R.A. would harm family life, advance abortions and force women into military combat roles."[53] One male Nevada representative and LDS physician commented, "I cannot pretend to think by legislation I can become equal to them."[54] Forty-five years after Congress approved the ERA, it continues to represent much more than its plain words opposing gender discrimination. In the present day, conservative representatives link the amendment to larger, usually unrelated fears of liberal feminism. When Illinois ratified the ERA less than a year later in 2018, the media clips could have been from that day or forty years earlier. The arguments had not changed. Illinois Rep. Peter Breen asserted that the ERA would "expand taxpayer funding of abortions, very well might roll back our parental notice (for minors to have an abortion) law and have other negative impacts on various abortion regulations."⁵⁵ When Virginia came extremely close to passing the ERA in January 2019 the *Federalist* published an article titled, "Today Virginia Could Ratify a U.S. Constitutional Amendment Forcing Women to Get Drafted and Share Hospital Rooms with Men," and included a photo of a terrified looking woman lying in a hospital bed. The article also added, "The Equal Rights Amendment could do great damage to the American constitutional order by inserting progressive identity politics into the highest law of the land."⁵⁶ When the ERA was up for debate in Utah in 2019 Mormons for ERA and the LDS faced off once again, ending with the Church reaffirming its stance against the amendment.⁵⁷ From privacy fears and forced gender mixing to women being drafted, the fear-based arguments utilized by opponents of the ERA continued on. The amendment still represented liberal and even "radical" ideas about gender and threatened the moral fabric of the United States by amending the nation's Constitution.

This was not just a local or western phenomenon either. National advertisements and articles from the Independent Women's Forum, a conservative women's organization, bought anti-ERA ads on YouTube stating, "The ERA is a bait and switch. It promises basic equality but leaves the door open for a radical progressive agenda to be implemented through the judiciary, without input from American voters, the majority of whom today are women." One particular article described the ERA as "nice-sounding words with potentially radical impact." The advertisements again utilized the term "radical" multiple times, promoting the notion that the ERA was not within the liberal tradition of the amendment process but was something both outside of legal means and unnecessary. Under a section for further reading on the amendment and how citizens can get involved, the article linked directly to Eagle Forum's website.⁵⁸

With one state technically needed for ratification, Arizona legislators again began to seriously work to get votes for ratification. After a tide-turning election in 2018, Democrats held the majority of the Arizona House for the first time since 1966, with thirty-one Democrats and twenty-nine Republicans.⁵⁹ In the Arizona Senate, party lines stood at seventeen Republicans and thirteen Democrats.

Then two moderate Republican House members, Michelle Ugenti and Heather Carter, ran and won in the Arizona Senate. While still in the Arizona House, the women co-sponsored the ERA. Representative Ugenti in particular was vocal about her support of the ERA, arguing that the amendment should not be a party issue. As a highly public pro-life supporter, she felt the need to defend her position on both seemingly unrelated issues, arguing that the amendment had suffered numerous "misconceptions" by many of her Republican colleagues, reminding them that the ERA was on the party's national platform until 1980.[60] As now senators, Ugenti and Carter promised to continue their support of the amendment, putting the ERA's tally in the Arizona Senate now at a likely even fifteen to fifteen if allowed to come to a vote.

Allowing Arizona legislators to even vote on the ERA was another issue. From 2016 to 2018 the amendment was not allowed out of committee and on the floor for a vote by the same man: Eddie Farnsworth, chairman of the Senate Judiciary Committee. Leading the newly invigorated charge to give the amendment a vote in Arizona, Rep. Victoria Steele (Seneca/Mingo) organized a media blitz and ERA rally at the capitol in March 2019 with the help of an old ally, the National Organization for Women (NOW), of which she was a board member. In an interview about the amendment she argued that the ERA "could be the most significant vote" she and her colleagues might ever have the chance to participate in.[61] The Democratic Party also argued that the amendment was necessary in the state in order to fix Arizona's still-present wage gap as well as further reinforce gender discrimination laws in the state. Janelle Wood, founder of the Black Mother's Forum, reminded voters that women of color in the state still make sixty-five cents on the dollar compared to men.[62] Other Arizonans asked their community to remember how a past leader, then state senator Sandra Day O'Connor, handled the ERA debate. Even without her Republican colleagues' backing, O'Connor continued to support and even sponsor the amendment in the Arizona Senate. When she could not secure enough votes to get it passed in the 1970s, she asked her fellow legislators to put the ERA to a referendum and let the citizens of Arizona vote on the issue.[63] Supporters in 2019 urged the Arizona legislature to allow, if nothing else, the amendment a vote. To further encourage Senator Farnsworth to allow the amendment on the floor, ERA supporters participated in a thirty-eight-mile march to the state capitol, similar to the march by ERA supporters in 1977 from Seneca Falls, New York, to the National Women's Conference in Houston, Texas. The marchers carried with them many of the same banners they themselves and the previous generation of supporters carried during the 1970s ERA ratification rallies in Arizona. Despite the internal and external support for the amendment at the Arizona State Capitol, Senator Farnsworth did not allow the ERA to be voted on. He argued, as in previous years, that the amendment was unnecessary due to federal regulations already protecting Americans from discrimination based on gender. He also added that states that passed the ERA had somehow used the amendment to prevent legislators from restricting reproductive rights and to keep abortions legal, a right already protected by the Supreme Court. When the news broke that the ERA would not be allowed on the floor of the Arizona Senate, it became hard for bystanders to differentiate between the present debate and the ERA debate forty years earlier. Just like in the 1970s ERA opponents thanked Senator Farnsworth and others for blocking the amendment with homemade baked goods. And just like in the past, opponents insisted that women were different than men and needed protecting more than they needed equal rights. "Women are sacred," Senator Farnsworth told the media. "The world is a better place because of their softness and femininity." Cathi Herrod, president of conservative watchdog organization Center for Arizona Policy, added, "It's really about abortion."[64] Activists, as they did in 1982, returned home without the ERA.

For both sides, conservatives and progressives, the ERA continues to represent the unfinished wave of feminism in the 1960s and 1970s. This is the legacy of the decades-long debate over its ratification. For supporters of the amendment the ERA became a public representation of liberal feminism's victory—a victory that would measurably improve women's lives. Those against the amendment also viewed the ERA as a representation of feminism and all the social disasters that movement portended for them. The defeat of the amendment was a way to publicly challenge that social change. Feminists argued the amendment was moderate and mainstream, a simple commitment to anti-discrimination, while opponents charged that it was a backdoor way to promote abortion and force children into state-run daycare centers.

Feminism in the West is just now recovering from the amendment's very public 1982 defeat and corresponding backlash. While 2018 may have been the next "year of the woman" in light of the Women's March, #MeToo movement, TIME'S UP, the one-hundredth anniversary of (white) women's suffrage, and a revitalization of female representatives, it is no coincidence that the ERA has returned with this new wave of feminism. On January 15, 2020, the Commonwealth of Virginia made history by ratifying the ERA and becoming the thirty-eighth and final state needed to reach a three-fourths majority.[65] While the amendment's ratification deadline expired on June 30, 1982, the ERA still has a chance at passage either through a deadline extension by Congress, which the House has already submitted, or the passage of a new ERA bill for states to vote on again. In either case the struggle to ratify the ERA remains. This amendment is still western women's unfinished business, as the ERA largely died in the West twice now and experienced some of the most extreme backlash against feminism in the 1980s through today.

This modern grassroots debate illuminates many of the similarities and challenges to western women's political activism in the past while also giving us a small glimpse into twenty-first-century trends. Tracing these current trends aligns with the call to action that many pioneers of western women's history highlighted in the last decades. The New Western History in the late 1980s and 1990s challenged historians to think outside of the classic western tropes of conquest and civilization, which all but glossed over the real experiences of western women. Patricia Limerick furthered this assertion in *A Legacy of Conquest*, pointing to the stand-in caricatures that historians and Wild West authors alike used in the place of real women.[66] Far from the "gentle tamers" and bonnet-clad pioneer mothers, western women left their mark on the region as well, often as colonizers themselves.[67] Women's suffrage was one of the only topics on women and politics in the West discussed in-depth in the historiography. Yet two theories remained popular about women in the West: the first, by "civilizing" the West women gained more economic and political freedom. Second, this made the West more progressive than other regions of the United States.[68] The ERA's failure in the region challenges both of these assumptions.

Histories of the West in previous decades are also limited when it comes to works on the twentieth and twenty-first centuries and, in particular, progressive and modern women. Many older works on the West aimed at complicating the often-preconceived stereotypes of western women. Joan M. Jenson and Darlis A. Miller wrote about these reoccurring images in 1980 with their article "The Gentle Tamers Revisited." The authors complicated the idea of women being the "civilizers" and moral authority in the West, arguing that women-focused works would break down the stereotypes of pioneer women being gentle tamers, helpmates, or hell-raisers.[69] Two aspects of western women's political lives have been carefully studied though. One is the suffrage movement, which holds many similarities to the ERA debate.[70] Rebecca J. Mead's *How the Vote Was Won* does an excellent job of breaking down the adaptability of women in western states and the strong and successful ties suffrage organizations made with populists and labor.[71] More local works on the ERA could also illuminate the strategies and political ties women's organizations made to try to secure their amendment. Researchers have also aptly covered the lives of conservative women in the West. Lisa McGirr's *Suburban Warriors* and Michelle M. Nickerson's *Mothers of Conservatism* both lay out important histories of the rise of the New Right in California, with Nickerson looking at conservative women activists particularly.[72] The ERA played a large role in uniting men and women against more liberal politics in the West, and the already established and thriving Christian Right provided the nationwide organization what they needed to succeed.

The ERA debate in the West expands our understanding of women's political activism and motivations in the region, which the New Western historians called for three decades ago. The amendment campaign highlights individual and local women's actions, especially those challenging "traditional" gender norms, while also expanding our understanding of how western women built up and navigated grassroots organizations across states. Many of the same cultural norms and challenges of women and politics from the nineteenth and twentieth centuries remain in the region today, namely religious and gender ideals, but in new and different ways. Here during the ongoing ERA debate we see both conservative *and* progressive women working for political campaigns, lobbying legislators, and running for public office, with both sides justifying their political activism in the shadow of their western suffragist grandmothers and great-grandmothers, under religious motivations, or on behalf of their families. In a sense the New Western historians called for western women's history to both expand as well as embrace the complicated reality that often defines women's lives. The ERA debate of the late twentieth and now twenty-first century allows for just that.

Notes

1. Title quote: Anne Lindeman, interview by Patricia Horstman, 1975, Patricia Horstman Collection, folder 3, box 1. Full text from the ERA: H.J. Res 208, January 26, 1971, RG 233, Records of the U.S. House of Representatives, National Archives.

2. Colin Dwyer, "Nevada Ratifies the Equal Rights Amendment . . . 35 Years After the Deadline," National Public Radio, March 21, 2017, https://www.npr.org/sections/thetwo-way/2017/03/21/520962541/nevada-on-cusp-of-ratifying-equal-rights-amendment-35-years-after-deadline.

3. David Montero, "Thirty-Five Years Past the Deadline Set by Congress, Nevada Ratifies the Equal Rights Amendment," *Los Angeles Times*, March 20, 2017, https://www.latimes.com/nation/la-na-nevada-era-2017-story.html.

4. Mack Burke, "Norman Urges Legislature to Ratify Equal Rights Amendment," *Norman Transcript* (Norman, Oklahoma), December 13, 2018, https://www.normantranscript.com/news/norman-urges-legislature-to-ratify-equal-rights-amendment/article_ca91457e-ff5f-11e8-8653-ab5bc706df02.html.

5. Debra Donwerth (treasurer of CLUW), in discussion with the author, February 8, 2019.

6. For individual histories of the ERA debate in each of these states, see Palmer, "Challenging Tradition"; Dziedziak, "The Gendering of Nevada Politics"; Ball, "From Red Dirt to Red State"; Bradley, *Pedestals and Podiums*.

7. See Ezekiel, *Feminism in the Heartland*; Matthews and De Hart, *Sex, Gender, and the Politics of the* ERA; Bradley, *Pedestals and Podiums*.

8. McGirr, *Suburban Warriors*, 3–10; Nickerson, *Mothers of Conservatism*, xiv, xvi–xvii. McGirr, like others, asserts the New Right came about in the 1960s by uniting libertarians and "Christian traditionalists." See also Dochuk, *From Bible Belt to Sunbelt*, 128–34.

9. "A Rebuke to Trump, A Century in the Making," *New York Times*, April 19, 2018, https://www.nytimes.com/2018/04/19/opinion/a-rebuke-to-trump-a-century-in-the-making.html.

10. Nick Thimmesch, "Supporters to Blame for ERA's Woes," *Daily Oklahoman*, June 6, 1978.

11. For a map of ratified and unratified states, including the dates of ratification, see "Equal Rights Amendment," Equal Rights Amendment, https://www.equalrightsamendment.org.

12. Critchlow, *Phyllis Schlafly and Grassroots Conservatism*, 221.

13. "Against ERA: Church's Stand Draws Opposition," *Equal Rights Monitor*, November and December 1976 issue, Jean Ford Papers, folder 3, box 30.

14. See Glasrud and Wintz, *Black Americans and the Civil Rights Movement in the West*.

15. Teall, *Black History in Oklahoma*, 228–31.

16. Emmily Bristol, "The Mothers Who Marched," *Vegas Seven*, March 3, 2016, https://issuu.com/vegasseven/docs/lv23238_vegas_seven_03_03; Orleck, *Storming Caesar's Palace*, 131–67.

17. Phyllis Schlafly, "Women's Liberation Amendment Would End 'Christian Age of Chivalry,'" *Thunderbolt*, March 1973, Jean Ford Papers, NOW of Las Vegas Collection, folder 3, box 4, part 2.

18. Donald Critchlow, *Phyllis Schlafly and Grassroots Conservatism*, 245.

19. "ERA Foes Will Continue Battle," *Tulsa Tribune*, February 21, 1977.

20. Dziedziak, "The Gendering of Nevada Politics," 169.

21. Palmer, "Challenging Tradition," 104.

22. Palmer, "Challenging Tradition," 74. See also Taylor and Herzog, "Impact Study of the Equal Rights Amendment."

23. Holland, "Salt Lake . . . Is Our Selma," 47, 55–58, 61, 115.

24. "State Legislative Council, Legal Service Division," memorandum, December 12, 1972, Hannah Diggs Atkins Collection, folder 19, box 4.

25. Ginger Hutton, "Views of a Black Woman Politician," *Arizona Republic*, July 8, 1972.

26. Warren Vieth, "Starting Over," *Oklahoma Monthly*, February 1981.

27. Penny Williams, interview by John Erling, *Voices of Oklahoma*, April 11, 2012, http://m.voicesofoklahoma.com/interview/williams-penny/.

28. Faludi, *Backlash*, 18–80, 82–118; Holland, "Salt Lake . . . Is Our Selma," 92.

29. Holland, "Salt Lake . . . Is Our Selma," 91.

30. Holland, "Salt Lake . . . Is Our Selma," 65.

31. "Chapter 2331: Nevada Commission for Women," Legislative State of Nevada, https://www.leg.state.nv.us/nrs/NRS-2331.html.

32. Palmer, "Challenging Tradition," 127.

33. Cammisa and Reingold, "Women in State Legislatures and State Legislative Research," 181–210, 181.

34. Richard C. Paddock, "Nevada Women Strike Electoral Gold," *Los Angeles Times*, January 31, 1993, https://www.latimes.com/archives/la-xpm-1993-01-31-mn-1214-story.html.

35. Palmer, "Challenging Tradition," 122.

36. Goodwin, "Women at Work in Las Vegas, 1940–1980s," 178, 190–91.

37. Goodwin, "Women at Work in Las Vegas, 1940–1980s," 191.

38. Palmer, "Challenging Tradition," 129.

39. Pat Reaves (Oklahoman ERA activist), in discussion with the author, March 15, 2019.
40. Bradley, *Pedestals and Podiums*, 442.
41. Cammisa and Reingold, "Women in State Legislatures," 191–92.
42. Wagner, "Through the Glass Ceiling: A Life in Nevada Politics," 125.
43. Cammisa and Reingold, "Women in State Legislatures," 205.
44. Leila Fadel, "A First: Women Take the Majority in Nevada Legislature and Colorado House," National Public Radio, February 4, 2019, https://www.npr.org/2019/02/04/691198416/a-first-women-take-the-majority-in-nevada-legislature-and-colorado-house.
45. Cammisa and Reingold, "Women in State Legislatures," 184–85.
46. Fadel, "A First," National Public Radio.
47. Fadel, "A First," National Public Radio.
48. Caroline Halter, "Oklahoma's Legislature Will Have More Women in 2019," High Plains Public Radio, November 8, 2018, https://www.hppr.org/post/oklahoma-s-legislature-will-have-more-women-2019.
49. Rose Dommu, "The 116th Congress Is Now the Queerest and Most Diverse in History," *Out*, January 3, 2019, https://www.out.com/news-opinion/2019/1/03/116th-congress-now-queerest-and-most-diverse-history.
50. Coral Davenport, "Biden Picks Deb Haaland to Lead Interior Department," *New York Times*, December 17, 2020, https://www.nytimes.com/2020/12/17/climate/deb-haaland-interior-department-native-american.html.
51. Fadel, "A First," National Public Radio.
52. Donwerth, discussion.
53. "Pumping Life into the Equal Rights Amendment," *New York Times*, March 25, 2017, https://www.nytimes.com/2017/03/25/opinion/sunday/pumping-life-into-the-equal-rights-amendment.html.
54. Sandra Chereb, "Nevada Ratifies the Equal Rights Amendment on 45th Anniversary of Passage by Congress," *Las Vegas Review-Journal*, March 22, 2017, https://www.reviewjournal.com/news/politics-and-government/nevada/nevada-ratifies-equal-rights-amendment-on-45th-anniversary-of-passage-by-congress/.
55. Rick Pearson and Bill Lukitsch, "Illinois Approves Equal Rights Amendment, 36 Years After Deadline," *Chicago Tribune*, May 31, 2018, https://www.chicagotribune.com/politics/ct-met-equal-rights-amendment-illinois-20180530-story.html.
56. Inez Feltscher Stepman, "Today Virginia Could Ratify a U.S. Constitutional Amendment Forcing Women to Get Drafted and Share Hospital Rooms with Men," *Federalist*, January 25, 2019, https://thefederalist.com/2019/01/25/today-virginia-ratify-u-s-constitutional-amendment-forcing-women-get-drafted-share-hospital-rooms-men/.
57. Becky Jacobs, "LDS Church Announces It Still Opposes Equal Rights Amendment as Supporters Rally at Capitol," *Salt Lake Tribune*, December 3, 2019, https://www.sltrib.com/news/2019/12/03/lds-church-announces-it/.
58. Inez Feltscher Stepman, "Policy Focus: Recipes for Rational Government: Equal Rights Amendment," *Independent Women's Forum*, February 2019, http://iwf.org/publications/2808672/Policy-Focus:-Equal-Rights-Amendment.
59. Dustin Gardiner, "Will Arizona Be Crucial 38th State to Ratify the Equal Rights Amendment?," *Arizona Republic*, January 19, 2019, https://www.azcentral.com/story/news

/politics/arizona/2019/01/19/equal-rights-amendment-why-arizona-could-state-put-over-top/2605903002/.

60. Gardiner, "Will Arizona Be Crucial 38th State?," *Arizona Republic*.

61. Dustin Gardiner, "Arizona Won't Make History: Representatives Block Vote on the Equal Rights Amendment," *Arizona Republic*, March 13, 2019, https://www.azcentral.com/story/news/politics/legislature/2019/03/13/equal-rights-amendment-arizona-democrats-try-force-senate-vote/3146269002/.

62. Gardiner, "Arizona Won't Make History," *Arizona Republic*.

63. E. J. Motini, "Arizona Lawmakers Can Honor Justice O'Connor By Passing the Equal Rights Amendment," *Arizona Republic*, January 16, 2019, https://www.azcentral.com/story/opinion/op-ed/ej-montini/2019/01/16/sandra-oconnor-equal-rights-amendment-arizona-legislature/2594106002/.

64. Gardiner, "Arizona Won't Make History," *Arizona Republic*.

65. Timothy Williams, "Virginia Approves the E.R.A, Becoming 38th State to Back It," *New York Times*, January 15, 2020, https://www.nytimes.com/2020/01/15/us/era-virginia-vote.html.

66. See Limerick, *A Legacy of Conquest*.

67. The term "gentle tamers" in reference to western women was made famous by Brown, *The Gentle Tamers*. Patricia Limerick, Elizabeth Jameson, Susan Armitage, and Virginia Scharff have all worked to challenge and complicate this view of women in the region.

68. For more on challenging these debates, see Jeffrey, *Frontier Women*, 4–6.

69. Jeffrey, *Frontier Women*, 5–6, 240–42; Jenson and Miller, "The Gentle Tamers," 9–15, 30–36.

70. See Jenson and Miller, "The Gentle Tamers."

71. See Mead, *How the Vote Was Won*.

72. See McGirr, *Suburban Warriors* and Nickerson, *Mothers of Conservatism*.

Bibliography

Archival Sources

Hannah Diggs Atkins Papers. Oklahoma State University Archives. Edmon Low Library.

Jean Ford Collection. Special Collections Archives. University of Nevada, Las Vegas libraries.

Patricia Horstman Collection. Special Collections and Archives. Northern Arizona University. Cline Library.

Published Works

Ball, Chelsea. "From Red Dirt to Red State: Oklahoma and the Equal Rights Amendment, 1972–1982." Master's thesis, University of Oklahoma, 2016.

Bradley, Martha Sontag. *Pedestals and Podiums: Utah Women, Religious Authority, and Equal Rights*. Salt Lake City: Signature Books, 2005.

Brown, Dee. *The Gentle Tamers: Women of the Old West*. Lincoln: University of Nebraska Press, 1981.

Cammisa, Anne Marie, and Beth Reingold. "Women in State Legislatures and State Legislative Research: Beyond Sameness and Difference." *State Policy Quarterly* 4, no. 2 (Summer 2004): 181–210.

Critchlow, Donald T. *Phyllis Schlafly and Grassroots Conservatism: A Woman's Crusade.* Princeton: Princeton University Press, 2005.

Dochuk, Darren. *From Bible Belt to Sunbelt: Plain-Folk Religion, Grassroots Politics, and the Rise of Evangelical Conservatism.* New York: W. W. Norton and Company, 2001.

Dziedziak, Caryll Batt. "The Gendering of Nevada Politics: The Equal Rights Amendment Ratification Campaign, 1973–1981." PhD diss., University of Nevada, Las Vegas, 2010.

Ezekiel, Judith. *Feminism in the Heartland.* Dayton: Ohio State University, 2002.

Faludi, Susan. *Backlash: The Undeclared War Against American Women.* New York: Three Rivers Press, 1991.

Glasrud, Bruce A., and Cary D. Wintz, eds. *Black Americans and the Civil Rights Movement in the West.* Norman: University of Oklahoma Press, 2019.

Goodwin, Joanne L. "Women at Work in Las Vegas, 1940–1980s." In *Oral History, Community, and Work in the American West*, edited by Jessie L. Embry, 175–96. Tucson: University of Arizona Press, 2013.

Holland, Jennifer L. "'Salt Lake . . . Is Our Selma': The Equal Rights Amendment and the Transformation of the Politics of Gender in Utah." Master's thesis, Utah State University, 2005.

Jeffrey, Julie Roy. *Frontier Women: "Civilizing" the West? 1840–1880.* New York: Hill and Wang, 1988.

Jenson, Joan M., and Darlis A. Miller. "The Gentle Tamers Revisited: New Approaches to the History of Women in the American West." *Pacific Historical Review* 49, no. 2 (1980): 173–213.

Limerick, Patricia Nelson. *A Legacy of Conquest: The Unbroken Past of the American West.* New York: W. W. Norton and Company, 1987.

Matthews, Donald G., and Jane Sherron De Hart. *Sex, Gender, and the Politics of the ERA: A State and the Nation.* Oxford: Oxford University Press, 1990.

McGirr, Lisa. *Suburban Warriors: The Origins of the New American Right.* Princeton: Princeton University Press, 2001.

Mead, Rebecca J. *How the Vote Was Won: Suffrage in the Western United States, 1868–1914.* New York: New York University Press, 2004.

Nickerson, Michelle M. *Mothers of Conservatism: Women and the Postwar Right.* Princeton: Princeton University Press, 2012.

Orleck, Annelise. *Storming Caesar's Palace: How Black Mothers Fought Their Own War on Poverty.* Boston: Beacon Press, 2005.

Palmer, Carl S. "Challenging Tradition: Arizona Women Fight for the Equal Rights Amendment." Master's thesis, Arizona State University, 2007.

Taylor, Charlene M., and Stuart Herzog. *Impact Study of the Equal Rights Amendment: The Arizona Constitution and Statues.* Tucson: Arizona State Historical Society and Archives, 1973.

Teall, Kay M. *Black History in Oklahoma: A Resource Book.* Oklahoma City: Oklahoma City Public Schools, 1971.

Wagner, Sue. "Through the Glass Ceiling: A Life in Nevada Politics." By Victoria Ford. University of Nevada Oral History Program (2005): https://archive.org/details/WagnerSue.

12

LGBTQ Civil Rights in Washington State Since 1977

An Unresolved History

PETER BOAG

On January 27, 2006, the Washington State Legislature added "sexual orientation," which it defined to include gender expression and gender identity, to its list of classes protected under its civil rights statute. The Evergreen State had begun developing that law in 1949 as a fair employment act protecting people based on their race, creed, and national origin. Fifty-seven years later it made illegal the discrimination against lesbian, gay, bisexual, transgender, and queer (LGBTQ) people in employment, credit and insurance transactions, public accommodations and amusements, and real estate property transactions.[1] For the state's LGBTQ people, this twenty-first-century achievement was one that they and their allies had been working for since at least 1977. Back in that year, Peter Francis, a state senator representing parts of Seattle and its northern suburbs, introduced the first bill to add sexual orientation to the state civil rights law. After the bill failed, supporters reintroduced similar legislation two years later and in every subsequent legislative session until its passage in 2006.

While there were many twists and turns during this thirty-year history, the trajectory was one of continuity. For one, through this period civil rights advocates persistently pursued expanding state protections for LGBTQ people. Part of this, of course, was LGBTQ people's continuing struggle for broader social acceptance. Continuity is also seen in civil rights advocates' efforts to thwart an increasingly shrill and chilling movement not just to hinder civil rights advancements for LGBTQ people but to create vicious laws to attack them.

Much of that effort was directed by conservative religious organizations and people who espoused fundamentalist ideas and readings of Christian scripture. Such efforts and a lack of complete acceptance of LGBTQ people yet continue in Washington, the American West, and elsewhere in the United States. This makes LGBTQ civil rights history, whether in Washington or in any imagined American West, one that is yet unresolved.

The excitement of the "New Western History" that began in the mid-1980s and continued at least into the early 1990s was something that did not consider the LGBTQ past. Additionally, although there was an established historiography on religion in the West, the rise of the new Christian Right in the region was also something that the New Western History did not much reflect on. In part, both were due to the fact that the struggle for LGBTQ rights and the rise of the Christian Right, and in particular its anti-LGBTQ campaign, were either becoming more apparent or just getting underway at the very time when the New Western History materialized.

Another reason that the New Western History ignored the LGBTQ past was that the field of LGBTQ history was only itself in its infancy at that time. To be sure, a (very) few LGBTQ titles that included coverage of the West existed or were coming out then, so to speak. But even in the twenty-first century, when more monographs and articles appeared on the history of LGBTQ people in the American West, these, like earlier exemplars, tended to be by scholars who did not identify as western historians per se and who did not argue specifically western regional themes in their work.[2]

Yet another reason why New Western History was largely bereft of LGBTQ content is that when the former emerged, it did so in a time (outlined in this essay) when it was yet difficult for professional historians to research the LGBTQ past, find funding for it, and then expect to land or even keep jobs in academia.[3] It was not until the Western History Association's annual conference in 1995 that the first session devoted to the region's LGBTQ history appeared on the program. Two of the three presenters did not consider themselves western historians; the third is the author of this piece. The principal reason why I organized that session was not because of enthusiasm for New Western History but rather to express resistance—the conference was held in Colorado where the majority of voters in the state had recently adopted the anti-LGBTQ Amendment 2, described briefly in this essay. I would add that only two years before then, historians of the American West had tried to dissuade me from exploring the LGBTQ past, explaining that it would ruin my career.

The history of Washington State's struggle for LGBTQ-inclusive civil rights legislation is a story that blends national, regional, and local developments. It emerged in the early 1970s when the same struggle was beginning in other progressive parts of the United States.[4] It was also part of the broader progressive revolution that had commenced during the 1960s. In 1973 Seattle became the first major city in the United States to adopt, and rather quietly so, an ordinance that protected lesbian and gay people from discrimination in employment. In 1975 the city council followed with a fair housing law. As a few other American municipalities began to do likewise—for example, Ann Arbor, Michigan (already in 1972), St. Paul, Minnesota, Eugene, Oregon, Wichita, Kansas, and Miami-Dade County, Florida—conservative forces galvanized in opposition.

The most visible opposition began in Florida. After Dade County commissioners adopted a law that prohibited discrimination based on sexual orientation in employment in 1977, local celebrity Anita Bryant led conservative religious forces in a successful effort to repeal that law. Bryant's organization took the name "Save Our Children," a phrase based in obsolete Freudian concepts, the strange belief that heterosexuality is somehow fragile and in need of protection, and the old stereotype that gays were "trying to recruit our children to homosexuality."[5]

Conservatives around the country took notice of Bryant's success and undertook similar repeal efforts in the few communities where ordinances protecting gays existed. In 1978 two Seattle police officers, who invoked fundamentalist Christian beliefs, formed Save Our Moral Ethics (SOME) and filed Proposition 13 to repeal that city's 1973 employment and 1975 fair housing ordinances. "I believe the laws of God don't change," one of the founders stated. "And it clearly states in the Bible that homosexual conduct is wrong." Florida's Save Our Children gave SOME funding, indicating a stiffening of resistance across the nation.⁶

To fight against Proposition 13, Seattle activists organized Citizens to Retain Fair Employment, Seattle Committee Against Thirteen, and Women Against Thirteen. They also made alliances across the city, receiving support from various local officials, some mainstream churches, the National Organization of Women, the League of Women Voters, and the Young Women's Christian Association. After a rancorous several months, in November 1978 Seattle residents handily defeated Proposition 13 by 63 percent to 37 percent. Seattle was among the first places in the United States wherein the electorate voted to retain a law that protected gay rights. The same election day in California, voters decided against an initiative (also supported by Bryant) that would have barred gays as teachers in public schools. Unlike in Seattle, however, California voters were not voting to uphold an existing law that protected civil rights. Less hopefully, conservative efforts that year rolled back protective legislation for lesbians and gays in St. Paul, Wichita, and Eugene.⁷

It was on the eve of the previously mentioned campaigns, and just after Washington legislators repealed the state's sodomy law (1976), that Sen. Peter Francis first proposed expanding civil rights statewide to include gays and lesbians. A broad range of supporters, including the mayor of Seattle, former professional (and University of Washington) football player who had come out as gay, David Kopay, psychologists, and the progressive Washington Association of Churches (today's Faith Action Network) spoke in hearings or wrote in favor of the bills. There were as many voices in opposition, including from conservative churches. The minister of a Foursquare church, for example, held that rights should not be extended to lesbians and gays because he believed such people to be immoral. A number of individuals who wrote to legislators against the bills quoted from scripture and made biblical references in opposition to gays. Many of these people, as well as speakers in public hearings, also expressed fear that should the legislation be adopted, lesbians and gays would be permitted to teach children, laws against child molestation would be rolled back, they would be forced by the law to associate with

LGBTQ people, landlords would be required to rent to LGBTQ people, and soon society would countenance group marriages.[8]

Not surprisingly, given the relatively early date, this civil rights legislation did not succeed. The 1980s and 1990s continued as a mixed bag of advances and setbacks. Advancements came about for interrelated reasons, in part as a continuation of a general liberalizing trend in attitudes in the United States that can be detected by the end of the 1960s. In part this liberalizing trend came as a result of the HIV/AIDS epidemic that claimed the lives of so many gay men beginning in the 1980s; it truly put a human and personalized face on sexual minorities and their struggles. In part the HIV/AIDS epidemic also spurred more vigorous activist efforts. At the local level lesbians and gays organized to feed, house, and provide care to the sick and dying when governments turned a blind eye to the tragedy. These community organizers then began to wage battle against this very governmental complacency by pushing for research into the disease, demanding the release of new drugs bottled up in the Food and Drug Administration, and working toward the protection of the rights of those infected.[9]

Overall advancement in legal protections for lesbians and gays in the 1980s and 1990s was also (counterintuitively) due to the rising conservative Christian lobby. The Christian Right had grown in strength and size across the United States, especially in the South and West, in the years following World War II. By the 1970s it could marshal a powerful voting bloc. It was structured through a loose national network of churches as well as through more formal organizations such as the Moral Majority, Focus on the Family, and the Christian Coalition. Well-funded, it had access to print and television media, including the Christian cable channel Trinity Broadcasting Network, founded in 1973. It began introducing a spate of referenda, initiatives, and legislation to repeal and deny gay rights across the country. But such efforts also had the effect of leading more gays and lesbians and a growing number of their allies to work yet harder for protections, especially beyond the municipal level. The greater the attack on them, the more lesbians and gays came out of the closet, chose visibility in order to fight back, and in the process made it clear that they and their lives did not differ from others. But the growing acceptance of gays and lesbians on the one hand, and the development of a more defined conservative coalition against them on the other, increased polarization in American society.[10]

The vigorous push by gays and lesbians and their allies in these years produced some successes across the nation. In 1982 Wisconsin became the first state to extend civil rights protections based on sexual orientation. Massachusetts became the second in 1989. By the early 1990s legislatures in a few other states had taken similar action: Connecticut and Hawaii (1991), California, New Jersey, and Vermont (1992), and Minnesota (1993). Some of these states extended a broad range of civil rights protections, while others only provided protections in public and private employment.[11]

In other instances, when state legislatures divided over civil rights for LGBTQ people, some progressive governors issued executive orders extending whatever protections they could. In 1985 Booth Gardner, governor of Washington, issued the first such order in the state's history. This made Washington the sixth state to establish some sort of protection for lesbians and gays against discrimination. Executive Order 85–09 was necessarily narrow. It directed that "no state agency or institution of higher education shall discriminate in employment solely based on an individual's sexual orientation." The order did not require state agencies or institutions of higher education to consider sexual orientation in affirmative action programs.[12]

Within a month of Gardner's action, conservative legislators in Olympia, the state capital, began efforts to overturn it. Rep. Glenn Dobbs, a Republican from Chehalis, with fourteen cosponsors from his party drew up House Bill 1969 that would have effectively barred state and local governments and school districts from hiring gays and lesbians and would require them to fire any who already worked for them. The proposed law also aimed to forbid counties and cities in the state from adopting ordinances similar to the governor's executive order. Dobbs voiced the opinion, "Washington citizens don't want this beautiful state to become the San Francisco of the Northwest, with all the risks and notoriety." The bill did not receive wide support, and even some fellow members of the Republican Party reacted against it.¹³ (It is worth mentioning that Dobbs also initiated a bill to re-criminalize sodomy, and one of his cosponsors, Dick Van Dyke from Bothell, at the same time considered sponsoring legislation to quarantine those infected with HIV.¹⁴)

After he failed in the legislature, Dobbs drew up Initiative 490 in hopes of repealing the governor's order at the ballot box. Essentially the same as his legislative bill, the law would have prohibited the government (including public schools) from employing those known to be "sexually deviant" and repealed local ordinances that prohibited discrimination based on sexual orientation. To support the initiative, Dobbs formed the Washington Family Coalition that drew in conservative women's groups, Christian organizations, and chambers of commerce. The initiative did not make it onto the ballot, but in the fall of 1986 a separate referendum supported by Dobbs did move forward in King County, where Seattle is located; it was an attempt to repeal an ordinance that county commissioners there adopted in 1985 extending employment protections to gays and lesbians. In this Dobbs failed yet again.¹⁵

Governor Gardner reaffirmed his executive order in 1991, and his successor, Mike Lowry, did so again in 1993 while also expanding it.¹⁶ Washington made progress in other areas of LGBTQ protections in the 1980s and 1990s. In 1988 it enacted the so-called "AIDS Omnibus Bill" that safeguarded the civil rights of Washingtonians who were HIV-positive. And in 1993 the legislature added sexual orientation to the state's hate crimes law. Washington was one of the first two states to adopt such legislation, Minnesota also doing so in 1993 (Washington DC adopted such an ordinance in 1989).¹⁷ Only days before the hate crimes law went into effect in Washington, members of the American Front Skinheads, in what seems to have been an act of defiance, bombed the National Association for the Advancement of Colored People headquarters in Tacoma and a gay bar in Seattle.¹⁸

During these years the greatest struggle over the civil rights of lesbians and gays in Washington, however, was tied to the campaign waged by the conservative Right to secure two regressive and punitive ballot measures in 1994 (608 and 610). These measures sought to ban all civil rights protections for LGBTQ people in the state; prohibit schools from teaching that being gay or lesbian is an appropriate lifestyle; and bar gays and lesbians from adopting, serving as foster parents, and even receiving custody of their own children.[19]

Regionally speaking, as had been the case with some other reactive movements—namely eugenical sterilization in the 1900s and 1910s and the Ku Klux Klan in the 1920s—the conservative anti-gay-rights campaign came to Washington in part from Oregon.[20] In 1986 Christian political activists in Oregon formed the Oregon Citizens Alliance (OCA). It was led by Lon Mabon, the campaign manager for a conservative Republican who attempted, unsuccessfully, in 1986 to unseat the moderate Republican U.S. senator Bob Packwood. In 1988 the OCA led a successful effort to repeal through the initiative process (Measure 8) an executive order that Gov. Neil Goldschmidt had issued in 1987 prohibiting job discrimination in state employment based on sexual orientation (the Oregon Court of Appeals invalidated Measure 8 in *Merrick v. Board of Higher Education* in 1992). The OCA built on its 1988 success and in 1992 gathered enough signatures to place Measure 9 before Oregon voters: it would have amended the state constitution to prohibit all state and local governments from using their money or property to promote, encourage, or facilitate homosexuality, pedophilia, sadism, or masochism. All levels of government, including public education, would also have had to teach that those aforementioned "behaviors are abnormal, wrong, unnatural and perverse and they are to be discouraged and avoided."[21] After an extremely bitter battle, Measure 9 failed by a vote of 56 percent to 44 percent. But the OCA returned in 1994 with two more anti-gay/lesbian initiatives that made it onto the Oregon ballot. Both failed but by narrower margins than two years earlier. The OCA received strong support from voters in nonurban Oregon counties and communities. Over the next few years the OCA turned its attention to these places, securing anti-gay-rights laws in twenty-seven smaller cities and rural counties. Oregon's 1993 legislature adopted a law that prohibited local communities from enforcing such discriminatory ordinances.[22]

The victories of the OCA emboldened it to spread into neighboring Washington and Idaho. The Idaho Citizens Alliance—founded by Lon Mabon's assistant, who had recently moved to that state—secured a ballot measure in 1994 similar to the one in Oregon. It failed by a slim margin, with 205,754 voting against it and 202,681 voting for it. On January 29, 1993, Mabon held a press conference in the rotunda of Olympia's capitol and announced that he would introduce an anti-gay initiative in Washington. The OCA then created the Citizens Alliance of Washington (CAW).[23]

Simultaneously a separate group of conservative churches within Washington also coalesced against LGBTQ people. It called itself the Washington Public Affairs Council (WPAC) and publicly promoted itself as the "Committee for Equal Rights—Not Special Rights." It expressed concern about the negative image that the OCA was developing in Oregon, as well as what it might look like to Washingtonian voters to have an Oregonian organization influencing politics there. As a result the WPAC and the CAW never reconciled and moved forward with separate efforts, each introducing its own initiative in 1994.[24]

In September 1992, before either CAW or WPAC formed, Seattle progressives, concerned about the ominous developments in Oregon, began organizing Citizens for Fairness Hands Off Washington (simply known as HOW). It preemptively went on the offensive. Although first forming in the liberal bastion of Seattle and drawing tremendous support from the Puget Sound region, ultimately HOW's success came from its broad appeal to diverse groups, reaching out to minorities of all types and to both rural and urban residents. For example, HOW made an appeal to African Americans when it learned that the WPAC received monetary support from the Populist Party (1984–1996) that had nominated David Duke (the Louisiana politician who was one-time Grand Wizard of the Knights of the Ku Klux Klan) for U.S. president in 1988. Organizers created chapters of HOW across the state in places as diverse as Walla Walla, Yakima, Bellingham, Spokane, Tri-Cities, and Wenatchee, purposely reaching across the Cascade Range into the more conservative and rural eastern reaches of the state. The board rotated its monthly meetings among communities throughout the state, something that increased its profile outside of Seattle and tapped into whatever goodwill and resources existed in those places.[25]

The early and expansive organizing efforts of HOW, along with its campaign to publicize the negative consequences of laws that CAW and WPAC proposed, slowed the efforts of those organizations. A number of mainstream religious bodies in the state, including the Catholic Church, publicly opposed CAW's and WPAC's efforts as well. The conservative groups ultimately failed to secure enough signatures on their initiatives to even place them on the ballot. In 1995 HOW continued its efforts when WPAC again attempted (and failed) to put two anti-LGBTQ legislative initiatives forward.[26]

Simultaneously through these years civil rights protections for lesbians and gays advanced in a few Washington municipalities. In 1986 Olympia adopted antidiscrimination protections based on sexual orientation in public employment, private employment, and housing. Vancouver began to protect gays and lesbians in public employment in 1993. In January 1999 the Spokane City Council adopted a Human Rights Ordinance that protected lesbians and gays in housing, employment, and public accommodations. Spokane voters retained the law when it was challenged at the polls that November. The situation in Tacoma was somewhat different. While the city council passed an ordinance prohibiting discrimination based on sexual orientation in 1989, voters overturned it later that year.[27]

In 1997 HOW, frustrated by the continued failure to secure a statewide civil rights law in the legislature and buoyed by its successful efforts at heading off anti-gay initiatives in 1994 and 1995, introduced its own initiative (I-677) that presented civil rights for lesbians and gays directly to the state's voters. Though HOW succeeded in obtaining the required signatures to place it on the ballot, Washingtonians defeated it by 20 percentage points (60 to 40).[28] On the one hand, given the broader, regressive developments in the 1990s, earning 40 percent popular support for a lesbian and gay civil rights bill in Washington was a remarkable achievement. And yet for those who see the glass as half empty (or in this case 60 percent empty), they would seek answers as to why the ballot measure was "unsuccessful."

There are various answers. First, even LGBTQ people in Washington divided over the initiative—some felt strongly that civil rights were not a matter for public voting to decide, an argument HOW actually made in its 1994 and 1995 battles. Some, for example the well-known columnist and activist Dan Savage, even publicly expressed their opposition to I-677 for that very reason.[29]

Second, outside of Seattle and King County, by the time of HOW's 1997 campaign, lesbians and gays in Washington experienced only rare civil rights victories at the ballot box. And in fact the only notable ballot-box victories in Seattle and King County had been turning back efforts to repeal civil rights in those places. To expect Washingtonians statewide in 1997 to ratify by popular vote something that they had never really done before, and seldom even at a local level, was a gamble.

Third, however successful HOW was in thwarting CAW and WPAC in 1994 and 1995, those organizations' failures were also a result of their own internal problems and sparring. They disagreed at times and could not present a united effort. It may be that when entering into the 1997 effort to secure civil rights at the ballot box, HOW had slightly confused CAW's and WPAC's own weaknesses for public sentiment in favor of wide-ranging civil rights for lesbians and gays.

Finally, one also has to look more broadly at what was happening in the 1990s. It was not a decade of unfettered progress for lesbian and gay rights. The battles in Oregon previously outlined suggest this, so, too, does the contentious battle in Colorado in 1992 when voters approved by a vote of 54 percent to 46 percent an amendment to the state constitution that prohibited LGBTQ anti-discrimination laws throughout the state (Amendment 2) and effectively repealed those where they existed, namely in the more progressive cities of Denver, Boulder, and Aspen. Like other such efforts, the one in Colorado was sponsored in part by Christian fundamentalists. Also in this era, in 1993 voters in Cincinnati, Ohio, by 62 percent to 38 percent, approved an amendment to the city charter, which prohibited it from adopting or enforcing any civil rights ordinance that protected people based on sexual orientation.[30]

Then there were the happenings at the federal level. In 1993 the U.S. government adopted the "Don't Ask, Don't Tell" policy, which deleteriously affected gays and lesbians in the military.³¹ Three years later came the Defense of Marriage Act (DOMA) that Congress overwhelmingly approved and Pres. William Clinton signed. The pretext for DOMA was in response to the shock out of Hawaii when, in 1993, courts determined that there was no compelling reason why they should not extend marriage rights to same-sex couples. Through DOMA, where same-sex couples might marry (though there was no place they could marry in the United States at that time), federal benefits would be disallowed; it also allowed states to refuse to recognize marriages between members of the same sex if those marriages might take place in states where it was legal. By 2006 forty states had adopted similar laws or even constitutional amendments, called mini-DOMAs, that reflected the federal legislation.³²

Washington was one state where the legislature adopted a mini-DOMA in 1998 over the governor's veto. Supporters of "defense of marriage" in Washington voiced views, some steeped in Christian conservatism, similar to those heard around the country. "Who are we to define what God has ordained and established?" Rep. John Koster (R-Shelton) asked. "When you talk about propagation of mankind," he continued, "that doesn't happen in a homosexual marriage. Who are we to say, 'God, you're wrong?' To redefine what God has defined as a relationship and what's normal, quite frankly. Whether you agree with the Bible or not, find me an authority higher than God." Rep. Val Stevens (R-Arlington) similarly espoused the view that heterosexual marriage is "God's choice and we ought to honor that. . . . I don't think we should minimize the sacredness of that union. It's for a man and a woman. Not two people. It's not about love. It's about responsibility to the children."³³

Despite some victories for gay and lesbian civil rights in the 1990s, the enactment of "defense of marriage" legislation by states and the federal government, "Don't Ask, Don't Tell," and any number of local- and state-level bans on the recognition of civil rights for lesbians and gays created an ominous atmosphere in the 1990s, even in Washington State. It was in this atmosphere that HOW undertook its efforts to obtain civil rights at the ballot box in 1997 and failed in doing so.

And still, in each legislative session in Washington during these years, bills appeared for adding sexual orientation to the state's civil rights law. Cal Anderson from Seattle—state representative, later senator, and Washington's first openly gay legislator—took up the cause in the late 1980s and early 1990s. Ed Murray (also openly gay) succeeded Anderson in his seat in 1995 (Anderson passed away due to complications from AIDS) and followed in his predecessor's footsteps, doggedly sponsoring the civil rights bill in Olympia over the next several years.[34]

By the early twenty-first century, the gloomy atmosphere for LGBTQ people began to lift somewhat in some parts of the United States. In Washington State it did so in a resounding way. The string of civil rights bill defeats that stretched back to 1977 ended on January 27, 2006, when the legislature finally added LGBTQ people to the state's civil rights law. House Bill 2661 was popularly known as the "Anderson-Murray Bill," a name that clearly demonstrates its connections to the past. But newer developments since the 1980s and 1990s were reflected in the bill, too. That is, the law included civil rights safeguards not only for lesbians and gays but also for transgender people when it employed language that provided protections for people based on their gender identity and expression. Given the historic marginalization of trans people in the larger LGBTQ movement, the 2006 law was an expansive and unprecedented piece of legislation in the state. The Washington House, as had been its pattern for several years, passed HB 2661 by a vote of 61 to 37. For the first time the Washington Senate also approved the statute. The vote there was 25 to 23, with two conservative Democrats voting against it and one Republican, Sen. Bill Finkbeiner from a district southeast of Seattle, voting in favor. Senator Finkbeiner had previously been in the opposition. News stories quoted him as explaining why he had switched to support the bill: "I've had a number of conversations over the past year that have led me to more fully understand the level of discrimination against gays and lesbians, and I now find it is both appropriate and necessary for the state to make it clear that this is not acceptable."[35]

Testimony before the legislature in support of the bill provided some statistical backing for the information that Finkbeiner had learned in his conversations, namely that 10 percent of discrimination complaints that the City of Spokane received and 5 percent that the City of Seattle received were based on matters of sexual identity. The testimony against the bill also captured the continuing prejudice that LGBTQ people in Washington faced. Much of the prejudice was based in religion. One speaker opposing Anderson-Murray claimed that gay people were an "abomination," and that Washington should "not try to legalize what God has clearly prohibited." Another claimed that the "foundations of this nation are based on the principles of God's words," and that HB 2661 "takes another hit at this foundation with a wrecking ball. . . . Jesus is the answer." And yet another explained, "Sexual immorality has not benefitted my Christian community, neighborhood, state, or county." Any number of other voices testifying against the bill rooted their prejudices in issues of morality and child welfare, while they also strenuously objected to the legislation because it would prevent people from being able to discriminate by invoking religious principles.[36]

Compared to some other states mentioned earlier, Washington's adoption of civil rights protections for sexual minorities seems rather late in coming. On the other hand, Washington was among a new wave of states in the new century that adopted various levels of civil rights protections for LGBTQ people at roughly the same time, with no discernable regional pattern, save that nowhere did this happen in the American South: New Mexico in 2003, Maine in 2005, Illinois in 2006, Iowa in 2007, Colorado in 2007, and Oregon in 2008. Moreover, several of the states that had acted much earlier than Washington revised and expanded civil rights laws for LGBTQ people in the first decade of the twenty-first century.[37]

Much had changed between 1997, when I-677 failed by 20 percentage points at the ballot box, and 2006 when the Washington State Legislature expanded its civil rights law to cover lesbians, gays, and trans people. In 2003 the U.S. Supreme Court had struck down the last remaining sodomy laws in the country, in so far as they applied to consenting adults (and also reversed its ruling in *Bowers v. Hardwick*, 1986, that proclaimed existing sodomy laws constitutional). It was also becoming abundantly clear to more and more people that the effects of "Don't Ask, Don't Tell" were blatantly discriminatory; during these years a majority of Americans came to support the idea of openly gay people serving in the military, perhaps in part due to numerous stories coming to light that many gay servicemen and lesbian servicewomen had served their country well, even heroically. One of these was Washington State's Col. Margarethe Cammermeyer, who had been dismissed from the National Guard in 1992 (after a thirty-some-year career in the military) for admitting to being a lesbian. This was just prior to the implementation of "Don't Ask, Don't Tell." Her 1994 book *Serving in Silence* was turned into an award-winning television film the following year that starred Glenn Close as Cammermeyer. Actions of Congress, federal courts, the secretary of defense, and the U.S. president ended "Don't Ask, Don't Tell" on September 20, 2011.[38]

But old prejudices had not somehow simply evaporated, whether in Washington or elsewhere in 2006. The accumulative effects of years of discriminatory laws that permitted, even encouraged, prejudice could not all of a sudden be undone with the signing of a piece of legislation. It is worth remembering that the support that Senator Finkbeiner had voiced that session was based on the very real stories of prejudice and discrimination that he had only finally opened his ears to. And in the state legislature that session one could loudly hear that very prejudice being voiced. Elected representatives who opposed the bill boldly brandished long-held negative views of LGBTQ people just as private citizens who also testified did, as noted previously. For example, Sen. Bob Oke (R-Port Orchard) expressed the position, "I believe that homosexuality is morally wrong," and that the Bible views it as an "abomination to God." Sen. Val Stevens (R-Arlington) and Sen. James Hargrove (D-Hoquiam) introduced an amendment to HB 2661 (later withdrawn) to clarify that the words "sexual orientation" in the law did not include "bestiality, necrophilia, incest, adultery, pedophilia, or sadomasochism." This was an effort deeply rooted in history that focused on behavior rather than personhood. Senator Stevens's term "labyrinth of perversion" that she used to describe LGBTQ people during the 2006 debates concisely sums up this tradition.[39]

The aforementioned senators from Arlington, Hoquiam, and Port Orchard were only three of the twenty-three senators who voted against HB 2661. Their views did not represent all the people in their districts, but their views are indicative of an anti-LGBTQ sentiment that yet predominates in many places in the state. Other senators who voted against HB 2661 came from districts within Yakima, Benton County, Walla Walla, Sunnyside, Wenatchee, and Spokane, all in the generally more conservative eastern side of Washington as well as from more rural districts on the western side of the state. That legislators from these places might so freely condemn LGBTQ people in the most mean-spirited words also demonstrates that a social and cultural atmosphere of bigotry confronted and continues to confront LGBTQ people in many places in Washington.

In the years following the adoption of federal and state DOMAs, views on same-sex relationships, like other civil rights safeguards, also continued to evolve, in part due to large businesses and some institutions of higher education being the first to extend domestic partner benefits to their gay and lesbian employees. Some municipalities and states slowly followed suit. And then in 2004 Massachusetts began recognizing same-sex marriage rights; it was followed in a few years by several other states. In 2007 the Washington State Legislature adopted a domestic partnership law and expanded it in 2008 and again in 2009.[40]

Washington's 2007 law partly grew from the success of same-sex couples who brought suit against the state's mini-DOMA (collectively referred to as the *Andersen* case). The King County Superior Court determined in 2006 that Washington's law allowing only opposite-sex couples to marry violated the state's constitution that provided equal protection under the law. The Washington Supreme Court narrowly (5 to 4) overturned this ruling, claiming among other things that the legislature "was entitled" to restrict marriage to opposite-sex couples because in so doing this "furthers procreation, essential to the survival of the human race, and furthers the well-being of children by encouraging families where children are reared in homes headed by the children's biological parents." (For all their learnedness, surely the justices knew that people had been procreating for years and raising children without the benefits or the drawbacks of marriage.) The court also, however, signaled to the legislature that it might revisit its DOMA.[41] It might be added that this 2006 defense of marriage—as an institution that "furthers procreation"—was an argument made in 1974 by the Washington Court of Appeals when it ruled against two men who filed suit when they were denied the right to marry in King County in 1971 (this was the first such case in Washington State). Notably, one of the concurring justices in this 1974 opinion was Charles Horowitz. He was later appointed to the Washington Supreme Court and would there decide it acceptable and legal for a public-school employee to be fired based solely on the fact that he was gay.[42]

Washington's 2009 domestic partner law provided both same- and opposite-sex couples, who entered into officially registered domestic partnerships, basically all the rights and privileges that "marriage" conferred (at the state level). In fact, the 2009 act was popularly known as the "Everything but Marriage" law because of this. Opponents (people who did not want same-sex couples to have even access to this form of recognition) secured a ballot measure to repeal it in 2009. It went down to defeat by 53 percent to 47 percent.[43]

Growing support for domestic partnerships in Washington—including the fact that they were in many ways similar to marriages—and changing sentiment elsewhere in the country that had led some other state legislatures to adopt marriage equality provided momentum to what changes began to occur in Washington State. In 2012 the Evergreen State's legislature rescinded the 1998 defense of marriage law and extended full marriage rights to same-sex couples. The vote in favor was not overwhelming (28 to 21 in the senate and 55 to 43 in the house). Many senators and representatives, as well as other observers, spoke out against it in long-recognizable ways. Sen. Dan Swecker (R-Rochester) declared, "I have to stick by my religious faith. I don't have any option." One Washingtonian present to observe the vote in the senate stated, "I'm a Christian, and this is not pleasing to God. I feel very grieved that the bill is even in question." She also explained that she had wished more Christians had been in attendance for "prayer support against this issue."[44]

Gov. Chris Gregoire signed the bill into law, but opponents quickly organized and sought a referendum to overturn the legislation at the November 2012 ballot box. The referendum went down to defeat, 54 percent to 46 percent (a slightly greater margin of defeat compared to the domestic partnership referendum's failure in 2009).[45] Washington voters became the first in the union to vote in favor of marriage equality.

In the early twenty-first century Washington made remarkable progress in eliminating laws that permitted discrimination against LGBTQ people. It has been a process that began in the 1970s, but the achievement is very new and in no way suggests that discrimination, let alone the prejudice that undergirds it, has disappeared. Despite the legislative passage and the voter approval of marriage for same-sex couples, majorities of voters in only ten of Washington's thirty-nine counties voted in defense of marriage for same-sex couples in 2012. All but one of those counties are in the more populated Puget Sound region. The one exception was Whitman County, located east of the Cascade mountains. It is dominated by Washington State University. The vote in Whitman County was actually quite close: 8,554 for marriage equality and 8,330 against it. Otherwise, every other county east of the Cascades (nineteen) voted against marriage rights for same-sex couples.[46]

The response of a longtime senator from eastern Washington, Republican Robert Morton, to the results of the 2012 referendum and the beginning of same-sex couples marrying in the state is instructive. For years Senator Morton (who arrived in Olympia in 1991) had promoted an effort to divide Washington into two states. He was displeased with the influence and power that the more populated and progressive Puget Sound region held over the areas east of the Cascades that he represented. In the twenty-four hours after marriage for same-sex couples became legal on December 6, 2012, the *Seattle Times* reported that some 450 such couples applied for licenses in King County (where Seattle is situated), while in Stevens County, part of Senator Morton's district in the extreme northeastern part of the state, no same-sex couples had done the same. To this piece of news, Senator Morton responded expansively of eastern Washington, "That's a good illustration of the difference in our philosophy and our basic beliefs." By the way, Morton simply ignored the 6,977 voters in Stevens County (31 percent of those who voted) who defended marriage equality.[47] Moreover, at the conclusion of one year after same-sex marriage became possible in Washington, each county in the state (save for Garfield, east of the Cascades) reported the marriage of same-sex couples within its bounds, and 17 percent of all marriages conducted in the state that year were between people of the same sex.[48]

Senator Morton is no longer living, but the views he held continue to animate many in the state, and, sadly, discrimination against LGBTQ people continues. The civil rights act of 2006 is thus regularly called into service. In 2015 and 2016, for example, in response to some people's concerns about transgender people using public restrooms (and also during the time of a similar and high-profile case in North Carolina), Washington's Human Rights Commission determined that transgender people in the state could use restrooms that comport to their identity and that this was in accord with the 2006 law. That same year the state legislature refused a bill that would alter that determination. An initiative that sought to change the law also failed to gather enough signatures to find its way onto the ballot.[49]

Some of the discrimination that persists also continues to find its roots in fundamentalist Christian prejudice. Increasingly common across the United States are specific cases wherein self-identified Christians refuse to provide services to LGBTQ people in governmental services and publicly operated businesses. For example, we have seen a county clerk in Kentucky refuse to issue marriage licenses to same-sex couples and bakers in Colorado and Oregon refuse to sell wedding cakes to same-sex couples all because such acts apparently transgress their religious beliefs. Such has occurred in Washington, too. In 2013 the proprietor of a florist shop in Richland, Washington, would not sell flower arrangements for the wedding of a same-sex couple with whom she had otherwise conducted business for years. She "simply declines to celebrate or participate in sacred events that violate her deeply held beliefs" and claimed that Washington State, in enforcing its civil rights law, "violated her religious beliefs" and therefore "compelled speech" on her part. That case wended its way through the Washington courts over several years with the state supreme court ruling unanimously against the florist in 2017. Her defense petitioned the U.S. Supreme Court to take up the case; that body returned the case to Washington for reconsideration. The Washington Supreme Court affirmed its decision in 2019. The florist's defense then asked the U.S. Supreme Court once again to take up the case. This time in July 2021 the U.S. Supreme Court denied the florist's petition, leaving the Washington Supreme Court's decision in favor of LGBTQ rights in place. Although this was a victory for Washington's LGBTQ people and the state's ever-evolving civil rights legislation, this likely does not resolve such matters, given that the court's decision provided no explanation, and there is no evidence that prejudicial thought was actually altered as a result. Left uncertain, then, are the rights of LGBTQ people in Washington to conduct their lives like others in a civil society free from the animus of those who try to prevent them from doing just that.[50]

Notes

1. For the full text of the law, see "Certification of Enrollment, Engrossed Substitute House Bill 2661, Chapter 4, Laws of 2006, 59th Legislature, 2006 Regular Session," Washington Legislature, http://lawfilesext.leg.wa.gov/biennium/2005-06/Pdf/Bills/Session%20laws/House/2661-S.SL.pdf?q=20210211081332.

2. Twentieth-century published histories of LGBTQ people that consider western American places, or histories relating to the American West that have some LGBTQ content are, Katz, *Gay American History*; D'Emilio, *Sexual Politics, Sexual Communities*; and one can more generally include Gutiérrez, *When Jesus Came, the Corn Mothers Went Away*. For a more thorough bibliography of late-twentieth- and early twenty-first-century titles, see Johnson et al., "Queer Wests: A Historiographical Conversation," 7–21. Likewise, the best studies of the rise of religious fundamentalism in the American West had also through the early twenty-first century been authored by scholars and journalists who are not "western" identified. Examples include McGirr, *Suburban Warriors*; Dochuk, *From Bible Belt to Sun Belt*; Perlstein, *Before the Storm*.

3. For a fuller discussion, see Boag, "Another Way West: An Introduction," 2–6.

4. Just as in places such as California, Chicago, and New York City in the 1950s and 1960s, there was a modest homophile movement underway in Seattle and Tacoma, where lesbian and gay people were mainly seeking better treatment from the local police. See Boag, "Does Portland Need a Homophile Society?," 23–27.

5. "Anita Bryant Battles Move for Gay Rights," *Seattle Times*, February 16, 1977; Eaklor, *Queer America*, 170.

6. He also claimed that gays were "emotionally disturbed," and that their "sickness" should be treated like alcoholism. See Ross Anderson, "Homosexual-Rights Battle: Gay City Clerk Steps into the Middle," *Seattle Times*, February 5, 1978; Atkins, *Gay Seattle*, 236, 255.

7. Atkins, *Gay Seattle*, 238–57; Alan J. Stein, "Marriage Equality and Gay Rights in Washington," HistoryLink, http://www.historylink.org/index.cfm?DisplayPage=output.cfm&file_id=10255; Eaklor, *Queer America*, 170–71. On California's "Briggs Initiative" more specifically, see Smith-Silverman, "Gay Teachers Fight Back!," 79–107.

8. "Washington State Legislature, Social & Health Services Committee Hearing, H-Hs03-23-1977, 03-23-1977, House of Representatives Committee Meeting Recordings, 1973–2002," Washington State Archives, https://www.digitalarchives.wa.gov; various items contained in the files of SB2734.

9. Stein, *Rethinking the Gay and Lesbian Movement*, 143–81; Chrystie Hill, "Queer History in Seattle, Part 2: After Stonewall," HistoryLink, https://www.historylink.org/File/4266.

10. See, for example, Fetner, *How the Religious Right Shaped Lesbian and Gay Activism*; Gallagher and Bull, *Perfect Enemies*.

11. Hunt, "A State-by-State Examination of Nondiscrimination Laws and Policies," Center for American Progress Action Fund.

12. Colvin, "Policy Entrepreneurs and Gay Rights Policies," 43; Booth Gardner, "Executive Order 85-09 of December 24, 1985, Prohibiting Discrimination and Establishing Affirmative Action Policy and Rescinding Executive Order 84-10," https://www.governor.wa.gov/sites/default/files/exe_order/eo_85-09.pdf.

13. "Bill Would Deny Gays Custody, State Jobs," *Seattle Times*, January 24, 1986; Don Jepsen, "Bill's Description of Deviance Scorches Legislators' Ears," *Oregonian*, February 5, 1986; "15 GOP Solons Aim at Gay-Rights Ordinances," *Oregonian*, January 25, 1986.

14. Jepsen, "Bill's Description," *Oregonian*, February 5, 1986; "15 GOP Solons," *Oregonian*, January 25, 1986; "Washington Legislator Dies in Apparent Case of Suicide," *Oregonian*, December 4, 1986.

15. Stone, *Gay Rights at the Ballot Box*, 17; Don Jepsen, "Initiative Would Ban Hiring Homosexuals," *Oregonian*, February 22, 1986.

16. Booth Gardner, "Executive Order 91–06 of September 6, 1991, Prohibiting Discrimination and Establishing Affirmative Action and Work Place Diversity Policy and Rescinding Executive Order 85–09," https://www.governor.wa.gov/sites/default/files/exe_order/eo_91-06.pdf; Lowry, "Executive Order 93–07 of September 27, 1993, Affirming Commitment to Diversity and Equity in Service Delivery and in the Communities of the State, Re-establishing Affirmative Action and Prohibiting Discrimination in State Workplaces and Rescinding Executive Order 91–06," https://www.governor.wa.gov/sites/default/files/exe_order/eo_93-07.pdf.

17. Washington State Legislature, RCW 9A.36.078, http://apps.leg.wa.gov/rcw/default.aspx?cite=9A.36.078; Barbara A. Serrano, "Senate Okays Harassment Protection for Gays," *Seattle Times*, April 14, 1993, C1; Atkins, *Gay Seattle*, 364.

18. Hewitt, *Political Violence and Terrorism in Modern America*, 162; Wayne Wurzer and Kery Murakami, "Skinhead Battle Cry," *Seattle Times*, August 22, 1993, B1.

19. "Initiative 608, 620—Putting Hatred on the Ballot," *Seattle Times*, July 6, 1994, B5; "Initiative Measure No. 608" and "Initiative Measure No. 610," Elections & Voting, Office of

the Washington Secretary of State, http://www.sos.wa.gov/elections/initiatives/statistics
_initiatives.aspx.

20. John Caldbick, "Ku Klux Klan in Washington, 1921–1925," HistoryLink, https://www.historylink.org/File/20718; Boag, *Same-Sex Affairs*, 207, 215.

21. Heather Burmeister, "Basic Rights Oregon," Oregon Encyclopedia, https://www.oregonencyclopedia.org/articles/basic_rights_oregon/#.YCb9wmo1ax0; Oregon Secretary of State, *Voters' Pamphlet: State of Oregon General Election, November 3, 1992*; see Young, "Measure 9: Oregon's 1992 Anti-Gay Initiative."

22. Peter Boag, "Gay and Lesbian Rights Movement," Oregon Encyclopedia, https://www.oregonencyclopedia.org/articles/gay_lesbian_rights_movement/#.YCwejmo1ax0.

23. Barbara A. Serrano and Alex Tizon, "Anti-Gay Group Branching Out—Oregon Coalition to Launch Efforts Here, In Idaho," *Seattle Times*, January 29, 1993, B1; Stone, *Gay Rights at the Ballot Box*, 24; "1994 Initiative General Election Results—Idaho," U.S. Election Atlas, https://uselectionatlas.org/RESULTS/state.php?fips=16&year=1994&f=0&off=61&elect=0.

24. See *We're Here to Stay*; Susan Gilmore, "Christian Coalition Takes New Approach," *Seattle Times*, March 12, 1994.

25. See *We're Here to Stay*.

26. See *We're Here to Stay*.

27. Eskridge, *Gaylaw*, 360; see *Washington—Sexual Orientation and Gender Identity Law and Documentation of Discrimination*; see Sears, Hunter, and Mallory, *Documenting Discrimination Based on Sexual Orientation and Gender Identity in State Employment*; "Spokane's LGBT Community," Inland Northwest Business Alliance, http://www.inbaspokane.org/spokanes-lgbt-community; City of Spokane Ordinance No. C-32232, legaljoint.net/humanrights.pdf.

28. Stone, *Gay Rights at the Ballot Box*, 116–17.

29. Dan Savage, "Risk vs. Rights: The Debate on I-677—Ballot Measure a Misstep that Jeopardizes Gay Gains," *Seattle Times*, May 4, 1997.

30. Stone, *Gay Rights at the Ballot Box*, 21–23; "Equality Foundation of Greater Cincinnati Inc. v. City of Cincinnati 94 3973 4280 3833," FindLaw, http://caselaw.findlaw.com/us-6th-circuit/1104057.html.

31. For example, see Huffman and Schultz, *The End of Don't Ask, Don't Tell*.

32. Koppelman, "The Difference the Mini-DOMAs Make," 265–66; Eaklor, *Queer America*, 215–16.

33. Lynda V. Mapes, "House Passes Ban on Gay Marriages—Backers Say Bill Defends 'God's Choice,'" *Seattle Times*, February 5, 1998, B1 (quoted); Andrew Garber, "State Gay-Rights Bill Okayed 29 Years After Effort Began," *Seattle Times*, January 28, 2006, A1.

34. Atkins, *Gay Seattle*, 357.

35. Andrew Garber, "Swing Vote Now Says He'll Vote Yes on Gay Civil Rights Bill," *Seattle Times*, January 9, 2006.

36. Washington State Legislature, "House Bill Report ESHB 2661," https://apps.leg.wa.gov/documents/billdocs/2005-06/Pdf/Bill%20reports/House/2661-S.HBR.pdf. It should also be noted that immediately upon the governor signing the law, conservative political activist Tim Eyman announced an initiative to repeal from the law its "sexual orientation" verbiage. His efforts made little headway, and he eventually withdrew the

proposed initiative. See Kit Oldham, "Governor Christine Gregoire Signs Bill Extending Civil Rights Laws to Gays and Lesbians on January 31, 2006," HistoryLink, https://historylink.org/File/7632.

37. The Human Rights Campaign website maintains ever-changing information on the history of states' LGBTQ civil rights at https://www.hrc.org/resources/state-maps.

38. See Cammermeyer, *Serving in Silence*; "Don't Ask, Don't Tell," *Encyclopedia Britannica*, https://www.britannica.com/event/Dont-Ask-Dont-Tell. For examples of lesbian and gay military "heroism," see Stephen Foley, "Gay American War Hero with Purple Heart Who Didn't Tell Unless Asked," *Independent*, July 29, 2008; "Born on the 4th of July: America's Gay and Lesbian War Heroes," *Queerty**, July 4, 2012.

39. See *Washington—Sexual Orientation and Gender Identity Law and Documentation of Discrimination*; Andrew Garber, "State House, Senate Pass Gay Rights Bill," *Seattle Times*, January 27, 2006.

40. Washington State Legislature, SB 5336-2007-08, http://apps.leg.wa.gov/billinfo/summary.aspx?bill=5336&year=2007; HB 3104-2007-08, http://apps.leg.wa.gov/billinfo/summary.aspx?bill=3104&year=2007; SB 5688-2009-10, http://apps.leg.wa.gov/billinfo/summary.aspx?bill=5688&year=2009.

41. See Andersen v. State of Washington, No. 75934–1, July 26, 2006, https://caselaw.findlaw.com/wa-supreme-court/1123318.html.

42. See Singer v. Hara, 11 Wn. App. 247, 522 P.2d 1187, https://casetext.com/case/singer-v-hara; Atkins, *Gay Seattle*, 227.

43. "Washington Domestic Partners Rights and Responsibilities, Referendum 71 (2009)," Ballot-Pedia, http://ballotpedia.org/Washington_Domestic_Partners_Rights_and_Responsibilities,_Referendum_71_%282009%29; "November 03, 2009 General Election Results," Washington Secretary of State, https://results.vote.wa.gov/results/20091103/referendum-measure-71-concerning-rights-and-responsibilities-of-state-registered-domestic-partners.html.

44. Andrew Garber, "Gay-Marriage Bill Easily Clears House," *Seattle Times*, February 9, 2012, A8 (quoted); Andrew Garber, "Gay-Marriage Bill Clears Senate Committee," *Seattle Times*, January 27, 2012, B1 (quoted): Andrew Garber, "Historic Senate Vote Clears Way for Gay Marriage," *Seattle Times*, February 2, 2012, A1 (quoted).

45. "B 6239-2011-12," *Washington State Legislature*, http://apps.leg.wa.gov/billinfo/summary.aspx?bill=6239&year=2011; "November 06, 2012, General Election Results, Referendum Measure No. 74," Washington Secretary of State, https://results.vote.wa.gov/results/20121106/referendum-measure-no-74-concerns-marriage-for-same-sex-couples_bycounty.html.

46. "November 06, 2012, General Election Results, Referendum Measure No. 74," Washington Secretary of State.

47. Kayla Webley, "A State Divided: As Washington Becomes More Liberal, Republicans Push Back," *Time*, January 15, 2013; "November 06, 2012, General Election Results, Referendum Measure No. 74," Washington Secretary of State.

48. Gene Balk, "Same-Sex Couples Now Account for 1 in 6 Washington Weddings," *Seattle Times*, December 5, 2013.

49. "Don't Change Transgender Law," *Seattle Times*, February 11, 2016, A13; Walker Orenstein, "Legislative Session: What Passed, Died, and Was Revived," *Seattle Times*, April 4,

2016, B2; Joseph O'Sullivan, "Effort to Overturn Transgender Bathroom Rule Falls Short," *Seattle Times*, July 8, 2016, B3.

50. David Gutman, "Court: Still Wrong to Refuse Gay Customer," *Seattle Times*, June 7, 2019, B1 (quoted); Lornet Turnbull, "State Sues Richland Florist over Gay Wedding," *Seattle Times*, April 10, 2013, B2; "A Bouquet for Defenders of Equality," *Seattle Times*, February 21, 2017, A13; Aryn Fields, "Human Rights Campaign President on Supreme Court Denying Certiorari for Ingersoll & Freed v. Arlene's Flowers, Inc.," *Human Rights Campaign*, July 2, 2021, https://www.hrc.org/press-releases/human-rights-campaign-president-on-supreme-court-denying-certiorari-for-ingersoll-freed-v-arlenes-flowers-inc.

Bibliography

Archival Sources

Washington State Archives. Washington Secretary of State Legislative Building.

Published Works

Atkins, Gary L. *Gay Seattle: Stories of Exile and Belonging.* Seattle: University of Washington Press, 2013.

Boag, Peter. "Another Way West: An Introduction." *Western History Association Newsletter* (Spring 2013): 2–6.

Boag, Peter. "'Does Portland Need a Homophile Society?' Gay Culture and Activism in the Rose City between World War II and Stonewall." *Oregon Historical Quarterly* 105, no. 1 (Spring 2004): 23–27.

Boag, Peter. *Same-Sex Affairs: Constructing and Controlling Homosexuality in the Pacific Northwest.* Berkeley: University of California Press, 2003.

Cammermeyer, Margarethe. *Serving in Silence.* New York: Viking, 1994.

Colvin, Roddrick A. "Policy Entrepreneurs and Gay Rights Policies: An Analysis of State-Level Laws." In *Handbook of Gay, Lesbian, Bisexual, and Transgender Administration and Policy*, edited by Wallace Swan, 33–68. New York: Marcel Dekker, 2004.

D'Emilio, John. *Sexual Politics, Sexual Communities: The Making of a Homosexual Minority in the United States.* Chicago: University of Chicago Press, 1983.

Dochuk, Darren. *From Bible Belt to Sun Belt: Plain Folk Religion, Grassroots Politics, and the Rise of Evangelical Conservatism.* New York: W. W. Norton, 2011.

Eaklor, Vicki L. *Queer America: A People's GLBT History of the United States.* New York: New Press, 2008.

Eskridge, William N. *Gaylaw: Challenging the Apartheid of the Closet.* Cambridge: Harvard University Press, 1999.

Fetner, Tina. *How the Religious Right Shaped Lesbian and Gay Activism.* Minneapolis: University of Minnesota Press, 2008.

Gallagher, John, and Chris Bull. *Perfect Enemies: The Battle between the Religious Right and the Gay Movement, Updated Edition.* Lanham MD: Madison Books, 1996.

Gutiérrez, Ramón A. *When Jesus Came, the Corn Mothers Went Away: Marriage, Sexuality, and Power in New Mexico, 1500–1846.* Stanford CA: Stanford University Press, 1991.

Hewitt, Christopher. *Political Violence and Terrorism in Modern America: A Chronology.* Westport CT: Praeger, 2005.

Huffman, J. Ford, and Tammy S. Schultz. *The End of Don't Ask, Don't Tell: The Impact in Studies and Personal Essays by Service Members and Veterans.* Quantico VA: Marine Corps University Press, 2012.

Hunt, Jerome. *A State-by-State Examination of Nondiscrimination Laws and Policies: State Nondiscrimination Policies Fill the Void but Federal Protections Are Still Needed.* Washington DC: Center for American Progress Action Fund, June 2012. https://www.americanprogress.org/wp-content/uploads/issues/2012/06/pdf/state_nondiscrimination.pdf.

Johnson, Susan Lee, Christopher Hommerding, Simon Fisher, and Johanna Lanner-Cusin. "Queer Wests: A Historiographical Conversation." *Western History Association Newsletter* (Spring 2013): 7–21.

Katz, Jonathan Ned. *Gay American History: Lesbians and Gay Men in the U.S.A., a Documentary.* New York: Crowell, 1976.

Koppelman, Andrew. "The Difference the Mini-DOMAs Make." *Loyola University Chicago Law Journal* 38, no. 2 (2007): 265–66.

Latham, Liz. *We're Here to Stay: A Documentary about the History of Hands Off Washington and the Politics of Hate in Washington State.* Seattle WA: Lizard Productions, 1998.

McGirr, Lisa. *Suburban Warriors: The Origins of the New American Right.* Princeton NJ: Princeton University Press, 2001.

Oregon Secretary of State. *Voters' Pamphlet: State of Oregon General Election, November 3, 1992.* Salem: State of Oregon, 1992.

Perlstein, Rick. *Before the Storm: Barry Goldwater and the Unmaking of the American Consensus.* New York: Hill and Wang, 2001.

Sears, Brad, Nan D. Hunter, and Christy Mallory. *Documenting Discrimination Based on Sexual Orientation and Gender Identity in State Employment.* Los Angeles: The Williams Institute, September 2009.

Smith-Silverman, Sara. "'Gay Teachers Fight Back!': Rank-and-File Gay and Lesbian Teachers' Activism against the Briggs Initiative, 1877–1978." *Journal of the History of Sexuality* 29, no. 1 (January 2020): 79–107.

Stein, Marc. *Rethinking the Gay and Lesbian Movement.* New York: Routledge, 2021.

Stone, Amy L. *Gay Rights at the Ballot Box.* Minneapolis: University of Minnesota Press, 2012.

Washington—Sexual Orientation and Gender Identity Law and Documentation of Discrimination. Los Angeles: The Williams Institute, 2009.

Young, Patricia Jean. "Measure 9: Oregon's 1992 Anti-Gay Initiative." Master's thesis, Portland State University, 1994.

13

The American West, Native Americans, and Controversies over the Antiquities Act

Bears Ears National Monument, a Utah Case Study

ANDREW GULLIFORD

> A lot of rocks, a lot of sand, more rocks, more sand, and wind to blow it away.
>
> —Cowboy description of San Juan County, Utah, 1938

> Rising from the center of the southeastern Utah landscape and visible from every direction are twin buttes so distinctive that in each of the native languages of the region their name is the same: Hoon'Naqvut, Shash Jaa, Kwiyagutu Nukavachi, Ansh An Lashokdiwe, or "Bears Ears." For hundreds of generations, native peoples lived in the surrounding deep sandstone canyons, desert mesas, and meadow mountaintops, which constitute one of the densest and most significant cultural landscapes in the United States.
>
> —Proclamation for Bears Ears National Monument, Pres. Barack Obama, 2016[1]

In an anthology of scholars writing about the modern American West, inevitably larger patterns must be discerned from localized case studies. In his excellent introduction to this volume Brenden Rensink has given us a superb summary of New West scholarship from a few decades back. If that was the New West in the 1980s and 1990s, perhaps we are now in the Next West. Regardless of the chronology, as Rensink argues we have gone beyond "settler mythologies," yet we remain "a nation and a region still wrestling with past and present problems." In several of her essays and books Patricia

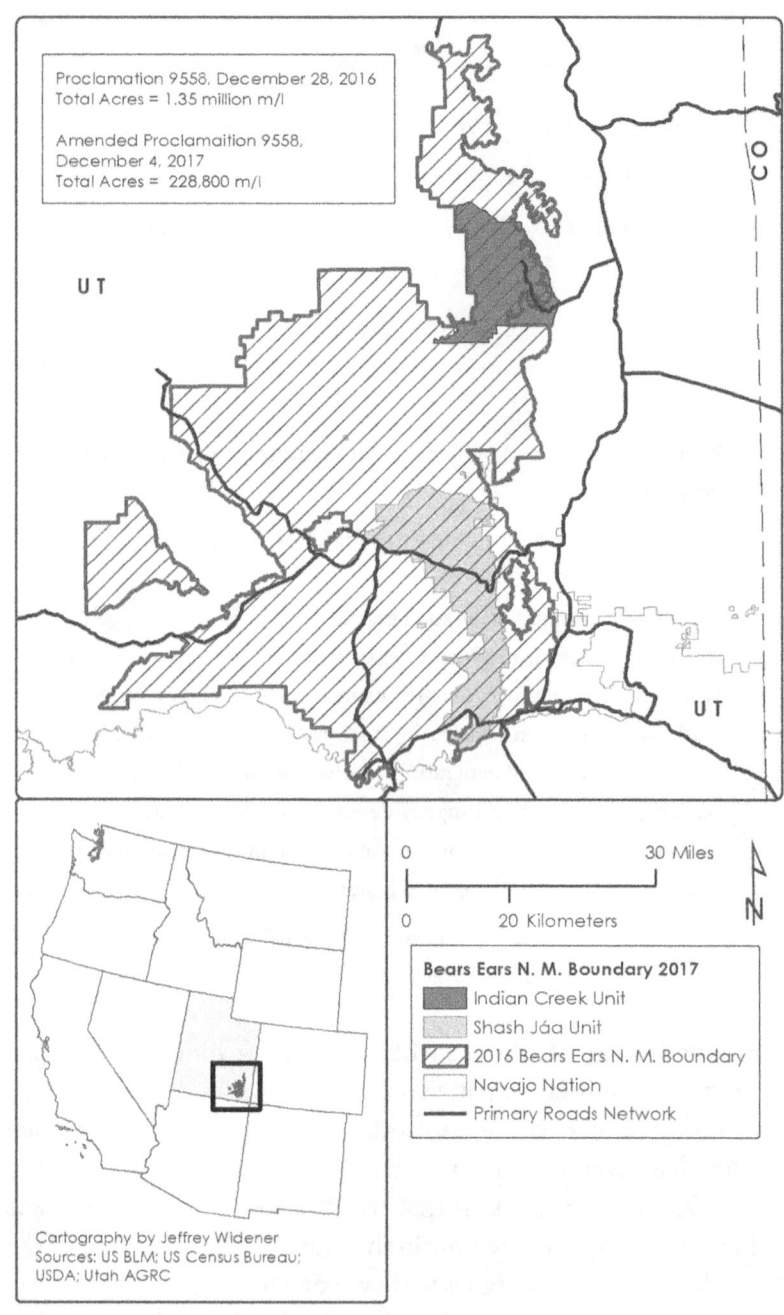

FIG. 30. Bears Ears National Monument boundaries and reduction.
Map by Jeffrey M. Widener.

Limerick has urged modern western residents to try to understand each other, to sit down and talk out old conflicts, and to seek resolution and common ground. One of the places where that needs to occur is southeast Utah, which is physically remote, far from the modern mainstream, and yet the center of controversy for one of the defining conundrums of the American West: how to manage, preserve, protect, and also utilize thousands of acres of public land.

A recent ongoing controversy over national monument designation in San Juan County, Utah, may define use of the Antiquities Act in the twenty-first-century American West. In desert, sagebrush, and canyon country, public land disputes mirror those from previous centuries. A case study is Bears Ears National Monument in southeast Utah, which has divided San Juan County and its Anglo and Native American residents.[2] What is it about this Bears Ears landscape that produces such intense feelings of home and sacredness? How has such a remote place with so few current inhabitants become nationally known, and how has it become a twenty-first-century case study over the future of conflicting views of the modern American West? In many ways, resolving conflicts concerning Bears Ears National Monument will serve as a litmus test for other western public lands issues.

For the first time in the century-old use of the Antiquities Act, American Indians are actively seeking protection of their prehistoric and historic sites as well as traditional cultural sites still used for plant gathering, prayers, and ceremonies.[3] San Juan County, Utah, has become a bullseye for conflict among states' rights advocates, local ranching and mining families, environmental groups, and Native American activists. "The Bears Ears monument has been very controversial, and Native Americans have been particularly involved in debates over the designation," notes anthropologist Soni Grant.[4] Legal and political issues swirl around Pres. Barack Obama's December 2016 1.35-million-acre Bears Ears National Monument proclamation in southeast Utah.[5] Since passage of the Antiquities Act in 1906, this is the first monument supported by five Native American tribes (members of the Bears Ears Inter-Tribal Coalition), yet Pres. Donald Trump, in an unprecedented action in 2017, shrunk the monument by 85 percent.[6] He did so because of intense local opposition from San Juan County and the Utah political delegation, which realized that Obama's designation withdrew mineral leasing.

Coalition members who are Navajo, Zuni, Hopi, Ute Mountain Ute, and Northern Ute representatives favor the original monument boundaries and protection of sacred sites. As envisioned this would be the first national monument with Native American comanagement. Native American tribes actively campaigned to protect thousand-year-old Ancestral Puebloan sites from vandalism, maintain access to Native cultural sites for ongoing ceremonies, and provide for hunting, plant gathering for herbs and medicines, and firewood collecting.

The Bears Ears Inter-Tribal Coalition explains, "The Bears Ears region is not a series of isolated objects, but the object itself, a connected, living landscape, where the place, not a collection of items, must be protected. You cannot reduce the size without harming the whole."[7] The struggle over Bears Ears is a contest over the soul of a landscape. Bears Ears is contested geography with different names in different languages for the same sites. It is being fought over by the descendants of Mormon families, who arrived via wagon in 1880 after the largest and longest eastbound wagon trek in American history, traveling through some of the most complicated canyons on the continent. The Hole-in-the-Rock expedition is a fundamental element of history and heritage for local followers of the Church of Jesus Christ of Latter-day Saints (LDS). Saints came to southeast Utah to build a community at Bluff as a buffer against non-Mormon, or gentile, encroachment from Colorado. They were called to do so in the last Mormon mission of the nineteenth century that resulted in Bluff, a new farming and ranching settlement. Part of their goal included working as Christian missionaries to the local Navajo, Ute, and Paiute tribes, who lived on both sides of the San Juan River and in the Bears Ears area.[8]

Several generations later local LDS members revere their families' rich heritage and religious devotion. Families proudly claim their connection to their ancestors who were "hole-in-the-rockers." Another group of local families are descended from Mormons who moved to Mexico to avoid the federal crackdown on polygamy in the

1890s. When the Mexican Revolution shattered their sense of peace and opportunity, they returned, almost penniless, to small towns like Blanding and Monticello that would take them in.

Yet if the attachment of Mormon families to this diverse canyon, mountain, and desert landscape stretches over several generations, Indigenous peoples' attachment goes back centuries and even millennia. They also love and respect the land but for very different reasons. If the Mormons arrived in 1880, Native peoples began building pit houses circa AD 650.[9]

Many groups use the area for hiking, camping, and hunting, but not all are conservationists or environmentalists. Cedar Mesa and the Bears Ears area is large enough to accommodate extended LDS families with trailers and ATVs camping out for long weekends, as well as backpackers dropping into the Grand Gulch Primitive Area after securing permits at the Kane Gulch Ranger Station. A mixed group utilizes this plateau landscape for recreation. From the very beginning of white settlement and the establishment of Bluff City as an outpost, San Juan County offered unique opportunities for adventure.

Hikers value the isolation and dark skies. The Obama monument boundaries include seven wilderness study areas, a variety of ecological habitats, and dozens of remote sandstone canyons. Archaeologists claim that the Bears Ears area, as an ancient homeland for the Basketmaker and Ancestral Puebloan peoples, has cultural resources found nowhere else. These include cliff dwellings tucked away on narrow stone ledges with dramatic drops to canyon floors. "An important aspect of cultural preservation, from the Hopi perspective, requires that one be able to journey back to those places and see first-hand how their ancestors lived," explains Hopi archaeologist Lyle Balenquah. "These experiences are afforded us because many of the landscapes of the Bears Ears remain in relatively pristine condition.... Protection of this landscape allows us to share with the outside world that we are more than historical footnotes, to show that our connections to ancestral lands traverse distance and time."[10]

Paleontologists assert that sites within Bears Ears are crucial to understanding deep time. Fossils found in the Valley of the Gods and at Indian Creek can help scientists explain how dinosaurs crowded out earlier life forms of crocodile-sized amphibians. "Paleontological resources in the Bears Ears area are among the richest and most significant in the United States," explained the Obama proclamation. Various sites are "teeming with fossils" from "ray-finned fish fossils" to dinosaurs with the possibility of yielding "insights into the transition of vertebrate life from reptiles to mammals."[11] Just as Southwest Indian tribes have entered litigation to protect Bears Ears, so have scientific researchers. "Scientists sue to protect Utah monument—and fossils that could rewrite Earth's history," proclaims a *Science Magazine* headline. A newly written report details over a century of paleontology within the Bears Ears boundaries.[12]

Federal lawsuits are now going forward against the Trump administration and the Bears Ears monument's reduced boundaries. What happens in San Juan County, Utah, may set new standards for local and state involvement in applying the Antiquities Act in western states that have large federal land holdings.

Using Utah's Public Lands

Public land use in San Juan County, and who gets to speak for its citizens and visitors, remains highly controversial. Some local citizens—both whites and Natives—deplore "outsider" environmentalists, while embracing "outsider" energy and mining companies. There is no question that mining and oil and gas revenue once filled county coffers from the 1950s through the 1970s, but like ranching, commodity values have tapered off. San Juan County is the largest in Utah and the poorest.[13] Economic development is vital, but how to achieve it remains elusive and debatable. Conflicts continue, and the media glare intensifies.[14] Visible almost anywhere across the landscape are the two distinctive rock outcroppings called Bears Ears as a 9,058-feet-tall landmark.

Environmental groups have long sought additional landscape protections in southeast Utah, because the state has one of the fewest number of wilderness acres in the American West. In 1989 the Southern Utah Wilderness Alliance launched an ambitious congressional campaign to pass a vast Redrock Wilderness Act with limited success. Great Old Broads for Wilderness, based in Durango, Colorado, has also been involved in Utah land issues. Friends of Cedar Mesa, based in Bluff, Utah, helped champion a Cedar Mesa National Conservation Area on Bureau of Land Management (BLM) lands, but it never got much momentum. Instead, a Native group emerged with broad Navajo support known as Diné Bikéyah, which translates as "Navajo homeland."

Historical disputes between Navajos and local white families resulted in the sprawling Navajo reservation, the biggest in the nation, to be largely south of the San Juan River, with the exception of lands near Montezuma Creek and Aneth. Navajos, however, had used the lands of Cedar Mesa and Bears Ears north of the San Juan River for centuries, and Navajos, Utes, and Paiute descendants represent more than half the county's population. Diné Bikéyah sought to revitalize interest in ancestral homelands north of the reservation's boundaries and to have some say in their management. By 2016 the patience and persistence of environmental and Native American groups paid off.

Sally Jewell, secretary of the interior, came to southern Utah to see the Bears Ears cultural landscape in summer 2016. She visited Moon House, a Pueblo II and Pueblo III ruins complex, and was awed by the site's remoteness and its preservation. In Bluff, Utah, the public comment meeting on a hot July day was standing-room-only, and speakers were allowed just three minutes to talk after they were chosen by a lottery system.[15]

More than a century earlier, Congress had passed, and Pres. Theodore Roosevelt had signed, the Antiquities Act of 1906. This unique legislation had two important functions. First, this was the first cultural resources law in the world to protect unmarked Indigenous burials. Henceforth, archaeologists would be required to have permits for any excavations, and looters and pothunters could be fined for illegal digging. Second, the law stipulated that as an executive privilege the president of the United States could "declare by public proclamation historic landmarks, historic and prehistoric structures, and other objects of historic or scientific interest that are situated on land owned or controlled by the Federal Government to be national monuments."[16] Furthermore, the president could "reserve parcels of land as part of the national monuments," but that the "limits of the parcels shall be confined to the smallest area compatible with the proper care and management of the objects to be protected."[17] Unlike national parks, national monuments could be declared without an act of Congress.

Pres. Theodore Roosevelt used the law to set aside eighteen national monuments including one in San Juan County. His cousin Franklin Delano Roosevelt (FDR) and Harold Ickes, FDR's secretary of the interior, considered a massive Escalante National Monument in Utah that would have taken in two hundred miles on both sides of the Colorado River and public land that later became Canyonlands National Park.[18] In the 1930s Utah legislators and politicians fought back against the size of the Escalante National Monument proposal. Conservationists let it drop, but on the Colorado Plateau the idea never completely disappeared.

In 1996 Pres. Bill Clinton used the Antiquities Act to declare a 1.8-million-acre Grand Staircase–Escalante National Monument out of BLM lands, much to the chagrin of locals, but there was minimal Native American involvement. That would change twenty years later with the Obama administration and a proposal presented by the Inter-Tribal Coalition. A large piece of the original 1930s Escalante monument idea from the FDR administration had been revived.

Like his Democratic predecessors, Pres. Barack Obama used the Antiquities Act to set aside 1.35 million acres in San Juan County, Utah, an expanse larger than Grand Canyon National Park.[19] The environmental community was ecstatic; citizens in Blanding and Monticello were not. Sen. Orrin Hatch (R-UT) complained about "Antiquities Act abuse" because of the size of the monument. Utah politicians accused President Obama of a "midnight land grab," because his declaration occurred within days of the end of his presidency. In truth Obama had waited years for a legislative solution to protect the area, but the Public Lands Initiative of Rep. Rob Bishop (R-UT) was flawed and never emerged from a congressional committee.[20]

Pres. Donald Trump took the unprecedented step of dramatically reducing Bears Ears National Monument, an action that plaintiffs claim "was unlawful" because the Antiquities Act "grants only two powers: The power to 'declare' a monument, and the power to 'reserve' land. It neither expressly nor implicitly, gives the President the *opposite* powers—to *revoke* or *remove* land from a national monument."[21] Instead, Congress alone reserves the right to modify national monuments. When in 1976 Congress passed the Federal Land Policy and Management Act (FLPMA), Congress reviewed, revised, and deleted public land laws. It did not touch the Antiquities Act.[22]

President Trump shrunk President Obama's conservation legacy into two much smaller units of only 228,784 acres. Trump eliminated important archaeological sites on Cedar Mesa. He did not include Grand Gulch, first explored and pothunted in the 1890s. He deleted the historic route the Mormon Hole-in-the-Rock Expedition took down Road Canyon and through The Twist. He ignored careful negotiation with diverse tribes seeking a common preservation goal.

This vast area of public lands has become a twenty-first-century target for conservation and environmental goals and alternatively for local Utah communities saying "no" to federal proclamations. For decades some local citizens have denied federal oversight of the Bears Ears area. Much of the history of nineteenth-century Southwestern archaeology begins within the Bears Ears boundaries and expeditions by McLoyd and Graham, occasional Durango, Colorado, prospectors. The five Wetherill brothers from Mancos, Colorado, also pulled thousands of artifacts out of southeast Utah canyons and sold them to collectors and museums. Pothunting, or digging of Native American human remains and artifacts, became illegal as one of the fundamental provisions of the 1906 Antiquities Act. Ranchers and others looted archaeological sites in the 1890s just as archaeologists were beginning to understand early Native American prehistory and as American archaeology was becoming a scientific discipline. Previously, academic archaeologists had turned only to Europe and the Middle East, not to the deserts and canyons of the American Southwest.

Pothunting flourished from the 1890s into the present in San Juan County, Utah. In winter, when water sources could be guaranteed, relic hunters dug up mummies, skeletons, baskets, pots, spearpoints, arrowheads, and ceramic mugs. Early looters made no distinction between mining for gold and silver on public lands and digging for ancient relics to be described, cataloged, and sold to the highest bidder.[23] The Wetherills explored and looted Cottonwood Wash, Butler Wash, and side canyons in Grand Gulch, which is a part of Cedar Mesa excluded under President Trump's monument boundaries. Richard Wetherill even homesteaded at Chaco Canyon in what is now Chaco Canyon National Historical Park, a World Heritage Site, where he built a trading post near the ancient walls of Pueblo Bonito. Trying to force Wetherill out became a major goal of H. E. Hewett, who campaigned for the Antiquities Act in Washington DC.[24]

Artifacts sold to individuals have long since disappeared, but thankfully major collections from San Juan County remain at the American Museum of Natural History in New York City, the Field Museum in Chicago, the History Colorado Center in Denver, the Natural History Museum of Utah, and the Edge of the Cedars State Park Museum in Blanding, Utah.[25] Despite intensive nineteenth- and twentieth-century looting, even today the area around Bears Ears is one of the last intact prehistoric cultural landscapes in the United States. It is an enormous area of public land contested by different groups.

The Politics of Place Names

The struggle over Bears Ears is also a fight over names upon the land and over whose stories demonstrate understanding of the landscape. Along Comb Ridge, a north-south sandstone outcropping preserved both by Obama and Trump, Mormon settlers christened a distinct outcropping "Highland Lady" to commemorate their Scottish and northern European roots.[26] For the Diné or Navajo, the same dramatic rocks are labeled "Big Sheep's Balls" as part of an historic hunting story of pursuing a large bighorn sheep ram to the top of the red rock cliffs. For cultural geographers, place is "a layered, shifting reality that is constituted, lived, and contested, in part, through narrative." Patricia L. Price explains, "If one digs into the history of any place, one is bound to uncover layer upon sedimented layer of historic claims to places by people who had come from other places."[27]

She adds, "One has only to witness the contemporary liberation struggles of ... Native Americans ... to appreciate the grim reality of the bloodshed and the hearts broken over such stories. These struggles are driven ultimately, by stories, often in direct conflict with the equally mythic, divine, or timeless claims of other groups."[28]

The importance of naming and cultural values is found in the name Bears Ears itself.[29] In *Comb Ridge and Its People: The Ethnohistory of a Rock*, Robert McPherson describes Navajo tradition and "the lengthy narrative of Changing Bear Maiden" as "a young virtuous woman who lives with her brothers. She denies many suitors but through Coyote's wily trickery, marries him and begins to change. She learns how to transform through witchcraft into an evil powerful bear that then tracks down and kills all of her brothers, except for the youngest one."[30] Feminist writer Amy Irvine explains Coyote's lust and sexual appetites. Coyote will connive a way to sleep with a girl, "and once he has her on all fours, howling and panting with abandon, no man will ever again satisfy her. When he realizes he cannot contain her newfound wildness, he kills and dismembers her. Her body parts are scattered across Cedar Mesa—two prominent landmarks called the Bears Ears are part of her remains."[31]

This Southwestern story hints of incest and rage as the virtuous maiden kills her brothers. It echoes the bear story from Devils Tower, the first national monument in Wyoming, in which a brother becomes a bear and pursues his sisters with sexual intent. The frightened girls climb a stump that rises into the air and transforms into a large rock outcropping clawed by the angry brother bear. The Creator saves the sisters by sending them skyward toward the heavens to become the constellation known as the Pleiades.[32] Just as with Devils Tower (named Bear Lodge by several Great Plains tribes), so Native stories about Bears Ears, and the dismemberment of the maiden who had become an angry bear, are powerful moral tales. Stories stick to sandstone and encompass vast landscapes. For Native peoples including Navajos, Zunis, Hopis, Ute Mountain Utes, and Utes, Bears Ears is a sacred landscape of stories, homes, storage areas, and artifacts from countless Indian generations. There are cliff dwellings, refuge sites, sweat lodges, world-class rock art of petroglyphs and pictograms, and potsherds scattered over roadless areas. It is a landscape of dry washes, steep canyons, sandstone cliffs, hidden springs, and pothole water tanks, or *tinajas*.

Land Stewardship vs. Oil and Gas Development

If the Native perspective is to leave land alone as the ancestors found it, and to preserve this ancient landscape for quiet, respectful visitation and traditional uses, many descendants of white Mormon settlers want development. They want oil and gas wells, mining, and public lands grazing. They want more roads and better wages that come with industrialization and a local future for their children and grandchildren. "To Mormons, wilderness has been not Eden but a fallen landscape to be redeemed: although they live in the midst of dramatic Western scenery, Mormon advocates for wild nature have been few," writes Mark Stoll in *American Wilderness: A New History*.[33]

New scholarship is challenging Stoll's notion both for historic LDS communities and for contemporary Mormons following their ancestors' precepts to make the desert "bloom like a rose." Land stewardship has been an important Mormon tenet. "The Saints carried a sacred obligation to build God's kingdom on earth as they exercised their stewardship over property in an environmentally responsible way," explains Thomas G. Alexander.[34] But the Mormon village concept of small irrigated farms on minimal acreage did not work in southeast Utah's rugged canyon country. Bluff, Utah, farmers transitioned to ranching, and later the county's economy focused on energy extraction.

The non-native vision of land use continues to be for extractive uses—holes in the ground for oil and gas wells, gouges in rock cliffs for potential uranium mines, and slender grasses clipped and eaten by cows in already overgrazed public pastures. But nothing is simple. Some Natives want development, some Anglos want preservation. There is both a conflicted vision of the past and a stark difference in perspectives on the future. Without doubt, the glory economic days of San Juan County, Utah, were the economic booms of both the discovery and production of the Aneth Oil Field and the post–World War II uranium frenzy. Both booms brought millions of dollars in tax revenue into the county, including steady, well-paying jobs, and modern streets, libraries, sewers, and municipal facilities—at least in Monticello and Blanding.[35]

Some residents feel the only economic future for the county is in oil and gas and mining. Though uranium mining and milling brought financial stability for many families, it also resulted in tragic deaths from radioactivity and related cancers and organ failures.[36] For other locals the Old West of extractive industries has become the New West of heritage tourism, eager hikers and vacationers, and a stable, sustainable economy based on a scenic landscape infused with the palpable remnants of a prehistoric past. "There is a complete blindness in small-town Utah about us out-of-state millennials. We're living in our vans. We're here for the recreation, the outdoors, and we can revitalize local communities if we're given a chance," explains a guide and outfitter. "State government does not understand. Small towns in the West can profit from their local outdoor recreation. We can make a new economy while maintaining local community character."[37]

The battle is over the twenty-first-century West and whether "the lords of yesteryear," to use law professor Charles Wilkinson's phrase, will prevail in a landscape that epitomizes congressional goals in the 1906 preservation of American Antiquities Act. The law states that presidents have the executive authority to set aside lands from the public domain for national monuments in the smallest acreage possible.[38]

Comb Ridge, Butler Wash, Comb Wash, Indian Creek, Beef Basin, Cedar Mesa, Tank Mesa, and all the canyons that drain Grand Gulch form vast, intact cultural landscapes. Their very value is their size. "Bears Ears, first and foremost, is indigenous land. It is a place essential to the physical, spiritual, and cultural identity of the Hopi, Zuni, Ute, and Navajo nations. Before the advent of European settlers in the West, these people were here," wrote Angelo Baca in the *New York Times*. "We listened to the direction that tribal leaders and elders provided. After weighing many options, they decided to pursue the national monument designation, which prohibits resource exploitation of these sacred lands while explicitly allowing us to continue our many traditional uses of this living cultural landscape that needs us as much as we need it."³⁹

This is the first national monument with active political support from many Native Americans, who want protection for their cultural heritage and traditional landscapes as defined by the law. President Trump reduced the size of Bears Ears upon the recommendations of Ryan Zinke, his former secretary of the interior. Trump's administration split the monument into two sections and gave each section new names. A part of Bears Ears is now called Shash Jaa, or Bears Ears in Navajo, but local Navajos were never consulted. The Native coalition had agreed on the name Bears Ears in English, and to change it to a Navajo word "tramples the Native American true history of the place," explains Gavin Noyes of Utah Diné Bikéyah, which had championed the original monument and its larger boundaries.⁴⁰

The Past and Future of the Antiquities Act

Never before has a president so drastically shrunk a national monument or so clearly ignored the conservation actions of a previous president. Nowhere in the Antiquities Act does it state that a president can undo the actions of a former administration. The implications of this action for the twenty-first-century American West are profound, but indeed monuments have been reduced in size in the past, and there are current restrictions on new monuments in Alaska and Wyoming.

In Wyoming in the 1930s ranchers expressed outrage that the Rockefeller family had secretly been purchasing property in the Jackson Hole valley to give to the federal government to create a new Grand Teton National Park. Pres. Franklin Roosevelt used his executive authority under the Antiquities Act to designate Jackson Hole National Monument from U.S. Forest Service lands to be joined with 33,562 acres of the valley floor owned by the Rockefellers.⁴¹ Outraged, Wyoming politicians sued in federal court. The judge ruled for the National Park Service, but as Senate Bill 3409 allowed the monument to be abolished and the park to be created in 1950, the legislation stipulated "no further extension or establishment of national parks or monuments in Wyoming may be undertaken except by express authorization of the Congress."⁴²

"Even though in 1943 Wyoming Governor Leslie Miller announced that the future of the state was in recreation instead of commercial resource extraction, the culture of the time and place argued strongly for the protection of the right to use land for grazing and even mining," notes historian Hal Rothman. "The battle between the Old and New Wests, between service and leisure on one side and commercial extraction on the other, has its roots in the showdown at Jackson Hole."[43]

Anger and judicial compromise also occurred in Alaska in the 1970s when Pres. Jimmy Carter declared seven new national monuments. Later, Congress voted those monuments into becoming national parks as part of the 1980 Alaska National Interest Lands Conservation Act (ANILCA), but similar to Wyoming, there can no longer be additional Alaskan national monuments set aside exclusively by the chief executive. Law professor Mark Squillace explains that ANILCA "specifically prohibits the president from making new withdrawals in Alaska in excess of 5,000 acres unless he provides notice in the *Federal Register* and unless Congress passes a joint resolution approving the withdrawal within one year after receiving notice."[44]

Many citizens in San Juan County and their elected politicians have felt that the county already has enough national monuments and federally designated areas because the county borders Glen Canyon National Recreation Area and Lake Powell. It contains Natural Bridges National Monument (1908), Rainbow Bridge National Monument (1910), and half of Hovenweep National Monument (1923) along with the Manti-La Sal National Forest and more than a million acres of BLM lands. White Mormon locals say that is enough. There is no need for a Bears Ears National Monument. They proclaimed it in signs in their front yards and in bumper stickers on their trucks. Large billboards stated, "No National Monument" after Obama's designation, yet tourism is vital to the county's economy. Still, San Juan County commissioners spent $500,000 in legal fees trying to oppose Bears Ears.[45] It worked. President Trump shrunk the monument.

Bears Ears Conflicts

Lawsuits have been filed. The environmental community is upset, yet many San Juan County citizens express satisfaction with their success. They are willing to gamble on the ups and downs of an energy and mining economy and county coffers utterly vulnerable to international markets rather than carefully build a more substantial tourist and recreation-based economy. For professional archaeologists, the Trump administration's decisions are a recipe for disaster. "This is the worst possible scenario," a federal archaeologist explains. "More people. No money. No management."[46] The opportunity exists to create and save a truly stunning landscape, yet city, county, and Utah state officials opposed Bears Ears National Monument. Navajos refer to places like Bears Ears as "Nahodishgish," or places to be left alone.[47]

In Utah popular national parks began as national monuments including Arches and Zion. Although local politicians called the Obama designation a "land grab," every single acre set aside by President Obama was already federal public land, although the monument boundaries also enclosed Utah state lands. The critical distinction is that by proclaiming a national monument, Obama used his executive authority to withdraw mineral leasing and oil exploration from within the monument.

Only 8 percent of San Juan County, which is almost the size of Massachusetts, is private property. It has two stoplights, but one just blinks. San Juan is "the largest county in Utah, a great triangular wedge of abysmally eroded and weathered sandstone bounded on the east by the Colorado line, on the south by the Arizona line, and all along its hypotenuse by the Colorado River," wrote Wallace Stegner in *Mormon Country*.[48] He added that its southern end is the Navajo reservation.

Navajos, who call the area Diné Bikéyah, or traditional tribal lands, played a major role in the creation of the Bears Ears National Monument. Though the seventeen-million-acre Navajo Nation lies primarily south of the San Juan River, its historic cultural area reached as far north as Monticello, Utah, and as far west as the confluence of the San Juan and Colorado Rivers. Tree ring dates, or dendrochronology, done in the 1950s as part of the Indian Claims Commission found Navajo hogans and sweat lodges far north of the San Juan River that date from the early 1600s.[49] In 1862 when Col. Kit Carson ordered Navajos to be rounded up and forced to walk east to

Fort Sumner and Bosque Redondo in New Mexico, Navajo headman Hashkeninii, or "one who passes out anger," fled west with his small band to avoid the Long Walk. The band learned to eke out a living in a sandstone maze. Navajo leader K'aayelli was born near Bears Ears as was Hastiin Chi'ihaajin, or Manuelito.

Protecting Native historic sites in Bears Ears National Monument will be as important as preserving prehistoric sites. Goals will be to safeguard thousand-year-old Ancestral Puebloan sites from vandalism, maintain access to Native cultural sites for ongoing ceremonies, and provide for hunting, plant gathering for herbs and medicines, and firewood collecting. The landscape is also contested terrain because it involves competing origin stories. For some Navajo and Ute bands, this place is their homeland. For Puebloan peoples, this is where their ancestors lived thousands of years ago. For LDS members, this is where they were called to a San Juan Mission in 1879. Their relatives endured privations along the Hole-in-the-Rock Trail to establish the village of Bluff in 1880 before moving north to create the towns of Blanding and Monticello.

Ten centuries ago the Bluff valley may have had two to three thousand Native people farming and living in small clusters. By 1900, twenty years after Mormons settled Bluff, there were two hundred residents. In 2018 there were still only 265 residents. Not much has changed, but it is about to. Too many visitors may overwhelm remote and underfunded public lands. Favorite canyons and ruins will see additional tourists. There will be more tire tracks, more crushed cacti and flattened delicate desert cryptobiotic soil.

"From earth to sky, the region is unsurpassed in wonders. The star-filled nights and natural quiet of the Bears Ears area transport visitors to an earlier eon. Against an absolutely black night sky, our galaxy and others more distant leap into view. As one of the most intact and vast roadless areas in the contiguous United States, Bears Ears has that rare and arresting quality of deafening silence," reads the Obama monument proclamation.[50] Yet local citizens want energy development with its concomitant roads, dust, and drilling rig lights. They want good paying gas well jobs, but most wells are drilled by transitory Oklahoma and Texas contractors. Energy development is not sustainable. Over time gas production diminishes. Wells falter and eventually fail. Pumpjacks squeak and groan and finally seize up. Corporations also abandon projects that they once embraced.[51] Just east of San Juan County, Montezuma County in Colorado is moving away from oil and gas. "The county is transitioning from an oil-and-gas-based economy to a sustainable and environmentally friendly tourism- and recreation-based economy," noted county commissioner Keenan Ertel.[52]

Utah favorite son Wallace Stegner wrote that mining communities often went out "like blown matches." That has happened with oil and gas but not with tourism. Recently there has been an hour-and-a-half queue to get into Arches National Park in adjacent Grand County. Park administrators may have to implement a reservation system. While other small, rural communities are dying, Moab, Utah, receives two million annual visitors, and each year new motels rise up along the highway. Yet Moab's crowded downtown streets are not a goal of San Juan County citizens; everyone agrees on that. They do not want what part-time Moab resident and environmental writer Edward Abbey scornfully termed "industrial tourism." They want quiet, not Jeep Jamborees.

The Future of a Cultural Landscape

Bluff, Utah, writer Ellen Meloy described the need for "a deep map of place." At Bears Ears, to the north of Bluff, the night sky and the ground beneath it can become an enduring resource for respectful, well-managed, heritage tourism. Terry Tempest Williams also expresses the power of the red rock desert. She writes in *Red: Passion and Patience in the Desert*, "For as far as I can see, the canyon country of southern Utah extends in all directions. No compass can orient me here, only a pledge to love and walk the terrifying distances before me. What I fear and desire most in this world is passion. I fear it because it promises to be spontaneous, out of my control, unnamed, beyond my reasonable self. I desire it because passion has color, like the landscape before me. It is not pale. It is not neutral. It reveals the backside of the heart."[53] Some of her passion was part of the national groundswell of conservation support for Bears

Ears. Williams explains, "As the world becomes more crowded and corroded by consumption and capitalism, this landscape of minimalism will take on greater significance, reminding us that through its blood red grandeur just how essential wild country is to our psychology, how precious the desert is to the soul of America."[54]

For writer Edward Abbey, the magic of the canyons resulted in slickrock seduction. He admitted to a love affair with rocks. Once, he left Bluff, Utah, headed west into "the Big Country" of Valley of the Gods and Monument Valley before it became a tribal park. He drove his aging vehicle to the top of the cut in Comb Ridge, in what is now Bears Ears National Monument, and he stared at the desert stretched out before him. "We went by dusty washboard road to Bluff on the San Juan and thought we were getting pretty near the end of the known world. Following a narrow wagon road through more or less ordinary desert we climbed a notch in Comb Ridge and looked down and out from there into something else," Abbey wrote. "Out *over* something else. A landscape that I had not only never seen before but that did not *resemble* anything I had seen before."[55] He was on the southern edge of Bears Ears.

Abbey explained he could not see "any sign of any kind of life, except a few acid-green cottonwoods in the canyon below. In the silence and the heat and the glare we gazed upon a seared wasteland, a sinister and savage desolation. And found it utterly fascinating."[56] Abbey turned around. He did not trust his car to continue westward. He worried about food, water, spare parts, radiator rupturing, tires splitting, bogging down in sand. But he would return "toward whatever lay back of that beyond."[57] On another trip he described, "Bear's Ears, Elk Ridge and more fine blank areas on the maps."[58]

What Cactus Ed luxuriated in during the 1970s—the vast desert wasteland, the inviting sandstone curves and cliffs, the lack of water, which meant few, if any, people—was exactly what terrified the early Mormon settlers in the 1880s. They just wanted to farm. These sons and daughters of European immigrants sought deep topsoil, shade, vegetable gardens, a pastoral landscape. Instead they got rock and sand and convoluted canyons so complex it would take decades to map and understand them. For millennia Native Americans had thrived in canyon country landscapes, which Wallace Stegner described "in hidden corners and pockets under its cliffs the sudden poetry of springs," where sandstone seeps produce hanging gardens of sweet-smelling flowers and luxuriant grasses protected by shade.[59] But acres of sustainable farmland? Not in southeast Utah.

"A country of drifting sand and bald rocks, a country of dry desolation gashed deeply with crooked gulches. Its surface had been carved by the winds into knobs and pinnacles and figures of fantastic patterns," wrote Mormon pioneer cowboy Albert Lyman. "The hellish howl of coyotes echoed back and forth in the darkness of its nights, and long green lizards raced over its hot hills in the day."[60] Sent on a mission to create a farming community at Montezuma Creek and to begin the political creation of what would become San Juan County, Utah, the hardy Mormon pioneers became exhausted and never made it. Their planned six-week trip had taken six months across some of the most complicated canyons on the continent. They stopped short and established the village of Bluff, which by 1890 optimistically called itself Bluff City.

Part of the Bears Ears story is their story and the story of their descendants still tenaciously working the land and living primarily in the communities of Mexican Hat, Blanding, and Monticello. The Native towns or villages are Monument Valley, Montezuma Creek, and Aneth for Navajo tribal members, and White Mesa for Paiute and Ute Indian families. Bears Ears, its past, present, and future, cannot be understood without also knowing something about the adjacent communities and the folks there struggling to make a living in one of the poorest parts of Utah. Local looting of ancient Native sites spurred tribes to seek federal protection of the landscape via national monument status. But a bitter archaeological undercover sting operation in San Juan County in 2009 galvanized residents against the federal government.

The *Washington Post* argued, "Trump's drastic policy shift—the largest federal land reduction in U.S. history—is in part about the tension stemming from the 2009 investigation" in which a Blanding physician committed suicide as did another defendant and a federal informer. The BLM and the Federal Bureau of Investigation both investigated the crimes. Operation Cerberus inflamed local opposition to federal public land oversight. No one served prison time. Three men committed suicide.[61]

A Devil's Bargain with Tourism

The same sandstone landscape that encouraged the beginnings of Southwestern pothunting and later professional archaeology, the landscape that befuddled farming Mormons and beguiled Ed Abbey as an adventure tourist, will continue to draw more visitors. But tourists have limited opportunities to find information about Bears Ears; there is no visitor center staffed by a federal agency.[62]

Instead, tourism is picking up in southern San Juan County along the San Juan River where it borders the Navajo reservation. A dozen new tourist cabins have been built in Bluff, Utah, along with a fifty-four-unit destination resort complete with conference rooms. The word is out. Tourists are coming to Bears Ears to embrace a new concept: visiting remote sites for archaeological adventure tourism. Unfortunately, so may pothunters, looters, and vandals. Without additional law enforcement rangers, archaeological sites will be picked over, potsherds and arrowheads stolen, and intact, thousand-year-old ruins damaged.

What are other conflicts with a tourist-based economy? Critics state, "Tourism is another form of exploitation ... in which avaricious mainstream society consumes the virtues of distinctive cultures in its midst."[63] Historian Hal Rothman argues, "In areas too weak to replace faltering economic activities, tourism has often come to play an important role in the regional economy.... People often find that the changes tourism brings outweigh the material advantages that accrue from its presence." Because, in Rothman's words, "Tourism is a devil's bargain, a choice between change and the remaking of sociocultural lines or stasis and ... on-going poverty.... In this sense, tourism is a trap, a sink to which places fall, an end-of-the-road option chosen above few others."[64] Tourism creates complex tensions not easy to resolve.

Some of the descendants of the original Hole-in-the-Rock Mormon settlers support an energy economy that does not yet have traction. They have forgotten their fling with uranium mining chronicled in Ellen Meloy's *The Last Cheater's Waltz*.[65] They have forgotten the hundreds of county residents who became sick or died from radiation exposure at the Monticello uranium mill, which cost American taxpayers $250 million to clean up the seventy-eight-acre site, now a wetland on the south side of Monticello.

The Trump administration cut Bears Ears National Monument and adjusted boundaries to favor uranium mining. The White Mesa mill, just a few miles from Blanding, is the only uranium mill with an active permit in the United States. The *Washington Post* reported that Energy Fuels Resources, a subsidiary of a Canadian firm, asked to shrink the monument in a May 25, 2017, letter to the Interior Department.[66] Historically, there were small uranium mines up Cottonwood Wash, which left potential hazardous waste in Cottonwood Creek adjacent to Ancestral Puebloan kivas, ruins, and rock art.[67] The *Washington Post* reported that a law firm was paid $30,000 to lobby for the monument's reduction in size to prepare for a new uranium boom linked to the aging 1978 White Mesa mill, with a capacity to process eight million pounds of uranium ore annually.[68] "A toxic history of failed uranium projects litter the Southwest, especially on tribal lands," stated Greg Zimmerman from the Center for Western Priorities. "That President Trump and Secretary Zinke have the audacity to sell out Bears Ears and its thousands of unique archaeological sites to a uranium extraction company is beyond the pale."[69]

The Obama monument designation states, "In recognition of the importance of tribal participation to the care and management of the objects identified above, and to ensure that management decisions affecting the monument reflect tribal expertise and traditional and historical knowledge, a Bears Ears Commission is hereby established to provide guidance and recommendations."[70] Such a commission had never happened before. It had not happened under the Trump administration. What has happened are lawsuits and pending legislation, which is why Bears Ears National Monument and the Bears Ears Inter-Tribal Coalition may help define the future of federal public lands in the twenty-first-century West. Legislation may die in committee or have a legislative life. Utah politicians propose gutting the Antiquities Act; other congresspeople and senators seek to strengthen it.

Judges have yet to rule on the pending federal lawsuits, but a major victory for plaintiffs has been to have their cases heard where they were filed in Washington DC rather than in federal court in Salt Lake City. The Navajo Nation is leading the legal charge to restore the boundaries of Bears Ears, though if its attorneys seek to use the argument of sacred sites as essential to Native American religious freedom, a previous law, the American Indian Religious Freedom Act (1978), did not fare well with the Supreme Court.[71]

Pres. Donald Trump's administration, to the applause of many rural Utahans, shrunk Bears Ears National Monument and left those lands vulnerable to oil, gas, and uranium exploration at a time when international markets for those resources have dramatically contracted, if not completely collapsed. "How much longer are we going to persist with the idea that the path to prosperity in some of the most beautiful places on earth is to drill oil wells and drag chains across the desert?" asked the editorial board of the *Salt Lake Tribune*, referring to both Bears Ears and Grand Staircase–Escalante National Monuments. "The reason they became national monuments is because they are unique. Shouldn't we trade on that rather than trying to use them to produce commodities that are already cheaper from elsewhere?"[72]

With the change in presidential administrations in 2021 and a return to valuing cultural resources and Indigenous perspectives, President Obama's boundaries for Bears Ears National Monument have been reinstated. Lawsuits may be dropped. Time will tell. Pres. Joe Biden's website proclaimed, "His administration will work with tribal governments and Congress to protect sacred sites and public lands and waters with high conservation and cultural values."[73] The Bears Ears shuffle began again. President Obama's boundaries were reinstated October 8, 2021, just in time for Indigenous Peoples' Day (the former Columbus Day). Biden's Proclamation 10285 states, "Few national monuments more clearly meet the Antiquities Act's criteria for protection than the Bears Ears buttes and surrounding areas." Biden referred often to President Obama's Proclamation 9558, reiterating "the compelling need to protect one of the most extraordinary cultural landscapes in the United States."

Utah's largely Mormon political delegation did not agree. By the end of October 2021 Utah's attorney general requested bids for a legal team and senior attorneys with "experience arguing appeals to the United States Supreme Court and United States Circuit Courts of Appeals." The State of Utah will sue the federal government over Biden's Bears Ears restoration to avenge a perceived "monumental insult."

Bears Ears will remain a poster child for presidential executive designation of the Antiquities Act and successful collaboration with Native peoples in the American West. Withdrawing special landscapes for scientific and historical purposes is at the heart of the Antiquities Act. Anthropologists, archaeologists, and historians continue to learn new truths about Bears Ears and the peoples who have lived in canyon country. As editor Rensink argues, "Our recent and most distant histories demand that we *do* pause, take careful stock of where we are, where we have come from, and where we wish to go."

Meanwhile, the land sits patiently waiting. An unequaled landscape of vivid night skies and sun-soaked canyons awaits the turn of hikers' boots on steep sandstone trails. "Landscape is a work of the mind. Its scenery is built up as much from strata of memory as from layers of rock," notes geographer Simon Schama. Surrounding Bears Ears, Glen Canyon Linear petroglyphs are five thousand years old. At Sand Island, a mammoth petroglyph may date from the Pleistocene at eleven thousand years.

Basketmaker images of males and females, anthropomorphs, and bighorn sheep reflect values, beliefs, and dreams from centuries ago. Opportunities exist for self-discovery, quiet campsites, and the thrill of finding ancient cliff dwellings in hidden alcoves. In one place, prehistory, history, Native voices, and future use of the Antiquities Act on public lands may all come together. But defining that future will take judges' rulings and court decisions. More than a century ago Pres. Theodore Roosevelt declared national monuments with ease, but the frontier West has filled up, and in the modern American West—even in remote, rural areas—everyone has a stake in public lands.

Notes

1. First quote: see Gregory, *The San Juan Country*. Second quote: Proclamation No. 9558, Fed. Reg. 82FR1139 (December 28, 2016).

2. Ruple "The Transfer of Public Lands Movement," 1; Gulliford, *The Woolly West*, 144–45; Gulliford, *The Woolly West*, chapter 6.

3. Native American resolutions supporting Bears Ears include: Resolution of the Naabik Iyati' Committee of the Navajo Nation Council, 23rd Navajo Nation Council, First Year 2015; Utah Diné Bikéyah; Resolution of the Navajo Utah Commission of the Navajo Nation Council, August 13, 2014; Resolution of the Navajo Mountain Chapter of the Navajo Nation, May 21, 2014; Teec Nos Pos Chapter Government, August 12, 2009; Red Mesa Chapter, August 9, 2010; Aneth Chapter, August 17, 2010; Oljato Chapter, November 9, 2014; Associated Students of Fort Lewis College, April 15, 2015; Hopi Tribe, September 30, 2014; Hualapai Tribal Council, February 9, 2015; Ysleta del Sur Pueblo, November 5, 2013; Ute Mountain Ute Tribe, August 12, 2015; Ute Indian Tribes, July 14, 2015; National Congress of American Indians, Resolution #EC-15–102, September 20, 2015.

4. I want to thank Soni Grant for her perceptive critiques as well as comments I incorporated from Marcus C. Macktima and P. Jane Hafen. A special thanks goes to editor Brenden Rensink.

5. Proclamation No. 9558.

6. Proclamation No. 9861, Fed. Reg. 82FR58081 (December 4, 2017).

7. "Bears Ears Inter-Tribal Coalition Condemns Zinke Recommendation to Eviscerate Bears Ears National Monument," press release, June 12, 2017, https://www.bearsearscoalition.org/bears-ears-inter-tribal-coalition-condemns-zinke-recommendation-to-eviscerate-bears-ears-national-monument/.

8. Miller, *Hole-in-the-Rock*, 137; Nelson, *Wrecks of Human Ambition*, 160–70.

9. Signs at the entrance to Bluff, Utah, "Founded 650 AD." See Cameron, *Chaco and After in the Northern San Juan*.

10. Balenquah, "Spirit of Place," 77–78.

11. Proclamation 9558.

12. Reese, "Scientists Sue to Protect Utah Monument," *Science Magazine*. Also see Uglesich et al., "Paleontology of Bears Ears."

13. See the later chapters in Powell, *San Juan County, Utah* and McPherson, *A History of San Juan County*.

14. Nordhaus, "Battle for the American West," *National Geographic*; Keeler, *Edge of Morning*, 111–62; Robinson, *Voices from Bears Ears*, 51–168; Strom, *Bears Ears: Views from a Sacred Land*, 13–20; KUED, "Battle Over Bears Ears," November 16, 2018.

15. Richard Robinson, email message to author, February 6, 2017.

16. *National Monuments* 54 U.S. Code 32031(a).

17. *National Monuments* 54 U.S. Code 32031(b).

18. See Kelly, "Proposed Escalante National Monument," *Desert Magazine* and Richardson, "Federal Park Policy in Utah."

19. Grand Canyon is 1.2 million acres because of various legislative expansions over the years. It began as an eight-hundred-thousand-acre national monument set aside by Pres. Theodore Roosevelt.

20. Jack Healy, "Remote Utah Enclave Becomes New Battleground Over Reach of U.S. Control," *New York Times*, March 13, 2016, https://www.nytimes.com/2016/03/13/us/remote-utah-enclave-new-battleground-over-reach-of-us-control.html; Editorial Board, "Antiquities Act Is a 'Land Grab' for All the Right Reasons," *Denver Post*, December 29, 2016, https://www.denverpost.com/2016/12/29/antiquities-act-is-a-land-grab-for-all-the-right-reasons/; Juliet Eilperin, "Trump Is Eager to Undo Sacred Tribal Monument, Says Orrin Hatch," *Washington Post*, January 27, 2017, https://www.washingtonpost.com/news/energy-environment/wp/2017/01/27/hatch-trump-is-eager-to-work-with-gop-lawmakers-to-undo-sacred-tribal-monument/; Orrin Hatch, "Working with the President to Fix Monumental Mess," *San Juan Record*, April 26, 2017.

21. Hopi Tribe v. Donald J. Trump; Utah Diné Bikéyah v. Donald J. Trump; Natural Resources Defense Council v. Donald J. Trump.

22. Pamela Baldwin, "Presidential Authority to Modify or Revoke National Monuments" (September 17, 2017), https://ur.booksc.eu/book/74049763/1f8e97; see Ruple, "Can Trump Redevelop America's Monumental Legacy?"; see Rasband, "Stroke of the Pen, Law of the Land?"; see Yoo and Gaziano, "Presidential Authority to Revoke or Reduce National Monument Designations."

23. McLoyd and Graham Catalog, "This Collection Is for Sale, Address McLoyd & Graham, P. O. Box 312, Durango, Colo., Explorers of Prehistoric Ruins and Collectors of Relics, 1894."

24. McNitt, *Richard Wetherill*, 188–90; Fletcher, *The Wetherills of Mesa Verde*, 277–89; Snead, *Ruins and Rivals*, 54–56.

25. Blackburn and Williamson, *Cowboys and Cave Dwellers*, 69–92.

26. McPherson, *Comb Ridge and Its People*, 24–25.

27. Price, *Dry Place*, xiii and xvi.

28. Price, *Dry Place*, 34.

29. See Macfarlane, *The Wild Places*; Basso, *Wisdom Sits in Places*; Hirst, *I Am the Grand Canyon*; Morehouse, *A Place Called Grand Canyon*.

30. McPherson, *Comb Ridge and Its People*, 76.

31. Irvine, *Trespass*, 110.

32. Rothman, *America's National Monuments*, 55–59; Momaday, *The Way to Rainy Mountain*, 5–12.

33. Stoll, "Religion Irradiates the Wilderness," 43.

34. Alexander, "Lost Memory and Environmentalism," 54.

35. See Shumway, "The Development of the Uranium Industry" and Payner, "The Effect of the Uranium and Petroleum Industries."

36. Andrew Gulliford, "A Poisonous Past: At Monticello Mill, the Story of Uranium's Deadly Legacy," *Durango Herald*, December 10, 2017, https://nsr.durangoherald.com/articles/199145-a-poisonous-past-at-monticello-mill-the-story-of-uraniums-deadly-legacy; Malin and Petrzelka, "Left in the Dust," 1187–200.

37. Anonymous Canyon Country guide, in discussion with the author, April 2016.

38. See Gulliford, "Canyons of the Ancients National Monument."

39. Angelo Baca, "Bears Ears Is Here to Stay," *New York Times*, December 8, 2017, https://www.nytimes.com/interactive/2017/12/08/opinion/bears-ears-monument.html; see Gulliford, "Bears Ears—Our New Backyard"; see Gulliford, "The Struggle Over Bears Ears."

40. Brian Maffly, "By Renaming New Utah Monument *Shash Jaa*, Is Trump Trying to Divide Native American Tribes?," *Salt Lake Tribune*, December 11, 2017, https://www.sltrib.com/news/environment/2017/12/11/by-renaming-new-utah-monument-shash-jaa-is-trump-trying-to-divide-native-american-tribes/.

41. Rothman, *America's National Monuments*, 214–22; Righter, *Crucible for Conservation*, 110–13; Harmon, McManamon, and Pitcaithley, *The Antiquities Act*, 81–92.

42. Righter, *Crucible for Conservation*, 140; Roberts, *Cody's Cave*, 14–15.

43. Rothman, "Showdown at Jackson Hole," 91.

44. Squillace, "Presidents Lack the Authority to Abolish or Diminish National Monuments," 55–71, 121.

45. "County Challenges in 2019," *San Juan Record*, January 2, 2019, https://www.sjrnews.com/archive/201910?page=1; Zak Podmore, "San Juan County Paid Nearly $500K to Louisiana Law Firm to Lobby for Bears Ears Reductions," *Salt Lake Tribune*, July 28, 2019, https://www.sltrib.com/news/2019/07/28/san-juan-county-paid/. Also see Gulliford, Andrew. Petitioner v. San Juan County. Respondent, Before the State Records Committee of the State of Utah. Decision and Order. Case No. 19–32 and subsequent stories by Podmore in the *Salt Lake Tribune*.

46. Julie Singer, email message to author, December 4, 2017.

47. Terry Tempest Williams, "Nahodishgish: A Place to Be Left Alone," *Durango Herald*, January 3, 2017, https://www.durangoherald.com/articles/nahodishgish-a-place-to-be-left-alone/.

48. Stegner, *Mormon Country*, 331.

49. Stokes and Smiley, "Tree Ring Dates," 8–18.

50. Proclamation 9558.

51. Gulliford, *Boomtown Blues*, 151–94.

52. "Congress Hears from County on Land Issue," *San Juan Record*, July 24, 2019.

53. Williams, *Red*, 195.

54. Williams, *Red*, 6.

55. Abbey, *Beyond the Wall*, 54.

56. Abbey, *Beyond the Wall*, 55.

57. Abbey, *Beyond the Wall*, 55.

58. Leopold, *A Sand County Almanac*, 158.

59. Stegner, *The Sound of Mountain Water*, 153.

60. Topping, *Glen Canyon and the San Juan Country*, 151.

61. Julie Cart, "Looting Indian Graves Is Big Business in Utah: BLM Agents Fight Continuing Battle Against Robbers," *Los Angeles Times*, April 8, 2001, https://www.sfgate.com/news/article/Looting-Indian-Grave-Sites-Is-Big-Business-in-2933483.php; Kyle Swenson, "Pilfered Artifacts, Three Suicides and the Struggle over Federal Land in Utah," *Washington Post*, December 5, 2017, https://www.washingtonpost.com/news/morning-mix/wp/2017/12/05/pilfered-artifacts-three-suicides-and-the-struggle-over-federal-land-in-utah/; see "In the News: Project Cerberus"; Paul Foy, "Feds Seek to Dismiss Artifact-Raid Lawsuit," *Cortez Journal*, June 16, 2012; Joe Mozingo, "A Sting in the Desert," *Los Angeles Times*, September 21, 2014, https://graphics.latimes.com/utah-sting/; William Yardley, "Utah Town Unsettled by Doctor's Suicide and an Inquiry of Indian Artifact Looting," *New York Times*, June 20, 2009, https://www.nytimes.com/2009/06/21/us/21blanding.html; Sharp, "An Exclusive Look," *Smithsonian Magazine*.

62. Andrew Gulliford, "From the Silver Dollar Bar to the Bears Ears Education Center," *Durango Herald*, August 3, 2018, https://nsr.durangoherald.com/articles/223488; Nick Davidson, "Bears Ears' Only Visitor Center Isn't Run by the Feds," *High Country News*, May 13, 2019, https://www.hcn.org/issues/51.8/bears-ears-national-monument-bears-ears-only-visitor-center-isnt-run-by-the-feds.

63. Rothman, "Pokey's Paradox," 91.

64. Rothman, "Pokey's Paradox," 91; *Devil's Bargains*, 338–70; see Stiles, *Brave New West*.

65. See Meloy, *The Last Cheater's Waltz*.

66. Juliet Eilperin, "Uranium Firm Sought Access to Bears Ears, Documents Say," *Washington Post*, December 8, 2017, https://www.washingtonpost.com/national/health-science/uranium-firm-urged-trump-officials-to-shrink-bears-ears-national-monument/2017/12/08/2eea39b6-dc31-11e7-b1a8-62589434a581_story.html; Eric Lipton and Lisa Friedman, "Oil Was Central in Decision to Shrink Bears Ears Monument, Emails Show," *New York Times*, March 2, 2018, https://www.nytimes.com/2018/03/02/climate/bears-ears-national-monument.html.

67. Shumway, "Cottonwood Mining," 1–81. See the entire issue to understand the extent of uranium mining in upper Cottonwood Wash.

68. Eilperin, "Uranium Firm Sought Access," *Washington Post*, December 8, 2017; Hiroko Tabuchi, "Uranium Miners Pushed Hard for a Comeback. They Got Their Wish," *New York Times*, January 13, 2018, https://www.nytimes.com/2018/01/13/climate/trump-uranium-bears-ears.html.

69. Missy Votel, "Radioactive Dealings: Energy Fuels Hired Big Guns to Lobby for Downsizing Bears Ears," *Durango Telegraph*, December 14, 2017, https://www.durangotelegraph.com/news/top-stories/radioactive-dealings/.

70. Proclamation 9558.

71. See King, *Cultural Resource Laws and Practice* to understand cultural resource laws and Native American perceptions; Gulliford, *Sacred Objects and Sacred Places*, 119–22.

72. "Tribune Editorial: Yesterday's Solutions Drive National Monument Plans," *Salt Lake Tribune*, February 10, 2020, https://www.sltrib.com/opinion/editorial/2020/02/08/tribune-editorial/.

73. Brian Maffly, "With a Biden Win, Bears Ears and Grand Staircase Monuments May Soon Be Restored," *Salt Lake Tribune*, November 10, 2020, https://www.sltrib.com/news/environment/2020/11/10/with-biden-win-utah/.

Bibliography

Archival Sources

Gulliford, Andrew. "Canyons of the Ancients National Monument: Interpreting and Administering the Proclamation." Appended to the CANM Management Plan. May 2008.

H.R. 3990. National Monument Creation and Protection Act. Introduced October 6, 2017.

H.R. 4518. Bears Ears National Monument Expansion Act. Introduced December 1, 2017.

H.R. 4532. To Create the First Tribally Managed National Monument and for Other Purposes. Shash Jaa National Monument and Indian Creek National Monument Act. January 30, 2018.

McLoyd and Graham Catalog. Special Collections. Brigham Young University Library.
Native American resolutions supporting Bears Ears include:
S.2354. America's Natural Treasures of Immeasurable Quality Unite, Inspire, and Together Improve the Economies of States Act of 2018—The Antiquities Act of 2018.
S.3193. Protecting Utah's Rural Economy (PURE) Act. July 11, 2018.
U.S. Department of the Interior, Bureau of Land Management. *Bears Ears National Monument: Draft Monument Management Plans and Environmental Impact Statement Shash Jaa and Indian Creek Units*. Executive Summary. August 2018.
United States District Court for the District of Columbia. Consolidated Cases: Hopi Tribe v. Donald J. Trump; Utah Diné Bikéyah v. Donald J. Trump; Natural Resources Defense Council v. Donald J. Trump. UDB Plaintiffs' Memorandum of Points and Authorities in Opposition to Federal Defendants' Motion to Dismiss. Filed November 15, 2018.

Published Works

Abbey, Edward. *Beyond the Wall*. New York: Henry Holt, 1984.
Alexander, Thomas G. "Lost Memory and Environmentalism: Mormons on the Wasatch Front, 1847–1930." In *The Earth Will Appear as the Garden of Eden: Essays on Mormon Environmental History*, edited by Jedediah S. Rogers and Mathew C. Godfrey, 47–68. Salt Lake City: University of Utah Press, 2019.
Balenquah, Lyle. "Spirit of Place: Preserving the Cultural Landscape of the Bears Ears." In *Edge of Morning: Native Voices Speak for the Bears Ears*, edited by Jacqueline Keeler, 75–82. Salt Lake City UT: Torrey House, 2017.
Basso, Keith. *Wisdom Sits in Places*. Albuquerque: University of New Mexico Press, 1996.
"Battle Over Bears Ears." Public Television. Salt Lake City UT: KUED, November 16, 2018.
Blackburn, Fred M., and Ray A. Williamson. *Cowboys and Cave Dwellers: Basketmaker Archaeology in Utah's Grand Gulch*. Santa Fe NM: School of American Research Press, 1997.
Cameron, Catherine. *Chaco and After in the Northern San Juan: Excavations at the Bluff Great House*. Tucson: University of Arizona Press, 2009.
Fletcher, Maurine S., ed. *The Wetherills of Mesa Verde: Autobiography of Benjamin Alfred Wetherill*. Lincoln: University of Nebraska Press, 1977.
Gregory, Herbert E. *The San Juan Country: A Geographic and Geologic Reconnaissance of Southeastern Utah*. U.S. Geological Survey: U.S. Government Printing Office, 1938.
Gulliford, Andrew. "Bears Ears—Our New Backyard." *Utah Adventure Journal* (Mid-Winter 2017).
Gulliford, Andrew. *Boomtown Blues: Colorado Oil Shale*. Boulder: University Press of Colorado, 2003.
Gulliford, Andrew. "Deadly Daughters, a Poisonous Past, and the Monticello Mill." *Utah Adventure Journal* (Early Spring 2018): 14–15.
Gulliford, Andrew. *Sacred Objects and Sacred Places: Preserving Tribal Traditions*. Boulder: University Press of Colorado, 2000.
Gulliford, Andrew. "The Struggle Over Bears Ears: Old West, New West, Next West." *Utah Adventure Journal* (Mid-Winter 2018).
Gulliford, Andrew. *The Woolly West: Colorado's Hidden History of Sheepscapes*. College Station: Texas A&M University Press, 2018.

Harmon, David, Francis P. McManamon, and Dwight T. Pitcaithley. *The Antiquities Act: A Century of American Archaeology, Historic Preservation, and Nature Conservation*. Tucson: University of Arizona Press, 2006.

Hirst, Stephen. *I Am the Grand Canyon: The Story of the Havasupai People*. Grand Canyon: Grand Canyon Association, 2006.

"In the News: Project Cerberus." *American Archaeology* 13, no. 3 (Fall 2009).

Irvine, Amy. *Trespass: Living at the Edge of the Promised Land*. New York: North Point, 2008.

Keeler, Jacqueline, ed. *Edge of Morning: Native Voices Speak for the Bears Ears*. Salt Lake City UT: Torrey House, 2017.

Kelly, Charles. "Proposed Escalante National Monument." *Desert Magazine* (February 1941): 21–22.

King, Thomas F. *Cultural Resource Laws and Practice*. Walnut Creek CA: AltaMira, 1998.

Leopold, Aldo. *A Sand County Almanac*. New York: Ballantine, 1970.

Lewis, Michael, ed. *American Wilderness: A New History*. New York: Oxford University Press, 2004.

Macfarlane, Robert. *The Wild Places*. New York: Penguin, 2007.

Malin, Stephanie A., and Peggy Petrzelka. "Left in the Dust: Uranium's Legacy and Victims of Mill Tailings Exposures in Monticello, Utah." *Society and Natural Resources* 23, no. 12 (2010): 1187–200.

McNitt, Frank. *Richard Wetherill: Anasazi*. Albuquerque: University of New Mexico Press, 1957.

McPherson, Robert S. *Comb Ridge and Its People: The Ethnohistory of a Rock*. Logan: Utah State University Press, 2009.

McPherson, Robert S. *A History of San Juan County*. Salt Lake City: Utah State Historical Society, San Juan County Commission, 1995.

Meloy, Ellen. *The Last Cheater's Waltz: Beauty and Violence in the Desert Southwest*. Tucson: University of Arizona Press, 1999.

Miller, David E. *Hole-in-the-Rock*. Salt Lake City: University of Utah Press, 1966.

Momaday, N. Scott. *The Way to Rainy Mountain*. Albuquerque: University of New Mexico Press, 1969.

Morehouse, Barbara J. *A Place Called Grand Canyon: Contested Geographies*. Tucson: University of Arizona Press, 1996.

Nelson, Paul T. *Wrecks of Human Ambition: A History of Utah's Canyon Country to 1936*. Salt Lake City: University of Utah Press, 2014.

Nordhaus, Hannah. "Battle for the American West." *National Geographic* (November 2018): 42–67.

Payner, Robert L. "The Effect of the Uranium and Petroleum Industries Upon the Economy of San Juan County, Utah." MA thesis, Brigham Young University, 1964.

Powell, Allan Kent. *San Juan County, Utah*. Salt Lake City: Utah State Historical Society, 1983.

Price, Patricia. *Dry Place: Landscapes of Belonging and Exclusion*. Minneapolis: University of Minnesota Press, 2004.

Rasband, James R. "Stroke of the Pen, Law of the Land?" J. Reuben Clark Law School, Brigham Young University, 2017. https://papers.ssrn.com/sol3/papers.cfm?abstract_id=3083777.

Reese, April. "Scientists Sue to Protect Utah Monument—and Fossils that Could Rewrite Earth's History." *Science Magazine* (January 17, 2019).

Richardson, Elmo. "Federal Park Policy in Utah: The Escalante National Monument Controversy of 1935–1940." *Utah Historical Quarterly* 33 (Spring 1965): 109–33.

Righter, Robert W. *Crucible for Conservation: The Struggle for Grand Teton National Park.* Moose WY: Grand Teton Natural History Association, 1982.

Roberts, Phil. *Cody's Cave: National Monuments and the Politics of Public Lands in the 20th Century West.* Laramie WY: Skyline West, 2012.

Robinson, Rebecca. *Voices from Bears Ears: Seeking Common Ground on Sacred Land.* Tucson: University of Arizona Press, 2018.

Rogers, Jedediah S., and Matthew C. Godfrey, eds. *The Earth Will Appear as the Garden of Eden: Essays on Mormon Environmental History.* Salt Lake City: University of Utah Press, 2019.

Rothman, Hal. *America's National Monuments: The Politics of Preservation.* Lawrence: University Press of Kansas, 1989.

Rothman, Hal. *Devil's Bargains: Tourism in the Twentieth Century American West.* Lawrence: University Press of Kansas, 1998.

Rothman, Hal. "Pokey's Paradox: Tourism and Transformation on the Western Navajo Reservation." In *Reopening the American West*, edited by Hal Rothman, 90–121. Tucson: University of Arizona Press, 1998.

Rothman, Hal. "Showdown at Jackson Hole." In *The Antiquities Act: A Century of American Archaeology, Historic Preservation, and Nature Conservation*, edited by David Harmon, Francis P. McManamon, and Dwight T. Pitcaithley, 81–92. Tucson: University of Arizona Press, 2006.

Ruple, John C. "Can Trump Redevelop America's Monumental Legacy?" *Public Land and Resources Committee Newsletter* (December 2017).

Ruple, John C. "The Transfer of Public Lands Movement: The Battle to Take 'Back' Lands That Were Never Theirs." *Colorado Natural Resources, Energy and Environmental Law Review* 29, no. 1 (January 2018): 3–78.

Schama, Simon. *Landscape and Memory.* New York: Vintage, 1996.

Sharp, Kathleen. "An Exclusive Look at the Greatest Haul of Native American Artifacts, Ever." *Smithsonian Magazine* (November 2015): 40–49.

Shumway, Gary, ed. "Cottonwood Mining." *Blue Mountain Shadows* 25 (Winter 2001): 1–81.

Shumway, Gary Lee. "The Development of the Uranium Industry in San Juan County, Utah." MA thesis, Brigham Young University, 1964.

Snead, James E. *Ruins and Rivals: The Making of Southwest Archaeology.* Tucson: University of Arizona Press, 2001.

Squillace, Mark, Eric Biber, Nicholas S. Bryner, and Sean B. Hecht. "Presidents Lack the Authority to Abolish or Diminish National Monuments." *Virginia Law Review* 103, no. 55 (2017): 55–71.

Stegner, Wallace. *Marking the Sparrow's Fall.* New York: Henry Holt, 1988.

Stegner, Wallace. *Mormon Country.* Lincoln: University of Nebraska Press, 1981. First published 1942 by Duell, Sloan & Pearce (Salt Lake City UT).

Stegner, Wallace. *The Sound of Mountain Water.* New York: E. P. Dutton, 1980.

Stiles, Jim. *Brave New West: Morphing Moab at the Speed of Greed*. Tucson: University of Arizona Press, 2007.

Stokes, M. A., and T. L. Smiley. "Tree Ring Dates from the Navajo Land Claim I, the Northern Sector." *Tree-Ring Bulletin* 25 (1963): 8–18.

Stoll, Mark. "Religion Irradiates the Wilderness." In *American Wilderness: A New History*, edited by Michael Lewis, 43. New York: Oxford University Press, 2004.

Strom, Stephen E. *Bears Ears: Views from a Sacred Land*. Tucson: George F. Thompson and University of Arizona Press, 2018.

Topping, Gary. *Glen Canyon and the San Juan Country*. Moscow: University of Idaho Press, 1997.

Uglesich, Jessica, Robert J. Gay, M. Allison Stegner, Adam K. Huttenlocker, and Randall B. Irmis. "Paleontology of Bears Ears National Monument (Utah, USA): History of Exploration, Study, and Designation." *Geology of the Intermountain West* 7 (2020). https://giw.utahgeology.org/giw/index.php/GIW/article/view/82.

Williams, Terry Tempest. *Red: Passion and Patience in the Desert*. New York: Vintage, 2002.

Yoo, John, and Todd Gaziano. *Presidential Authority to Revoke or Reduce National Monument Designations*. Washington DC: American Enterprise Institute, March 2017. https://www.aei.org/wp-content/uploads/2017/03/Presidential-Authority-to-Revoke-or-Reduce-National-Monument-Designations.pdf.

Afterword

FRANK BERGON

After reading these essays I wonder if an alternative title for the book might be, *Crises and Disasters in the Twenty-First-Century American West*. Devastating wildfires, prolonged drought, poisoned soil, depleted aquifers, oil spills, toxic dumps, cancer clusters, abandoned mines, and despoiled wilderness join tornados, blizzards, floods, dust storms, and cyclone bombs, many the most severe on record, to mark a region on the edge of environmental collapse. Social disasters scar the contemporary West as well. We read about destructive gentrification and exploited workers, unaffordable housing and vanished farms, declining wages and obscene private profit, corporate sexism and community racism, the imprisonment of children and the separation of families, political malfeasance and impoverished towns, social-class warfare and gender discrimination, all broadcasting a litany of accelerating inequality across a blighted land.

Once upon a time, not so long ago, a pantheon of legendary western frontiersmen displayed to the world an image of a nation on the march. This triumphant myth was not without justice in the world's recognition of the United States as a flourishing democracy of unequaled richness and international strength. No more. As political commentators tell us daily, "The reputation is now gone." In recent decades and gaining traction during Donald Trump's presidency, a worldview emerged of the United States in decline. Today's fractured West often leads the way in displaying the plight of our polarized nation. Across a dry, pest-ridden, dead and dying land, former western heroes vanish into a blotted sunset, unseen behind a garish smoke-filled sky.

Historian and editor Brenden W. Rensink approaches the contemporary West as "a region in turmoil," yet his herculean efforts offer both insight and guidance to chart a positive future. In what he calls "modern West history," I admire the range of multidisciplinary contributors from geography, sociology, anthropology, ethnic studies, environmental studies, and several other fields and disciplines, along with history, to aptly identify what's evolving into "Modern West Studies."

Although several essays focus on topics also headlined in the daily news, I wonder about news not found in today's headlines. Revisionist western historians often upset common views like the revelation that more people were killed in hydraulic mines of the Old West than in gunfights. They spotlight how overlooked incidents of America's worst racial violence took place in the New West, such as Tulsa's Black Wall Street Massacre. In a twist on historians' habitual revisions of the past, this book proposes "a handful of case studies" to illuminate the present. Some of these academics assume the techniques of investigative journalists, skirting the roles of political advocates or community boosters and the even more threatening complacency of the self-righteous.

This book makes visible the normally invisible, the news behind the news, as indicated in the title of an Ellis Island exhibition about a western phenomenon: *Hidden in Plain Sight: The Basques*. As a writer of novels and general nonfiction about the rural West, including misunderstood minorities like the Basques and overlooked events such as the 1911 Nevada massacre of Hukandeka Shoshone, I welcome this book's unveiling of people and events hidden in plain sight. No-till agriculture, while not headline news, is a healthy method of contemporary eco-farming to help save western farmland, a practice shattering the notion of *rain follows the plough*. For every debunked myth, though, a new one pops up. A current belief in how technology can save farming is limited. Replacement of flood irrigation with drip hoses, for instance, does save water, yet it also allows hillier cropland to be planted and irrigated, ultimately using more water.

U-pick farms, winery tours, peach festivals, and other forms of agritourism reflect the enormous economic shift explored in these essays from the agricultural to the recreational West. Former polluted mining towns erase the past to rebrand themselves as "Dream Towns" attractive to amenity migrants. Retirement communities, vacation resorts, and sporting haunts simultaneously tout wilderness preservation even as they degrade it. A social media post about a visitor overlook on the Colorado River recently caused a jump in tourists from a thousand a year to four thousand a day.

Now that nine out of ten westerners are urbanites, the metro West understandably becomes a focus of attention in the shift from the industrial to the high-tech West. New company towns and exploited "shadow workers" accompany a 2.0 tech boom. The aerospace industry has moved into cyberspace. Startups flourish in the service of profit rather than human need. Traditional Latino businesses close while many urban Black people leave their homes. Digital robber barons are said to duplicate the nineteenth-century era Mark Twain named "The Gilded Age," when a corrupt western mining king and U.S. senator dominating politics was, in Twain's words, "as rotten a human being as can be found under the flag." As I type this page I see in the day's news that California's Bay Area is reported to be more segregated than thirty years ago.

Contemporary California, dismissed often as its own entity apart from the rest of the West, assumes its proper position in this book as the extreme West. "Don't Californicate Our State," other westerners hollered. But it was useless. California as the extreme West frequently showed the way the West was going and simply got there first. It has the costliest wildfires and most toxic dump in the West, but it's also the first western state in the twenty-first century with laws to protect both gender identity and sexual orientation against discrimination.

We live in a divided America, we're told, and these essays certainly show we live in a divided West, most often represented in the political split between interior, deep-red states and those of coastal and borderland blue states. A look at a California map of the last presidential election shows something different: 40 percent of the state is red. A central swath of red, rural counties helped California give loser Trump more votes than any state except Florida and Texas. Rural America originally put him in the White House. Cities spurned him. The gulf between the urban and rural West most accurately reflects a way the United States has become two separate countries. In blue-state Nevada 90 percent of the counties are bright red; only two harboring the cities of Reno and Las Vegas are blue.

The western rift between city and country affects people of all social classes and ethnicities. In 2019 analysis of income per capita demonstrated that the richest U.S. county wasn't in Silicon Valley or Connecticut but Wyoming.[1] Billionaires build second homes and enjoy resorts in the Rockies serviced by the working and commuting poor, often undocumented immigrants, who wash the dishes, cut the grass, and clean the rooms, showing that the American West doesn't stop at the border. This expansion of borders came home to me after a young Chamula *indigene* called my wife in the Hudson Valley, asking her to phone me in Chiapas, Mexico, to tell his father, Xalik, that his son had successfully crossed the desert with a *coyote* into the United States wearing the Brooks Beast running shoes I'd given him. A Native American network was now shuttling him across the Southwest to a job as a gardener.

Whether in the Great Basin or the San Joaquin Valley, I've heard the same complaint from rural Americans: "It's like we don't exist. We're invisible." It is a refrain that again cuts across economic and ethnic lines. Many Latinos in the West, as we see in these pages, tend to hold conservative beliefs, brandishing a desire for success through individualistic western gumption and not handouts. If you fail, you're a *pendejo*. One self-described Mexican American in Arizona said that as an eighteen-year-old registering to vote it was explained to him Democrats are for the poor, Republicans for the rich. "Well, that made it easy," he said. Another Latino commented that if you're not getting ahead, "You're going to have the same kind of rage we've long seen with white, working-class voters."

That rage extends from western workers to ranch owners in the country, where only one out of ten people now live. Older ways of living off the land may be dying, but they're not dead. Nine of the ten biggest U.S. coal mines are in Wyoming. Those struggling in the mines and fracking fields of the rural West often voice awareness of liberal academic and political disdain for white, working-class people. Years ago Martin Luther King Jr. warned about the need of "rescuing a large stratum of the forgotten white poor [and] many white workers whose economic condition is not too far removed from the economic condition of his black brother."

How do we get out of this new-millennial mess fueled by systematic inequality and a burning planet? Again and again in this book we see that appeals to the better natures of company officials don't bring corporate giants like Monsanto, Bayer, W. R. Grace, Pacific Gas and Electric, and TC Energy to their knees. Nor do neo-Christian concepts of "sacred sites" and "holy ground" from "time immemorial" halt encroachments on Native American land. State and federal legislation, court rulings, and executive orders do.

At the moment I'm writing, in mid-2021, the Nebraska Ponca Nation has joined an alliance of other Indigenous groups, environmental activists, climate scientists, ranchers, and farmers in celebrating the termination of the Keystone XL Pipeline running twelve hundred miles down the Great Plains to Texas. With three hundred miles of the line completed, unused pipes lie abandoned in Montana. For all the importance of thirteen years of vehement protests, the developer didn't pull the plug on the project until President Biden put pen to paper to rescind a federal permit to build the line.

Activist nonprofit lawyers behind the scenes emerge in these revisionist accounts to do more than headline-grabbing union leaders for the well-being of rural farmworker communities. In California vineyards, machines now pick most of the wine grapes, and low tilling makes weed control possible without poisons of earlier years. Waste disposal becomes a new threat. It's unfortunate that urban environmentalist activists for alternative energy, like Mothers for Nuclear Energy, downplay the disposal of highly radioactive nuclear rods too hot to remain in power plants, a danger for everyone, especially poor rural communities where toxic waste dumps show up. This book is valuable in clarifying such western struggles of today and tomorrow. As in battles for minority rights, equal rights for women, same-sex marriage, and LGBTQ rights, we see how fighters for environmental justice in the West have learned to draw strength through legislation and court cases tied to civil rights.

With a stroke of the pen, President Trump lopped off two million acres from Bear Ears National Monument and Grand Staircase-Escalante National Monument in Utah. Only one-fifth of the area remained in the biggest rollback of federal land protection in the nation's history. This year in Washington DC a member of New Mexico's Laguna Pueblo named Debra Anne Haaland, the first woman and the first Native American to head the U.S. Department of Interior, has recommended presidential restoration of the lands to their original boundaries. Perhaps there's not a new dawn but at least a glimmer of light in the eastern sky.

Notes

1. See https://www.bea.gov/news/2019/local-area-personal-income-2018.

CONTRIBUTORS

Chelsea Ball, assistant professor, West Texas A&M University, Department of History.

Frank Bergon, professor emeritus, Vassar College, Department of English.

Peter Boag, professor and Columbia Chair in the History of the American West, Washington State University Vancouver, Department of History.

Taylor Cozzens, PhD student, University of Oklahoma, Department of History.

Jennifer Dunn, PhD candidate, Montana State University, Department of History.

Soni Grant, Killam postdoctoral fellow, Dalhousie University, Department of Sociology and Social Anthropology.

Andrew Gulliford, professor, Fort Lewis College, Department of History.

Layne Karafantis, The Huntington-USC Institute on California and the West.

Stuart W. Leslie, professor, Johns Hopkins University, History of Science Department.

Patricia Nelson Limerick, professor, University of Colorado Boulder, Department of History, and director, Center for the American West.

Marcus C. Macktima, San Carlos Apache, PhD candidate, University of Oklahoma, Department of History.

Ivón Padilla-Rodríguez, Bridge-to-Faculty postdoctoral scholar, University of Illinois, Chicago.

Brenden W. Rensink, associate director, Charles Redd Center for Western Studies, and associate professor, Brigham Young University, Department of History.

Ernesto Sagás, professor, Colorado State University, Department of Ethnic Studies.

David D. Vail, associate professor, University of Nebraska at Kearney, Department of History.

Jeffrey M. Widener, business analyst, Williams, Tulsa OK.

Lindsey Passenger Wieck, associate professor, St. Mary's University, Department of History.

INDEX

Abbey, Edward, 348–51
abortion, 283, 286, 293, 296–97
Adams, Juliann, 185
aerospace, 115, 117, 121–24, 127, 131, 365; Ford Aerospace, 117
African Americans (Blacks): and Black Mother's Forum, 295; and environmental justice, 220, 229; and the ERA, 285–86, 292; and gentrification, 124, 365; labor of, 111–12, 115, 367; and racial identities and slavery, 83; and same-sex marriage, 313; in Silicon Valley, 118; Tulsa Massacre of, 364
Agricultural Research Service, 41
agritourism, xxviii, 170–75, 180–90, 365
AIDS, 156, 309, 311, 317. *See also* HIV
Alaska National Interest Lands Conservation Act (ANILCA), 345
Alley, E. N., 7
Amazon, 110–16, 124
American Indians, 292, 333; Congress of American Indians, 86
American Indian Religious Freedom Act (1978), 353
Anderson, Cal, 317
Anderson-Murray Bill, 317
Andrade, Sammy, 125
Angelita C. et al. v. California Department of Pesticide Regulation, 232, 236, 240–41
Antiquities Act, 333, 336–40, 343, 353–54
Apaches (San Carlos): Apache Survival Coalition, 68; Aravaipas, 65, 77; Elders Cultural Advisory Council, 74–75; and environmental protection, xxvii, 59–64, 76–78; and the federal government, 69–73; history with mining elements, 64–69; nationalism of, 73–76; Pinal, 62, 65; San Carlos Apache Reservation, 62–64, 66, 74–78; San Carlos Indian Reservation, 60, 64; White Mountain, 65, 74
Apache Leap Mountain, 61
Apple, 110, 116, 119
Arguello, Erick, 158
Arizona: Arizona Coalition for ERA, 289; Center Against Sexual Assault, 290; Center for Arizona Policy, 296; Legislature, 294–95; Southeast Arizona Land Exchange and Conservation Act (2007), 61, 64, 71, 73
Arndt, Deke, 30
art: and agritourism, 176, 187; and gentrification, xii, xxviii, 154–60; in the Mission District, 141–48, 161–63
artists: and Día de los Muertos, 160; and eviction, 153–57; in the Mission District, 141–51, 161, 163; studio, 125
asbestos: Community Asbestos Memorial Project (CAMP), 21; health risks of, 237; at Libby, 3, 6–21; and toxic waste, xxvi, 237
Atkins, Hannah, 285, 287
Autry, Greg, 123
Ayala, Martina, 160
Aztecs, 147, 157

Baca, Herman, 203, 210–12
Bagby, M. O., 43
Barerra, Rudy Elmer, 210
Basques, 364

Bayer, 219, 367
Bears Ears National Monument: and Bears Ears Inter-Tribal Coalition work, xiii, 334, 343–44; future of, 348–51; government protections of, 59, 86, 336–40; Obama statement on, 331; and place name politics, 340–42; and public land use, xxx, 333–36, 345–48; and tourism, 351–54
Belvado, William, 68–69
Berget, Tony, 10
Bernal, José Celso, 255
Berryhill, Clare, 225
Bezos, Jeff, 113, 115
Biden, Joseph R., Jr., 292, 353–54, 367
Binz, Ron, 178
Biotech Beach, 110, 126
Bishop, Rob, 338
Black. *See* African Americans (Blacks)
Boeing, 111–16: McDonnell-Douglas merger with, 112
borders: Arizona-New Mexico, 75; and borderlands, 211, 272–73; and Border Patrol, 199–205, 208–12; crossing, 211, 259; deaths at, 159, 205; Mexican, 251; on reservation, 66, 82; towns at, 258; U.S.-Mexico, xiii–xxix, 199, 272. *See also* migrant youth detention
Bowers v. Hardwick (1986), 318–19
Breen, Peter, 293
Brin, Sergey, 116
Bronzan, Bruce, 225
Bryant, Anita, 307–8
Buecheler, Rondo, 186
Burnham Institute for Medical Research, 129
Burns, Conrad, 10
Bush, George W., 212, 272

Cactus Ed, 349
CAL EPA, 237–41
California: *Angelita C. et al. v. California Department of Pesticide Regulation*, 232, 236, 240–41;
California Department of Agriculture, 221
California Department of Pesticide Regulation (CDPR), 235, 241
California Department of Public Health, 239
California Department of Toxic Substance Control (DTSC), 237–41
California Environmental Quality Act (CEQA), 125
California Rural Legal Assistance (CRLA), 220–25, 228–37, 240–42
California Stem Cell Agency, 130
Camarena, Adriana, 156
Cammermeyer, Margarethe, 319
Camp Grant Massacre, 65
cancer, 7–8, 15, 18, 129, 153, 224–25, 343, 363
capitalism, 13, 116, 150, 181, 255, 285, 349; and disruptive innovation, 131
Carney, Eileen, 20–21
Carrasco, Jose, 158
Carrasco, Paul, 205
Carrillo-Estrada, Humberto, 203
Carson, Kit, 346–47
Carson, Rachel, 224
Carter, Heather, 295
Carter, Jimmy, 200, 203, 210, 345
Cassadore, Ola, 68
Castillo, Leonel, 203–5
Cedar Mesa National Conservation Area, 335–43
Center for Western Priorities, 352
Central America, 156, 200–201, 204, 209–11, 259, 264, 270–71
Chaco Culture National Historical Park, 352
Chamulas, 366
Chapman, Leonard, 203
Chapter House, 87, 96
Chavez, Cesar, 147, 223
Chavez, José, 257
chemicals: agriculture, 33, 219–24, 228–33, 236, 239; and fracking, 85, 87; and pollution, xii, xxix, 5, 33, 42. *See also* Monsanto; pesticides
Chemical Waste Management, 231
Chi'chil Biłdagoteel: and Apache identity, 64–69, 77; and Apache nationalism, 73–76; and federal governmental action, 69–72; and sacred lands, xxvii, 59–64
Chi'ihaajin, Hastiin (Manuelito), 347
Chicanos/a/x, 146–47, 157, 256–57, 260, 266–73; Chipsters, 152; Committee on Chicano Rights, 203
children: and birth defects, 224–25, 238–40; and border militarization, 200–205; and Bracero descendants, 256, 268–70; Child & Migrant Services, 268; detention of, xxix, 199–200, 205–12, 363; and ERA battles, 288–89, 297; immigrant, xiii; and labor, 223–24,

372   Index

228, 232–39; and LGBTQ+ civil rights battles, 312, 316, 320–21; "Save Our Children," 307–8; and welfare, 285–86, 318
China and Chinese, 110–11, 221
Christian Right, 298, 306, 309
Church of Jesus Christ of Latter-day Saints (LDS or Mormon), 273, 284–85, 293–94, 334–35, 340–42, 345–54
Citizens to Retain Fair Employment, 308
civil rights: for Blacks, 283; Civil Rights Act, 231; environmental, 229, 235–37, 241–42. *See* Equal Rights Amendment (ERA)
Clark, R. Nolan, 43
class: civil rights concerns of, 285; creative, 110, 113, 131; middle, 117, 126, 256, 268–70 291; tech, 118; upper, 291; warfare, 363; working, xii, 113, 127, 131, 141, 143, 152–53, 163, 289, 366–67
climate, xii, 30–32, 35–39, 42, 46–48, 367
Clinton, William J. (Bill), 212, 229, 316, 338
Cobell, Eloise, 92
Cobell v. Salazar (2009), 92
Cold War, 37–38, 94, 109–12, 117, 121–22, 126–28, 131
Cole, Edward D., 203
Cole, Luke, 230–231, 234
Collier, John, 94
Colorado: Association for Viticulture and Enology, 178–80, 183, 185; Department of Agriculture, 173, 185; Fruit and Wine Byway, 180–85; HB 1280, 181; Mountain Winefest, 175–80; State Demography Office, 260; Tourism Office, 172–73, 181–88; Western Colorado Latino Chamber of Commerce, 268
Commons, Julie and Bob, 186–87
Community Action Against Rape, 289
Compañeros, 268
Convair (Consolidated Aircraft), 126–27
Cooper, Sandie, 183, 185
Copper Basin Jobs Act, 70
Cuba, 157, 200

Defense of Marriage Act (DOMA), 316, 320–21
DeLeon, Rafael, 235
desert, 35, 61, 88, 204, 259, 333, 335, 339, 342, 347–49, 353, 366
detention sites: El Centro, 206; Metropolitan Correctional Center (MCC), 206; San Ysidro, 206

Development, Relief, and Education for Alien Minors (DREAM) Act, 269
Día de los Muertos, 143–48, 156–60
Dinés: and Bears Ears National Monument, 334, 337, 340–47, 350–53; and Comb Ridge, 340; Diné Bikéyahs, 337, 344, 346; and federal land dealings, 88–95; land buy-back, 92; North Escavada Unit, 82; and oil extraction on Diné land, 81–88; oil spill remediation plan, 95–97; and sovereignty, xxviii, 97.
Dixon, Frank, 128–29
Dobbs, Glenn, 310–11
Donwerth, Debra, 293
Dore, Tim, 181–82
Dougherty, Michael, 120
Dropbox, 150
drought: xxvii, 29, 46–48, 190, 363; Eisenhower's Drought Tour, 37–40; University of Nebraska's Drought Monitoring Institute, 48
Duke, David, 313
Dził Nchaa Si An (Mount Graham), 60, 66–68, 73, 77

Eagle Forum, 284, 294. *See also* Schlafly, Phyllis
Easterling, William, 46
Edelman, Gerald, 129
Eisenhower, Dwight, 38–39; and Public Order 1229, 69
Ellis Act, 154–56, 161
El Pueblo Para el Aire y Agua Limpio v. County of Kings, 230
energy, renewable, 36, 43–44
Enos-Martinez, Cindy, 269
environment: cleanup of, 3–6, 10–18; crises for, xxvi, xxvii, 14; degradation of, 3, 18, 31, 42, 131, 365; Earth Institute, 48; and environmental impact reports, 72, 125, 231; hazardous waste and, 3, 14, 17, 229, 236–37, 352; justice for, xiii, 220–21, 229–31, 234–36, 240–42, 368; stewardship of, 342–44. *See also* Environmental Protection Agency (EPA); resource extraction
Environmental Protection Agency (EPA): CAL EPA, 237–41; at Libby, 3, 5–6, 9–11, 14–18; Office of Civil Rights, 235–36; and pesticides, 219, 224–25, 230–37, 240–41; Superfund, 3, 5–6, 12–19

Equal Rights Amendment (ERA): Equal Rights Coalition, 289; Mormons for ERA, 294; opposition to, 285–87; origins, 284–85; and race, 286; remaining hurdles to passage of, 293–99; in the West, xiii, xxx, 281–84; women politicians and, 289–93
Ertel, Keenan, 348
Estes, Nick, 59
eviction: Anti-Eviction Mapping Project, 161–62; in Los Angeles, 124; in the Mission District, xxviii, 141–43, 149–63; Our Mission No Eviction, 158–59
executive orders, 63–65, 72, 93, 229, 310–12, 365

Facebook, 109–10, 115–16, 120
Farnsworth, Eddie, 295–96
Federal Bureau of Investigation (FBI), 350–51
Federal Communications Commission (FCC), 132
Federal Emergency Management Agency (FEMA), 29
Federal Land Policy and Management Act (FLPMA), 339
feminism, xiii, 282–93, 296–97
Ferrick, Robert M., 204
Finkbeiner, Bill, 317, 319
fire: and agricultural risk, 29–30, 33; forest, 15; megafires, xii; oil, 81; Pyrocene, xxvii; and wildfire, xxvii, 30, 363, 365
Fishman, Lillian and William, 128
Flake, Jeff, 70
flooding, 29–33, 46, 363–64
Flores, Jenny Lisette (Flores Settlement) (1997), 212
Food and Agriculture Department (CA), 225
Foster, Norman, 116
Foursquare Church, 308
Francis, Peter, 305, 308
frontier: high-tech, 110–11; mythic imagery, xvii–xviii, xix–xxv, xxxi, 363; the West as, 271, 273, 354. See also Turner, Frederick Jackson

Gadsden Purchase, 64
Galería de la Raza: Día de los Muertos, 143, 146–48, 156–60; and gentrification, 153, 156–58, 163; origins, 141–49
Garcetti, Eric, 123
Gardner, Booth, 310–11

Gehry, Frank, 116
gender: and the ERA, xxx, 282, 285–88, 291, 294–99; and femininity, 296; identity, expression, and, 305, 317, 365; and inequality, xxviii, 110, 115, 291, 293, 363; and masculinity, 286; and transgender people, 305, 317, 323
General Allotment Act (1887), 91
General Land Office, 94
gentrification, xii, xxviii–xxix, 126, 131: in the Mission District, 141–43, 149–53, 159–63, 363
Gilded Age, 131, 365
Goeppert-Mayer, Marie, 129
Goldschmidt, Neil, 312
Gómez-Peña, Guillermo, 151–54
Good Samaritan Family Resource Center, 158
Goodwin, Grenville, 65, 74–75
Google, 109–10, 113, 116–21, 141, 150
Gorman, Howard, 88
Grand Gulch Primitive Area, 335, 339–40, 343
Grand Teton National Park, 344
Grant, Ulysses S., 64–65
Great Old Broads for Wilderness, 337
Great Plains Agricultural Council (GPAC), xxvii, 36, 36–49
Great Plains Tree Pest Council (GPTPC), 41
Grey, Laura, 172
Grijalva, Raúl, 70
Güereca, Sergio Adrián Hernández, 204
Guzmán, Rocío, 263

Haaland, Debra Anne, 292, 368
Haiti, 200
Hanway, D. G., 44–45
Hardeman, Edwin, 219–20
Hargrove, James, 319
Harold, John, 269
Hart, Steinberg, 124
Hashkeninii (Navajo), 347
Hatch, Orrin, 338
Hawthorne Arts Complex, 125
Hawthorne Municipal Airport, 123–24
healthcare, 20, 118–19, 143, 154
Hellickson, Mylo A., 44
Helling, Charles S., 41–42
Herman, Renee, 176–77
Hernández, Luis Eduardo, 204
Hernandez, Robert, 158

Hernandez v. Mesa (2020), 204
Hickenlooper, John, 181
Hispanics, xxix, 115, 118, 131, 229, 260–61, 264, 270; Hispanic Affairs Project, 264, 268
Hispanos, 254–57, 260, 268–73
HIV, 309, 311. *See also* AIDS
Hix, Anita, 182
Hoffmeyer, Brian, 120
Holtrop, Joel, 71
Homesteading Act (1862), 89–90
Hopis, 334–35, 341, 343
Horowitz, Charles, 321
housing, fair, 307; LGBTQ+, 309; rent, xxviii, 115–17, 124–26, 149–56, 163, 261–63, 309; rent-control, 153–56. *See also* eviction; gentrification
Hualapais, 65
Hughes, Allison, 289
Hughes Aircraft, 109, 122
Human Rights Commission, 323
Human Rights Ordinance, 314
Hybritech, 129

IBM, 113
Ickes, Harold, 338
Idaho Citizens Alliance, 313
immigration: children and, xiii; community creation, 268–69; coyotes and, 199–205, 208, 211, 366; and criminality narratives, 200–211; and detention, 199–200; and family separation, 199, 205–12; Immigration and Customs Enforcement Agency (ICE), 212; and labor, xxix, 222, 251–53, 255–57; Midwest Coalition in Defense of Immigrants, 205; after NAFTA, 257–68, 270–73; National Immigration Law Center, 205; and undocumented persons, 199–207, 212, 269, 366; and violence, xxix. *See also* Immigration and Naturalization Service (INS)
Immigration and Nationality Act (1965), 201
Immigration and Naturalization Service (INS), 199–211
Immigration Reform and Control Act (1986), 202
Independent Women's Forum, 294
India, 110
Indians: and allotment lands, 82, 84, 89–91; Bureau of Indian Affairs, 93–94; ecological trope about, 61; Indian Appropriations Act (1871), 64; Indian Claims Commission, 346; Indian Reorganization Act (Indian New Deal), 60, 65, 76–77, 94; Individual Indian Money accounts, 92; military defeats, 254; policies covering, xxvii; and sacred space, 59, 341. *See also* American Indians; Indigenous people; Native Americans
Indigenous people: absent from frontier mythology, xviii; from central Mexico, 264; Indigenous Peoples' Day, 353; mixed racial identities of, xii, 83; racialization of, 270; resistance in Colorado by, 254, 272–73; and sacred space, 337, 353; sovereignty of, xxvii–xxviii, 84–86, 91, 94, 367; symbols, 147; and tourism, xxx. *See also* American Indians; Chi'chil Biłdagoteel; Indians; Native Americans
Ingels, Bjarke, 116
Inglewood stadium project, 124
Intel, 117
Irvine, Alexander, 90
Ishizaka, Kimishige and Teruko, 129

Jackson, Lisa P., 234
Jackson Hole National Monument, 344–45
Jacobs, Ilene, 242
Jesus Christ, 147, 318
Jewell, Sally, 337
Jobs, Steve, 110, 116
John Paul II (Pope), 68
Johnson, Cory, 187
Johnson, Dewayne, 219–20, 223
Johnson, Lyndon B., 223
Johnson and Johnson, 130
Jones, Karen Kitcheyan, 73

K'aayelli (Navajo), 347
Kahlo, Frida, 147
Kahn, Louis, 128
Kaiyé, Bija Gush, 65
Kan, Pearl, 233
Keystone XL Pipeline, 367
Kimball, Spencer W., 284–85
Kitcheyan, Buck, 67, 73
Kolbe, Jim, 68
Kootenai National Forest, 3, 7
Koster, John, 316
Ku Klux Klan, 286, 312–13
Kyl, Jon, 63, 71

labor: and agritourism, 185–88; blue-collar, 118, 123, 131; Chinese, 221; Citizens to Retain Fair Employment, 308; Coalition of Labor Union Women (CLUW), 281, 293; contingent, 117–20; contractors, 96, 110, 117–19, 124, 127–28, 222, 347; farmers, xxviii, 31–43, 46, 169–75, 180–83, 188–90, 222, 239, 251, 258, 269, 342, 367; farmworkers, 220–25, 228–42, 271, 367; high-paying, 127, 131; hospitality, 258, 262, 264, 266, 271; immigrant workers, 263–64, 269; Mexican labor is western labor, 271–72; mining, 5, 8, 11, 17, 20, 254; stoop, 255, 271; TVC workers (Google), 119; unemployment, 17, 201, 257; white-collar, 112, 118, 269

La Jolla Institute for Allergy and Immunology, 129

Lanham Defense Housing Act, 127

Latin Americans, 143–47, 159, 200–203, 210, 271–72

Latinos/as/x: in Colorado, 251, 254–66; community formation among, 268–70; and environmental justice, 220–22, 228, 234–38, 242; and gentrification, xxviii, 141–43, 153–64, 365; and immigration violence, 199–203, 210; in Las Vegas, 285; *La Voz del Pueblo*, 268; new migrations of, 148–52, 270–73; origins in the Mission District, 143–48; and stereotypes about work, 366; Western Colorado Latino Chamber of Commerce, 268

Law Enforcement Assistance Administration, 210

League of Women Voters, 289, 308

Lee, Ed, 150

Levy, Rebecca, 180

LGBTQ+ people: *Andersen* case, 316, 320; and anti-LGBTQ+ candidates, 292; and the Bible, 307, 319; bisexual, 292, 305; and civil rights in Washington, xiii, xxx, 368; and domestic partnerships, 320–22; and "Don't Ask Don't Tell," 315–16, 319; and the ERA, 286; lesbian, 286, 292, 305, 307–20; queer, 144, 292; and same-sex marriage, 316, 320–23, 367–68; Save Our Children, 307–8; transgender, 317–18. *See also* Bryant, Anita

Lilly, Eli, 129–30

Lockheed Missiles and Space, 117, 122

Lopez, Fred, 125

Lopez, Jesús, 222

López, Yolanda and Leo, 153,156

Los Angeles International Airport (LAX), 109, 123

Lower Twenty-Fourth Street Merchants and Neighbors Association, 158

Lucero, Plácida, 255
Lyman, Albert, 350

Mabon, Lon, 312–13
Maradiaga, Ralph, 141, 144, 147
Maravilla, Leticia, 228
marriage: intermarriage, 268; law, 287; among LGBTQ+ people, 368
Martz, Judy, 12–13
Matthews, Glenna, 120
Matute, Juan, 125
McCain, John, 63–66, 70–73, 77
McClure, Florence Shilling, 289
McDonald, Howard, 18
McGrath, Mike, 13
McLoyd and Graham, 339
Mejia, Daniel Romero, 211
Meloy, Ellen, 348, 352
Menke, Steve, 185
Merrick v. Board of Higher Education (1992), 312
Messmer, Terry, 46
#MeToo Movement, 284, 291, 297
Meuter, Michael, 234
Mexico and Mexicans: artists, 141, 157, 159; Bracero Program, 201, 255–56; and the Camp Grant Massacre, 65; on Colorado's Western Slope, 254–57, 259–68, 270–73; family separation at U.S.-Mexico border, 199–11; immigrant communities, 268–70; immigrants harmed by pesticide, 222; immigration to Colorado, 251–54; International Monetary Fund, 258; invisibility of, 366; Mexican-American War, 254; Mormons and, 334–35; and NAFTA, 257–59; United Mexican American Students, 257; U.S.-Mexico border, xiii, xxix. *See also* pesticide
Microsoft, 111–14
Midwest Coalition in Defense of Immigrants, 205
migrant youth detention, xxix, 201–11
Miles, Dale, 73
Miller, Leslie, 345
mines and mining: abandoned, 363; at Bears Ears, 333, 336, 340–48, 352; Berkeley Pit, 18; at Chi'chil Biłdagoteel, xxvii, 59–63, 69–72, 77; coal , 85, 94, 257, 367; on Diné lands, xxviii; Hecla Mining Company, 19; historic Colorado industries, 251, 254; and Latino labor, 271; at Libby, 3, 5–8, 11–21; and mineral leasing, 69, 94, 334, 346; and mineral

rights, 87–91, 94–96; and the mythic West, 254, 364; Resolution Copper, 61–64, 66, 69–73, 77; and tourism, xv, 263, 266, 270, 365; vermiculite, 3, 7–8, 14–18. *See also* resource extraction
Mission District (San Francisco), 141–64
Monsanto, 219, 367
Montana Department of Environmental Quality, 15
Monterey County Agricultural Commissioner, 233
Moral Majority, 309
Mormons. *See* Church of Jesus Christ of Latter-day Saints
Morton, Robert, 322–23
Mothers for Nuclear Energy, 367
Mount Graham International Observatory, 66–67, 73
Murray, Ed, 317
Musk, Elon, 121, 124–25

Nason, George, 46
National Association for the Advancement of Colored People (NAACP), 286, 311
National Center for Immigrants' Rights (National Immigration Law Center), 205
National Congress of American Indians, 86
National Defense Authorization Act (NDAA), 64, 66
National Environmental Policy Act (NEPA), 71–72
National Historic Preservation Act, 67, 72
National Institutes of Health, 129, 132
National Oceanic and Atmospheric Administration (NOAA), 29–30
National Organization for Women (NOW), 295, 308
National Park Service, 344
National Security Agency (NSA), 121
National Women's Conference, 286, 296
Native Americans: ancestors of, 59, 75–77, 87, 335, 342, 347; as ancient peoples, 254; and economic crises, 367; in federal government, 292, 368; as laborers, 221; and Mexican immigration, 366; trust funds of, 92; violence against, 5. *See also* American Indians; Bears Ears National Monument; Indians; Indigenous people

Navajo Nation, xxvii, 86; and Bears Ears National Monument, 334, 337, 340–47, 350–53; and federal lands disputes, 90, 94–95; and land buy-backs, 92; and national governments, 81, 88, 93; reservations, 82, 89, 91, 93, 254; treaties, 87, 89. *See also* Dinés
New Mexico: Boundary Bill, 88; Oil Conservation Division (NMOCD), 81, 96
Niitsítapi Blackfoot Confederacy, 92
NIMBY-ism (Not in My Back Yard), 125
Nixon, Richard M., 200, 203
North American Aviation, 122
North American Free Trade Agreement (NAFTA), xxix, 251–53, 257–60, 264–66, 269–70
North Central Weed Control Conference (NCWCC), 41
Northrop Corporation, 121–23
Nosie, Wendsler, 60–61, 71
Novartis, 130
Noyes, Gavin, 344

Obama, Barack, 64, 212, 272, 331–40, 345–47, 352–53
Obregon, Nancy, 158
O'Connor, Sandra Day, 295
Odegaard, Shirley, 289
oil: development, 90; on Diné lands, xxviii, 81–83, 87–88, 93–97, 336, 342–49, 353; extraction, 251, 253, 257, 272; fracking, 84–87, 367; spills, 81, 87, 95–97, 363
Oke, Bob, 319
Omar, Ilhan, 292
Operation Cerberus, 351
Oregon Citizens Alliance (OCA), 312–13
Orozco, José Clemente, 141
Our Mission No Eviction, 153–61

Pacific Gas and Electrine, 367
Packwood, Bob, 312
Page, Larry, 116
Paiutes, 334, 337, 350
Palisade Peach Festival, 171, 175–77
Papalas, Carol, 289–90
Peach Street Distillers, 180, 182
People of Color Environmental Leadership Summit, 229
Pérez, Ricardo, 264
Peronard, Paul, 10–12

Index 377

pesticides: and environmental change, 33, 41–42; paradigm of, 220; toxicity of, 36; workers' exposure to, xiii, xxix, 159, 220–25, 228–36, 239–41. *See also* California Rural Legal Assistance (CRLA); chemicals
Pfizer, 129–30
Pichai, Sundar, 119
Pilliod, Alva and Alberta, 219–20
police: brutality, 143, 159–60; in Calexico, 203; Mexican, 211; officers, 263; in San Francisco, 160; in Seattle, 307
pollution, xxvi, xxix, 3, 5, 13–14, 19, 41, 97, 116, 124, 230, 240, 365. *See also* environment, justice for; Environmental Protection Agency (EPA)
Ponca Nation, 367
populism, 132, 298, 313
Posada, José Guadalupe, 159
poverty, 118, 125, 131, 204, 228–32, 240, 351; programs to fight, 289; War on Poverty, 223
Powell, John Wesley, 33–35, 44, 48
property rights, 83–84, 90–91, 97, 342
public health, xxvii, 3, 10, 20, 225, 235, 239–42. *See also* environment, justice for
public lands, xxx, 69, 71, 94: and Bears Ears, 333, 338–42, 346–47, 351–54; and land grant institutions, 36, 43, 48; and Public Lands Initiative, 338; and Senate Committee on Natural Resources, 61, 70–72. *See also* Bears Ears National Monument
Pueblo Indians, 85–86, 334–37, 340, 347, 352, 385; All Pueblo Council of Governors, 86; Laguna, 292, 368

race: Asians, 131, 272; and the ERA, 285–86; eugenics, 12; and housing, 110, 112, 143, 146, 150–52, 158, 161, 231–32, 242, 285; and labor, 221, 256, 268, 272; and property rights, 83–84; racializing and, xxix, 83, 270–72, 285; and racism, 126, 131, 230, 363; and violence in the Old West, 364. *See also* African Americans (Blacks); American Indians; Indians; Indigenous people; Latinos/as/x; Native Americans; settler colonialism; whites and whiteness
railroads, 84, 89, 93–94, 172, 254–55, 271
Rambler, Terry, 72, 75
Ramirez, Ana Margarita, 199–200
Ramirez, Orlando, 199–200

rape, 259, 286; and Community Action Against Rape, 289
Reagan, Ronald, 211, 288
Reaves, Pat, 290
regulations, government, xv, 13–14, 31, 82, 96, 131–32, 228, 231–33, 241, 294, 296
Republican Party, 112, 282, 284, 293–95, 310, 312, 317, 322, 366
Resolution Copper, 61, 64–66, 69–73, 77. *See also* Rio Tinto
resource extraction: copper, 19, 61, 64–66, 69–73, 77; extractive industries, xii, xxvi, xxx, 3, 5, 257, 271, 343; gas, 82–90, 94–96, 251, 253, 336, 342–43, 347–48, 353, 367; gold, 7, 340; silver, 19, 64, 340; timber, 3, 15–19; uranium, 85, 94, 257, 342–43, 352–53. *See also* mines and mining; oil
Rettig, Mel, 180
Revelle, Roger, 127–28
Rio Tinto, 60–61, 69
Rivas, Para Rosa, 208–9
Rivera, Diego, 141
Roe v. Wade (1973), 283
Roman Catholicism, 67–68, 147, 231, 314: Catholic Community Services, 199, 209; Virgen de Guadalupe, 147
Roosevelt, Franklin Delano, 36, 344
Roosevelt, Theodore, 93, 337–38, 354
rural areas: and agritourism, 172–73, 181; in California, 201, 230–33; in Colorado, 257, 259, 265–66, 269–72; in Great Plains, 36, 39–44, 46, 49; in Mexico, 251; in Oregon, 312; in Utah, 348, 353–54; in Washington, 313, 320; in the West, 14, 30, 364–67. *See also* California Rural Legal Assistance (CRLA)

sacred space, 59–64; at Bears Ears, 333–34, 341–43, 353; earth as, 229; protection of, 86, 367. *See also* Chi'chil Biłdagoteel
Sales, Richard, 180
Salisbury, David, 71
Salk, Jonas, 128–30
Salvation Army, 199, 209
Sanford Consortium for Regenerative Medicine, 110, 130
Savage, Dan, 315
scarcity, xii, 31, 33, 38–41, 169; watersheds, 34
Schlafly, Phyllis, 284, 286

Schmidt, Claude, 42–43
Schroeder, Roger, 46
Schwarzenegger, Arnold, 239
Scripps Research Institute, 128–29
Seattle Committee Against Thirteen, 308
settler colonialism: and agriculture, 170; and Anglo-American settlement, 89–90, 93, 254–56, 270–71, 333; and displacement, 255; environmental impact of, 34; and Latino settlement in Colorado, 254–55, 270; legacies of, xxxi; Mormon, 340, 342, 347, 349–52; and oil extraction in Dinétah, 82–84, 87–97; state-sanctioned, 59; and western mythology, xvii–xviii. *See also* Bears Ears National Monument; Chi'chil Biłdagoteel
sexism, 115, 282, 287–88, 363
Sherman, William Tecumseh, 89
Shoshone, Hukandeka, 364
Shull, Cassidee, 183
Sierra Club, 230
Silicon Valley, 110–11, 115–21, 130, 132, 150, 169–70, 190, 366
Sinema, Krysten, 292
Sioux Indians: Lower Brule, 59; Standing Rock Sioux Nation, 86
Siqueiros, David Alfaro, 141
skiing, 161, 173, 186, 253, 258, 261–66
soil: and agritourism, 171; erosion of, 33, 37–39, 45–48, 94; fertile, 31; and GPAC, 43; and pollution, 14–15, 48, 232–33, 363; studies of, 36–42; and vermiculite for soil conditioning, 8
Soliz, Juan Manuel, 205
Southern Utah Wilderness Alliance, 336–37
SpaceX, 110, 121–25
Spearman, Pat, 292–93
Standing Rock (#NoDAPL), 59, 69, 86
Steele, Victoria, 295
Stegner, Wallace, 35, 169, 190, 346, 348, 350
Stevens, Val, 316, 319
sugar beets, 255, 257
Sullins, Martha, 189
Swecker, Dan, 321

Tabor, Daniel, 124
Taft, William Howard, 93
Talbott, Bruce, 179–82
Talgo, Harrison, 68–69, 73
Taylor Grazing Act (1934), 94

TC Energy, 367
technology: biotech, 110, 126–32; booms, 143, 149–50, 161, 365; and the dot-com boom, 149–50; high-tech, xii, xxviii, 109–13, 116–17, 121, 124, 127, 132, 174, 251, 365; industries, 17, 109–11, 126–27, 131–32, 169–70, 257–58
Teck, Ron, 178
Tesla Design Center, 124
The Boring Company, 124–25
Thomas, Jack, 68
Tlaib, Rashida, 292
Tockstein, George, 201
Tohono O'odhams, 65
Tonto National Forest, 61
Torre, David de la, 159
tourism: and Bears Ears National Monument, xxx, 343, 345–48, 351–54; economies of, xiv–xv, 5–6, 10, 16–20, 161, 263; and gentrification, xxix, 156; heritage, xxvii, 343; and Latino labor, 251, 258, 262–63, 267, 271. *See also* agritourism; skiing
Trump, Donald J.: and Bears Ears, 333, 336–40, 344–46, 350–53, 368; and frontier mythology, xvii–xviii, 363; and immigration, xiii, xxix, 199, 207, 209, 212, 272; and rural/urban divide, 366; and women's concerns, 284
TRW Automotive, 122
Tso, Daniel, 81, 86
Turner, Frederick Jackson, xvii–xviii, xx, 111, 132

Ugenti, Michelle, 295
United Church of Christ, 229
United Farm Workers (UFW), 220–21
urbanism: and agritourism, 169–72; and Cold War growth, 111–13; and environmentalism, 49, 230, 367; and the ERA, 283, 285; and Hispano immigrants, 256; and LGBTQ+ politics, 313; in the Mission District, 148–53; in the West, xxiv–xxviii, 365–66
Urey, Harold, 128
U.S. Border Patrol, 199–205, 208–12
U.S. Bureau of Land Management (BLM), 86, 94, 337; and Navajo Occupancy Resolution Program, 94–95
U.S. Census Bureau, 260
U.S. Constitution, Nineteenth Amendment, 291
U.S. Department of Agriculture (USDA), 42–43, 67, 69, 172–73, 185, 221

U.S. Department of Defense, 132
U.S. Department of the Interior, 292, 352; and Buy-Back Program for Tribal Nations, 92
U.S. Forest Service, 67–72, 344
U.S. House of Representatives and the ERA, 60–61, 297; Subcommittee on Energy and Minerals, 72; Subcommittee on National Parks, Forests, and Public Lands, 61, 70–71
U.S. Indian Affairs, 93–94
U.S. Marshals Service, 199, 206–9
U.S. Navy, 126–28
U.S. Office of Economic Opportunity, 223
U.S. Senate, 70, 344; Subcommittee on Public Lands, Forests, and Mining, 72
Utah: Fruit Way in, 188; Natural History Museum, 340
Utes, 254, 334, 337, 341, 343, 347, 350, Northern, 334; Ute Mountain, 334, 341

Van Dyke, Dick, 311
Varian Associates, 117
Vietnam War, 203
violence: domestic and sexual, 288–90; and immigration, xxix, 200–204, 209–11, 259; against Native Americans, 5; and the police, 143, 159–60; structural, in West, 364. *See also* rape
Virgin, Emily, 281

Wallis, Cynthia, 153–54, 161
Warren, Elizabeth, 121
Washington: Citizens Alliance of Washington (CAW), 313–15; Citizens for Fairness Hands Off Washington (HOW), 313–17; Proposition 13, 307–8;
Washington Association of Churches (Faith Action Network), 308
Washington Family Coalition, 311
Washington National Guard, 319
Washington Public Affairs Council (WPAC), 313
water: aquifers, 41, 46, 48, 363; and infrastructure, 127; and irrigation, 29, 34, 171–72, 181, 189, 221, 255, 364; and land conversation, 169–72, 189–90; and mining, 7, 19; and Native Americans, 59, 61, 63, 81, 84–86, 90, 93, 96; pollution, 14, 36, 41–42, 46, 228, 236, 239–41; public, 353; rights, 34

weather, 30–34, 37, 39, 42, 115, 186, 257; blizzards, 29–33, 363; tornadoes, 30, 363
Webster, Barbara, 188
welfare, 200, 209, 212, 285–86, 318; corporate, 116
Westworld (HBO), 109–10, 132
Wetherill brothers, 339–40
whites and whiteness, 83, 271; artists, 146; and Latinos, 256, 267, 269; nationalist, 286; privilege, 131; settlers, 89–90, 93, 254–56, 270–71, 333; suffrage, 297; and Utah's public lands, 336–37, 342, 345; in the West, 285–86; white-collar, 111, 118, 123, 269, 291; workforce, 115, 127, 150, 220, 230, 234, 366–67
Wicks, Gail, 45
wildfires: Starbuck Fire, 30
wine: in agritourism, 173–74, 177–85, 365; Colorado Wine Industry Development Act, 178; Colorado Wine Industry Development Board, 178
women: Governor's Commission on the Status of Women (Nevada), 288–89; Governor's Commission on the Status of Women (Utah), 288; political caucus of, 289; Relief Society (LDS), 284; and suffrage, xiii, 282, 297–99; as tamers, 297–98; Women Against Thirteen, 308; Women's March, 284; Year of the Woman (1992), 291, 297. *See also* Equal Rights Amendment (ERA)
Wood, Janelle, 295
World War I, 255
World War II, 14, 48, 111, 122, 126, 221, 255, 342: post-, 110, 143, 285, 289
W. R. Grace Company: and environmental catastrophe, 367; poisoning of Libby MT, 5, 8–14, 17, 367

Yañez, René, 141–49, 153–63
Yates, Sidney, 68
Yavapais, 65, 70–71
Young Women's Christian Association, 308
YouTube, 109, 115

Zadrozny, Carol, 174, 181
Zarate, Martin, 203
Zimmerman, Greg, 352
Zuckerberg, Mark, 116–17
Zunis, 334, 341, 343

www.ingramcontent.com/pod-product-compliance
Lightning Source LLC
Chambersburg PA
CBHW020057100326
40955CB00017B/766